EGYPT'S UNCERTAIN
REVOLUTION UNDER
NASSER AND SADAT

EGYPT'S UNCERTAIN REVOLUTION UNDER NASSER AND SADAT

Raymond William Baker

HARVARD UNIVERSITY PRESS
Cambridge, Massachusetts
and London, England • 1978

Library of Congress Cataloging in Publication Data

Baker, Raymond William, 1942-
    Egypt's uncertain revolution under Nasser and Sadat.

    Bibliography: p.
    Includes index.
    1. Egypt—History—1952-   I. Title.
DT107.825.B34   962'.05   78-18356
ISBN 0-674-24154-1

962.05
B 168

To my mother,
Dorothy M. Baker—
my first and wisest teacher

Preface

From the July 1952 coup d'état led by Gamal Abdul Nasser emerged a regime charged with the social reconstruction of Egypt. There were ambiguities in that charge from the outset. Nasser's Free Officers were military conspirators who nevertheless were affected by Egypt's broader nationalist movement. Even though their coup preempted a revolutionary situation that existed in the early 1950s, Nasser subsequently used his power to effect certain fundamental changes. The political processes within which Egyptians are today enmeshed derive from this complex revolutionary experience.

The new Egyptian regime and its record in both ruling and transforming Egypt are examined in this book. After a brief historical introduction, Part One analyzes the enduring patterns in the political evolution of post-1952 Egypt. The dynamics of Free Officer rule are characterized by studying the interplay of power, ideas, and social change under Nasser and his successor, Anwar es-Sadat. Part Two—case studies of social change in critical areas of industry, agriculture, and rural welfare—evaluates the actual performance of the regime as closely as available evidence allows. While the primary focus is on domestic developments, internal changes are correlated also with important shifts in Egypt's global role. Throughout, the Egyptian understanding of these multiple transformations of their political life in the quarter-century from 1952 to the present is stressed.

The analytical viewpoint that underlies *Egypt's Uncertain Revolution* developed gradually in the course of my ten-year encounter with Egypt and the Egyptians. The character of that encounter was shaped by my training as a comparative political scientist and an orientalist. It has not, I hope, been limited by it. Nor will my study be easily classified with either tradition. The skills and insights of these often antagonistic scholarly disciplines have been raided repeatedly, even as some of their conventions and minor obsessions have been ignored. My text, written in everyday language, is aimed at the informed public as well as at students and specialists. Unadorned with the neologisms and other exotic vocabulary that we comparativists have come to favor, it makes no effort to ensnare Egypt in yet another formal and ahistorical taxonomy. Moreover, despite the wisely cautionary attitudes that I acquired from orientalist teachers and colleagues, the book treats Egypt's recent history.

In seeking to understand Egyptian political life, I have consorted with all manner of social scientists, cultural observers, and journalists—with anyone, in fact, who has engaged in worthwhile reflection about Egyptians and their society. Most helpful, of course, have been Egyptians themselves. An important correlate has been my extensive qualitative acquaintance with Egypt: long-term residence, linguistic and cultural competence, and meaningful interaction with Egyptians. The best evidence available to me, ranging from government documents to literary works to local and international newspapers and journals, has been synthesized to present as accurate and thorough an interpretation as possible of contemporary issues.

But in an important sense the study remains preliminary: it is an attempt at an overall understanding of Egypt's contemporary domestic development, one that I hope will prepare the way for more definitive studies as the essential documentation becomes available. Certainly present evidence does not permit conclusive judgments about many key questions of Egypt's modern political history. A statistical base of reliable aggregate and survey data bearing on fundamental questions is still largely unavailable. The monographs that form the few brave exceptions are of sharply limited compass.

Nonetheless, in presenting my general interpretation of the Egyptian political experience, I have tried to ask important questions (meaningful to Egyptians as well as to students of Egyptian political life)—questions that will yield more or less lasting answers, expressed in words as attentive as possible to broad applicability and to logical relationships. The search for regularities in empirical observations of Egyptian political behavior was aided by my comparative experiential as well as professional base. Egypt is not the only foreign culture I have intensely experienced; I have come to know France as well, and the Soviet Union perhaps more fully. But the major source of analytical discipline for this book was the systematic effort during research to subject my explanations for specific patterns of political behavior to as rigorous a testing procedure as a single-case study allows. The multiple social implications of any broad explanation of a given aspect of Egyptian political life were used to generate expectations about political behavior in other Egyptian milieus. If those expectations were not fulfilled, the status of the explanation as a generality was undermined. This rough technique generated the crucial capacity for rejection of uncorroborated theoretical explanations—one advantage of the otherwise intimidating effort to see a society whole.

All translations from French and Russian and most from Arabic are my own. The Egyptian government does issue translations of important documents and presidential speeches, and they have been used here. In addition, selected materials are frequently translated from Arabic in publications like the *Middle East Economic Digest* and the *Arab Record and Report* that monitor Arabic-language newspapers and journals. Whenever possible, I have verified such materials against the originals. Conventional and consistent transliterations have been employed for Arabic and Russian proper names and special terms in the text, although spelling variations do appear in cited materials or in references to works that have been published with a different spelling of the author's name.

During the early preparation of this study Professors Adam Ulam, the late Merle Fainsod, and Nadav Safran of Harvard gave beneficial counsel. From them I learned that political phenomena can best be understood in terms of the total cultural and historical matrix in which they are set. Later, while I was at Boston University, Professors Paul Breines and Marcene Marcoux and Mr. Wodek Szemberg helped me see the importance to my work of an explicit interdisciplinary perspective and the relevance of new developments in critical theory and phenomenology.

In the course of teaching and preparing the final version of this study at Harvard and at Williams College, discussions of Middle East affairs with colleagues at those two institutions and elsewhere were extremely helpful. Through every stage in the preparation of the manuscript Professor Safran offered generous professional support. Others who taught me a great deal—whether through brief exchanges, correspondence, or hours of conversation—were Professors L. Carl Brown of Princeton University, Noam Chomsky of MIT, Fred Greene of Williams, and Richard P. Mitchell of the University of Michigan. A special debt is owed Professor Amr Barrada, formerly of Williams, for his incisive criticism of the entire manuscript. At Harvard University Press my two editors, Aida Donald and Vivian Wheeler, provided indispensable help in improving the organization and readability of the book. John Hopkins, a student at Williams, has been a superlative research assistant.

For financial support of extensive field research in Egypt, Lebanon, Syria, Algeria, and the Soviet Union, I am grateful to the Harvard University Government Department Staff Travel Grant Program, the Foreign Area Fellowship Program, and the Boston University Grants-in-Aid Program. In Egypt, I was helped immensely by many Egyptians. In the Soviet Union, scholars concerned with Egypt in major Middle East centers shared their findings and insights with an American colleague. I have thanked individuals in both groups privately.

Williams College has been extremely kind in supporting later stages of my research and responding to my numerous requests for assistance. If "kind" is an unusual adjective to apply to an institution, then Williams is an unusual institution. Typists Donna Alpi, Barbara Boltz, Louise Gilotti, and Mary Jane Paradise were especially thoughtful in helping me meet deadlines. I am also appreciative of the indispensable resources and pleasant environments of the Center for Middle Eastern Studies and the Russian Research Center of Harvard University, where I have been a research associate while writing this book.

Finally, my friends Richard Bentley, Dorian Bowman, Nick Fritz, Pink Horwitt, Gary Jacobsohn, and Grahame Smith gave much-needed encouragement. And above all, I am grateful to my wife, Elaine; readers will never know how much they owe to her ruthless substantive and editorial criticism of every page.

Contents

EGYPT'S UNCERTAIN REVOLUTION UNDER NASSER AND SADAT

INTRODUCTION

Colonialism and Nationalism

Every revolution is shaped by the history of the people involved and by their distinctive genius that gives shared meaning to the formative events of their past. Undoubtedly among the factors that created a revolutionary situation in Egypt in the middle of the twentieth century were the pressures of beginning industrialization, the dislocations occasioned by World War II, and the loss of the war in Palestine in 1948. But to Egyptians revolution had come to mean above all the negation of Egypt's colonial past and the promise of political community. In the exhilaration of a revolutionary period, Egyptians seemed to step forward as the creative makers of their own history. Yet inevitably they did so under historical and social circumstances not of their own choosing. Both the negation and the promise central to Egypt's revolution clearly manifested the scars of a colonial past.

THE COLONIAL LEGACY

The colonization of Egypt began with nineteenth-century commercial penetration, included direct British occupation, and ended with Egyptian nationalization of the Suez Canal in 1956. Central throughout was the role of the British. For convenience their domination may be dated from 1839, when Britain intervened effectively to curtail the power of the parvenu former Albanian officer Muhammad Aly (1805-1849), who founded the last of the foreign dynasties to rule over Egyptians. Under Muhammad Aly's dynastic successors British influence in Egypt grew in rivalry with that of the French. Direct British occupation, however, did not come until 1882, in the wake of a successful army revolt by Colonel Ahmed Arabi, the first hero of Egyptian nationalism. The year 1919 brought a second wave of nationalist revolt. Wartime conditions had contributed to the creation of serious food shortages and a staggering rate of inflation. Nationalist leaders like Saad Zaghloul gave voice to the popular resentment of foreign rule aggravated by these conditions. The rejection of Zaghloul's request for an Egyptian delegation to the Paris

Peace Conference sparked a wave of armed rebellion and strikes that paralyzed the country. Under the pressure of these nationalist disturbances Britain unilaterally ended the protectorate it had established. Egypt was declared an independent monarchy in 1922.

In actuality the 1922 declaration merely veiled the continuance of British power, since its political arrangements expressly qualified Egypt's independence. Important responsibilities, including security of communications, Egyptian defense, and protection of foreign nationals in Egypt and the Sudan, were reserved to the British. A later 1936 agreement did officially end the British occupation of Egypt and undertake to abolish the special privileges that had been guaranteed to foreigners. Nevertheless, Britain still retained the right to station troops in the Suez Canal and to fly over Egyptian territory. The agreement also provided for British defense of Egypt against aggression, in return for Egyptian assistance in a British war. These qualifications meant that one of the four major political forces in the country until the Nasserist revolution was the British—along with the Egyptian king, the aristocracy, and the nationalist party known as the Wafd.

Although the British dominated events in Egypt, they failed to create a genuine political community, which can be defined as one that commands allegiance as the basic moral authority for the individual. British rule succeeded instead in imposing and stabilizing a colonial authority with the aid of indigenous allies. That authority proved capable of maintaining itself, spreading its values among part of the population, and earning recognition of its legitimacy from other imperial authorities such as the French. In short, despite the heavy veils of indirect rule which at times screened British power, one recognizes in Egypt's history the process of colonization and its inevitable result: a colonial situation that led to the rise of nationalist resistance. That recognition provides orientation today for analysts of Egypt's political history just as it provided orientation at the time for those who are the primary object of study: the successful nationalist revolutionaries.[1]

Of course, the foreign domination of Egypt had some unique characteristics. The country was never a colony for large-scale settlement by the British, nor was the Egyptian elite ever totally excluded from political activity. To be sure, power to make the crucial decisions that determined the course of Egypt's history was reserved to the British. Still, the indigenous elite was given just enough of a taste of political power to be tantalized and kept off balance in a position of calculated inferiority not without racist overtones.[2]

In his classic study of the colonial experience Albert Memmi observed: "It is remarkable that racism is a part of all colonialisms under all conditions." British colonialism in Egypt proved no exception, despite the undoubted achievements registered by the British in the spheres of agriculture, finance, and communications. Lord Cromer, the all-powerful British proconsul from 1882 to 1907, best recorded the racist underside of British colonial rule. In his memoir, *Modern Egypt*, Cromer eloquently defended Britain's role in civilizing "barbarous" Egypt. To read Cromer is to understand the cultural amnesia of the colonized Egyptian: better to forget the "coarseness" of his literature, the "cruelty" of his mores, and "the lack of harmony" of his music. To become human is to leave this cultural wreckage and barbarism of a "subject race." But to go where? The Egyptian cannot retrieve his humanity by assimilation, for to adopt the ways of the colonizer is to become the clever monkey, the good imitator, but never the genuine article. Cromer unintentionally has revealed the essential frustration of the colonial situation: for the colonized Egyptian there is no way out.[3]

THE SITUATION OF THE NATIONALISTS

Nationalist revolutionaries, faced with the trauma of colonization, have everywhere claimed history as an ally. What better way to shake the certitude of ruling aliens and undercut their tendency to eternalize the status quo than to reveal the colonial situation as the result of a historical process.[4] Such a condition, after all, could be comprehended and transformed by the actions of men and women in history.

For Egyptian nationalists, Cromer's bald pronouncements could not but stir the historical imagination. How, precisely, had "civilized" Britain laid hand on "barbarous" or "semi-civilized" Egypt—and how could that process be reversed? What did it mean to be a "subject race"—and how could that situation be transformed? History from the selective point of view reflected by these questions is the history of interest to the nationalists—and to those who would understand the nationalists and the meaning of their actions.[5] These are the questions that continue to haunt Egyptians to the present day.

For the occupied Egyptians an understanding of the origins and consequences of British rule was crucial, since they faced a situation for which their traditional culture provided little orientation. Once again Cromer has eloquently described the particular colonial world created in Egypt by the British presence:

> Egypt may now almost be said to form part of Europe. It is on the high road to the far East. It can never cease to be an object of interest to all the Powers of Europe, and especially to England. A numerous and intelligent body of Europeans and of non-Egyptian Orientals have made Egypt their home. European capital to a large extent has been sunk in the country. The rights and privileges of Europeans

are jealously guarded, and, moreover, give rise to complicated questions, which it requires no small amount of ingenuity and technical
knowledge to solve. *Exotic institutions have sprung up and have
taken root in the country.*[6]

To understand the Egyptian nationalist revolutionary (and the modern-
day heirs of his legacy), one must grapple with this colonized Egypt de-
picted by Cromer. For the Egyptian, such an Egypt constituted a new,
"exotic," and profoundly disorienting situation. Behavior could no
longer reliably be guided by traditional patterns. The Egyptian culture in
isolation no longer existed; it had been shattered as a coherent whole by
the process of British colonization. To be sure, fragments of the cultural
past survived—important fragments such as religious beliefs and patterns
of interpersonal relations. Egyptians naturally sought refuge in those
fragments in their time of troubles. Some even sought to piece them together in creative responses to their situation, as in new religious movements, for example. However, such shattered cultural constructs were
now parts of the colonial situation. Their importance in giving meaning
to the world could no longer be grasped by relating them to a theoretical
reconstruction of the disrupted traditional culture.[7] After the occupation
of 1882, Egyptians were made aware that they coexisted with the British.
In their actions they were more and more responsive to the demands of a
colonial world. History had thrust that world upon them, and Egyptian
nationalists looked to history to understand it.

The Egyptian experience with outside domination could be considered
as part of a global, multifaceted Western expansion. From such a perspective the Egyptian nationalist soon recognized that real power lay outside the national boundaries. Egypt had been drawn into a global web of
Western economic and political forces beyond its control. History also
revealed that Egyptian national resistance had been crushed by British
power which, though screened by the manipulation of compromised
segments of the indigenous elite, retained the capability to secure its own
ends. The British held power sufficient to allow them to create Egyptian
dependency and promote the myths that sustained it. Whatever the reluctance of the British to occupy Egypt directly, overwhelming power was
available to do so; and it was exercised. The forces of Arabi's nationalist
revolt, ten thousand roughly trained men and a rabble of peasants, were
crushed by an occupying British force of thirty thousand.[8] History is
memory, and memory revealed that Egyptian resistance was not silent, it
was silenced—and never for long.

Equally important was history's confirmation of the colonial situation
as an objectively verifiable reality characterized not only by the damming
of nationalist aspirations but also by the destruction of Egypt's past. The
Islamic belief system was disrupted and was no longer congruent with ex-

perienced social life. The surgery of colonization was discovered to have profoundly affected key institutions of the traditional socioeconomic framework, destroying the bedouin tribal units and urban guilds and weakening the village community. While clinging to traditional family and religious structures, men and women were nevertheless forced into dependencies on the new and unaccustomed institutions of the colonial situation in Egypt.[9]

Finally, history revealed to the colonized Egyptian that resistance was both part of his legacy and essential to him if his humanity was to be rescued from the racism of colonial rule. This aspect of the nationalist response to the British and the compromised Egyptian monarchy holds particular fascination, for British rule in Egypt was not without an impressive record of positive material achievement. Furthermore, Egypt under the British passed through a relatively brief period of direct occupation and then entered a quasi-independent, constitutional phase. Yet British-sponsored liberalism failed in Egypt and the liberal age ended with revolution.

THE FAILURE OF LIBERALISM

In their social thought and political action, nationalist Egyptians attempted to deal with the shattering impact of the British presence. Egyptian intellectuals were concerned even during the period of direct British occupation to provide their community with a new basis for legitimate, indigenous political authority. Two orientations competed for the loyalties of the intellectuals: reformist Islam and liberal nationalism. Both were moderate; that is, both compromised with British power. Muhammad Abdou, the outstanding figure of the reformist Islam trend, argued that only an Islam that had broken out of traditional confines and come to terms with science and the modern world could provide the underpinnings for a just and viable political community. In contrast, the liberal nationalists represented by such figures as Mustapha Kamel and especially Lutfi Sayid aimed to establish social and political life on the principle of the nation, supplementing that fundamental concept with some of the ideals and values of Western liberalism and constitutionalism.

The Revolution of 1919 seemed to mean that the liberal nationalist alternative had registered a brilliant success. In his defiance of the British, the nationalist leader Zaghloul had rallied all elements of Egyptian society. In February 1922 Britain proclaimed Egyptian independence; Egypt's new constitution enshrined liberal nationalist ideas. The country had entered its constitutional era, which was to last until the Revolution of 1952.

The euphoria of the early years of independence tended to obscure some damaging qualifications to the apparent triumph of liberal nationalism. It was the conservative members of the landowning class who, alarmed by the broader social implications of the 1919 revolution, had urged British issuance of the unilateral declaration of Egyptian independence in 1922. And that independence came with critical reservations, which not only ensured a continuing British role in Egyptian political life but also left the dominance of the Egyptian landowning class intact. Moreover, the Egyptian masses supported the Revolution of 1919 out of a raw nationalism unencumbered by liberal principles. Consequently, in the Egyptian context liberal constitutionalism meant the perpetuation of upper-class Egyptian rule and the continuance of British influence. Conservative, landowning Egyptians who had developed a stake in the colonial situation manipulated the electoral system. The British, guaranteed a military presence in Egypt, had little trouble in protecting their own interests. Not surprisingly, Egypt's pressing national needs—the attainment of full independence and the overcoming of social and economic backwardness—were not met. Blame for the failure of the constitutional regime must be shared by all key political forces: the Egyptian aristocratic parties, the king, and the Wafd, as well as the British.

The aristocratic groups in Egypt who had masterminded the compromise of 1922 organized themselves into the Liberal Constitutionalist Party. When it became apparent that they could not match the popularity of the nationalist Wafd Party headed by Zaghloul, the Liberal Constitutionalists did not hesitate to call on the Egyptian king and the British to defend their interests in ways directly subversive of the constitutional order. Thus, although the Wafd won the right to form a government in every relatively honest election, Wafdist governments were invariably dismissed by the king or compelled by a conflict with the British to resign. In these interim periods the aristocratic groups ruled dictatorially: the constitution was suspended, modified, or abrogated with devastating effects on the legitimacy of the political system. With time the Wafd itself became corrupt and inefficient, as control passed from lawyers and professionals, who initially led it, to landowning elements.

A stagnant economy provided the background for these depressing political developments. The free-enterprise system of Egypt's constitutional period displayed little capacity for raising the deplorable living standards of the masses. In fact, the annual per capita income of the population declined from $109.50 in 1907 to $63.50 in 1950. This drop was precipitated by an increase in population disproportionate to the increase in other resources, including land brought under cultivation. The acceleration in population had begun in the nineteenth century. Egypt's population rose from 9.72 million in 1897 to 19.00 million in 1947. The rate of growth was especially rapid in the 1940s and 1950s. From 1945 through 1952 overall national output barely kept pace with this population increase. Even more telling than the debilitating effects of the population explosion was the attitude of the government. Viewing population growth as a source of a cheap and abundant labor supply rather than as a cause of human misery, successive governments in Egypt not only were willing to allow the population to multiply but actually took steps to stimulate it.[10]

Agriculture, the primary source of output, employment, and foreign exchange, did not have much room for the kind of advance necessary to offset this spurt in population growth. Technically, Egypt had already experienced its agricultural revolution during the nineteenth century when it was integrated into the world market as essentially a cotton producer. Monoculture fostered a lopsided development pattern that endures to this day. Still, the nineteenth-century agricultural revolution had produced high yields on major crops. In the present century, significant expansion could no longer be achieved by land reclamation or by cheap improvements in techniques of cultivation.

Reform of the shockingly inequitable distribution of land in the villages would have helped to alleviate poverty. By 1952, 65 percent of the cultivated land in Egypt was owned by only 6 percent of Egypt's landowners. Change was consistently blocked by the large landowners, who dominated the government. So severe was the problem that land reform in the Egyptian context of an ever greater population pressure on the land would have been at best a palliative measure.

With prospects for advance in agriculture so limited and with mineral resources so scarce, rapid industrialization was an urgent priority. Important beginnings were made by the Egyptian ancien régime. Between 1938 and 1951 industrial production rose by 138 percent, a simple annual rate of increase of a little over 10 percent. However, this was no more than a beginning. Industry in 1950 made only a 15 percent contribution to national output and employed 10 percent of the labor force. Modern industry in Egypt dated only from the 1920s and was limited essentially to textiles and food processing. Existing firms were inefficiently run, and the rates of savings and industrial investments declined in the forties. Furthermore, the rate of growth of industrial production was not sufficient to offset the stagnation of per capita agricultural output and thereby provide Egypt with any overall economic progress. Under the free enterprise system of the ancien régime the government abstained from taking vigorous leadership in the industrial sphere. Left in the hands of private entrepreneurs more interested in conspicuous consumption than in production, industrialization advanced too slowly to meet Egypt's needs.[11]

Disillusioned with the performance of the constitutional regime, large numbers of Egyptians by the mid-thirties had begun to look for alternative forms of political organization. Of the variety of nonliberal political movements, the Moslem Brotherhood elicited the most impressive response. A true mass movement founded by the charismatic Hassan el-Banna in 1928, the brotherhood looked, in el-Banna's words, to the "Islamizing" of Egypt as the means of redemption from the "slow annihilation and profound and complete corruption" occasioned by the British colonial presence. While the movement activists accepted the basic premises of modernization, they lashed out both against the British and against the Egyptians who cooperated with them and slavishly imitated Western ways. The brotherhood's analysis of imperialism was a sophisticated one. It distinguished between "external imperialism," the naked force of the occupying power, and "domestic imperialism," those Egyptian groups and individuals who served the occupiers consciously or unconsciously and profited from their presence. The brotherhood was particularly sensitive to the dangers imperialism posed to the Moslem community's cultural identity. Egyptians were warned against this "cultural imperialism, which entered the minds of the people with its teachings and thoughts" and which tried "to dominate the social situation in the country." Hassan el-Banna described the destruction wrought by such domination:

> Young men were lost, and the educated were in a state of doubt and confusion . . . I saw that the social life of the beloved Egyptian nation was oscillating between her dear and precious Islamism which she had inherited, defended, lived with and become accustomed to, and made powerful during thirteen centuries, and this severe Western invasion which is armed and equipped with all the destructive and degenerative influences of money, wealth, prestige, ostentation, material enjoyment, power, and means of propaganda.

This onslaught of the West was deadly and effective, the brothers argued; it produced "dejection and moral defeat: a dead pacifism, lowly humiliation and acceptance of the status quo." Throwing off all loyalties to the established order, the brotherhood exuded a spirit of revolution. By 1948 the society could claim, without exaggeration, to speak for a million Egyptians. This astounding success was an indicator of the bankruptcy of the regular political groups and the constitutional order itself.[12]

Already weakened by a corrupt and inefficient ruling class, Egypt's constitutional order had been shaken by an array of unfavorable historical circumstances in the forties. Britain leaned heavily on Egypt in World War II and did not hesitate to claim its wartime rights—and more—under the 1936 agreement. While fighting was under way in North Africa, the Egyptian King Farouk in 1942 moved to form a government headed by a minister suspected of pro-Axis sympathies. An alarmed British ambassador instructed the commander of British troops in Egypt to surround Farouk's palace. Farouk was ordered to install a Wafdist government under Nahas Pasha, who was viewed as more amenable to British influence. The king yielded to this British show of force, and the leader of the nationalist Wafd came to power under the protection of British guns! The prestige of both the crown and the Wafd was seriously undermined by this incident.

Political life in the forties was marked by the meaningless circulation of Wafdist and minority governments, all of which were incapable of instituting reform or securing the evacuation of the British. The Palestine War of 1948 might have diverted attention from Egypt's domestic ills and even restored King Farouk's sagging popular esteem, but rapid Egyptian defeat crushed those possibilities. In 1950 the Wafd led by Nahas Pasha won a last victory at the polls. Temporarily buoyed by an artificial boom in cotton prices brought on by the Korean War, the new government was soon weakened by charges of widespread official corruption, involving the Nahas family itself. In the last stages before the Revolution of 1952 the instances of imprisonments, violent strikes and demonstrations, killings and assassinations, and plots and purges increased sharply.[13]

In 1951, in an effort to strengthen his position, Wafdist head of government Nahas inaugurated a struggle against the British by unilaterally abrogating the 1936 Anglo-Egyptian treaty, which provided the legal basis for British presence in Egypt. A program of sabotage and guerrilla attacks against the British base in the Suez Canal Zone was begun, with the Wafdist government relying on the Moslem Brotherhood and left-wing groups to carry out the attacks. The struggle threatened to end in stalemate. The Egyptians did not possess the means to defeat the British army of eighty thousand, although they could make maintenance of the British base in the Canal Zone difficult and costly. The British government was unwilling to reoccupy Egypt proper in order to secure its position; it chose instead to respond with limited guerrilla counterattacks.

One such attack had far-reaching effects. On January 25, 1952, the British announced their intention of expelling from the Canal Zone all units of Egyptian police suspected of aiding the guerrillas. Heavily armed British troops and tanks surrounded the Egyptian police headquarters in Ismailia and demanded surrender. On orders from Cairo, the Egyptian police refused to submit. The British opened fire. Before they were compelled to surrender, the Egyptians had lost forty-one men, with seventy-two wounded, to only three deaths for the British. In Cairo the incident was regarded as a massacre. Reaction was explosive and aimed as much against the government for its inept handling of the incident as against the British. A large section of central Cairo was looted and burned by angry crowds and about a dozen lives were lost before the Egyptian army restored order.

Farouk dismissed Nahas, head of the Wafd government, the next day and thereby initiated a period of crisis from which the ancien régime never recovered. In the next five months no one proved capable of forming a strong government.

EGYPT IN REVOLUTION

Subjective signs that Egypt was approaching a revolutionary moment in its history were seen in the late forties and early fifties in the growing appeal of radical thought and movements of the left and right. The perceived relevance of the several varieties of Marxism that took root in Egypt derived from Marxism's acceptance of aspects of the Western achievement while at the same time it called for revolt against it. Marxism sounded the call for industrialization, but for an industrialization cleansed by social revolution of the Western capitalist contagion. It provided a persuasive demonology to explain the disruptions and disorientations experienced in the colonial situation. And Marxism gave expression to the instinctive anarchist feeling of a society that had been profoundly dislocated in its fundamental socioeconomic structures.[14]

Marxism was not the only ideology that served to canalize the sense of social disintegration born during the colonial confrontation and its aftermath. The history of revolutionary politics in Egypt often reveals congeries of conspirators who had held Islamic fundamentalist as well as Marxist views. There have even been individuals who fluctuated between the two ideologies. This apparent anomaly disappears when it is realized that in Egypt the evocative power of "Islamic" theoretical formulations was used by the brotherhood to appeal to the same discontented groups that might have been attracted to Marxism. The Moslem Brotherhood assuaged the trauma of the disintegrating colonial situation with the promise of a "conservative transition," modernization cleansed by Islam of racist, individualistic, corrupt capitalism as well as of atheistic, tyrannical, and materialist communism.[15]

The call for revolution from both the left and the right was increasingly heard as the bankruptcy of Egypt's liberal age became apparent. From the wide array of contenders for the nationalist mantle, it was a movement of military conspirators—the Free Officers led by Gamal Abdul Nasser—that ultimately destroyed the monarchy and eliminated the colonial presence. It was from their coup d'état of July 1952 that the instruments were forged to make possible a real break with the colonial past.

And it was Nasser who led the Egyptian people at Suez in 1956, when the colonial legacy was at last repudiated.

How did the military conspirators orient themselves and demarcate the arena for their decisive social action? How did they understand the "logic of their situation"? Through their words and behavior the Free Officers expressly defined this realm of their social action, and they have thereby left a concrete record for its reconstruction here. But the significance of that reconstruction is not limited to Egypt. For the recognition and destruction of a colonial situation in Egypt by the Free Officers was understood by them to be related to the larger historical process of decolonization. Egypt's revolution was seen as partaking of that "repossession of the world" and that "call for its remaking" which has marked the modern era.[16]

The Free Officers saw themselves as vindicators of the promise of Egypt's nationalist movement. That claim was challenged, by the Moslem Brothers among others. Yet through their efforts to destroy Egypt's colonial dependency the military conspirators did give new meaning to a history that for the mass of Egyptians had become meaningless. By seizing power and using it to destroy the material and cultural structures of colonial domination, they placed the revolutionary transformation of Egypt and the redefinition of its role in global politics on the historical agenda. The coup d'état moved toward revolution. The process of building an authentic political community was at last begun. Egypt's revolutionaries aimed to transform their society, and that transformation was itself part of the global drama of decolonization and national renaissance. The meaning of their actions must be measured by an appropriate criterion that focuses on the forging of the necessary links between power and ideas. The framework must be one of creativity in a concretely defined historical situation.

The attempt in this book to gauge the scope and depth of Egypt's transformation under Nasser and Sadat is given focus by a conceptual scheme of six basic propositions in social theory, which reflect the value and methodological assumptions of this study and determine its logical substructure:

(1) Any given society can be understood only in terms of the specific historical period in which its exists.

(2) The social structures, the ideas, the kinds of social behavior prevailing in any given society in any given historical period constitute a unique pattern. That pattern may be compared with other patterns, it may be discerned by means other than intuition; but it must first be entered into on its own terms.

(3) The situational analysis of purposive social action taking place

within a society so understood is of necessity a study of social ideas as well. No purposive activity, especially no such social activity, can be carried on without some theory, no matter how rudimentary or tentative, which explains for the actors the practical reality involved and the practical means to maintain or change it.

(4) The determination of the potentialities of a concrete social situation (the key to arriving at appropriate standards for evaluating a given process of social change) can only be a historical determination grounded in meaning-analysis. Potentialities are relevant to the study of a process of social change only as real (experienced) economic and political questions that deal with human relations in the productive process, the patterns of generation and distribution of the product of social labor, and people's active participation in the economic and political administration of the social whole. Comparative historical studies reveal that a central preoccupation of thought and action in a society changing from a preindustrial to an industrial pattern has been with the relation between political power and the market as competing principles and instruments of social organization—the political versus the market solution to the problem of social order.

(5) The study of a process of purposive social change aimed at accelerating passage from the preindustrial to the modern world—here the pursuit by the Egyptian Free Officers of the means to develop their society—is aided by both a subjective and an objective referent. Crucial to any interpretation of such a process is a critical analysis of the subjective understanding by the actors of the meaning of their political behavior. Similarly, analysis is guided by an appreciation that the resolution of the question of political power versus the market is a crucial objective determinant of the nature of a given social order. Any particular resolution of this core problem will involve domestic as well as international political and economic forces and will be reflected on both macro and micro levels of society.

(6) The measure of the creativity of those who by virtue of their historical situation are able to act to bring about change is the degree to which their thought and action successfully oppose reality with a better alternative—which is here understood as the closest possible approximation, given existing material and intellectual resources, to a free and rational society, a society in which a people can collectively regulate their lives in accordance with their needs.[17]

What have been the successes—and equally important—the failures and unintended consequences of Egypt's revolutionaries in generating plans to direct revolutionary social changes in Egypt and in creating the organizational means to carry them out? The literature on contemporary

Egypt is rich. But the historians, the comparative social scientists, and the orientalists who have most systematically studied Egypt for the most part have had different concerns. The answer to this fundamental question requires more than a generalized account of recent Egyptian history, more than a comparative study that classifies Egypt among the nations of the world, more than the orientalist preoccupation with Egypt's traditional Islamic culture and the tasks of adjusting it to the modern world. The present study brings a new focus: explicit analysis of the obstacles, both domestic and foreign, that Egyptians have confronted in their efforts to create the politics and administration of revolutionary social reconstruction. The general argument can be briefly stated:

(1) Egypt's revolutionary rulers as yet have been unable to generate the institutions, systems, and relations which they themselves see as essential to the social reconstruction of their country.

(2) There have been many causes for the failures of Nasser and Sadat, but most critical has been the absence among the Free Officers of organization and of ideology.

(3) This lack of institutionalization and ideology has hampered a coherent, self-generated approach to the problems Egypt has faced since 1952. Basic decisions on the character of Egypt's new political-economic order, and correlative regional and international alignments, were too long delayed. Despite the domestic roots of their core motivations, Egypt's new rulers allowed their regime to be defined to an excessive degree by the responses made to external crisis stimuli and to the counter-responses of the environment. The Free Officers have been unable to devise and carry out the basic public policies demanded by their own vision of change.

(4) In Egypt a political-economic order has taken form that is characterized by sharply limited competence for the tasks of modernization. It is an order without secure social moorings, an order in which political power is both personalized and bureaucratized. The essential question of the relation of the market mechanism to political authority in regulating society has not been resolved. Ironically, such a system of social organization itself erects new and formidable barriers to the task set by the Free Officers for themselves and their people: the revolutionary transformation of Egypt.

PART ONE

RULING EGYPT

Anwar es-Sadat in his autobiography, *In Search of Identity*, writes of the nationalist legends that penetrated to the Nile Delta village of his birth and enlightened his childhood imagination. For Sadat, most moving was the ballad of Zahran, the hero of Denshway. A village only a few miles from his own, Denshway was the site of a real incident:

> British soldiers were shooting pigeons in Denshway, the ballad goes, when a stray bullet caused a wheat silo to catch fire. Farmers gathered and a British soldier fired at them and ran away; they ran after him and in the ensuing scuffle the British soldier died. Many people were arrested. Scaffolds were erected before sentences were passed; a number of farmers were whipped, others hanged.

In the oral tradition of Egypt's villages, Zahran became a nationalist martyr, celebrated for "his courage and doggedness in the battle, how he walked with head held high to the scaffold" (pp. 5-6).

Sadat saw the overthrow of the Egyptian monarchy in 1952 and the eventual expulsion of the British as a vindication of Zahran's courage. At last, with power in their own hands, Egyptians would have the opportunity to create a new Egypt:

> The revolution took place in 1952, and I played a part in it. My participation was not in itself important to me. What was important to me was that the revolution actually took place and that the dream I had from early childhood was realized. It was this that made me live with Nasser for eighteen years without ever clashing with him. I was happy to work in any capacity.   (p. 78)

For Sadat, Gamal Abdul Nasser—the man who led the July coup—was the legitimate heir of the nationalist resistance despite all the later failings of his rule. Understanding the politics of Egypt today requires an encounter with Nasser and the nationalist Free Officers who surrounded him.

1. The Military Conspirators

A prediction of revolution for Egypt at midcentury would have required no great prescience: the ancien régime was clearly losing its grip on power and there was no dearth of rival claimants in the field. But to have predicted that the Muhammad Aly dynasty would fall to a coup d'état by an obscure band of conspirators from the military would have been an accomplishment of quite a different order.

Following the successful establishment of the new regime, a contrary impression of inevitability was created around the July coup and the particular pattern of revolutionary changes that ensued. In a curious way both hostile and sympathetic Western observers have largely accepted the regime's own myth that Free Officer rule was the necessary denouement to the drama of the rise of nationalist resistance and the disintegration of the old order.[1]

Whatever the usefulness to the regime of this aura of inevitability, the myth is a misleading one that makes it difficult to assess accurately the Free Officers movement. To understand the major changes the Free Officers underwent as they developed from unknowns in a secret society to Egypt's ruling elite requires an unvarnished view of their origins and their early struggles for power. The patterns of rule that characterized Nasser's Egypt were shaped by the responses of the Free Officers to actual or potential challenges to their power. There were alternatives to the regime of the military conspirators and to the particular ways in which they mobilized Egypt's material and intellectual resources. Any analysis of the nature of the regime established by the Free Officers is well served by a sense of historical contingency.

Part of the fascination of a revolutionary period lies precisely in its open-endedness. In Egypt at midcentury new social groups and formations emerged to speak the language appropriate to a turbulent age. A young Egyptian author, Fathy Ghanem, provided an immanent view of this revolutionary situation in his novel *The Man Who Lost His Shadow*. One character, Shodi Pasha, is a corrupt newspaper publisher who illustrates the bankruptcy of the journalistic politics of the traditional nationalist opposition. For all its rhetoric of criticism, that opposition had in fact compromised and integrated itself into the old order. Through Shodi Pasha, Ghanem conveys the opportunistic desperation of all those tied to the old order as Egypt moved into a revolutionary age:

> Now's no time for intrigues. This thing is bigger than all of us. Let anyone come to power—foe or friend—and I'll support him provided he rids us of these criminals. The country's being ruined by trash . . . Communists . . . Muslim Brothers . . . Socialists . . . Nationalists. They're all paupers with nothing to lose. But we have everything to lose.

Shodi Pasha seeks to use the ambitious and unscrupulous reporter Yusif to simulate the new language of Egypt in a revolutionary age. He hopes thereby to mask the ties of his paper *al-Ayyam* to the old order and to survive in a situation so threatening to his position of privilege.

> [Shodi Pasha] "I have recently read every word you wrote. When you analyze crimes, you trace them to poverty, to the social situation. You talk like the communist papers."
> [Yusif]: "But I'm not a communist."
> "Of course not, or I shouldn't have received you."
> "And I would have been in prison."
> "You are too intelligent to be a communist," he continued, "and too ambitious. You want to get on, to become something."
> I nodded. "I am trying hard."
> "And you can! You can even be editor-in-chief of *Al-Ayyam*."
> He saw the look of shock on my face but continued.
> "We need new blood. I am a gambler, someone who loves a risk. If I trust a young man, I put him in charge of my largest companies. Muhammed is splendid for fighting the old politicians, for teasing the Palace. But that's *vieux jeu* [an old game]. The new struggle is between socialists, communists, and the Muslim Brotherhood. They write in a way that attracts university students. I need someone who can write in their idiom, someone whom they can believe."[2]

Striking in Ghanem's dialogue is the intuitive understanding that both the extreme right and the extreme left spoke in terms that for increasing numbers made sense out of an apparently senseless world. Eclipsed was not only the old order, but its traditional nationalist opposition as well. The Wafd, legitimate heir to the nationalist legacy, was compromised by involvement with the intrigues of the palace; the Moslem Brothers and the Marxists moved to claim the nationalist mantle.

THE MILITARY AS SEEDBED FOR REVOLUTION

Yet it was from the military that the successful blow against the ancien régime was struck. Revolution came to Egypt in the form of a coup d'état by military conspirators. Their military origins and their preparation of the coup in a military environment had a profound impact on the nature of the regime Egypt's Free Officers eventually established. An understanding of that regime begins with a realistic assessment of the Egyptian army from which it grew. General Aziz el-Masri, commander in chief of the Egyptian military before World War II and a hero to Nasser's Free Officers, has provided a sharply critical view of the Egyptian military:

> Of course the Egyptian army is worthless. It was the British who organized it, and they had their reasons for making a poor thing of it.[3]

General Masri's blunt assessment and its raw insight provides a necessary corrective to the popular and misleading views of Egyptian military apologists who have sought to explain Egypt's military revolution by portraying the Egyptian army before 1952 as a technologically advanced island in a sea of backwardness and as the vanguard of the Egyptian nationalist tradition.

Although the army had been the main center of Egyptian national power from the time of Muhammad Aly until the Arabi revolt, its fate had been determined by its defeat at the hands of the occupying British at Tel-el-Kebir in 1882. Its epitaph was provided one week later by the khedive's short notice: "The Egyptian army is disbanded." The army that was built to replace it was completely the creature of the British and of the Egyptian crown. Thus, while the Arabi revolt became an important part of nationalist symbolism, the reconstituted Egyptian army itself could in no way claim to speak for the nation. With the khedival disbanding of the army, direct military links to the Arabi tradition were broken.

In the protracted struggle for Egypt's independence—the dominant political motif of the early twentieth century—the role of the army was negligible. Spokesmen for the Free Officers later argued that their action in 1952 was the fruit of a continuous tradition of military leadership of the nationalist movement dating from the Arabi revolt. Though useful to the regime, such a view is historically untenable. Any continuing significance of the Arabi tradition lay rather in its impact on the broader nationalist movement that animated Egyptian society during the first half of the twentieth century. In the idiom of the Egyptian left, the Arabi army, although destroyed, "nevertheless left deep impressions on the spirit of the whole nation; impressions that kept chasing colonialism and disturbing its sleep."[4]

Whatever the pronouncements of the official propaganda apparatus after 1952, Nasser recognized that the military never occupied a vanguard role in the nationalist movement. Echoing General Masri, he commented: "The Egyptian army had not been a good one. It was in the interests of the British to keep it so." Egyptian analysts of the pre-1952 military have made that judgment more specific by explaining that rank in the high command was much more a reflection of family connections than of martial skills. The other end of the military scale—that is, the mass of the soldiery—were considered to belong to "the basest of occupations." The British and the reactionaries were blamed for a system whereby financial payments could be accepted in lieu of military service. The result was that "the military profession appeared to be confined to the poorest of the poor and the most ignorant of the ignorants, and not as a national honor."[5]

More promising than these two extremes were the younger, lower-rank officers from whose number actually emerged the Free Officers. However, before attributing the vanguard role to these young officers as a group, a frequently overlooked qualification must be made. The low prestige of a military career did little to attract the more able and ambitious of Egypt's youth. With the exception of the highest ranks, the officer corps in general was placed by a status-conscious society below the merchants, if still above the thieves.[6]

This picture changed somewhat in the period following the 1936 treaty when the Royal Military Academy was opened to classes other than the landowning aristocracy. Although the new prospect of a military career must have looked attractive to talented men of modest means, considerations of nationalism or national service were still unlikely to have figured largely in that attraction. Muhammad Naguib, who was to be the figurehead for the Free Officers movement, described in his autobiography the attitude of his father (himself an army officer) toward his son's choice of the military as a career. In this attitude one can see, from a nationalist perspective, the limitations of a military career:

> The Egyptian Army, he said, was not all that it was supposed to be.
> It was not really an army at all, but rather an auxiliary corps in
> which Egyptians were expected to take orders from the British.

Naguib writes that since he had been a good student, his father argued that "it would be better for . . . me to be a lawyer or an engineer. I could do more for my country in civilian clothes."[7]

Despite the fact that the military as an institution had forfeited its earlier identification with the national idea, it nevertheless remains true that men of strong nationalist inclination did undertake military careers. As a result of the change in the policy of admissions to the academy the following men, who were to play central roles in the revolution, became officers: Abdul Hakim Amer, Abdul Latif el-Baghdadi, Kamal el-Din Hussein, Hassan Ibrahim, Zakariya Muhieddin, Gamal Abdul Nasser, Anwar es-Sadat, Gamal and Salah Salem, and Hussein el-Shafei. However, available biographical data on these men, including Nasser himself, suggest that their nationalist orientation had already been formed before they joined the military. Nasser's own example suggests that these men tended to regard the military not as a "school for nationalism" but rather as the recalcitrant object of nationalist instruction that they themselves furnished.

Gamal Abdul Nasser began his political involvement at the age of twelve. By the time he was seventeen he had been elected president of the Nationalist Secondary Students' Executive Committee, organized mass student protests, and been wounded by the police in the course of a street demonstration. Such student political activism was the byword of the Egypt of the 1930s. A letter written by Nasser in 1935 at the age of seventeen to his friend Hassan el-Nashar indicates the tone and the nationalist thrust of that movement:

> God has said: "We must prepare ourselves and mobilize all our forces against them." Where is this force we have prepared against them? Today the situation is critical and Egypt has reached an impasse. I feel the country is in a state of hopeless despair. Who can remove this feeling? The Egyptian government is based on corruption and favors. Who can change it? The constitution has been suspended. A protectorate will be proclaimed. Who can cry halt to the imperialists? There are men in Egypt with dignity who do not want to be allowed to die like dogs. But where is the growing nationalism of 1919? Where are the men ready to give their lives for their country's independence? Where is the man to rebuild the country so that the weak and the humiliated Egyptian people can rise up again and live as free and independent men?[8]

Egypt's schoolboys, impatient with the ineffectiveness of the older generation, had taken to the political field. Their political and social ideas were barely developed, and abrupt swings from right to left were not infrequent. But they were all ardent nationalists.

In *Revolt on the Nile* Anwar es-Sadat paid tribute to these student nationalists:

> The university has a fine record of active political demonstration, and it was the students—instinctively on the side of the proletariat and the oppressed—who effected the spiritual revolution so necessary to our political revolution.

The army, Sadat made clear, could itself make no such bid for nationalist laurels, for it was generally regarded as "a weapon in the hands of the King which he would use to tame his subjects should they rise in protest." In discussing his own formation as a revolutionary, Nasser likewise revealed the sources of the nationalist spirit that moved him:

I have often been asked when I first became a revolutionary. It is an impossible question to answer; this was something conditioned by my family background and upbringing, allied to a general feeling of dissatisfaction and defiance that spread throughout the whole of my generation in schools, universities, and *subsequently* in the armed forces.

Indeed, Nasser was initially rejected for the Royal Military Academy, partly because he was the grandson of a fellah but mainly because of his nationalist activities. The reasons Nasser gave, at least on one occasion, for his choice of a military career have little to do with his nationalist proclivities:

I went into the army as a career for financial reasons. I had been studying law, but my disagreements with my father now meant that I had to keep myself; and the army, with its security, appeared the natural opening.[9]

Once embarked on a military career, though, it was inevitable that Nasser should view the army in terms of its potential for the realization of his nationalist aims for Egypt. Such prospects did not seem overly bright. The Egyptian military, Nasser was to learn, was neither very promising nor very suitable as a seedbed for revolution. In fact, the eventual success of the Free Officers owed much more to historical accident than to any advantages of their situation in the military.

A leftist Free Officer, Khaled Muhieddin, writing in 1966, offered a simple and compelling explanation for the success of the July military coup. "The army," Muhieddin observed, "emerged as the only national force which had not been hit." Earlier the ancien régime had been successful enough in dealing with overt civilian threats to its rule: the Moslem Brotherhood had been weakened first by the assassination of its leader Hassan el-Banna and then by the imposition of martial law following the burning of Cairo in January 1952. This action also facilitated the arrest of the brotherhood's guerrilla contingents. The left was similarly undermined by police persecution and arrests. M. H. Haikal, editor of *al-Ahram* and Nasser's confidant, has explained that the Free Officers movement "only acted to fill a void which had revealed itself in the political milieu before 1952. Their movement to tell the truth had the character of a shock or reaction." Had it not been for the special circumstances that cleared the field of rival contenders, the army was, in Haikal's view, the last place where revolution should have broken out.[10]

It is, paradoxically, the generally low esteem in which the military was held that explains how King Farouk lost control over it. Farouk was aware that the nationalist movement had found an echo among certain circles of army officers. Free Officer pamphlets had appeared throughout 1951, and police investigations had led to the arrest of some peripheral associates of the Free Officers and to the questioning of Nasser himself. Yet the regime never moved as effectively against the Free Officers as it did against its civilian challengers. It was the record of traditional subservience of the army to the British and to the crown that dulled Farouk's vigil. The king was certain that by manipulating his firm control over the high command he could ensure its loyalty.

Farouk's confidence in the army proved naive, but an incident involving General Fuad Sadek showed how the king could have been misled. Sadek had commanded the Egyptian forces in the Palestine War of 1948 and was respected by the Free Officers for having acquitted himself honorably. Convinced of the importance of a top military leader to win the loyalty of the mass of soldiers to their movement, the Free Officers approached General Sadek to back them. Earlier, General Aziz el-Masri, the favorite of the conspirators, had declined because of his advanced age to be their figurehead. While Sadek was negotiating (the Free Officers were willing to trade his support for their coup for the position of chief of staff), a rumor reached him that the king planned to appoint him to the same post. Preferring the prospect of a royal appointment, Sadek ended his discussion with the Free Officers, who then turned to General Naguib. Thus, at the upper levels and among Egypt's most honorable commanders, the crown could still command support.

Assured of the loyalty of the highest commanders, the ancien régime lapsed into fateful complacency. When finally persuaded that a threat did exist from conspirators among the middle-rank officers, the army high command met on the night of July 23, 1952, to plan the elimination of the dissidents. Their intended blow was never delivered, for that same night the Free Officers brought their conspiracy to fruition.

THE CHARACTER OF THE CONSPIRACY

During the formative period of a regime conceived in conspiracy habits of thought, organization, and action are acquired that leave a lasting imprint on that regime. The ideological persuasions of the young men who coalesced around Gamal Abdul Nasser covered the full range of political thought from right to left, from Moslem fundamentalism to Marxism. The exigencies of conspiracy impelled Nasser to minimize these differences. With great skill he maintained the unity of the core participants by avoiding discussion of the kind of society the Free Officers eventually would build. Attention was riveted instead on the immediate task of consummating the revolution. Ideological differences were submerged in an emotionally powerful nationalism, which evoked the shared dream of Egyptain independence and purification.

Interestingly, some of the intensity of that commitment to the nationalist idea may have resulted from the very difficulty of sustaining a nationalist orientation in the military environment. Nasser has graphically recorded the steadfastness of his own determination to contribute to Egypt's renewal despite the lack of reinforcement for such ideas. From the garrison at Mankabad, to which Nasser had been stationed after graduation from the academy, he wrote to Nashar:

> I am happy to tell you that my character is still firm. Gamal at Mankabad is the Gamal you know for a long time—the one who is seeking in his imagination for reasons to hope . . . but his hopes vanish like clouds.

Nasser's disappointment suggests that while the more open admissions policy that the Royal Military Academy adopted in 1936 did inject new blood into the Egyptian military, the extent of the change was not great. The nationalist officers of the new type, talented men of modest means who were susceptible to a nationalist orientation, remained a small minority.[11]

In a description of his first army assignment Nasser described his disillusionment with the majority of his fellow officers:

> All three of us [Nasser, Sadat, and Z. Muhieddin] were posted to a remote garrison at Mankabad, near Assiut, in Upper Egypt. We went there full of ideals but were soon disillusioned. Most of the staff officers were inefficient and corrupt. Some of my fellow officers were so shocked that they resigned. I could see no point in this, although I was as incensed as the others.

For a man "seeking for reasons to hope" despair was alleviated by his comradeship with those few young officers who did share his views. For although Nasser had no illusions about the military as a whole, he did believe that "now, however, it began to have a new class of officers, men who saw their army careers only as part of a greater struggle to win freedom for their people."[12]

An army marked by modern technology, merit, and a sense of national mission would indeed have attracted the most enterprising of Egypt's sons and perhaps would have created the natural, even inevitable, military revolution so many claimed to have found in the July Revolution. But Egypt's army was not such an army and Egypt's revolution was not such a revolution.

The Free Officers found themselves in an environment not very hospitable to their nationalist dreams. As a result, they drew together and strengthened their conspiratorial ties with more personal bonds. Sadat, describing the embryonic beginnings at Mankabad of what was to become the Free Officers movement, has conveyed some of the flavor of the relationship.

> One evening . . . we were beneath the Gabal al-Sharif mountain preparing our modest meal . . . We were celebrating Gamal Abdel Nasser's birthday with lentils, which we had cooked ourselves on the fire and sugar cane. In honor of the special occasion we had also brought chestnuts from Assiut. While we were laughing and joking Gamal said in his usual quiet voice: "Let us make something lasting out of this meeting. Let it be the date on which a real brotherhood between us was founded. I assure you that in this spirit with God's will we shall overcome all our obstacles."

In fact, the ties forged at Mankabad were to prove significant, even as the careers of the young and idealistic officers scattered them throughout Egypt. Sadat's autobiography, *In Search of Identity*, describes his own subsequent conspiratorial efforts that led to the formation of a grouping of nationalist officers in 1939. But he recognizes that Nasser tightened the organizational thrust of nationalist activities within the army with his resort to a structure of secret cells. Nasser himself regarded the activities of circles such as Sadat's as merely broadly preparatory. He dated the real origins of the Free Officers movement much later: beginnings in 1942, first regular meetings in 1944, serious organization only after 1949.[13]

Personal, noninstitutional ties were the cement of the conspiratorial movement. Yet once the Free Officers had taken power, such linkages were translated into a generalized and ultimately debilitating personalization of power. The nature of the ties, it became apparent later, made it difficult to open the core group to new members as responsibilities expanded. The men invited to affirm their nationalist commitment through the conspiratorial movement were drawn solely from the officer corps. What is known of the revolutionary tracts distributed by the movement indicates that they were aimed at persuasion of the officers and not of the mass of soldiers. There was to be no revolutionary disruption of the ranks. From its inception the Free Officers movement was elitist, even within the military context.

Although the exact number of the elite group of officers is not known, its nucleus comprised ten to fifteen officers, each surrounded by several dozen followers. Nasser's central position within the organization is revealed by the fact that only he and his closest friend, Abdul Hakim Amer, knew the names of all the members. This inner core was characterized by a profound distrust of all political parties and groupings, a distrust that led Nasser to guard jealously the autonomy of the movement. To be sure, individual Free Officers did at times pursue intense relationships with particular political figures and groups. In later years Nasser himself acknowledged contacts with the right-wing Young Egypt, the Wafd, the Moslem Brotherhood, and the Marxists; and his experience was by no means unique. Despite dialogue with all active political forces, the Free Officers would act in concert with none.[14] The official view of the revolution would have it that the officers acted alone in order to preserve the purity of their aims from the contamination of civilian corruption. Be that as it may, the essential point is that in 1952 the Free Officers did act without dependence on any civilian groups or foreign powers.

The final success of the Free Officers' coup in July of 1952 was greatly facilitated by the passive acquiescence it was granted by both the Western powers and the leading actors on the domestic political scene. Assurances that the coup would not adversely affect their interests were given both to the British and to the Americans, who were rapidly replacing them as the preeminent Western power in the Middle East. Rival domestic political forces were lulled by the expectation that the military conspirators were acting in their favor. The Wafdists, for example, hoped to exploit their ties to Free Officer Sarwat Okasha and Nasser himself through the progressive journalist Ahmed Aboul Fath. The Moslem Brothers were confident that their interests would be served, thanks to the connections of key members of their Guidance Bureau with leading Free Officers including Nasser and Sadat. The Free Officers, along with other revolutionary currents in the army, had from the earliest days received support and encouragement from the brotherhood. Nasser, meeting with the head of the Moslem Brotherhood in 1944, had received this advice:

> Begin to organize in the army groups which have faith in what we believe so that when the time comes, we will be organized in one rank, making it impossible for our enemies to crush us.

Little wonder that the Brotherhood welcomed the coup and cooperated in the first days of the revolution to preserve order and security. Similarly, the Marxists were confident that political dividends would flow from the contacts of Ahmed Fuad and other party militants with Nasser, Khaled Muhieddin, Yussef Saddiq, and Aly Sabry. All were ultimately disappointed, but not until their initial expectant passivity had helped facilitate the Free Officers' strike for power.[15]

THE SEIZURE OF POWER

The actual seizure of power by these fundamentally nonideological, elitist military conspirators was marked by an almost complete absence of violence. The ease of this takeover did much to reinforce significant traits of the movement, such as habits of secrecy, personalization of power relationships, reliance on the military, and absence of independent civilian allies.

Success in July 1952 undoubtedly owed much to the conspiratorial skills of Nasser and his fellow Free Officers. However, their own accounts of the coup caution against overestimating the organizational efficiency of the military revolutionaries. Nasser himself was nearly arrested by conspirators who initiated the coup an hour earlier than planned and did not know that he was president of the Free Officers. The firebrand Anwar es-Sadat, unaware of a shift in planning, was at a movie on the crucial evening and almost missed the action. Still, Nasser was confident. One Free Officer has written of the night of the coup:

> Toward nine-thirty I saw a tall young man in sports clothes pull up outside. It was Gamal. He was very calm. He told me that the time for the operation had been advanced, and added in English: "Saroit, don't let your feelings run away with you. And don't imagine you're at the cinema. We have 99 chances out of 100 of succeeding."[16]

In this judgment, Nasser was proved correct. Mistakes were made in the execution of the coup, but they were not fatal. Once it was realized that the British would not intervene on behalf of the Egyptian crown, no one was willing to fight for the old order. The dynasty founded by Muhammed Aly simply collapsed.

In later years the regime realized that, strangely enough, the ease with which it had accomplished the revolution from a long-term perspective constituted a drawback. The rapid downfall of the old order obviated any necessity to organize and mobilize political support against it. Such an effort might have forced the conspirators to broaden their organization by reaching into the civilian population for allies; a legitimate and independent political base for the regime might have resulted. In 1952, however, the absence of a popular role in the July events was considered highly desirable by the Free Officers, no matter how the views of some of them (including Nasser) changed later. Explanations for the lack of popular participation in the revolution have made too much of the fatalism and passivity of the Egyptian populace. The historical record of violent popular unrest right up to 1952 had been impressive; in 1951 alone a total of forty-nine workers' strikes and several bloody peasant uprisings took place. The January 1952 burning of Cairo should be proof enough that the possibility of large-scale urban unrest was very real. During the so-called Black Saturday riots in January 1952, Nasser was serving with the army in Cairo. His response is instructive. Although undoubtedly encouraged by the nationalist fervor of the masses when stirred into action,

Nasser sought to preempt the revolutionary situation by a coup d'état aimed at bringing the Wafd to power. Contact was made, but Wafdist head Nahas recoiled from a proposal he regarded as too risky.[17]

Nasser's response to Black Saturday suggests an explanation for the inactive role of the populace when the Free Officers struck in July. Such passivity was considered by the military conspirators to be crucial for the success of the coup and they worked to secure it. In 1952 there were still approximately eighty thousand British troops stationed on Egyptian soil in the base at Suez. The Free Officers, haunted by memories of 1882 when popular disorders in Alexandria were exploited as a pretext for the original British occupation of Egypt, were concerned lest any popular outburst (and threat to foreign lives and property) again justify foreign intervention. For the Free Officers a successful revolution would have to be an orderly revolution. They dared not appeal to the hatred of the masses for the ancien régime, out of fear that such hatred could not be controlled. Just as the Free Officers had in the pre-1952 period eschewed any binding alliance with civilian political forces, they now sought to curb, as completely as possible, any popular role in the revolution.

This closed character of the Free Officers' political action meant, of course, that there was to be no correction to the movement's early habits of intrigue and to the potential for the abuse of power that intrigue fosters. M. H. Haikal argued later that the secrecy in the revolutionary cells established by Nasser created "veils" that screened individual abuses of authority and petty tyrannies by the nationalist officers. Haikal suggested that "bad seeds" were nurtured, whose actions marred the regime's performance and allowed "many errors to be perpetuated in shadows." Nasser himself on numerous occasions admitted that he had been a conspirator for so long that he could not break the habit of suspicion. It is just such a cautious, wary, and untrusting Nasser that Sadat describes with devastating flair in *In Search for Identity,* whatever the later motivations for Sadat's criticisms. Undoubtedly, the repressive aspect of Nasser's system of rule did owe much to these characteristics.[18]

The conscious decision to avoid binding involvement with civilian allies and to curtail popular participation in the strike for power meant also that the Free Officers depended exclusively on military resources not only for the recruitment of core members but also for the launching of their coup. This fact has profoundly affected all subsequent Egyptian political development by creating a precedent for reliance on military cadres and methods. Given the severe limitations ingrained in the Egyptian military by its history of subservience to foreign rule and Egyptian reactionaries, the precedent has not been a felicitous one.

To say that the conspirators were dependent solely on military resources is to disagree with the official view developed later that the Free Officers acted in some corporate sense for the entire Egyptian military against a corrupt civilian regime. The Free Officers, conspirators drawn from the middle-rank officers, were rebelling as much against their military superiors as against the monarchial regime. With verve Nasser presented his indictment of the military high command:

> They were overfed, lazy, and selfish and they spent their time eating, drinking, gambling, carousing, smoking hashish, and engaging in many different forms of tyranny and corruption. They had the most unmilitary stomachs I ever saw on army officers anywhere. They were fawning and subservient to the British Military Mission, and a disgrace to the uniform they wore. They spent money that belonged to the Egyptian army on food and drink for themselves.[19]

While the revulsion provoked by this spectacle—notably increased by rumors of high-command complicity in the sale of defective arms to Egypt's forces in the Palestine War—may be assumed to have been widely shared by the younger officers, even they as a group were by no means synonymous with the Free Officers. Coterminous with no official military ranks or groupings, the Free Officers were a secret society centered on a handful of close friends. The point is a telling one, for their separation in attitudes from the officer corps as a whole explains the later splits between the regime and the military establishment.

If the Free Officers were not an instrument or a vanguard of the military, it is nonetheless true that they were deeply influenced by their military environment. Although personally successful as a student leader, Nasser had concluded that mass civilian demonstrations were ultimately ineffectual. Recalling those politically active years in his *Philosophy of the Revolution,* Nasser remarked:

> In those earlier days, I led demonstrations in the Nahda Secondary School, and I shouted from my heart for complete independence, and many others behind me shouted, too. But our shouts only raised dust blown by the wind, and produced only weak echoes which shook no mountains and shattered no rocks.

Such early disappointments induced in Nasser and other Free Officers a deep appreciation for the clear-cut hierarchies of military life. In a revolutionary situation, Nasser reasoned, the military could be an important organizational weapon:

> The situation demanded the existence of a force set in one cohesive framework, far removed from the conflict between individuals and classes, and drawn from the heart of the people: a force composed

of men able to trust each other; a force with enough material strength at its disposal to guarantee a swift and decisive action. The conditions could be met only by the Army.

So while the Egyptian military was not the vanguard of national and social reform that some have claimed, and while it by no means possessed a monopoly or even a noticeable lead in the modernity of its training and educational programs, it did have a strong advantage in its basic organizational coherence and, ultimately, in the power rationalized by that coherence.[20]

The hierarchical principles of military organization left their mark; the Free Officers worked consciously to prevent the subversion of those principles in a revolutionary situation. Sadat reminds us that although the Free Officers movement was illegal, with members working "in darkness" and using "secret signs," military rank was as consistently observed inside the movement as it was in the army. Furthermore, the leaders of the movement (middle-rank officers) enjoyed a sound professional reputation among Egyptian officers quite apart from their revolutionary activity. From 1943 until the Palestine War, Nasser taught tactics at the Royal Military Academy—an excellent vantage point from which to become acquainted with the young officers. Thus, although Nasser was unknown to society at large, the majority of young officers had served him, heard his lectures, or knew his reputation. Strengthened by recognition as a hero in the Palestine War, Nasser's professional standing served him well both in building up his movement and in securing broad military support for it once the revolution had taken place. While it is true, and vital to later developments, that the Free Officers worked secretly within the army and that they plotted against the high command, it is equally true and equally vital that they never intended to subvert the organizational principles of the military. Their view was that by purging the army of a corrupt and inefficient high command—"a disgrace to the uniform they wore"—they would free the army to realize its true potential. In any case, once the corrupt elements at the top were eliminated, the command structure was to remain essentially intact.[21]

The Free Officers believed that the organizational integrity of the military was essential for two reasons: any serious breakdown of military coherence might draw the masses into factional strike and engender the disorder that could serve to provoke foreign intervention; and disruption in the normal chain of command might confuse the loyalties of the common soldiers. No attempt had been made by the Free Officers to indoctrinate these soldiers with more radical principles. For their loyalties the movement was counting on the habits of obedience instilled in Egypt's "peasants in uniform."

With the success of the revolution, the establishment of a strong national army was announced as a basic goal. This goal was given substance by the fact that, although nearly all the top military personnel were removed following the coup (more than four hundred officers, including most of the colonels and nearly all men of higher rank), these purged posts were not filled specifically by Free Officers. Rather, while the Free Officers themselves took political positions, they made military appointments based on both reliability and competence. When Nasser made his closest friend Amer a general and commander of the armed forces, it was the only accelerated promotion that followed the 1952 coup. By acting in this manner, Nasser was able to secure the loyalties of many officers and preserve the organizational integrity of the military.[22]

As a conspiratorial nationalist group whose monopoly of power rested on control of the captured armed forces, the Free Officers produced a regime with a profoundly ambivalent attitude toward the military establishment. From the meager resources of the military milieu they had forged their movement, an instrument of national revolt and revival. At the same time, a strong element of solicitude and even dependence on the military—itself in part a deserved target of that very revolt—was built into their attitudes and actions. This ambivalence was later to plague Free Officer rule.

THE CONSOLIDATION OF POWER

The official mythology of the revolution would have it that the Free Officers never intended to rule. Nasser in his *Philosophy of the Revolution* conceptualized their purported role as that of a vanguard which, once having swept away the ancien régime, would step aside as the Egyptian people took command of their own destiny. With flair he described his "disappointment" when reality did not follow this hope and the Free Officers were "compelled" by circumstances to retain the reins of power:

> For a long time it [the vanguard of Free Officers] waited. Crowds did eventually come, and they came in endless droves—but how different is the reality from the dream! The masses that came were disunited, divided groups of stragglers. The sacred advance toward the great objective was stalled, and the picture that emerged on that day looked dark and ominous; it boded danger. At this moment I felt with sorrow and bitterness, that the task of the vanguard, far from being completed, had only begun.

The suggested notion of Nasser as "reluctant dictator" has gained wide credence. The absence of a Free Officer blueprint for the new society coupled with Nasser's early avoidance of publicity was seen as evidence to support such a view.[23]

An alternate interpretation of the original motives of Nasser and his lieutenants is suggested by their overriding concern for preservation of the institutional integrity of the military and their jealous guarding of its independence from civilian groups. As seen earlier, the avoidance of discussion of the new society was justified by the Free Officers in these terms. Furthermore, Nasser explained his own early shying from publicity with a parallel argument:

> I ordered that no name be given any publicity except that of Naguib's. I wanted all the light cast on him. I gave this order principally to avoid a split in the Free Officers. We were all of us either thirty-two, thirty-three, or thirty-four years old, except Khaled Mohieddin, who was a little younger. We were all about equal in rank. I knew how the British and our internal enemies would try to pit us one against the other, if we gave them a chance. But if we had the sense to let an older man like Naguib be the figurehead, we could retain our unity.

Seen in this light, the evidence leads to a rejection of the widely accepted official view and to an argument that the Free Officers intended to wield decisive power, but to wield it indirectly. They would rule through the captured military establishment, acting as a kind of political stage manager—above politics, yet preserving the monopoly of decisive power.[24]

This explanation makes sense of both the evident willfulness with which the Free Officers overthrew the ancien régime and their apparent reluctance to assume power. The initial attempt by the Free Officers to concentrate on preservation of the military power base by avoiding the divisive and problematic question of what actually to do with power solidified a basic attitude that later had a formative influence on the regime. Their rule was marked by a pronounced tendency to regard ideology that prescribed how power was to be used as a divisive threat to the unity of their movement rather than as an instrument to augment their power.

A political stage manager role for Nasser and the Free Officers might have become reality if General Naguib had remained content as front for the Free Officers. But Naguib reached for the substance as well as the form of power. A bitter struggle with Nasser ensued. Naguib, faced with Nasser's dominant position within the Free Officers movement, reached for allies to civilian groupings, including elements of all political coloration from Moslem Brothers to Marxists. Speaking of the necessity to reinstate political parties, he appeared to gain strength from a growing mass popularity. Naguib, to Nasser's alarm, succeeded in drawing into the political equation those very elements Nasser had sought to exclude.

Still more disconcerting was the fact that Naguib's maneuvers had the effect of beginning to crack the solid front of the Free Officers on which Nasser counted most of all. The defection to Naguib of the leftist officer Khaled Muhieddin, influential with the cavalry officers, was a case in point. Ideologically the Free Officers included members sympathetic to all the major trends of political thought; each group that rallied behind Naguib thus was a potential source of further defection from the Free Officers' united front. Faced with this threat, Nasser made some concessions to Naguib. For instance, he agreed that Naguib would be declared president as well as prime minister. But he was adamant on two demands. Over the objections of Naguib, Nasser insisted that Abdul Hakim Amer, his devoted friend, be appointed commander in chief of the army. He likewise insisted that control of the Ministry of the Interior rest in his own hands. Nasser argued that for "almost a year . . . he and he alone had been watching the machinations, the plotting, of the opposition. He could do it better if he had the machinery of security under his direct control." [25]

When the showdown with Naguib came in the months of February, March, and April of 1954, Nasser could draw on two strong resources: the mobilized support of a section of the working class organized by the first of the regime's mass mobilization parties, the Liberation Rally; and control of the instruments of coercion—that is, both the police and the army. [26] With these tools Nasser was able to gain complete control of Egypt by the spring of 1954. Formal recognition of this fact did not come until two years later, in June 1956, when Nasser was elected president of the republic. Here was a significant indication that in revolutionary Egypt form was to mean but little—control of the military and police everything.

Gamal Abdul Nasser, with the military as the bedrock of his support, was now the master of Egypt. With power in his hands, he was confronted starkly with the question assiduously avoided for so long: power for what?

Had the movement actually been able to assume the stage manager role originally envisioned, the nationalism that motivated the Free Officers most likely would have proved sufficient to legitimize their indirect rule. In the situation of the direct assumption of power it provided only the barest beginnings of an answer. To be sure, the shared nationalist dream called for a revolution that was to be anti-imperialist and anti-feudal. The Free Officers were also pledged to build a strong army and to use that army to clean up the government. Experience was to demonstrate that this purely nationalist orientation was not enough. For any government must eventually face the "who gets what" dimension of ruling power. Social support would be needed as hard political choices were made and Egypt redefined its role in global politics.

In time "the revolution in power" did evolve and progressively define itself by adding to its basic nationalism the neutralist, pan-Arab, and (still later) socialist colorings that came to distinguish it. In the struggle to consolidate power can be discerned early and far-reaching implications for that process of evolution. The power struggle with Naguib helped shape Nasser's own conception of the social bases of his support. The small but influential middle class, the political parties, and the Moslem Brotherhood rallied to Naguib against him, apparently enjoying the spontaneous support of the masses. The army and the police, controlled by loyal Free Officers as well as a segment of the working class mobilized by the Liberation Rally, supported Nasser. Not surprisingly, a distrust for the middle classes (including the intellectuals), for political spontaneity, and for politics in general came to characterize the new regime. To the consternation of large segments of the intellectual community, the activities of political parties were first suspended and then outlawed. A strong reliance on the military and security forces supplemented only by those civilian elements that could be carefully controlled was to be the preferred method of rule.[27]

Reflecting on the experience of the Free Officers, one of Egypt's most prominent publicists, Ihsan Abdul Kudus, has observed:

> When ideology precedes revolution it can decide exactly who its enemies are and who its supporters are. It can also define its positions toward them: who are to be destroyed, with whom to compromise, and towards whom to look for help.[28]

The Egyptian revolution, as Kudus stresses, was based on a vague nationalism rather than a coherent ideology. Essential decisions were made purely on the basis of power considerations. Of paramount importance was the alienation of a considerable segment of Egypt's intellectuals. Having sided overwhelmingly with Naguib, the intellectuals were never again fully trusted by the Nasser regime. The loss of their talents was to be a serious one.

CHARISMA AND FOREIGN POLICY

The momentum that Nasser was to give Egypt's foreign policy makes it difficult to recall that basic continuity in foreign policy rather than a sharp break with the past characterized the new regime in its earliest years. Like their predecessors Egypt's new rulers structured their foreign policy around a few principles that remained constant: termination of the British military presence, leadership both in the Arab unity movement and in the Arab hostility to Israel, neutrality in the East-West Cold War, and rapid military modernization.[29] On the other hand, the new regime did bring a change in style—and that change was soon to startle the world.

In the eyes of the Free Officers the outstanding foreign policy concern was the evacuation of the British from Egyptian territory. After prolonged negotiation the Anglo-Egyptian Treaty of October 19, 1954, settled the issue by providing that within twenty months all British troops would be evacuated from Suez. Anthony Nutting, who signed the treaty for Britain, has described how deeply moved Nasser was by what he took to be resolution of the national question for Egypt:

> Even in this sentient atmosphere, his sense of humour did not desert him. As his aide, Ali Sabry, put the treaty in front of me for signature, I discovered that my fountain pen had run out of ink and I had to borrow Nasser's. Then, having signed my name, as an automatic reflex I put the pen in my breast-pocket. Nasser held out his hand and with a broad grin said, "I think you have already got enough out of me in this treaty. Please can I have my pen back."

Nasser was not the only one who thought Egypt had conceded too much. Most vocal were factions within the Moslem Brothers. Objections were raised to the base facilities granted to the British in the Canal Zone, as well as to the "reactivization" clause of the treaty, which provided that if the area were involved in a war with an outside power, Britain and Egypt would be allies. Nasser was denounced for his "act of treason" in signing a treaty that "gave away the rights of the nation."[30]

Equally suspect from a radical nationalist position was Nasser's early moderation vis-à-vis Israel—a moderation out of step with much nationalist feeling. The Moslem Brotherhood had a long and proud history of active support for the Palestinian Arabs. The earliest of the society's journals reflect the brotherhood's concern for Palestine—as Egyptians, as Arabs, and as Moslems. With the general strike of the Palestinian Arabs in 1936, that concern was translated into concrete support. Supplies, equipment, and (most likely) volunteers were sent in support of the Palestinian cause. In similar, if somewhat less activist, fashion the mainstream of the nationalist movement in Egypt opposed the consolidation of a Zionist state. The only exception was a segment of the left, which followed Moscow's example of seeing a progressive dimension to the Zionist presence in Palestine as an anti-British force. Nevertheless, most Egyptian nationalists saw the struggle of the Palestinian Arabs against the British and the Zionists as part of their own anti-imperialist battle.[31]

Nasser and the Free Officers were themselves veterans of the fighting in Palestine: "When I look around me today," Nasser wrote in his *Memoirs of the First Palestine War,* "I see many faces in the Free Officers Organization which I met for the first time in the trenches during that strange period of our lives which we spent in Palestine."[32]

Yet the major lesson learned in Palestine by the Free Officers appears to have been the necessity for revolution in Egypt. Nasser frequently quoted the remark of a dying Egyptian officer: "The main battle is in Egypt." In his *Memoirs* Nasser recorded the sense of frustration that overwhelmed him as he realized the disastrous position of the Egyptian army as a result of the ineptness of those ruling Egypt and directing its participation in the war:

> The first officer I met as I was emerging from the maize fields told me that Ismail Mohieddin had been killed. I do not think I have a right to conceal today the simple human feelings that swept over me as I heard this. I will straightaway confess that I lost all control over my feelings and my tears started to fall. I found myself sobbing with a bitterness I had never before experienced in my life. I was weeping for a brave comrade in arms who had fallen in battle. But I also wept for the battle itself whose reins had been entrusted to the winds.

Little wonder that Nasser diverted part of his energies in Palestine to recruitment for the Free Officers movement—the movement intended to seize the reins of power and give Egypt direction:

> I grew restless at H.Q. and went out on a tour of our positions in order to ascertain the mood of the officers. I will not deny that I was really trying to enlist some of them in our Free Officers Organization. In my conversations with the officers I did not come directly to the point. I did not want to distract their minds from their immediate environment, nor to divert their attention from the enemy who was lying in wait for them. My method at this time aimed at two things. First, to win the confidence of those I met and secondly to strengthen my personal relationship with them as much as possible. I was sure—and this has been amply justified by my experience— that trust and personal friendship were certain to turn into something deeper when the opportune moment arose.[33]

Given this preoccupation with revolution at home, it should not be surprising that once in power Nasser pursued a policy toward Israel that can be described as moderate and Egypt centered. Despite opposition in the junta and the country at large, Nasser argued against the engagement of Egypt's slender resources in confrontation with Israel. At the beginning of 1954 reliable French journalists witnessed Naguib, Nasser, and

Salah Salem greeted at the University of Cairo by actual jeering and the cry: "Give us arms for the Canal and for Palestine." Richard Crossman, a pro-Zionist future British labor minister, who interviewed Nasser during this period, remarks: "At that time he judged that Israel ought not to distract him from the problems of Egypt, those of the social revolution." For Nasser a sense of commitment to the cause of Arab Palestine was always tempered by a pragmatic concern for Egypt's own national interests. For Palestinians these limitations—not fully recognized until after 1967—were a source of perpetual disappointment and increasing frustration.[34]

In the early fifties, then, especially because of the exigencies of power consolidation, the Palestine question was not a salient one for the new regime. Nevertheless a dangerous pattern of violent interaction was developing: small groups of Palestinian raiders, including some operating from Gaza, which was then under Egyptian administration, were infiltrating Israel's borders. In October 1953 Israel, judging unacceptable the level of violence that accompanied the raids, inaugurated the policy of large-scale retaliation.[35]

Responsibility for the worsening situation is not easy to determine. There is considerable evidence that the Egyptians were not spoiling for a fight. During this period Nasser maintained a secret contact with the Israeli prime minister, Moshe Sharett, through the press office of the Egyptian embassy in Paris and occasionally through other channels as well. Moreover, Nasser claimed that the raids that did occur were mounted by his political enemies (probably the Moslem Brothers). However, this attempt to disallow responsibility for the more limited attacks from the Gaza Strip has been challenged by independent French journalists, who report that in fact the Egyptian government in the spring of 1954 had given authorization to the Gaza refugees to harass Israel.[36]

From the mass of charges and countercharges one thing can be stated with certainty: a devastating Israeli retaliatory raid on Gaza in February 1955 sharply escalated the level of violence. The attacking Israelis lost eight men, with thirteen more wounded; they left behind thirty-eight dead Egyptians—thirty-seven men and a seven-year-old boy. The raid dramatized the military weakness of the Egyptians, particularly galling for a regime that relied essentially on the military for its support. From the very genesis of their movement the Free Officers had pledged themselves to the creation of a strong national army. Their inability to respond in kind to the Israeli raid revealed to all the world—notably to the Egyptian military itself—that this pledge had not yet been kept.[37]

The conditions for the resolution of Egypt's dilemma were created in the arena of great power politics and by seemingly unrelated considera-

tions. The United States and Britain proposed an alliance project, later to
be known as the Baghdad Pact, which sought to join the Eastern Arab
countries with Turkey, Iran, Pakistan, and the two Western countries
into a regional grouping transparently directed against the Soviet Union.
The Egyptians objected violently to this project, and for reasons other
than any great solicitude for the Soviet Union. Pursuant to the traditional policy aimed at securing Egyptian leadership in Arab affairs, Nasser had formulated his own project for an exclusively Arab alliance,
which would avoid appearing too closely identified with the "imperialist" powers while at the same time making possible extensive political,
economic, and military links with the West. Such an alliance would enhance Egypt's stature and its claim to large-scale Western aid.

Nasser, then, opposed the Baghdad Pact not simply on nationalist
grounds but also because it meant that his own scheme for an Arab alliance under Egyptian leadership was being challenged.[38] In addition, the
pact thrust Iraq, Egypt's traditional rival in Arab affairs, into prominence; it promised to bring to Iraq those resources of material and prestige that Nasser had sought for Egypt. The conservative Iraqi regime did
not have Nasser's reservations about a close and open identification with
the West. Nasser, moved by Egypt's national interests, launched his
attack against the Baghdad Pact, expressing his opposition in the dramatic and evocative language of "anti-imperialism." The decision to initiate
this overt attack against the West was not undertaken lightly. Faced with
Egypt's overwhelming problems, Nasser believed that one great hope for
the country lay in large doses of foreign aid. In the early 1950s the West
appeared the most likely source, and Nasser had given many indications
that he was not averse to working with the Western powers to secure that
aid. Yet there were limitations to the openness with which he could pursue such a policy.

The justification for the military revolution in 1952 had been expressed
largely in nationalist terms, and the fact is that the Egyptian military
never enjoyed a monopoly on the Egyptian nationalist tradition. One
group that could offer substantial rival claims to speak for that tradition
was the Moslem Brotherhood. The brotherhood earlier had spearheaded
various guerilla attacks against the British in Suez and earned acclaim as
brave fighters for the Arab cause in the Palestine War. Their nationalist
credentials were well established when they attacked the treaty negotiated
by Nasser with the British as a sellout to the imperialists.[39] Although Nasser, on the heels of an inept assassination attempt instigated by the brotherhood, succeeded in crushing the immediate threat of the movement, he
must have been affected by the response evoked by their charge of com-
promising the nationalist tradition. A too close relationship with the
recently ousted Western powers was not a prescription conducive to the
regime's domestic good health.

It was these basic considerations of the regime's power position, Egypt's national needs, and its role in inter-Arab affairs that determined Nasser's opposition to the Baghdad Pact. The emotion-charged, anti-Western presentation called forth a strong positive response from the masses of the Arab world. And it happened that Nasser's opposition to the Western-sponsored scheme coincided with the interests of the Soviet Union.

The Soviet Union initially had been unimpressed with the Nasser regime. Early characterizations tended to view the Free Officers as a group of reactionaries connected with the United States. The post-Stalinist period, however, was marked by a growing Soviet interest in the liberation movements of the Third World. The havoc wrought by Nasser's virulent and effective opposition to the Baghdad Pact could not but attract favorable Soviet attention. The altered Soviet attitudes led to a resolution of Nasser's problem of military impotence; in September 1955 an arms agreement between Egypt and Czechoslovakia was signed to provide a large influx of arms from the Soviet bloc to the Egyptian army. The West's ill-fated Baghdad Pact had borne its first bitter fruit, Nasser's triumph was complete.

Domestically, Nasser's military power base reveled in the windfall of Soviet arms. It is doubtful that second thoughts about the source of those arms in any way spoiled the revelry, especially when one remembers that the Free Officers' movement before the coup had clearly proclaimed: "We demand arms for the army from all countries which sell us weapons, either from the East or West." Moreover, the idea of an arms deal with the East was not new; it had been given favorable consideration intermittently by the Wafd government from 1950 to 1952.[40]

Equally advantageous was the skyrocketing of the regime's reputation. All of the previously mentioned reservations about its nationalist credentials were swept aside and forgotten in the popular euphoria that greeted the news of the arms deal. Nasser, or so it seemed to his own people, had openly defied the foreigners who had dominated Egypt for so long. And he had triumphed.[41]

The victory on the inter-Arab level was, if possible, still more impressive. In terms of immediate objectives, the military advantages that had accrued to Iraq as a result of the Baghdad Pact were more than offset. More dramatic and ultimately more significant, though, was the reaction of the masses throughout the Arab world. Nasser's recent suppression of the Moslem Brotherhood had been the occasion of huge anti-Nasser demonstrations in the streets of Damascus, Amman, Baghdad, Khartoum, and Karachi. Although the brotherhood had never won broad mass support beyond Egypt's borders, it had earned the reputation of being a patriotic organization, especially during the Palestine campaign. The arms deal prompted an instant forgiveness: overnight Nasser was hailed as a new Saladin, the savior of Arabs everywhere, the modern symbol of Arab unity. With this response Nasser was first awakened to the political possibilities of pan-Arabism.[42]

On the plane of international politics the arms agreement was no less important. In a sense it represented the first of the successive nationalizations that were to punctuate the Nasser years: Egypt's foreign policy, Nasser announced to the world, was henceforth to bear the label "made in Cairo." The explicit formulation of "positive neutrality" still lay ahead, but the arms deal, by opening the door to the East, clearly laid the foundations for it. And the fundamental characteristic of that later policy could already be recognized: in the name of Egypt's own conception of its national interests, support from both East and West would be graciously accepted—or, depending on one's perspective, ungraciously extorted.

It seems clear that Nasser would have agreed to tacit alliance with the West and the aid that would have made it worthwhile had that alliance and that aid been offered in a form he deemed safe. Ahmed Aboul Fath, a liberal Egyptian journalist, has recorded Nasser's early disbelief in the possibility of a pure and literal neutrality for Egypt: "It is impossible . . . Do you wish to isolate Egypt from the rest of the world? West or East, one must choose. You must have a strong ally to aid and support you."[43] The arms deal demonstrated that Egypt intended to exercise that choice—and exercise it according to Egypt's own felt interests. Such an approach, in an area where Western domination had been so pronounced, was dramatic enough. Still more telling was the fact that three months after Nasser revealed the arms deal to the world, the United States announced its willingness to support construction of the massive Aswan Dam, the keystone of the regime's domestic development plan. Nasser, it appeared, had secured not only the independence to choose between East and West, but also the special grace to choose both. The Egyptian leader's performance dazzled the world and gained for Egypt an unprecedented role in international affairs.

This initial phase of Egypt's courtship from both sides was short-lived, ending rudely with the withdrawal by the United States of its offer to help Egypt build the High Dam. U. S. Secretary of State John Foster Dulles' reappraisal was prompted essentially by Nasser's continued attacks on the Baghdad Pact, compounded both by his apparent role in promoting an overturn of the government of Jordan and his boldness in recognizing Communist China.[44] Nasser's response is well-recorded history: nationalization of the Suez Canal Company, followed by the Israeli-British-French invasion—all ending with the canal firmly in Egypt's hands and its enemies out of Egyptian territory. Nasser had won what was to be the greatest victory of his astonishing career.

It was at Suez that Egypt's nationalist revolution found its voice. Stung by withdrawal of the Western offer to finance the dam, Nasser expressed in his anger the full depth of historical humiliation built into Egypt's colonial dependency; he also expressed its new defiance. To hear Nasser announce the nationalization of the canal was to hear for the first time the authentic voice of a new Egypt.

The French journalist Jean Lacouture was there that day in Alexandria and marveled at the transformation in Nasser as he made his speech. Gone was the earlier austerity and the awkwardness of a young leader striving for a noble public style. Nasser spoke colloquially, regaling his audience with anecdotes about the American diplomats and statesmen who had sought to humiliate Egypt: "Poor Mr. Allen! He comes into my office with the note—I drive him out; he returns without having delivered the note—Mr. Dulles drives him out. What can be done for poor Mr. Allen?" Nasser lampooned and ridiculed, as the crowd roared approval. But then the tone changed. Speaking, many felt, for the first time as the authentic voice of Egyptian nationalist resistance, Nasser laid down his challenge: "We are going to take back the profits which this imperialist company, this state within the state, deprived us of while we were dying of hunger." With his audience exultant, Nasser shared the historic moment:

> As I speak to you, government agents are taking possession of the company . . . The canal will pay for the dam! Four years ago, in this very place, Farouk fled Egypt. Today I seize the canal, in the name of the people...This night our canal shall be Egyptian, controlled by Egyptians.

Nasser had become a true national hero. As Sadat put it much later: "Egypt, a small country, was at last capable of speaking loud and clear in defiance of the biggest power on earth. It was a turning point in the history of our revolution, and in the entire history of Egypt." Who could forget that after the high drama of the nationalization, Nasser stood firmly with his people under siege. In the face of the tripartite invasion of Egypt by Israel, France, and Britain he defiantly broadcast the vow to resist; his own family remained in Cairo. From the pulpit of al-Azhar mosque Nasser pledged that the invaders would be fought from village to village, from house to house. He then plunged into the crowds and toured Cairo in an open car so that his people would know he was among them.[45]

From the Suez experience Nasser of course drew his own lesson. Despite the nationalist fervor aroused in Egypt, he understood that Egypt's salvation had been secured by the successful manipulation of global political forces. Later Nasser coolly acknowledged that the decisive element in his victory had been American diplomacy, which exerted pressure for withdrawal of the British, French, and Israelis. For Nasser Egypt's new defiance rested on his own sure grasp of the logic of international politics.

To Egypt's people it seemed clear that their country had at last shed its legacy of colonial dependency; the Egyptians relished their triumph. Nasser as a charismatic figure to the Egyptian and wider Arab masses was born with these successes in foreign policy. Nasser has admitted being somewhat startled by the emotional intensity of the popular response to his moves against the West:

> Even then I had not realized the acclaim this would receive not only from my own people but throughout the Arab world. Almost for the first time there was complete Arab unity in support of my action.[46]

Nasser, or so Egyptians thought, had at last succeeded in throwing off the aggressive attack of the West. Power had been answered with power.

NASSER'S VISION OF A NEW EGYPT

Under the impact of these experiences in domestic and international politics Nasser's regime began to take shape. The power struggle with Naguib and then with the Moslem Brotherhood was decisive in solidifying the essentially nationalist thrust of Egypt's revolutionary regime with a military and authoritarian, yet popular and secular, cast. Early experience in foreign policy pointed to the positive neutralism and pan-Arabism that came to distinguish the regime. And the dramatic successes that crowned the foreign policy of the new government provided the emotional capital to carry Nasser and his regime through almost two decades of rule.

The revolutionary changes during the Nasser era do not alter the fact that the Nasserist regime did originate as a military putsch rather than a major social and political revolution. There can be no doubt that the potential for such a revolution existed in Egypt at midcentury; however, that potential was preempted by the coup d'état executed on July 23, 1952, by Gamal Abdul Nasser as leader of the Free Officers conspiratorial society. Much later Sadat was to remark that the Free Officers movement "saved the country from civil war."[47]

With the resolution by the mid-fifties of an initial period of confusion and uncertainty, the vision animating Nasser's revolution from above crystallized around five major goals:

(1) The elitist, restrictive, and nonideological Free Officers had moved from conspiracy to a rule closely tied to but not identical with the military from which they had emerged. A regime marked by these origins

took shape and gave the preservation of its hold on power top priority.

(2) As a ruling group, the Free Officers were inevitably faced with the question: power for what? Guided by no systematic ideology that might have provided a pattern or model for socioeconomic change, they were left with a vague but widely shared dream of a purified, developed, and strong Egypt, purged of its colonial past. In his *Philosophy of the Revolution*, written in 1953, Nasser called gamely for a "social revolution" that would develop Egypt. It is symptomatic that the implementation of such a revolution was not really begun until 1961.

(3) In the mid-fifties attention was necessarily riveted on foreign policy. Nasser's successful maneuvers in the arena of great-power politics had earned for him the adulation of the Arab masses and suggested the enormous advantages that would flow to an Egypt which spearheaded the drive for Arab unity. The essentially Egyptian nationalism behind the coup was shaded into an Arab nationalism that profoundly influenced Egypt's modern course of development. The ill-starred merger with Syria in 1958 and the disastrous war in Yemen in 1961 were a direct outgrowth of the aim of advancing Arab unity.

(4) The confrontation with Israel was inevitably raised to a new level. If Egypt was to reap the advantages of its role as leader of the Arabs, it had to address itself directly to the task of confronting the primary enemy of Arab nationalism—Israel.

(5) While its attitude toward the course of domestic change remained ambivalent for years, the regime's preoccupation with foreign policy early crystallized a concern with the enhancement of Egypt's international standing as a major aim.

Each of these goals was seen as a means to advance each and all of the others. It was such revolutionizing, interrelated ideas that gave Nasser's rule its tremendous flexibility and dynamism. Nasser's Egypt—in triumph and defeat—can only be understood in the context of this complex vision as it found historical expression during the almost two decades of Nasser's rule.[48] The continuing resonance of that vision for large segments of Egyptian society suggests that it was both conditioned by and addressed to their situation. Embracing both internal and external political forces, the vision gave meaning to the pressures that impinged on Egyptians at midcentury. And perhaps more importantly, Nasser's vision promised to the Egyptian people liberation from their dependency.

2. Building a Political-Economic Order

Gamal Abdul Nasser's performance at Suez in 1956 tested and ultimately strengthened his hold on power. The successful defiance of Israeli, French, and British forces earned the Free Officers widespread domestic support. From Nasser's defeated rival, General Naguib, came a significant pledge of unqualified loyalty and support at the time of the tripartite invasion. But for the men who had made Egypt's revolution, their own political survival was not an end in itself. Nasser and his lieutenants saw themselves as heirs of the nationalist tradition, charged with the mission of achieving greatness for Egypt. As the conspirators transformed themselves into a ruling elite, they developed a clearer understanding of the obstacles to the building of a strong and independent Egypt. Nasser spoke bitterly of his inheritance of "a handful of cinders from the ancien régime."[1] New means, both material and intellectual, were needed for the social reconstruction of Egypt. Like revolutionaries everywhere, the Free Officers learned that they must fashion instruments of power, cadres, and ideology if they were to harness the creative energies to realize their dreams. Ironically, the search for resources complicated their task by drawing Egypt further into the diverting tangle of global politics.

THE STRATEGY FOR DEVELOPMENT AND ITS COSTS

At the heart of the Nasserist vision of Egypt's destiny was a grasp of the necessary linkage between domestic and international politics. Such an understanding was natural to one who viewed Egypt's history from a nationalist perspective, for the country's fate had so often been decided by outside forces. Nasser now sought to exploit this link to the outside world to supplement Egypt's meager resources, while at the same time preserving his own monopoly on power.

The outlines of a strategy aimed at both the necessity for development and the maintenance of Free Officer rule can be seen in Nasser's earliest writings. If Egypt's resources in themselves offered little, Nasser reasoned, Egypt's role in relation to its Arab neighbors promised a great deal. Nasser insisted that collectively the Arabs were strong as a result of several factors: the moral and material ties that bound the Arab countries into a homogeneous whole, the strategic position of the Arab countries, and Arab oil. Moreover, in a much quoted passage of *Philosophy of the Revolution,* written not long after the Free Officers seized power, Nasser had spoken of destiny's beckoning Egypt to play a role in the three circles of the Arab world, the Moslem world, and Africa. Nasser understood that the strong collective position of the Arabs was not built on inherent strength but on their relation to the rest of the world. Strategic importance and oil are eminently salable, but hardly consumable products for the Arabs. Implicit in Nasser's thinking was the idea that in such a situation politics can be made to assert primacy over economics. And Egypt, while poor economically, could claim a position of political leadership among the Arabs. Location at the crossroads of the Arab world, a large and relatively well-trained population, and the cultural importance of Cairo guaranteed that much.[2]

Nasser reasoned further that a strong international political position could be made to pay economic dividends in a variety of ways. Had he not sought earlier to place Egypt at the head of an Arab alliance, which would cooperate with the West while positioning Egypt to receive both large-scale aid and prestige? When the Baghdad Pact undermined those plans, Nasser adroitly turned his attack on the pact into a strong anti-imperialist position. With the important Soviet arms pact of 1955, East-West competitive courtship of Egypt began in earnest. "Foreign policy," explained Nasser's confidant M. H. Haikal, "was not a charge but a motive force for our economy."[3] The payoff from its investment in foreign policy was to become Egypt's greatest resource.

For the period 1957 to 1965 foreign loans and credits totaled $3.43 billion. It would have been difficult at this time to question Haikal's judgment that Egypt derived more aid per capita from both the West and the communist bloc than any other country, with the aim of "building a base for progress on its soil." Nasser had early reached the fundamental decision that "there is no alternative for us but to become an industrial power in the shortest possible time." The financial resources for such an industrialization program, Nasser further concluded, could only come from foreign aid.[4]

Nasser was frequently accused by foreign and domestic critics alike of grandstanding in the international arena to the detriment of Egypt's domestic development. Reality was more complex. To his own people Nasser on numerous occasions explained the rationale of his foreign policy and the way in which it was responsive to the international logic of power and to Egypt's developmental needs. In one such address Nasser

bluntly acknowledged that Egypt could never realize its investment goals
if it relied solely on its own domestic resources. He explained that it was
only with an activist foreign policy that Egypt could assure its independence and the large-scale aid required. It was, as Nasser put it, "Egypt's
participation in the problems of the contemporary world" that stimulated the flow of foreign loans and credits. In addition to these national-
interest considerations, there was an ideological component to Nasser's
reasoning. He saw Egypt's struggle as but one part of a worldwide movement for "the eradication of imperialism, and . . . the liberation of all
colonized and subjugated peoples." Cairo during the Nasser years did
become a center for liberation movements struggling against colonial
rule. Yet in Nasser's view commitment to anti-imperialism and aid to
colonized peoples did not preclude a strikingly businesslike concern for
Egypt's own interests.[5]

The logic of looking to foreign policy activism to generate resources
has not been lost on Nasser's successor. Anwar es-Sadat, looking back
on the situation before the October War of 1973, frankly acknowledged
that without the war Egypt would have failed to meet its debt installments in January 1974. "Nor could I have bought a grain of wheat in
1974," Sadat confided. "There wouldn't have been bread for the people." Sadat then explained that the October War regained for Egypt the
initiative in foreign relations, which promptly paid economic dividends.
"As soon as the battle of October 6 was over," Sadat reported, "our
Arab brethren came to our aid with $500 million . . . and this sum would
never have come had we not taken effective action."[6] Nasser's manipulation of foreign policy issues established precedents still of relevance today.

The attempt to extract resources for development from Egypt's foreign
involvements represented a creative response to the country's difficult
situation at midcentury. In the face of overwhelming pressures from both
domestic and international environments, it aimed to fulfull Nasser's
dynamic vision of Egypt's future. Investment in foreign policy would
mask Egypt's weakness and generate new sources of strength.

These much vaunted advantages notwithstanding, the fundamental
Nasserist strategy eventually proved to have its costs. For one thing, Nasser was obliged to devote an inordinate amount of time and energy to
foreign policy considerations. It was in part the force of Nasser's personal commitment to the task of modernizing Egypt that saved the Free
Officers movement from degenerating into a military tyranny interested
in power for its own sake. The channeling of his energies into foreign
policy represented a serious loss for Egypt. And the same process continued under his successor. It is striking that although Sadat in the process
of consolidating his power did launch a "Corrective Revolution," calling

for a national dialogue about the domestic character of the regime, his own efforts appear also to have been directed disproportionately to the conduct of foreign affairs. It was only with the large-scale urban riots of January 1977 that Sadat showed signs of redressing that imbalance.

Preoccupation with international affairs also clouded comprehension of the magnitude of the task of modernizing Egypt. It encouraged a simplistic engineering approach. In the early years of his rule Nasser apparently believed that with enough foreign aid and enough technical skill Egypt could be dragged into the twentieth century. It was a euphoric phase not without its triumphs (notably the High Dam). By the mid-sixties, however, Nasser realized that he had deceived himself and Egypt. The internal challenge of modernity—the challenge of ideas and values linked to social change—had not been met. Through the painfully gained experience of the Nasser years, Sadat came to power with a fuller understanding of this fundamental challenge confronting Egypt. In a major programmatic statement, *The October Working Paper of 1974,* Sadat observed:

> The real challenge confronting peoples with deep-rooted origins who are facing the problem of civilizational progress is precisely how to renovate their civilization. They should not reject the past in the name of the present and should not renounce the modern in the name of the past, but they should take of the new without losing sight of their origins.

Raising the issue of values and social change, Sadat continued:

> The modern society and nation are not such [*sic*] insofar as their material manifestations alone are concerned, and their setting up is not completed once they have acquired modern commodities and products. Modernism is knowing the right order of priorities as to our requirements of these tools. *Then we should set up the institutions, systems and relations capable of transforming these tools in Arab hands from hackneyed, inanimate tools into creative, productive ones.* Next, we should compose the suitable environment and necessary stage of development which will make us capable of invention and creativeness and consequently of a true contribution to human civilization.

This improved comprehension was one important lesson learned from the failures of the Nasser era.[7]

Despite such awareness, Free Officer rule to this day has been unable to create those "institutions, systems and relations" to which Sadat referred. The beginnings of an explanation for this continuing failure lie in the final cost of the strategy of investment in foreign policy: such an approach demanded a radical flexibility and freedom of tactical movement for the highest political leadership. The insulation of foreign policy from potentially constraining domestic pressures was therefore considered essential. Nasser was already conditioned by his experiences of conspiracy and revolt to regard such independence of movement as desirable. Once in power he met the requirement of freedom from societal constraints, which the strategy of investment in foreign policy imposed, by basing his regime solidly on the military and dependent administrative apparatus. Such a political system proved severely limiting as an instrument of social transformation.

The Military Dimension of Power

Nasser spoke of the role of the military in his regime as "the vanguard and shield" of the revolution.[8] This formulation is vague, and appropriately so, for it reflects a basic ambiguity in the relations between the Free Officers movement and the larger military establishment. The conspiratorial origins of the Free Officers and the mediation through friendships of their ties to the military make it difficult to define a vanguard or shield relationship. Still, such conceptualizations do recognize a salient reality of Egyptian political life: ruling power in Nasser's Egypt had a pronounced military coloration. Sadat's assumption of power has not altered this fact.

The military dimension of power in the Egypt of the Free Officers has been manifested in the prominence of military men in key political positions. Reliance on military personnel in turn has reinforced the insulation of the ruling group from the larger society. A crippling retardation of political institutionalization has been the overall result. In the formative years immediately following the revolution, decisive power in Egypt was consistently concentrated in the hands of Nasser and approximately a dozen fellow officers, most of them veterans of the Free Officers movement. The institutional locus of Free Officer power was the Executive Committee, which after January 1953 was known as the Revolutionary Command Council. In 1956 the council was dissolved in an effort to deemphasize the military aspect of Free Officer rule. Nasser and his key lieutenants resigned their military commissions to assume what ostensibly were to be civilian positions in a government outlined by a newly ratified constitution.

Despite a certain symbolic importance, these costume changes did not alter the fact that the same military personalities, led by Gamal Abdul Nasser, continued to play the leading roles. In all governments after 1952 the top positions have been held by officers. Furthermore, the presence of the military at the ministerial level generally has been impressive: of the sixty-five men who held portfolios in the government between 1962 and 1967, twenty-seven were former officers.[9] Such heavy reliance on military and security personnel freed the new regime of the necessity to ally itself closely and irrevocably with any social class or stratum. A quite remarkable insulation from normal domestic pressures, at least in the short run, resulted. As the "revolution in power" began to make those unavoidable decisions that shaped its orientations in foreign policy and domestic development, it enjoyed a striking tactical flexibility. Only much later was it realized that this isolation of Egypt's rulers made the tasks of social reconstruction more difficult.

The relation of the military regime to the urban business groups in Egypt provides one example of the social isolation of the Free Officers. The first years of military rule were marked by a strong conservatism in economic affairs. Egypt's political revolution of 1952 only began to have its counterpart in the economic sphere after 1956. The military regime's early courtship of business groups is reflected in a whole series of measures. There were, first of all, policy statements transparently designed to reassure the middle classes. Thus, the influential minister of national guidance, Gamal Salem, explained: "We are not socialists: I think our economy can only prosper under free enterprise."[10] Such statements were given credibility by the early purging from the leadership circle of left-wing elements, as well as by the imprisoning of communists. Certain key policies long advocated by the Egyptian Federation of Industries, which represented the interests of Egyptian business groups, were speedily implemented. The regime raised tariffs and lowered custom duties on raw materials and capital goods, as the federation had frequently urged. Generous tax exemptions and benefits were extended to new and existing joint stock companies. Finance for development became more easily obtainable when the government strengthened its financial support of the industrial bank. New privileges were also accorded to foreign investors.

During these first years of the Free Officers' rule it seemed clear that the regime inclined toward a partnership with the business-oriented sections of the middle class. But by 1962 the economic policy of the Nasser regime had been completely reversed. Cooperation with Egypt's businessmen had been replaced by nationalization of all important industrial establishments, and free-enterprise capitalism had given way to a centrally directed economy. The breathtaking ease with which this change was accomplished was largely a reflection of the fact that the early partnership with business groups was strictly confined to the economic realm. With the bedrock of its support in the military, the regime was not required and definitely not inclined to any effective sharing of political power. Consequently, when the regime's purposes had been served, a complete reversal of the previous relationship with business groups was perfectly feasible and speedily accomplished.

The lack of social roots reflected in this maneuverability might have been a more significant problem for the Free Officers were it not for their special relationship with Egypt's peasantry. Nasser and his lieutenants were perceived by the peasants as representatives of peasant interests. Such a situation has been a fortuitous one for Egypt's rulers.

The peasants constitute a social class to the degree that they live under distinctive and similar economic conditions. This shared way of life sets them apart from other classes and groups. However, the relative isolation and self-containment of their communities hampers the development of a full-blown class identity. Consequently, Egypt's peasants can have a class interest only to a limited degree, and they are quite incapable of defending that interest. In winning peasant support the Free Officers were helped by themselves being in many cases provincials and the grandsons of peasants. For the first time, rulers spoke a language understood by the people. An impression was created that the problems of the village were understood and that someone was concerned to solve them.[11]

Although the material conditions of the rural population have not improved in any dramatic way under the revolutionary regime, the relations between the Free Officers and the peasants nonetheless have been mutually beneficial. For the regime, they have provided an unstructured popular underpinning, a diffuse but important approbation for military rule. Peasant aspirations have been simply for the improvement of their lot and thus can be manipulated and shaped to conform to any ideological or institutional patterns desired by the regime. The support of the peasantry in no way lessened the freedom of maneuver of the regime, notably in foreign policy. For example, pan-Arabism had only to be given an Islamic flavor to win popular support. In addition, as spokesman and benefactor of the masses, the regime acquired a certain moral justification for rule. For their part, the peasants could see at least some actions taken on their behalf, such as agrarian reform and improvements in rural health care and education. They could also enjoy the presumed psychic satisfactions of an unprecedented honorific status. In revolutionary Egypt one-half of the seats in the National Assembly were reserved to peasants and workers.

The freedom from societal constraints demanded by the ruling style of the Free Officers, whatever its justification for the conduct of Egypt's foreign affairs, was secured at devastating cost to the institutionalization of Free Officer rule. "Everyone knew," reported Soviet specialist G. I. Mirsky, "that the real power in the country was the army and important questions were decided by President Nasser." Description of constitutional and political party arrangements devised by the regime over the years can safely be left to traditional institutional historians: effective power for decision making has consistently lain elsewhere.[12]

M. H. Haikal, in an incisive article published during the self-critical period after the 1967 defeat, wrote that in Nasser's Egypt "the dominant element is the old military element that took part in the operation of July 23, 1952 or were in contact with those who did have a direct part." This inner core, strengthened during the period of conspiracy and revolt, was then supplemented by "a large number of civilian elements . . . led by the necessity of political or technical activity to draw near to the group in power and to integrate themselves with it." Finally, Haikal bluntly acknowledged that "the ensemble of those who hold power does not constitute a single but rather several 'formations' the strongest of which without doubt is represented by an alliance between elements of the Army High Command and the Secret Police." The most recent changes inaugurated by Sadat, for all their promise of reform, have yet to alter significantly the realities of power revealed in these stark generalizations.[13]

Whatever its value to their own political survival, the basic strategy for Egypt's development devised by Nasser and the Free Officers held little hope for the creation of an effective political community. Popular energies were aroused by the successes of the Free Officers, but they could not be canalized by fraudulent political and constitutional arrangements. Before long those energies were lost to Egypt's development.

Prototype for the Mandate System

Real power in Nasser's Egypt did not flow through the officially prescribed constitutional channels. Crucial to the actual system of rule was the relationship established by Nasser between his regime and the military establishment. Since that relationship set a pattern characteristic of Nasser's rule generally, it merits close study. Given the fact that power mechanisms in Nasser's Egypt were highly personalized, analysis here will focus on the appointment of Abdul Hakim Amer as military commander in chief.

The Free Officers came to power with an ambivalent attitude toward the military establishment. On the one hand, Nasser and his followers were contemptuous of an institution that had been reduced by the ancien régime to a mere police force or parade unit charged with "participation in celebrations and the putting up of decorations."[14] Yet the Free Officers also saw clearly the potential of the army as an organizational weapon to destroy the old order and to help build a new, strong Egypt. This potential, Nasser had argued, could be realized by capturing the military institution with its organizational structure intact. The military could then be bent to the achievement of nationalist aims. Such a project, by its nature, engendered an attitude of both solicitude and wariness toward the military establishment. Although the army was not to be fully trusted, it was to be fully used to guarantee Free Officer power and the success of the revolution. It was from the struggle with these conflicting pressures that Nasser created the prototype for the mandate system of rule, the single political mechanism most characteristic of his regime.

Once their coup had succeeded, the Free Officers were deeply concerned to win over those military officers still uncommitted to the movement. That concern is reflected in the initial choice of General Naguib to act as figurehead for the younger officers. Naguib has recorded that earlier, when he contemplated resigning from the army as a result of what he considered to be a demotion without cause, Nasser and Amer had begged him to reconsider: "If I resigned, they said, the Free Officers movement would be left without a single general to represent them." When discussing the choice of a figurehead, Nasser said that the man chosen should be "a middle-aged man. Some senior officer, older than any of us; someone whose name will command the respect of the entire army, and lead the people."[15]

When Naguib became the first president of the Egyptian Republic in June 1953, he was succeeded (at Nasser's insistence) as commander in chief by Abdul Hakim Amer. From that time until just before his reported suicide after Egypt's defeat in 1967, Amer retained that position. The choice of Amer is instructive. As a veteran Free Officer, his revolutionary credentials were impeccable. Equally important is the fact that of all the Free Officers Amer was Nasser's closest personal friend. The liberal Egyptian journalist Aboul Fath, who at the time enjoyed the confidence of the Free Officers, has provided an illuminating description of the discussions that preceded Amer's appointment. Aboul Fath suggests that Nasser was concerned primarily lest the Free Officers lose their recently established control over the larger military establishment. He quotes Nasser as arguing:

> We cannot leave the army without control . . . We will all be threatened if we do not establish an effective control over it. You have ascertained that there is a certain malaise which has begun to make itself felt in the units. I would not be surprised if a faction of the army one night carried out our arrest. But the whole army loves Abdul Hakim Amer and that is why I insist that he be nominated commander in chief.[16]

Nasser made it clear that the choice of Amer was based not only on his personal loyalty and veteran status in the Free Officers movement, but also on his popularity with the officers corps as a whole.

Amer's prestige with the military rested on a sound professional reputation. An instructor in the Army School of Administration, Amer was well known among younger officers. He was a member of the distinguished class of May 1948 graduating from the Staff College, one of twenty-six chosen to attend from approximately a thousand eligible officers. Nasser recalled that Amer, along with two other members of the Revolutionary Command Council, "were given exceptional promotions on the field of battle in Palestine."[17]

Such a man was the ideal choice to consolidate support for the Free Officers in the military and ensure their ultimate control over it: Amer was both loyal to the Free Officers and more than satisfactory to the military. Aboul Fath has characterized Amer as a "sincere patriot" aspiring to "rid the country of British occupation" and to "raise the level of the Egyptian army." Amer's attitude toward the army is reflected in the fact that he originally declined the post of commander in chief by arguing that his promotion from major to brigadier—necessary if he were to assume the post—was completely contrary to military tradition. Eventually Nasser was able to persuade Amer to take the position by convincing him that it would provide the opportunity to raise the level of the army. From the outset Amer was a man with more than one loyalty.[18]

With complete trust in Amer, Nasser, in the words of the Soviet analyst Mirsky, "was anxious to bring his [Amer's] influence in the army and the country to bear in the interests of the revolution." It would be a mistake, though, to ignore the fact that there is tension implicit in such a dual commitment as Amer's. Inevitably, time strengthened Amer's attachment to the particular interests of the military. Aboul Fath described the process:

> Officers have their problems, their demands, their wishes. It is Amer who listens to their complaints, resolves their problems and realizes their wishes . . . It is this attitude which has avoided for Nasser up to the present many difficulties which the officers would have been able to cause him.

Amer, then, became the spokesman for military interests. Whatever its short-term advantages in binding the military to Free Officer rule, such a role gradually put pressure on Amer's unquestioning loyalty to Nasser.[19]

A documented incident in the 1954 power struggle between Naguib and Nasser provides a very early example of the tension built into Amer's dual dedication. The leftist Khaled Muhieddin had defected to Naguib, bringing with him the support of the important cavalry officers. Aboul Fath reports that the question of using force against the dissidents was raised within the Revolutionary Command Council. He identifies Salah Salem and Anwar es-Sadat as the leading proponents of such an approach, strongly supported by Gamal Salem, Baghdadi, and Ibrahim. With the help of the army Nasser undoubtedly could have crushed the cavalry's threat. In this situation Amer's position as commander in chief was clearly of pivotal importance. And Amer, despite his friendship for Nasser, refused to identify himself openly with either Nasser or the dissidents. Amer would not "sanction a civil war between the different corps of the army." Pressured by partisans of Nasser who advocated the use of force, Amer threatened resignation: "I cannot remain commander in chief of an army in which orders are given to launch a civil war between different units." As it happened, Nasser was able to outmaneuver Muhieddin and Naguib without resort to force and Amer was spared making a more definite choice. The incident, nevertheless, served to dramatize the fact that from the very beginning the outcome of such a decision was by no means clear.[20]

In the early years the disruptive possibilities built into Nasser's mandate system for dealing with the regime-military relationship were not realized. Amer's dual commitment to Nasser and the military establishment was harmonized by the mutually beneficial relationship between the revolutionary government and the army. Whatever his original intentions, Nasser's own fate was bound up with the army insofar as he derived power from it; the army in its turn would owe a great deal to the new regime.[21]

Nasser's insistence that Amer accept the position of commander in chief reflected his awareness that control could best be maintained by persuading the army that the rule of the Free Officers was in its best corporate interest. To be sure, these positive efforts were supplemented by coercive instruments such as intelligence networks in the armed forces and periodic purges of all uncooperative elements. Yet even the purges were remarkable for their lack of vindictiveness and their evident concern with avoiding disruption and alienation of the military. There have been numerous examples of potential dissidents eased, even promoted, out of positions where they could have been a threat. Service in the diplomatic corps, followed by generous retirement, has frequently been used to short-circuit a potentially dangerous career. Nasser has explained the rationale of this policy, pursued with Amer's help:

> I have made a careful study of the army. And I have concluded that each officer has at least five other officers with him a hundred per cent. And each of those has five others, and so on. If I begin purging the army, I run the risk of alienating big blocs of men in the army. In the end, I would undermine my own position and invite a coup d'état against my regime.

The mandate system secured for Nasser the essential support of the Egyptian army until Amer's own loyalty apparently broke under the strain of the defeat by Israel in 1967. Until that time and despite the strains that surfaced after 1961, Nasser could congratulate himself for the success of the Amer appointment in securing the military as the basic prop for his regime.[22]

Little wonder, then, that the mandate system became Nasser's major political mechanism. Having come to power without ideologically motivated cadres from whom he could draw for appointments, Nasser assigned key responsibilities to individuals (technically qualified, if possible) who enjoyed his personal confidence. These mandated personalities, like Amer, were then given considerable autonomy. Such figures became powerful fixtures in the edifice of Nasser's rule. They owed their power not to officially sanctioned institutional roles, but rather to their direct relation to Nasser and to the roots they established in their respective domains.

CADRES AND IDEOLOGY IN NASSER'S EGYPT

The mandate system provided Nasser with the top-level appointments for his regime. But it did not resolve the broader task of staffing the revolution in power at lower levels and providing it with coherent intellectual underpinnings. The Egyptian revolution still required both a new political elite and a full-blown official ideology.

Nasser's New Elite

Nasser responded to the regime's need for lower-echelon staff by creating a ruling caste, composed of former military officers complemented by civilians with needed technical skills. The conspicuousness of officers at the upper levels of government has been noted. Their prominence was merely symptomatic: the army came to represent for Nasser a personnel pool for far-reaching extramilitary tasks. Below the ministerial level, the military has been strongly in evidence throughout the political, administrative, and economic hierarchies. The pool from which these men have been drawn for government service comprises the approximately thirty-five hundred members of the officer corps who remained after the first purge of the promonarchy elements in the armed forces immediately following the revolution. Since about twenty-three hundred of that group continued to pursue army careers, it can be figured that roughly a thousand officers over the years have been drawn into the service of the state in administrative or economic capacities. In 1961, for example, an estimated three hundred men of military background were serving in the various ministries. As late as 1964, at least twenty-two of the twenty-six provincial governors were active or retired officers of the security forces.[23]

These military figures undoubtedly stabilized Nasser's regime and guaranteed the political survival of Free Officer rule. It remains now to add that Egypt has paid dearly for such advantages. Perhaps the greatest cost has been the failure of the governmental bureaucracies so heavily permeated by army officers to restrain the budgetary appetites of the military establishment. External developments (including Israel's hard-line Arab policy and Nasser's commitment to Arab unity) have provided an impetus for arms growth. Without the fiscal restraint a more heavily civilian regime might have provided, the Egyptian military has easily dominated the appropriations contest. Had the army not played so strong a role, a better case might have been made for concentrating Egypt's resources on the creation of a modern, industrialized society, which ultimately would be more effective in confronting Israel. Granted, the Israeli Gaza raid of 1955 and the Suez invasion of 1956 weakened such a case. Nasser sought to use Arab fears of Israeli military power to solidify pan-Arabism under Egyptian leadership, ultimately for Egypt's benefit. Whatever Nasser's intentions, it is the consequences of his actions that are important: Egypt was weakened and its long-term development slighted as the arms race with Israel spiraled.

In his speeches to the defense establishment Nasser repeatedly stressed that "the nation and the people have not failed to provide their Armed Forces with all their requirements." The fruits of this solicitude have been very generous indeed. One careful study concludes that defense expenditures increased almost sevenfold in the fifteen-year period from 1950 to 1965. Especially significant is the sharp rise in defense outlays (as percentage of GNP) from an estimated 3.90 percent in 1950-51 to 12.30 percent in 1964-65. Official spokesmen have argued that such expenditures have been eminently justified, even modest, when considered in the light of the threat posed by Israel. It does seem clear that under any regime the Egyptian military would have been able to make a good case for a generous share of the budget. For a regime originating in the army and ultimately depending on it for power, a good case became an overpowering one.[24]

The results of such an allocation policy have been disastrous for Egypt. During the six years following the Suez War in 1956, Egypt's national product per capita had increased steadily by over 3 percent annually and its aggregate output rose by about 6 percent per year. By 1963 Egypt appeared to be entering a period of sustained growth. However, such optimism was short-lived, for it was precisely in 1963 that Egypt began to feel the effects of participation in the Yemeni Civil War. Involvement in Yemen had been expected to be limited and brief. But the resilience of the Yemeni royalist forces drew Egypt deeper into the conflict, and defense costs soared. With the Egyptian economy thrown severely out of balance, the overall growth rate slowed. Egypt began the downward spiral that reached its nadir in the wake of the June 1967 war with Israel. As defense appropriations increased still further, development came to a standstill.[25]

The continuing rise in defense expenditures found its social reflection in the inflation of the military administration. Room was created for greater numbers of well-paid, high-ranking officers (an Egyptian general reportedly receives a salary twice that of a minister). An expansive conception of the army's extramilitary role also provided justification for its rising share of the budget. "The role of the army," Nasser never tired of repeating, "did not end on July 23, 1952." Arguing that "the army is not isolated from the people," Nasser described a revolutionary role for Egypt's men in uniform. Addressing noncommissioned officers in 1962, he observed that each officer represented a "revolutionary cell among the mass of the people."[26]

This impressive buildup of defense resources created pressures for their use on some larger scale. Nasser's early foreign-policy triumphs—the successful attack on the Baghdad Pact, the arms agreement, and Suez—culminated with the union of Egypt and Syria announced in February 1958. That union provided a dramatic first occasion for the exploitation of the expanded resources. Unionist sentiment in Egypt had never been strong—a fact attested to by Nasser in his satisfaction with his success "in converting the isolationist current, which was in our country, to an Arab current." The military and administrative apparatuses provided two natural and early converts. In a speech addressed to troops returning from the Yemen War, President Nasser obliquely confirmed this view: "You, men; you, heroes; you were the first to proclaim Arab nationalism and to implement this nationalism during the period of the unity." The ensured approval of his initiatives in foreign policy by the dependent military and administrative establishments had its obvious advantages for Nasser; one may also speculate that "union" from the perspective of those establishments must have looked like an agreeable expansion of their own spheres of activity.[27]

Nasser accurately characterized the military as the force that implemented the Syrian union. The integration of the Egyptian and Syrian armies, naturally under Egyptian domination, was to serve as a binding force. Not surprisingly, Nasser's reliance on the military to rule in Egypt was reflected in his policies toward Syria. The activities of the Egyptian military in Syria included not only the retraining of the army but active participation in the civilian administration. Egypt's bureaucrats likewise were given their opportunity in Syria. To complement his officer cadres, Nasser sent scores of civilian officials to man the purged Syrian administrative apparatus.[28]

The collapse of the union with Syria in 1961 was a severe blow to Nasser's prestige. Consequently, when the Yemeni Civil War broke out in the fall of 1962, he readily exploited support for the republican cause there as a means to restore his position in the Arab world. The temptation to intervene in Yemen was strengthened by the belief that Egypt had the military and administrative resources to do so successfully. If the inflated size of the defense establishment created pressures for its misuse abroad, there were abundant temptations for its corruption at home as well. The presence of officer appointees at the higher levels of the regime was clearly intended to infuse new life into the bureaucracy and bend it to the will of the new military masters of Egypt. On this score the regime's efforts ended in failure. That the traditional self-serving orientation of the bureaucracy had not been significantly altered was a fact frequently decried by Nasser himself. In his speech on the occasion of the breakup of the union with Syria, for example, he admitted:

> We could not develop the government machinery up to the revolutionary level . . . Sometimes, this machinery could not convey to the people the feeling of its being a mere servant of their interests but, on the contrary, the interests of the people have been exploited for the service of the government machinery with all its defects and drawbacks.[29]

One reason for this failure was the sheer weight and influence of the bureaucratic tradition—rather than reform it, countless officer appointees succumbed to it themselves. Even in those cases where the appointee had the technical expertise appropriate to his new position, immunity could not be guaranteed. An article in *al-Ahram* describes how even an innovative and competent technician, once assigned to a position of administrative authority, "is influenced by his administrative employees who will evidence fear of responsibility and drag the new director into the routine of delay and into a negative attitude."[30]

An Egyptian minister of labor has described the seduction process whereby leadership elements are turned into insensitive and careerist bureaucrats. When they take over a powerful position in the administrative apparatus, the minister explained, "a type of vanity takes hold of them. They look down on the masses." That the former military officials would be subject to such behavior suggests that even before appointment they had lost some of the spirit of self-sacrifice and patriotic zeal attributed to them by Nasser. Still, the regime treated corruption cases involving former officers with striking leniency. Illustrative are some comments by the minister of the interior Sharawi Gomaa in October of 1968. In a meeting with over two hundred police officers, a high percentage of whom were former military officers, the minister remarked that "an officer is not barred from promotion because in the past he has accepted a bribe." Institutional protection of the officers is emphasized throughout his speech. Such a defensive attitude toward corruption and deviation is not the most effective method to curb it.[31]

Whatever patriotic zeal officers might feel has also been eroded by the very considerable privileges they have come to expect in Egypt. Quite apart from its status as the preferred recruiting ground for the highest-level personnel in civilian life, the military owes a great deal to the revolutionary regime. It has been profitable to be an officer in the new Egypt. Officers have found themselves at the top of the social pyramid, and great care has been taken to shield them from difficult or abrasive aspects of daily living. They have been spared the indignities of Egypt's over-crowded public transportation facilities: army transportation is regularly available for their use. Officers have their own impressive social clubs in Cairo and Alexandria. They have regularly been paid better than their civilian counterparts, and those salaries go even further with a whole network of consumer privileges, including special high-cost living allowances and well-provisioned cooperative stores for their exclusive use.[32]

Especially since the defeat of 1967, discussion of the corrupting effects of special military privileges has greatly increased in the Egyptian press. For example, journalist Ahmed Bahaeddin has argued that the effectiveness of the Egyptian army has been undermined by these benefits. Bahaeddin suggests that the extensive extramilitary role assumed by the officers under Nasser's system of rule has eroded their combat readiness. For many Egyptians an army career has been viewed simply as an unavoidable preliminary to a transfer to potentially lucrative posts in the administrative and economic hierarchies. Nonetheless, the military establishment has fostered this trend by encouraging officers to undertake the advanced training that would make them more qualified for these civilian appointments.[33]

Such training efforts, in addition to raising the technical level of the officer cadres, has furthered their susceptibility to corruption. Soviet commentators on Egyptian affairs have usually emphasized a loss of innocence in describing this process:

A part of the officers, assuming supervisory administrative functions, were subject to "embourgeoisement." To the degree that they blended with the society of the capital, bourgeois in its essence, to the degree that they advanced to its heights, their former fresh romanticism, revolutionary enthusiasm, and modesty were strongly dimmed.

But at times the condemnation of the erosion of revolutionary enthusiasm has taken a strident tone:

The relation of many officers to their service in the armed forces has significantly changed. They use their privileges for the improvement of their own well-being. Leaving the army after the expiration of their term of service, many generals and colonels receive, as a general rule, high positions in the industrial and state apparatus. The state often addresses itself to the military with a call for help to bring order into one or another state enterprise . . . In their new positions they receive wide opportunities for the improvement of their well-being. These generals and former officers acquire checkbooks and bank accounts. Cases have been recorded where accounts have been opened in foreign banks to which are transferred sums in foreign currencies. There appeared the type of the officer businessman who was more interested in business than in the military preparation of soldiers and sergeants.[34]

Within Egypt, as the nationalist euphoria stimulated by the 1952 coup and the 1956 Suez triumph settled, the limitations of Nasser's new elite for the revolutionary transformation of Egypt became apparent. It was widely understood that political loyalty to the regime was the touchstone for success and material profit in Egyptian public life.

One frequently discussed solution to the difficulties raised by this predominance of materialistic motives in attracting Egyptians to the military and governmental bureaucracies was the prospect of providing an ideological impetus for genuine service to the government. If a sense of real mission, of real responsibility for the fate of Egypt, could be generated— so the argument ran—the debilitating effects of a reliance on material inducement could be overcome.

Socialism in Nasser's Egypt

The socialist component of the official ideology spelled out in the early sixties might have provided impetus to Nasser's "revolution from above." That it did not is explained in part by Nasser's deep-seated antipathy and distrust of any orientation that could command independent loyalty. While quasi-Marxist and socialist conceptions of the world were very much a part of Egypt's general intellectual climate, official socialism originated in the narrow imperatives of power, as understood by Nasser. Furthermore, Nasser's interpretation of Egypt's foreign as opposed to domestic needs determined the timing of adoption of the socialist strand in the official ideology.

Mindful that jobs in the bureaucracy were an important source of political loyalties, Nasser heartily enjoyed contrasting the expanded functions of his own government with the prerevolutionary state. Before 1952, Nasser argued, the state was "a group of clerks" charged essentially with maintaining order and issuing passports and licenses. After the revolution, the state's activities were vastly increased. "Today the state is raising poultry and breeding cattle,'' boasted Nasser. "There is a development plan. We want to provide jobs for so many workers.''[35] Of course, this does not mean that Nasser would have accepted the interpretation that Egypt's socialist era was inaugurated in order to expand the power of the ruling elite. According to Nasser's own official explanation, government control over Egypt's major economic resources was essential in order to forestall an attack on the revolution by the wealthy middle classes and to ensure the most efficient use of those resources for Egypt's development.

In an address to the National Assembly in 1964 President Nasser cogently summarized this case:

> If economic power is monopolized in the hands of the minority as was the case in 1954, this implies that political power still remained in the hands of this minority whatever high-sounding slogans were used.

Speaking later of the "revolutionary alliance of working powers,'' Nasser warned that "the enemies of this alliance by nature could, if we had left them the weapon of money, attack it and destroy it or deprive it of all effectiveness.'' The economic aspect of the official argument emphasized the failure of the possessing classes to cooperate with the government's new central plan for the development of the United Arab Republic (UAR). In the President's oft-repeated explanation, the middle classes shied away from investment in the basic industries and found ways of making speculative profits in nonproductive activities such as the building of luxury apartments. If the country were to progress at the desired rate and in the desired direction, Nasser claimed, the socialist solution was inevitable.

There is a great plausibility to this basic explanation for the socialist conversion of Egypt. The government's assumption of direct control over a considerable portion of Egypt's resources in the form of a public sector did make sense in these domestic political and economic terms. However, there are several things wrong with the official interpretation offered by President Nasser. It is difficult to take seriously his charge of the political threat of the middle class. Shortly after coming to power, the Free Officers had passed an Agrarian Reform Law that limited land ownership to 200 feddans (1 feddan equals 1.04 acre) per person and thus weakened the power of the landowning class. The subsequent record of Egypt's middle class was one of impressive political docility. It is instructive that the most dramatic response to the government's nationalizations was a petition to the commander in chief of the military forces, Abdul Hakim Amer, asking him to put an end to the dictatorship. Not unexpectedly, the government's response to this "move against the revolution" was harsh, swift, and effective: representative members of Egypt's leading middle-class families were arrested and the property of several hundred people from the wealthy classes was sequestered. Politically, the nationalization measures looked at most like a preventive measure rather than a response to any imminent danger.[36]

The economic aspect of President Nasser's interpretation also seems to have been enriched with a generous amount of deliberate mythology: the valiant young revolutionaries "forced" to abandon cooperation with the greedy, self-interested capitalists in the name of Egypt's higher good. Such a view overlooks the fact that while the middle class was indeed hesitant to invest its wealth along the lines suggested by the regime, the measures taken to induce compliance hardly indicated the regime's own wholehearted belief in the proposed partnership. Its early attempts to cooperate with Egypt's businessmen were soon abandoned. They were not consulted on the five-year plan, drawn up in 1957, which aimed to increase dramatically industrial investment and growth. Nor were any institutions established to coordinate the public and private sectors in the construction and timing of joint projects. In an interview published in *al-Ishtiraki* late in December 1966 Aly Sabry, then vice-president and general director of the Arab Socialist Union, himself exploded the myth that the regime had ever seriously intended to cooperate with Egyptian capitalists. Asked if the issuance of the 1961 laws nationalizing major industries could have been delayed had local capital played an active part in development, Sabry replied: "Capitalism in our calculation was not a part of the forces of the working masses. The socialist decrees should have been issued prior to 1961. They were delayed because of the Syrian Unity of 1958."[37]

The official characterization of the adoption of the socialist solution and its institutional arrangements as the natural or technically optimal answer to economic problems also appears dubious. In drawing up its first five-year plan, the regime did indeed consult—only to disregard—expert opinion. The government set up six mixed committees of public and private representatives (for industry, agriculture, irrigation, transport, public services, and economic and financial problems) on which approximately five hundred persons served. According to the director-general of the Ministry of Planning, they represented "all government departments and agencies, all private business, social and labor institutions, as well as private individuals." On the crucial question of the volume of available resources for the achievement of a higher rate of growth, a difference of opinion arose between the Mixed Committee on Economic and Financial Problems and the purely governmental National Planning Committee, established by presidential decree in January 1957.

The mixed committee claimed that the rate of growth suggested by the planning committee was unrealistic in its optimism. Nasser's eventual decision to select an even higher growth rate confounded both committees.[38]

In his speech of November 12, 1964, to the National Assembly, President Nasser spoke of this disregard for expert opinion in arriving at the target of doubling the national income in ten years:

> Discussions took place in the Council of Ministers for several days. Those in the planning said that it could not be done. They said that it could be done in 18 years but we insisted that it should be 10 years. They said 15, but we said 10. Again they said 12 and again we said 10. Had we not worked on that basis, and had we not faced the problem in that manner, our efforts would have been to no avail.[39]

The fundamental decisions affecting Egypt's development were clearly responsive to politically defined imperatives. The institutional changes that converted Egypt from an essentially free-enterprise economy in 1952 into a mixed economy with state ownership of all large-scale enterprises represented a dramatic expansion of the government's control over Egypt's resources. These changes flowed from a narrow political rather than an economic, technical, or even ideological calculus.[40] However, the restructuring of Egypt's economy cannot be fully explained in terms of domestic power considerations alone. While such considerations did make it useful for Nasser to develop the socialist orientation, the timing of the changes derived from pressures originating in the international sphere. More specifically, the impact of three events on Egypt are vital: the Suez War of 1956, the nonaccession of republican Iraq to the UAR after the 1958 Iraqi coup, and finally the Syrian secession in 1961 from union with Egypt.

For an economic history of modern Egypt the year 1956 with the Suez crisis represents a landmark of even greater importance than 1952 with the July revolution. From 1952 to 1956 military rule brought basic continuity in economic policy based on private enterprise. Suez altered this picture in several drastic ways. With the Egyptianization and subsequent nationalization of "enemy property" (largely British, French, and Jewish banks, insurance companies, industrial enterprises, and landholdings) a new attitude toward private property was born. The strengthening of the public sector by the accession of these holdings prompted the regime to adopt comprehensive planning, scheduled to begin in July 1960. Control of these financial institutions and their credit policies likewise enhanced the government's role in capital formation. These developments were justified in nationalist rather than socialist terms.[41]

The impact of the nonaccession of republican Iraq to the UAR, although perhaps more diffuse, was just as crucial for the emergence of Egypt's socialist system. The pan-Arabism that Nasser sought to exploit in order to enhance Egypt's standing in the world and consequent eligibility for large-scale economic assistance had eventuated in Egypt's union with Syria in 1958. That union further stimulated the pan-Arab momentum. The most promising candidate for union was oil-rich Iraq, which had just undergone a coup d'état initially thought to have been engineered by Nasser. Although Iraq's new military regime, headed by General Abdul Karim Kassem, did repudiate the Baghdad Pact, orient its foreign policy to the East, and declare its solidarity with republican Egypt, it soon became clear that union on the Syrian pattern was not in the offing. Kassem desired a more significant role in Arab affairs than Egypt had in mind. Before long, relations between Egypt and Iraq degenerated into bitter recriminations. The situation was complicated by the fact that the Soviet Union, impressed by the scope of leftist activities in Iraq, sided with that country against Egypt.

The nonaccession of Iraq to the UAR represented a first important break in the long string of successes that President Nasser had enjoyed in international politics. It prompted a reappraisal of Egypt's strategy for securing the resources for its development by investment in foreign policy. While Egypt's rulers by no means abandoned this strategy (which continued to pay dividends until 1965), the checkmate in Iraq served to suggest its intrinsic dangers. While nonaccession meant first of all that Egypt would not share in Iraq's oil resources, equally instructive for the Egyptians was the behavior of the Russians. Russian defection to the Iraqi side dramatically highlighted the precariousness of reliance on outside assistance for development. So, newly apprised of the uncertainties of foreign relations, Egypt's rulers moved to shore up their domestic position. While there is no evidence that Nasser believed that the UAR could afford an isolationist strategy on the model of "socialism in one country," he did begin to pay more serious attention after 1958 to the development of the resources of the UAR. This shift in attention manifested itself above all in a drive to maximize state control over those resources: thus was socialism born in the UAR.

The progress of nationalization began with the largest banking concern, expanded to take over half the capital of 86 companies, with government participation in 147 others, and finally culminated in full nationalization after two or three years. Later cloaked in the rhetoric of an ideologically inspired social revolution, such a pattern in actuality reflected extension of government control over the economy in the hopes that pressures from the uncertainties of foreign affairs would be ameliorated by firm domestic control of a planned economy. The nationalizations of February 1960 and of June and early July 1961 were not defended on socialist grounds. Once again, simple national interest was adduced.

There is a certain irony in the way the Syrian secession, the last of the three foreign-policy events affected Egyptian developments. On the one hand, the secession itself was sparked partly by resentment of the nationalization decrees, which were applied to both Egypt and Syria. The new concern for a consolidation of the UAR's resources had resulted instead in destruction of the union with Syria. On the other hand, the additional disruptions caused by the secession made the policy of tighter control over Egypt's resources imperative to the regime. It was only the defection of Syria that induced Egypt's military leaders to take the nationalization policy seriously.[42]

One salient indicator of this new attitude was the subsequent elaboration of a full-fledged socialist ideology for Egypt. In a 1965 speech dealing with the breakup of the union, Nasser recalled that the "setback which destroyed half the state of the union, the secession, had a most violent reaction in the second half, here in Egypt." Commenting on the precise nature of that reaction, Nasser remarked that "after secession, there was a great movement towards the clarification of the socialist thought."[43]

Nasser's comment is significant for its explicit recognition of the Syrian secession as the impetus for elaboration of the socialist doctrine. More usual was the claim that socialism had been implicit in the intentions of the Free Officers as reflected in the famous Six Principles announced shortly after the revolution. Those principles called for the destruction of imperialism, the eradication of feudalism, the ending of monopoly and domination of capital over the government, the establishment of social justice, the building of a strong national army, and the creation of a sound democratic system. While certainly vague enough to accommodate a socialist interpretation, the Six Principles could have been used to justify a wide variety of social systems. The first explicit mention of socialism seems to have come in April 1955 when Nasser proclaimed: "The Revolution aims at creating a socialist society without class distinction." But then another two and a half years passed before socialism again figured in his declarations. In a speech at a convention for cooperation in December 1957, the goal of the revolution was defined as the creation of a "cooperative, democratic, socialist society." Careful consideration of the meaning of socialism in Egypt did not come until after the Syrian secession.[44]

Mirsky has called Nasser's famous postmortem speech on the Syrian secession the most significant of all the president's addresses—and with good reason. In that speech Nasser presented his interpretation of the causes for the breakdown of the union with Syria; that interpretation was to have momentous consequences for Egypt's development. Nasser's thesis was simple: "reactionaries" alarmed by the socialist laws (nationalizations) had struck the blow that destroyed the union. Calling on Egyptians "to face with courage and honor the mistakes that made it possible for the reactionaries' movement to make its assault," Nasser continued with a masterfully disingenuous self-criticism. "We fell victims," Nasser explained, "to a dangerous illusion . . . we made the mistake of making peace with reaction." In a later passage the president made his meaning clearer:

> Closely connected with this illusion is another illusion, that it is possible to reach a compromise with reaction on national grounds; for at the time when we declared our faith in the possibilities of removing class distinction peacefully within the framework of national unity, reaction was following a different path, opposite to ours.

In these passages were presaged the fundamental shift from nationalism (first Egyptian, then Arab) to socialism in the official ideology developed in the early sixties. The impetus for that change in emphasis lay in the Syrian secession.[45]

Nasser needed both a convincing and an exonerating explanation for the breakup of the union. Nationalism, which had flourished on the demand for unity, could not provide it. Socialism, in contrast, had a more discriminating vocabulary, which allowed for that now crucial distinction between progressive and reactionary Arabs. While Nasser's blaming of the reactionaries for the secession has not gone unchallenged, the argument was at least plausible. Wealthy Syrians did indeed resent the July 1961 measures as well as an earlier land reform and severe currency-exchange controls. Postsecession developments in Syria offered little in the way of refutation of Nasser's charges: parliamentary elections resulted in an exceptionally strong showing by conservative politicians, who promptly repealed the nationalization decrees, amended the land reform, and voted themselves a 333 percent increase in salary![46]

By focusing blame for the secession on the reactionaries, President Nasser was also careful to deflect it from the Egyptian military and administrative establishments. He could hardly afford to acknowledge that the main props of his own regime, behaving in a repressive manner familiar to Egyptians, had so alienated the Syrians as to make the break inevitable. Yet Egyptian military and administrative heavy-handedness was undoubtedly a major irritant leading to the dissolution of the union with Syria.[47]

Nasser painted a rather different picture. Asking rhetorically where the Egyptian military was when the secession broke out, he commented that "the Egyptian officers in Syria, brethren, were at the Front. They were on the firing line. They were on the Israeli frontier. They were doing their duty." Asked what other Egyptians went to Syria, Nasser replied: "There were engineers . . . There were also doctors . . . They lived in the villages to perform their duty towards the people of their Republic."[48] Devoted military patriots and unselfish technicians—these were the Egyptians that Nasser claimed to have sent to Syria, these were the Egyptians "betrayed" by the Syrian reactionaries.

There were, though, revealing limits to President Nasser's whitewash: no mention was made of the Egyptian bureaucrat. Of the Egyptian civilian personnel in Syria only the technicians—the engineers and doctors— were acknowledged, while large numbers of bureaucrats had gone there also. The Syrian administrative system itself was only modestly developed (Nasser once characterized it as scarcely worthy of a grocery shop). Consequently, when new sets of currency, wage, and import regulations were instituted after the union, large numbers of Egyptian officials were needed to implement the new methods. Ultimate Syrian disenchantment with the union was fed by quiet outrage engendered by the interminable procedures imported with these Egyptian bureaucrats. Although Nasser did not explicitly attribute blame for the breakup of the union to the bureaucrats, his postmortem speech did include the following criticism: "We could not develop the government's machinery up to the revolutionary level."[49]

There are several other factors that help to explain Nasser's wholehearted adoption of a socialist ideology after 1961. In addition to explaining the Syrian secession and exonerating the Egyptians from any blame for it, Nasser's ideological interpretation of the episode by no means necessitated an abandonment of pan-Arabism. Since the mid-fifties the regime had attached great importance to a pan-Arab policy designed to secure an Egyptian position of leadership in the Arab world. Nasser had no intention of abandoning that strategy, especially when the union with Syria had demonstrated that such a policy might, under the right conditions, mean access for Egypt to the resources of its neighbors.

The new socialist additive to Egypt's official ideology served to define those conditions. Henceforth, it was announced by M. H. Haikal, there would be two Egypts—Egypt as a state and Egypt as a revolution. As a state it should deal with all Arab governments, whatever their social and political systems, in such forums as the United Nations and the Arab League. But as a revolution "Egypt should deal only with the people," announced Haikal. "This does not mean interference in the affairs of others, since the fundamental premise of our struggle is that the Arab people are a single nation." By the people Haikal meant an alliance of workers, peasants, national capitalists, soldiers, and intellectuals against the alliance of exploitative capitalists, feudalists, and other reactionaries held responsible for the secession. Arab unity according to President Nasser now had social revolution as its first condition. With this formulation Nasser fostered new tension in inter-Arab affairs and clearly hoped to exploit Egypt's revolutionary socialist stance in order to regain the initiative.[50]

Furthermore, a series of measures undertaken in the wake of the secession and in the name of socialism gave Egypt's rulers economic power and control approaching the political monopoly they had enjoyed since 1954. These included consolidation and extension of the July 1961 nationalizations; revision of the 1952 land reform, lowering the maximum ownership from 200 to 100 feddans; a wave of arrests, property sequestrations, and political isolation directed against the upper classes; dissolution of the "reactionary ridden" National Union and parliament, accompanied by the creation of what was intended to be a more tightly organized political movement called the Arab Socialist Union; and adoption of the National Charter, a formal ideological program for Egypt that embodied its revolutionary socialist principles.[51]

Although Egyptian officials have seen in these changes their "socialist revolution" and "economic Suez," non-Egyptian observers have been inclined to deny Egypt the socialist-revolutionary designation. Responsible Soviet commentators, while praising the progressive expansion of the state sector, do not conceal their disappointment over Nasser's rejection of proletarian dictatorship and his preference for "his own nebulous conception of democracy." For those Westerners whose conception of socialism involves distributive justice, the decrees that nationalized property and redistributed income had too slight an impact on the mass of Egyptians to warrant the socialist title. Still, there is substantial agreement on all sides that, however interpreted, the postsecession developments in Egypt meant a very significant extension of government control over the economy—an extension justified and explained by a new radicalized version of the official ideology.[52]

The suitability of socialism for such a role rests on several considerations. Explicit references to socialism (even if infrequent and vaguely formulated) had been made by the president when explaining his political views as far back as 1955: he could therefore with at least a claim to plausibility characterize his ideological position outlined in the charter as a "clarification" of views held at the time of the revolution itself. The most important break with past thinking centered on acceptance of the Marxian emphasis on class struggle. Earlier, in keeping with the nationalist impulse, Nasser had claimed that peace and cooperation between classes did exist: "We achieved it for the first time in history." Now, however, Nasser wished to exploit the reactionary-progressive dichotomy so much a part of socialist vocabulary—internationally in order to explain the Syrian debacle and domestically in order to move against the owning classes. With great ingenuity he accomplished this reversal of position by "confessing" that he had in his earlier vision been too good-heartedly naive—with the result that reaction had taken advantage of the situation. This reasoning, as indicated earlier, was used to explain the secession; the arguments used for the domestic situation were similar. The president first pointed out that since 1952 as a result of the revolution's benign policies the wealthy had been flourishing. Nasser claimed that the number of those with yearly incomes over $28,000 had almost doubled the year before and that the nation's wealth was concentrated in less than 5 percent of the people. Nasser concluded: "We were therefore facing the question: who really rules the country?" He was then "forced" to admit that Egypt had not after all achieved class harmony: "We have not been over successful in resolving the contradictions by peaceful means." By presenting himself as a man who had previously exhausted peaceful means even to the point of foolhardiness, Nasser was providing himself with the moral justification for his subsequent use of force against the recalcitrant reactionaries.[53]

Furthermore, the regime's expanded role in the economic realm looked natural in a socialist context, where a large and active role for the state in economic development was expected. "Socialist justice" and other such borrowings from Marxist and socialist theories likewise helped to justify these incursions. By the early 1960s such a socialist orientation was by no means too radical for a regime that still counted on its ability to win economic assistance from the West. The world had already witnessed the heyday of the Third World conferences, and Nasser had associated on the world stage with men of the stature of Tito, Sukarno, and Nehru. For them, socialism (each defining it differently) was the answer to all the problems of the developing countries and they had demonstrated that a socialist position did not preclude large-scale aid from the West. During the Kennedy years Nasser enjoyed some acceptance in selling his socialism as an alternative to communism.[54]

But for Egypt, more important would be the effectiveness of Nasser's development strategy and the instruments of rule (both cadres and ideology) it engendered. Nasser had frequently observed that the real question of power was not acquiring or even holding it. The test would come in how that power would be used for the social reconstruction of Egypt.

3. Bureaucratic Feudalism

The Free Officers brought vitality to the conduct of foreign policy and stability to Egypt's domestic political affairs. Far less successful was their creation of institutional means to effect Egypt's internal transformation. By the mid-sixties it was apparent that Nasser's "revolution from above" had been slowed by bureaucratic ossification.

To some extent the ways of bureaucracy are everywhere the same. The narrowness of viewpoint, the rigidity of routine, the self-serving protection of "domain," and the hoarding of expertise: all these classic symptoms were to be found in the new Egypt. At the same time Nasser's mandate system of rule imposed a certain structure beneath the surface phenomenon of bureaucratic behavior. The combination of the two produced a political system of personalized and bureaucratized power best characterized as bureaucratic feudalism. Such a system generated unproductive and potentially disintegrative political rivalries; it proved totally inadequate to the task of revolutionary transformation.

THE GROWTH OF THE BUREAUCRACY

The impact of bureaucratic proliferation on Egypt's development has been a major theme of postrevolutionary Egyptian literature. Among the most effective social critics is the playwright Aly Salem. In his biting farce, *The Well of Wheat*, Salem dramatizes the plight of the inventive and the imaginative when subjected to the ravages of cancerous bureaucratic growth.[1] The plot of the play, which opened in Cairo in 1968, revolves around three characters (Basyuni, Mutwali, and Uncle Hussein) who have discovered a vast Pharoanic wheat storage bin under the sands of the desert. The heroes promptly report their discovery of "the well of wheat" to Cairo and are as promptly overwhelmed by an invasion of bureaucrats—all under the direction of the distinguished Dr. One, whose earlier researches had established conclusively the impossibility of such wells of wheat in the desert. Dr. One asserts his authority with a command: Desks! In a flash the stage is bustling with workmen carrying on desks; they push Mutwali, Basyuni, and Uncle Hussein first off the stage and then right out of the theater. The desks are soon all over the stage and down into the aisles as well.

> DR. ONE: (shouting) Bureaucrats!
> (Like lightning bureaucrats invade the stage and take their places at their desks. On the chest of each is a number: 1, 2, 3, etc.)

With the heroes pushed into the background, the hoards of bureaucrats soon engulf the stage with reams of papers. They then proceed to make demands on Dr. One. To introduce some discipline and curb the growing chaos, Dr. One is forced to call in Dr. Cop. The logic of the policeman completes the logic of the bureaucrat.

> DR. COP: . . . I'll introduce myself. I'm Dr. Cop. Despite my great respect for Dr. One, who was, after all, my professor, I still can't believe that he could have arranged the desks in this manner. I know that he specialized in the arrangement of desks, but what he did here is totally wrong; if he is responsible for this then he is a prize ass . . . (The bureaucrats change places quickly causing total pandemonium, but when they are finally reseated, it is obvious that they are all back exactly where they started).

Dr. Cop continues with his reforms, eventually expelling Uncle Hussein and Mutwali from the project. Since Basyuni has already left, all three of the original discoverers of the well of wheat are now gone. Then a missive from Cairo arrives, asking for a production report on the desert project. Dr. Cop makes a painful discovery.

> DR. COP: . . . I've got a letter from Cairo asking what our level of production is.
> BUREAUCRAT: Production of what?
> DR. COP: Production of what? You mean you don't know.

Furious, Dr. Cop begins an investigation of the aim of the project. He interrogates each bureaucrat.

> DR. COP: . . . What do you do?
> BUREAUCRAT: Public relations.
> DR. COP: And you?
> BUREAUCRAT: Promotions and demotions.
> DR. COP: And you?
> BUREAUCRAT: Documentation and compilation.
> DR. COP: And you?
> BUREAUCRAT: Investigations.
> DR. COP: And you?
> BUREAUCRAT: Programmation and computerization.
> DR. COP: And you?

BUREAUCRAT: Transportation.
(As the questioning proceeds, the bureaucrats simply reply to Dr.
    Cop, 'tions, 'tions, 'tions . . .)
DR. COP: (furious) This must be some sort of plot against me. You
    people want to destroy me. All of you are 'tions, 'tions, 'tions. No
    one knows what this project is.

Bureaucrats, as Aly Salem's play suggests, have fared well in the Egypt
of the Free Officers. Initially, Egypt's new rulers were little inclined to
disturb the functioning of the traditional bureaucracy. Saddled overnight
with the responsibilities of power, the Free Officers had "neither plans,
nor program, nor cadres, nor organized masses" on which to draw.[2]
Lacking the personnel for a complete purge or even a substantial restaff-
ing of the state apparatus, the new military rulers preferred bureaucratic
continuity to chaos. For their part, the bureaucrats adjusted easily to
their new masters. The thin crowning layer of ex-military men assigned to
top positions left the various governmental hierarchies with their well-
established, self-serving traditions comfortably intact.

While this explanation does elucidate the origins of the improbable
rapprochement between Egypt's ardent young military revolutionaries
and its ageless and unchanging bureaucrats, it does not suffice to explain
its endurance. Egypt's bureaucrats provided the regime with more than
smooth continuity in the performance of essential government functions;
they provided a surrogate for the social base the regime lacked. Egypt's
new rulers came to power in such a way that they could not naturally
command the loyalty and service of any particular civilian groups or
classes aside from the peasantry, whose support was diffuse and inarticu-
late. The civil service provided the ideal supplement to the military power
base of a still unsure regime. Dependent on the military rulers for their
jobs, Egypt's bureaucrats provided Nasser with the human material to
create an artificial caste for which the regime's survival would be a necessity.

So, like the military, the bureaucracy flourished. The government ex-
penditure pattern for the period 1959 through 1967 reveals that the rate
of increase of civil nongrowth expenditures—in other words, the costs of
ordinary administration—was second only to that of defense. The actual
size increase in the civil service, reflected in these figures, was enormous.
A quarter of a million employees at the time of the revolution had grown
to over a million by the early seventies. While this inflation reflects in
part the expanded role of the government in all fields of economic and
social activity, it also measures the failure of the Egyptian economy to
grow rapidly enough to absorb its more educated manpower. With that
failure, irresistible pressures mounted for the regime to create jobs in an
already bloated bureaucracy.[3]

Nasser did not initially view this inflation of the military and civilian bureaucracies negatively. Aware of their rapid growth, he sought rather to justify and even institutionalize such growth as beneficial for development. Throughout his early career Nasser remained impressed with the fact that Egypt's overwhelming edge in human resources constituted perhaps the soundest basis for its claim to leadership in the Arab world. In the context of a development strategy based on financing industrialization with large-scale foreign aid or by somehow tapping the resources of neighboring states, the numerous Egyptian bureaucrats and specialists were an advantage. Surplus Egyptian personnel came to play important roles in the surrounding Arab countries: Egyptian teachers today are found in every Arab state; the civil codes of Syria and Iraq were drawn up by Egyptian lawyers; important public works projects in Jordan have been undertaken by Egyptian contracting companies. And this is but a sampling of the kind of productive activities that engage Egyptians throughout the Arab world. By monumental efforts to improve Egypt's educational system through the university level, President Nasser vastly increased this pool of skilled human resources. The institutionalization of their employ in the service of the state came with the 1962 law that guaranteed jobs for all graduates of Egyptian universities. Socialism as an ideology, with its vocabulary of public welfare, provided a convenient rationalization for the unnecessary overstaffing of governmental structures.[4]

BUREAUCRATIC POLITICS

In contemporary Egypt the bureaucratic forms that seemed to dominate public life by the 1960s were in fact grafted onto a mechanism of rule—the mandate system—designed in quintessentially political terms. The basis of political life in Nasser's Egypt was not administrative or bureaucratic in nature, as some have argued.[5] Nor was the vision or self-understanding of the ruling elite cast in administrative rather than political terms. Though Egypt's leaders did adopt rapid economic development as a national goal, the organizational imperatives of development were contained within a political logic that dictated the survival of Free Officer rule.[6] Furthermore, while the tone of Egyptian public life has been marked by a deceptive surface blandness, that blandness has screened intense political activity.[7]

To understand bureaucratic politics in Nasser's Egypt, it is helpful to recognize that the expansion of bureaucratic forms resulted from the unintended consequences of Free Officer decisions. M. H. Haikal has recorded the awareness in ruling circles that from the 1920s on the effectiveness of the Egyptian civil service had been steadily eroding. The corruption of the political system during Egypt's "liberal age," Haikal has explained, inevitably infected the bureaucracy and was manifested in the twin forms of political patronage and involvement in the extensive black market of the war years. Despite their misgivings, the Free Officers were forced by political constraints to turn to the bureaucracy. Their coup had relied for its mass cadres on a docile soldiery, untouched by revolutionary agitation. Furthermore, previously active civilian elements had played no direct part in the seizure of power and were soon alienated from the military regime. Only the bureaucracy remained. Haikal has made it clear that the Free Officers turned to the bureaucrats with no great relish: "The regime was aware of the incapacity of the old bureaucratic forms which were incapable of serving its objectives, but it was unable to do without them."[8]

Of course, the bureaucrats welcomed reliance on administrative means despite the rhetoric of revolutionary change. However, they were disturbed by Free Officer justification of their new authority in the name of the improvement of the condition of the masses. Such an orientation implicitly challenged their own privileged status and the traditional exploitative attitudes of the bureaucrats toward the Egyptian people. Again, Haikal is a useful guide to the reaction of the bureaucrats to the new regime. A period of malaise, Haikal observes, was followed by fear as the bureaucrats were forced to deal with new superiors as well as new demands. In order to survive, they avoided responsibility whenever possible and channeled their energies into elaborate and unproductive stratagems of self-justification. From the beginning, Haikal makes clear, there was tension in the regime's relations with the traditional bureaucracy.[9]

The shape of politics in Nasser's Egypt was determined by the interaction of the mandate system of rule with the proliferation of bureaucratic forms. The essential personal power rivalries built into Free Officer rule acquired institutional weight as Nasser's appointees and their respective staffs organized themselves into rival centers of power. It is within such an arena that Egypt's new men—army officers, security officials, technocrats, bureaucrats, and leftists—struggled for influence and privilege in Nasser's imposing shadow.

A strong personality was not enough to explain the emergence of a center of power; there had to be also an administrative or political institutional base. Cohesiveness was derived from three key factors: the personal charisma of the mandated personality, enhanced by status as a Nasser appointee; the material inducements that such figures could offer as the heads of influential institutions; and the reinforcement that came from drawing similar types together in a given institutional setting (for example, the tendency for the military to dominate the police apparatus, for the technocrats to play an important role in economic organizations, and for the leftists to gravitate toward the communications and propaganda networks). The existence of such centers led to a feudalization of political power.[10]

The rival power bases that structured political life in the new Egypt derived either from the carving up of the inherited state apparatus or from the formation of new administrative bodies. Whatever the difficulties caused by the defensive behavior of the bureaucracy when faced with Egypt's rulers, its abject if obdurate spirit made it possible for Nasser to infiltrate his own largely military appointees into the state apparatus. He then divided it into functional fiefdoms, which were allotted to trusted lieutenants. Such was the case of the security apparatus, a preserve for years of Free Officer Zakariya Muhieddin. By 1961 more than 3,400 of the 4,100 employees in the Ministry of the Interior were either active or retired military officers. This staff was the core of a pervasive internal security system and a powerful fiefdom in Nasser's Egypt: it was the real social embodiment of that "logic of the cop" caricatured by Aly Salem in *The Well of Wheat*. Abuses by the security establishment were frequent in these years.[11]

Nasser thus was able to assert control over the inherited bureaucracy by segmenting it according to the logic of the mandate system. But the commitment to radical social reconstruction called for more than effective control: it would be necessary to expand the scope of state activity. Faced with sharply limited areas of inherited administrative expertise, the regime had to either broaden traditional bureaucratic capabilities or organize new structures. Early desultory attempts at reform merely revealed the immensity of that task. One of the first measures of the regime had been a purge of the state apparatus. However, the aim then was removal of disloyal individuals rather than any fundamental restructuring, which required a long-term vision and sense of direction that the regime simply did not have. "State authority," Haikal explained, "had passed into the hands of revolutionaries who had not precisely determined the sense to give to the revolution." Instead, Nasser proceeded on an ad hoc basis to establish state bodies to manage expanding functions. A pattern of bypassing the inherited bureaucracy emerged, which can be seen in the case of the Suez Canal Authority.[12]

Egyptians have been widely praised for their efficient management of the canal, especially since so many doubts had been expressed prior to the nationalization in 1956. In a 1964 article in *al-Ahram* M. H. Haikal provided details on the circumstances surrounding the formation of the Canal Authority. President Nasser's direct involvement is revealing. To head the organization Nasser personally chose Mahmoud Yunes, who had joined the army in 1937 after studying engineering. Yunes had been an instructor-colleague of Nasser at the Staff College in 1951. Discussing the qualifications that led to the choice of Yunes, Haikal stressed his technical competence and his political reliability: "He had the technical capability as a professor and an expert in administrative matters . . . He was fully aware of his political obligations as a citizen having faith in the July Revolution." Once the nationalization had been announced, Yunes (according to Haikal) was accorded the maximum possible degree of independence in the performance of his task: "One refrained from submerging him with instructions and orders . . . Moreover, Gamal Abdul Nasser ordered Cairo not to communicate too frequently with Yunes, even for purposes of encouragement." Still more significant was the fact that "after the storm, Yunes was provided with the authority to reorganize the administration of the Canal on new bases which he judged useful after discussion of the subject . . . At the same time, the traditional government apparatus was prevented from invading the domain which had just been conquered." In sum, the new administrative bodies were created by a pattern of appointments that conformed to the logic of the mandate system of rule, with the addition of a concern for technical competence.[13]

Linked directly to the highest political authorities, such administrative structures have been responsible for the greatest successes achieved by the new regime: advances in industrialization, land reform, the High Dam, and administration of the Suez Canal. During its first decade, as the need arose and frequently spurred by happenings in foreign affairs, the military regime created the Council for Production, the Ministry of Industry, the Economic Organization, the Suez Canal Authority, the High Dam Organization, and the Organization for Land Improvement and Desert Reclamation. These bodies have provided the primary institutional setting for extensive recruitment of technocratic talent, recognized as essential to the development of Egypt. Haikal reported in 1964, for example, that 40 percent of the directors of large organizations and societies were engineers. Concentrated within the new organizations, university graduates with backgrounds in economics, engineering, and science, along with former managers and experts from private companies, have become the favored partners of the military officers in power.[14]

THE LIMITATIONS OF BUREAUCRATIC FEUDALISM

Modernization, Nasser learned, entails much more than engineering. Enthusiasm for governmental organizations to mobilize technocratic talent dimmed as Nasser learned that programs crucial to radical social transformation do not lend themselves to treatment by bureaucratic means. Population control was one such challenge. Furthermore, the personalization of power and bureaucratic rivalries endemic to Nasser's regime dulled its effectiveness as a political instrument for social reconstruction in general.

Birth Control

The failure of Egypt's population control effort prompted an Egyptian analyst to ask in April 1973:

> How can we build the High Dam . . . How can we plunge into the job of building the iron and steel complex and move ahead with it and yet, at the same time, stumble over a project such as the family planning project?

The lack of progress in controlling population growth did not stem from any lack of awareness by Egypt's new ruling group of the significance of that issue. The population explosion, Nasser explained in the 1962 charter, was the "most serious obstacle to the efforts of the Egyptian people in their drive to increase levels of production." Almost a decade later, in his Program for National Action, Nasser's successor acknowledged: "This phenomenon [rapid population growth] if it continues would not only condemn all our hopes for evolution and progress but threaten the simple maintenance of our present level." Sadat's alarm was fully justified. After a decade of effort Egyptian demographers warned that at current rates of increase the number of inhabitants of the Nile Valley would double in the next twenty-five years.[15]

Birth control as a developmental problem simply did not lend itself to the kind of engineering solution possible through the new administrative instruments. Effective population planning required alteration, through persuasion and coercion, of mass attitudes, values, and practices. The regime had neither the necessary ideological impetus nor the cadres even to contemplate such a massive undertaking. Instead, Egypt's leaders viewed the population question as primarily a technical issue, linked to the broader problem of economic development. In the early years of the regime it was felt that the drive to industrialize would itself solve the population problem: an industrialized Egypt would provide, if necessary, for a larger number of Egyptians; and a birth control mentality would be an inevitable by-product of life in an industrialized society.

Consequently, population planning was viewed as a low-priority, low-budget medical problem. Responsibility for the program was lodged not in a separate ministry but rather in a prestigious but largely symbolic and inoperative interministerial body, the Supreme Council for Family Planning. Created in 1965, the council was to bring together a group of officials of ministerial rank including the prime minister and the ministers of public health, higher education, national guidance (now information), planning, religious affairs, social affairs, the head of the central agency for mobilization and statistics, and the ministers of state for prime minister's affairs and local administration. However impressive the titles, the supreme council accomplished little. Initially charged to meet fortnightly, this body of overworked ministers rarely met as a group. In addition, the rapid turnover at the ministerial level typical of Egypt served to undermine its organizational coherence.

The problem of ministerial rivalries has been even more debilitating than these top-level impediments to the birth control effort. Since the population question was initially viewed primarily in its technical (medical) dimension, basic responsibility for the program went to the Ministry of Health, where it was consistently challenged over the years by the Ministry of Social Affairs. Typical of the infighting was a 1973 claim by the minister of social affairs to supervision of the program. Family planning, the minister argued, is fundamentally a social rather than a medical problem and it was originally studied by the Ministry of Social Affairs. Intolerable, according to the minister, were the efforts of the Ministry of Health to "monopolize the project." Little wonder that the press has spoken of the family planning project as an "open battlefield for a power struggle" between the two ministries.[16]

Rivalries at the center had devastating results in the field, where personnel were frequently caught in the crossfire. Increasingly, accounts of such clashes found their way into the Egyptian press. *Al-Ahram* in April 1973 reported on one such typical incident at a family planning center in Lower Egypt. An inspector from the Ministry of Health was annoyed with a doctor who refused him inventory information that the doctor had already given to the Ministry of Social Affairs. The health department officials retaliated by submitting a report to the provincial governor accusing the doctor in question of smuggling birth control devices to Lebanon! The overlap between the two ministries has also resulted in wasteful duplication. In one area two family planning centers operated within 90 meters of one another—one administered by the Ministry of Health, the other by the Ministry of Social Affairs. When the duplication was brought to the attention of the central authorities, "both Social Affairs and Health dug in their heels with regard to their centers and, in order to resolve the dispute, the governor decided that each center should operate three days a week. However, the rivalry was the same and the dispute continued."[17]

The difficulties flowing from the competition of the two central ministries were further compounded by the more traditional inefficiencies of each individual ministry. Officials in the Ministry of Health, for example, were wary of involvement in the population program, since its ostensibly interministerial character did place it somewhat outside the regular patterns for career advancement. Fearing that their professional rise through the grades would be adversely affected, the health ministry bureaucrats connived to transfer out of the program. Attempts to stimulate commitment led with inexorable bureaucratic logic to further corruption. Dr. Khalil Mazhar, professor of gynecology at Cairo University and first chairman of the executive board of the Supreme Council for Family Planning, initiated a system of incentives for medical workers engaged in population control activities. Proceeds from the sale of birth control pills and a special payment for the insertion of each intrauterine device (IUD) were divided among the clinic staff, with 40 percent going to the doctor, 25 percent to the social worker, 25 percent to the midwife and/or nurse, and 10 percent to the janitor.[18]

Abuses soon appeared. After 1967, when Dr. Mazhar left the program, incentive payments were no longer made on the spot as originally planned, but had to be cleared at the center. This procedural change greatly expanded the paperwork for medical personnel. But the bureaucratic logic—and interest—behind the measure was clear: the change was advocated forcefully by the Ministry of Finance, which now took 10 piasters in tax on every 40 paid to the doctors!

Even more disruptive than the problems of increased red tape have been the corrupt practices evolved to maximize health workers' "profits" on the incentive program. Patients have been forced to buy pills while obtaining other medical services at clinics; government-issued birth control devices have been resold to pharmacies for a profit; there have also been reports of large quantities of pills reaching the Lebanese market, where their resale value is even higher. The populace generally has also sought to play the incentive system to advantage. When the program was first set up, new users as well as those who recruited them were rewarded financially. Before long, roving teams of recruiters and users were making the rounds of area clinics, putting in IUDs and taking them out—all the while enjoying the multiple monetary rewards of their exemplary civic virtue. Exposés have often revealed that clinic staffs actively connived in the whole process.

The severe limitations of the population control effort translated into depressing statistics. From 1960 to 1966 the population of Egypt grew 2.54 percent annually. The decade from 1966 to 1976 registered only a slight drop to an increase rate of 2.31 percent. That still meant that each year nearly one million more Egyptians pressed on the country's slender resources. By the mid-seventies foreign and Egyptian specialists were agreed that the failure to contain this rapid growth was Egypt's single most pressing problem. As quickly as gains were made in industrial or agricultural productivity, they were negated by population increase.[19]

Feudalization of Power

Feudalization of power not only meant that the developmental successes of Nasser's revolution from above were confined within severe functional limitations, as the study of population control reveals; the nature of ruling power in Nasser's Egypt created problems even in those areas of social life to which the engineering approach of the new administrative bodies could be applied. A pair of important disabilities was built in: critical personalization of power, and unanticipated hostility between the old and the new administrative structures.

Mandated personalities in Nasser's Egypt were widely understood to derive their power from the highest political authorities. The vague, non-institutional character of their appointments served to enhance, in the eyes of subordinates, the aura of mysterious power that surrounded these men. Moreover, that power did not appear to be circumscribed by any rigorous method of functional accountability. Leftist Free Officer Khaled Muhieddin pointed out that the regime, although successful in verifying and controlling the basic political loyalty of its key appointees, in fact has devised no effective system to monitor their performance. Enormous responsibilities, Muhieddin charged, were entrusted to individuals with no means of exercising control over them and verifying independently the quality of their work. Such a situation has encouraged in subordinates an attitude of loyalty to persons rather than to principles, with success linked to pleasing and strengthening one's ties to powerful personalities rather than to an outstanding record of work performance.[20]

Impressionistic evidence suggests that these widely understood realities of power produced a generalized pattern of abuses that severely hampered the regime's capacity to direct socioeconomic change. Self-protective "family circles" took shape, with subordinates aiming above all to ingratiate themselves to superiors and superiors defending their hangers-on from the possible ill effects of any functional accountability. The methods of "flattery and hypocrisy," an Egyptian minister of labor has explained, took precedence over any concept of service to the nation: "Dishonest elements submit misleading and erroneous reports to their leaders in order to remain constantly on their bandwagon." The complicity of high-level appointees in these distortions is exemplified by the directors of companies in the nationalized, public sector industries. Under the pressure of competition for scarce investment resources, directors encouraged their subordinates to falsify the project reports submitted to the central authorities, as a normal part of administrative behavior.[21]

Nasser created administrative bodies to expand the functional capabilities of his regime. Yet one consequence of that policy was an intensification of the traditional, destructive bureaucratic rivalries illustrated by the case study of population control. The inherited state apparatus regarded the new organizations as "cancerous proliferations depriving it of all hope of survival." For their part, the recent structures disdained the state apparatus as "a stone which blocks the way." Such colorful journalistic characterizations of the competition were grounded in some hard facts. Resentments were stirred by the higher salaries offered in the new organizations. Differences in training and background also reinforced the competition. Whereas the latest structures attracted men with a practical, technocratic orientation, the state bureaucracy remained the stronghold of men with liberal arts training. Actual bureaucratic infighting has taken various forms. Egyptian sources report, for example, that the traditional state apparatus has used its control function to harass and undermine the new administrations. In *al-Ahram* of December 1964 M. H. Haikal noted: "Sometimes many administrations receive daggers in the back, although under the pretext of inspection and control."[22]

Patterns of Conflict

The underlying cleavages in Egyptian public life were determined by the competition of the rival centers of power in the mandate system of rule. The differences among the centers were heightened by the location of some in new public bodies, whereas others were based in established bureaucracies. Into an environment structured by such institutionalized rivalries stepped the bureaucrat, the technocrat, the leftist, and the security or military figure, establishing an individual level of competitive interaction. The tensions of public life experienced by these figures cannot be measured with any great precision. However, the flavor and style of their interactions can be conveyed by a look at several of the more important patterns of individual-level conflict.

The rivalry of the bureaucrat and the technocrat has long been an established fact of Egyptian public life. Analysts have gone so far as to claim that "the conflict between technicians and bureaucrats, which inhibits progress, is therefore the most serious problem in government administration." In their opposition to the technocrats, the state bureaucrats have found an occasional ally in the Egyptian left. There have been two distinct wings of that left: the Marxist intellectuals, writing in such journals as *al-Katib* and *al-Tali'ah* and represented intermittently at the upper governmental levels by Khaled Muhieddin; and those who, in Muhieddin's words, "have rallied to the cause of socialism in terms of their own experience." During the Nasser era this second wing was represented in government by Aly Sabry.[23]

Egypt's Marxist intellectuals have been in many ways the critical conscience of a regime by which they have been both courted and persecuted. The incisiveness of their analyses of the regime's shortcomings has given their critical voice an importance belied by their numbers. Moreover, the views of the Marxist doctors at times have been picked up by the official left and thereby have entered into ongoing political struggles.

The antipathy of the Marxist intellectuals for the technocrats is based on a sophisticated analysis that covers both domestic and international considerations. Their arguments begin with a recognition of the extreme heterogeneity of the technocrats' social origins. The technocrats are described as emerging from the "petite bourgeoisie." However, that term is given an elastic meaning, which excludes only the urban and rural masses on the one hand and the former landlord and industrial class on the other. It is the middle-range elements between these two extremes that is designated the petite bourgeoisie and it is recognized by Marxist analysts that it is not a homogeneous class. Typically included are such groups as students, professionals, artists, and industrial foremen, in addition to small entrepreneurs and wealthier peasants.[24]

What distinguishes the technocrats from other elements of the petite bourgeoisie is their specialized training, vital to an industrializing Egypt. The Marxists, while acknowledging the functional role of the technocrats, bemoan the fact that their ideological formation has not kept pace with their professional training. This failing is explained by the absence in Egypt of experienced political cadres who could train technical personnel in the proper socialist spirit. Consequently, the revolution is forced to depend on a technocratic caste with a class mentality that considers technical expertise as private property. The technocrats do not oppose the revolutionary changes introduced by the new regime, essentially because they see themselves as inheritors of the privileges of the former propertied classes. But they do oppose mass political action, since an active role of the masses is viewed as a threat to their own positions. The Marxists warn that the technocrats, if they cannot halt political action, will at least attempt to obstruct it.[25]

In their opposition to political action, the technocrats are very close to the initial attitudes of the Free Officers. Perhaps for this very reason, the leftists attempted to clothe their attacks on the technocrats with the mantle of Nasser's authority. A leftist intellectual, writing in *al-Katib* of October 1967, first noted the expanded role of the technocrats in the economy and then identified that phenomenon with a warning by Nasser against the rise of a new privileged class in Egypt:

Those are the categories which took over the positions of the old managers, factory owners, members of the boards of directors. They also took over corresponding positions in the political organization and in government administrations . . . This is what increases the danger of the new class which President Gamal Abdel Nasser so often warned against.

Such an enlistment of Nasser's support is something of a distortion, for the president's frequent remarks directed against the "new class" appear in context to be aimed instead at the bureaucrats. However, this distinction is easily blurred for Marxist intellectuals who have become critical and suspicious of the bureaucrats of Egypt's expanding public sector as well as of its technocrats. They would like to see both elements subordinated to an ideologically oriented political party. This principle has been embraced officially many times and embodied in Egypt's successive mass parties. Professor Lutfy el-Kholy explained in 1961 the failure to implement the principle in terms of the opposition it has engendered; his comments provide a rare insight into the types of tensions and conflicts that must color political debate at the highest levels of the UAR:

The authority of the leadership of the political mass organization over all sectors of the state is the correct starting point for revolutionary action. But this principle (i.e. giving the newly planned popular mass organization real authority) was strongly opposed by the reformist and bureaucratic circles as "illegal interference with state affairs."

At those influential levels leftists have sustained one defeat after another.[26]

Leftist opposition to the autonomous power of both bureaucrats and technocrats in the public sector is heightened by their fears that the support of these groups for socialist transformations is purely opportunistic. They are therefore susceptible, the leftists argue, to the blandishments of neocolonialist arguments, which seek to replace a genuine socialist revolution in the interest of the workers and peasants with a technological one for the benefit of the bureaucrats and technocrats. The *al-Katib* article of October 1967 contained a warning against the pernicious influence of the doctrines of a managerial revolution typified by James Burnham or the equally misleading "convergence theory" identified with W. W. Rostow. In a 1967 study Dr. Muhammad Anis, a leading leftist intellectual, argued that the untutored self-interest of the technocrats leads them into the arms of the neoimperialists who hide behind such theories. Technical personnel with narrow class horizons are easily persuaded by arguments that the technological revolution is minimizing the differences between capitalism and socialism, and that technical advance is capable of creating an abundance within the reach of all. Anis made it clear that the triumph of this outlook would have disastrous results for the left. For if the technological revolution can be substituted for the social revolution, "there is no longer a need for the social revolution, nor for its tool, i.e. the revolutionary political organization, nor for its theories, i.e. the socialist concepts." Society would simply hand itself over to the technicians who are "confident that they can achieve abundance and progress for it."[27] The leftist intellectuals saw in Nasser's engineering approach to modernization (embodied in the new administrative structures) the Egyptian variant of a technological revolution. As a substitute for the social revolution they desired, this was unacceptable.

One implication of these arguments is significant. It will be recalled that the highest bureaucratic and technocratic positions in Egypt frequently were assigned to resigned military officers. This was a fact which escaped no informed Egyptian and which meant that the left's criticism of the bureaucrats and technocrats carried with it an implicit attack on the military. By and large, the attack remained implicit, although there were occasional lapses even before the 1967 defeat encouraged overt hostility. In the April 1966 issue of *al-Katib,* during the course of a roundtable discussion including Egypt's leading leftist intellectuals and dealing with the theme of "the new face of colonialism and its inside agents," Zulfikar Sabry (brother of Aly) made the startling comment: "There may be sometimes a technical, administrative, and military class that has interests linked to colonialism."[28] The implication was clear that elements within the Egyptian military were playing a reactionary role.

The general thrust of this Marxist critique of the military was eventually absorbed by the official left, headed by Aly Sabry. From January 1967 until the outbreak of the June war a series of over a hundred articles by Sabry appeared in *al-Jumhuriyyah,* analyzing Egyptian society and political development. Sabry's discussions echoed the Marxists with repeated attacks against highly placed bureaucrats, technocrats, even the military. On January 4 he charged that "certain high functionaries and technical directors have tried to obtain personal profits for themselves or their circle by exploiting their functions or their specializations to that end." In case studies of such "deviations" (see, for example, his articles dealing with the construction industry in *al-Jumhuriyyah* from February 25 to March 9) Sabry never mentioned the retired military officers, although he exposed many of the illicit practices that after the June defeat were attributed to the "military bourgeoisie."

In several late March articles Sabry did address himself more directly to a study of the military and its role in Egyptian society. The articles are cautious, yet they do provide insights into the relation between Egypt's

sole political party and the military. Most important are Sabry's revelation that no satisfactory formula had yet been found for participation of
the military in political work and his pointed hints at dissatisfaction with
that state of affairs.

In his article of March 20, Sabry stressed the desire of the majority of
the soldiers for an active political role. He claimed that in colloquiums
organized for the armed forces and police he had noted a "pressing desire to participate positively in daily political work . . . in order to serve
the masses." This kind of incursion into the military sphere could not
have been enthusiastically received by tradition-oriented officers. Since
the hold of the officer caste over their men depended on the institutional
factors of command and obedience habits, infusion of politics into the
military, especially from the bottom, could seriously endanger its control. Although it might be hard to prove that this was the reaction of the
military to the threatened incursion, it does seem clear that Sabry himself
anticipated such a reaction. In an article on March 23 he remarked that at
the highest levels of the socialist union (those involving the officer corps
itself), the soldiers were well represented. At the lower levels, though,
Sabry commented merely that the problem of their representation was
under study. Enumerating the specific barriers encountered in finding the
right formula for political participation by soldiers, Sabry alluded to the
institutional defensiveness of the military. He emphasized that the formula adopted must "preserve the military traditions and the organic stat-
utes of the army which are of a special nature."

The sensitivity of the military to any interference from the Arab Socialist Union (ASU) was shared by the security establishment, which was
heavily commanded by former military figures. During a meeting between the minister of the interior, Sharawi Gomaa, and over two hundred officers, the relation of the police to the ASU was raised. The minister responded with pointed references to the tradition of rank within the
security apparatus (to parry any attempt by the left to appeal over the
heads of the officers to the ordinary police) and to the need for deferring
action until "after the effects of the aggression are eliminated" (to consign the whole question to the distant future).[29]

These same tensions between the military and the left are reflected in
an article by Khaled Muhieddin in the *Démocratie nouvelle* of February
1968. In an explicit and appreciative reference to Sabry's extended analysis in the *al-Jumhuriyyah* series, Muhieddin first raised the inflammatory issue of relations between soldiers and officers: "It does not mean
establishing equality between the officers and soldiers, but creating humane and revolutionary relations between the different ranks." Then, in
line with the previously unheard of direct criticism of the military that

had followed the 1967 defeat, Muhieddin called for direct control over the military by the ASU. The army in Muhieddin's view should end its isolation from society by a wall of favors and privileges. Nor did Muhieddin shrink from suggesting that the party must penetrate the military's institutional structure and work from within to ensure that the army officers "do not form a caste escaping from control of the political direction." Similarly, the journalist Ahmed Bahaeddin charged that the army, despite its earlier great services, "has exhausted its revolutionary potential and its role has become negative." Bahaeddin developed his theme of the necessity for basic changes in Egypt's military-dominated system more subtly in the Egyptian press with a call for the "creation of a modern state." In the popular journal *al-Mussawwar* he argued that the struggle with Israel was a "civilization struggle" that could only be won "by the establishment of a sound, modern, civilized society." Bahaeddin's critique strikes at the heart of Nasser's strategy for Egypt's development and at the system of rule that flowed from it.[30]

The deemphasis on the military—and by extension on military confrontation with Israel—fundamental to Bahaeddin's argument produced the expected virulent reaction in the Egyptian press. The military's preeminent claim on Egypt's resources has rested on its role as shield of the revolution, and it was not eager to allow that role to be questioned. In the wake of the 1967 military disaster Bahaeddin's was not the only voice to do just that. The celebrated author Abdul Rahman el-Sharkawy wrote bitterly of the "new class" that occupied key posts in the state and created ideas and values fundamentally opposed to the people. Sharkawy made it clear that he viewed the military establishment as the core of that new class: "The external dangers menacing our republic helped it [the new class] to reinforce its influence." The last years of Nasser's rule were marked by rising tension between the military/police and the leftists who argued for a truly effective political party.[31]

Gamal Abdul Nasser came to power without an ideologically motivated political party or organization. In the absence of such a party both the mandate concept and a tendency to rely on administrative means were imposed. Bureaucratic feudalism was the result.

Egypt's political arena was dominated by new men who were not cut of one cloth: the army officer, the security official, the bureaucrat, the technocrat, the leftist each came to have a somewhat different vision of Egypt's future and his role in that future. In a political arena structured around rival centers of power, these men struggled for influence. Nasser's tie to the military/police complex and his control over the mandate appointments contained these pressures. His tremendous prestige acted as a cohesive, noninstitutionalized force to prevent the total fractionalization of power implicit in the mandate system. Still, there was no denying the danger of the pressures built into the political system over which Nasser presided. "Such conditions," wrote Haikal starkly, "could lead to a struggle for power."[32] By 1965 Nasser was groping for new political beginnings.

4. Nasser's Search for a New Way

The Egyptian revolution by the mid-sixties had fallen on difficult times. As the domestic revolution stalled, the brilliant foreign policy successes of the fifties were tarnished by a string of disappointments and failures. Revolutionary Iraq's refusal to join the UAR in 1958, followed by the traumatic collapse of the union itself in 1961, set the stage for Nasser's desperate attempt to regain the initiative in Arab affairs. Egypt plunged into "revolutionary war" in Yemen. The costs of that war, political as well as financial, were fateful for Egypt: its domestic economy worsened; it became more isolated in inter-Arab affairs; and its relations with the United States deteriorated as the Americans took the Saudi side in the Saudi-Egyptian proxy war fought in Yemen. Then in 1964 the fall of Nikita Khrushchev aroused fears in Egypt of a cooling of Soviet enthusiasm for the Egyptian revolutionary experience. Such a trend seemed to solidify in 1966 with the advent of a radical regime in Syria. In the 1964-1965 period of Arab summitry the Egyptians had been concerned primarily to moderate the radical Syrian approach to the Israeli issue. Now, in its disputes with Syria, Egypt frequently found the Soviets backing the Syrian regime.

On the international, domestic, and regional levels the mid-sixties were a period of great and dangerous frustration for Nasser's Egypt. They were also a time for reassessment. Along with a clear sense of the limitations of the Free Officer achievement came a conscious search for new direction. For a while at least, Nasser considered a political radicalization of his revolution.

ALTERNATIVE DIRECTIONS

Nasser's view of the international scene in the mid-sixties was dominated by concern with the deterioration of the Egyptian-American relationship and with signs of strain in the Egyptian-Soviet connection. He realized that these troubles in Egypt's relations with the superpowers were symptomatic of a basic shift in the global configuration of power:

> In the international sphere we have moved from the age of the two blocs to the age of diversity of positions, and from the probability of a nuclear war to its impossibility. All these are new conditions and positions for which we cannot prepare ourselves without restudy and reassessment.

Nasser had no difficulty in assessing the meaning for Egypt of Soviet-American détente: "the sources of foreign financing have become strained." By muting superpower competition, détente made questionable Nasser's justification of activism in world affairs as an investment that would earn large-scale foreign aid from both East and West.[1]

Nasser moved to decrease the level of Egypt's involvement abroad and to emphasize the development of the country in terms of its own resources. Egypt's traditional moderation of the Israeli issue was more openly reaffirmed. Nasser also indicated a loss of enthusiasm for the doctrine of unity through social revolution that had prompted Egyptian intervention in Yemen, although Egypt's presence there dragged on until 1967. Egyptians, Nasser warned, could no longer rely on windfalls from abroad. Incremental resources for investment would have to be secured by the more demanding road of a decisive increase in production. Egypt, in short, would have to depend on itself and its own hard work.[2]

The moderation in foreign policy suggested by Nasser's changed view of the global situation was eventually swept away by the events leading to Egypt's ruinous war with Israel in 1967. Nevertheless, in the mid-sixties there were signs that the abandonment of an activist foreign policy was intended to accompany a serious program of domestic retrenchment and reorientation. Up until 1964 Nasser had governed Egypt through the mandate system with virtually no organized consultation of the popular will. Successive attempts to create popular institutions had been half-hearted and invariably put aside under the pressure of outside events.[3] The first such effort came in 1956 with the promulgation of a constitution that called for a National Union to replace all political parties and with the ill-defined Liberation Rally, founded by Nasser shortly after the revolution. The Suez crisis diverted Nasser's attention from these efforts, although the union did play a leading role in electing a National Assembly in July 1957. But both the union and the assembly were correctly perceived as mere rubber stamps for Nasser's power.

A second attempt to create an institutionalized political system for Egypt came in the wake of the Syrian seccession from union with Egypt in 1961. A charter announced in 1962 outlined a new political order for Egypt and called for the creation of yet another single party, the Arab

Socialist Union. In March of 1964 elections were held for a National Assembly and Nasser announced a provisional constitution. Egypt, by official pronouncement, was to be a "democratic, socialist state."

Despite the continued high-handedness, there was a seriousness to such efforts to reshape Egypt's formal political institutions. That attitude, while it never went so far as to involve a real devolution of authority to the new popular institutions, is important as a reflection of loss of that previous easy confidence that Egypt could be modernized by an administrative revolution from above. In a speech to the National Assembly on May 16, 1965, Nasser announced: "The stage of revolutionary administrative means is over." In the press the president's spokesmen explained that the stage of dramatic proclamations from on high, such as the announcements of the arms deal and the nationalization of the Suez Canal Company, was over. Henceforth, the political leadership would be concerned with production figures and the challenge of raising the national income. Explicit in the critique of the regime's earlier performance offered by Nasser and his closest collaborators was a call for new directions.[4]

For all the promise of these grand pronouncements, little of substance had been accomplished by 1967, when the entire effort was overwhelmed in the wake of the defeat by Israel. Faced with the dilemma of a stalled revolution at home and a global context that no longer favored Egypt's interests as he saw them, Nasser hesitated between two alternate views of the proper direction for Egypt's development: a political versus an economic solution.

The political solution was a left alternative, which called for a tilt toward the Soviet Union on the global level and a reliance on political mobilization rather than administrative means to spur the economy at home. The economic solution was a right alternative, which relied on an American connection and implied technocratic control of a retrenched economy with discipline enforced by a streamlined security apparatus. Both orientations were Nasserist, even though both did demand a significant departure from past practices by recognizing that a closer identification with either the Soviet Union or the United States would be necessary if high levels of support were to be received. Two of Nasser's closest associates, Aly Sabry and Zakariya Muhieddin, became associated with the left and right alternatives respectively. Nasser's own uncertainties about the most fruitful direction for Egypt are reflected in his alternation of the two men as prime minister.

The right alternative got a brief play when in October 1965 Nasser appointed Muhieddin as prime minister with a mandate to implement an austerity program for the economy and to improve relations with the United States. Muhieddin called for a policy of economic accommodation with the United States and economic retrenchment at home. Prices and taxes were raised, consumer subsidies lowered, private investment encouraged, and efforts made to reduce imports and reschedule the repayment of short-term foreign credits. Nasser's successor was to return after the October War of 1973 to a grander version of this right alternative. But Nasser in the mid-sixties soon abandoned it. Muhieddin was dismissed in September 1966. The West, it seems, was too slow in responding to Nasser's overtures, and it made its response conditional on financial reforms and final Egyptian withdrawal from Yemen. Nasser was unwilling to be pressured on either issue. Consequently, in the mid-sixties it was the left alternative that he considered most earnestly. In the process he learned that any reorientation of Egypt's pattern of domestic development would prove difficult.

DOMESTIC CONSTRAINTS

The radical freedom that Nasser had enjoyed in conducting Egypt's foreign policy evaporated once attention was turned to domestic affairs. Powerful forces, Nasser discovered, had developed a stake in the bureaucratized mandate system of rule. Both the political and economic solutions, since each called for a new direction in domestic affairs, appeared to threaten some of those interests. Nasser learned that the pliant military and administrative props for his regime could be constraints as well.

One common denominator of the projected left and right solutions was antipathy to the proliferation of bureaucratic structures. Political activists and technocrats alike agreed on the proposition that the bureaucrats were the impediment to Nasser's newly announced goal of increased self-reliance through expanded production. Accordingly, in the sixties the regime's critical attitude toward the bureaucracy became sharply accentuated. That attitude had been somewhat mollified earlier by an appreciation of the bureaucracy as a compliant instrument that helped to soak up and deaden political energies. But as Egypt moved into the sixties, the longstanding complaints against the inefficiency and arrogance of the bureaucracy were compounded with rising resentment over abuses of privilege. In a speech to the National Assembly in March 1964 Nasser gave voice to this resentment in a warning against the rise of a "new class" of privileged bureaucrats. Eight months later Nasser added that it was the earlier reliance by the regime on the state apparatus that allowed the bureaucrats to emerge as just such a dangerous social force. Nasser suggested that the bureaucrats would need disciplining, either by a more vigilant security apparatus or by a mobilized political arm.[5]

The difficulties that had befallen Egypt's revolution in the sixties helped clarify for Nasser more than just the dangers posed by the bureaucratization of his regime. Nasser learned that the feudalization of power concomitant with the mandate system of appointments was even more damaging. For any projected reorientation of domestic affairs in the sixties had to confront entrenched centers of power, of which the military was the strongest. As Nasser sought to reactivate the revolution, there were threatening signs of strain with the military.

In many ways it is remarkable that such tension did not surface sooner. The appointment of Abdul Hakim Amer as head of the military establishment incorporated a certain dichotomy. For Amer was not only Nasser's closest comrade in arms; he was also a professional with strong and independent loyalties to the army. Inevitably, those loyalties deepened over the years, as Amer continued to represent and defend military interests. His role as spokesman for the military on major issues can be seen clearly during Nasser's 1959 falling-out with the Soviets. Stung by Khrushchev's support for Iraq during a period of stress between Egypt and Iraq and by alleged Soviet meddling in Cairo's domestic affairs, Nasser had responded with a bold verbal counterattack. Amer urged caution and conciliation. The Egyptian military, he pointed out, was dependent on the Russians for spare parts and anticipated further arms. The argument proved persuasive, and Nasser was soon mending fences with the Soviets.[6] This representative incident suggests one important reason why an independent position for Amer did not materialize early: in the first years of rule Nasser himself was acutely aware of and responsive to military interests. Such fundamental agreement, coupled with Amer's apparent lack of independent political ambition, helped to forestall any wedge between them.

Nasser appears to have first encountered serious difficulties with the military in 1962, in the wake of the 1961 nationalizations that launched Egypt's socialism. In the formative stage of the Free Officers movement Nasser had avoided all discussion of the social content of his revolution. The same kind of ambiguity was preserved in the heroic years of the nationalist phase, when attention was focused on foreign affairs. This vagueness about the precise social meaning of the revolution was undoubtedly important in cementing the loyalties of an officer corps that had not changed in social composition from the prerevolutionary period. But the nationalizations and attendant socialist ideology meant that the regime had begun to take on a form the character of which disquieted elements within the military. "It would be difficult," observed two Soviet journalists, "to imagine that generals or high officers, the interests of whose families would be infringed by the reforms would with enthusiasm support these reforms."[7]

Much later the minister of war, Shams Badran, corroborated this view in the course of testimony at his treason trial for complicity in a coup attempt. (Badran was one of several key officials tried for attempting to reinstate Amer after Nasser removed him as commander in chief subsequent to the 1967 defeat. Amer apparently committed suicide before he could be tried.) Badran claimed that as far back as 1962, in the wake of the nationalization decrees and the failure of the union with Syria, Nasser had intended to deprive Amer of exclusive control over all questions involving the army. However, when Nasser prepared an order to that effect, Amer threatened resignation. Unprepared for that extreme action, Nasser backed off. From that time, Haikal explained in *al-Ahram,* a situation of dual power developed:

> The trials which have recently taken place before the Tribune of the Revolution have revealed, among other things, that in 1962 there took place a "peaceful coup d'état." From the time of that peaceful coup the state powers began to suffer from a phenomenon of pluralism.

Sadat in *In Search of Identity* presented a dramatic version of Nasser's despair as Amer, having survived the attempt to remove him, consolidated his position. Sadat claimed that "the day came when Amer actually wanted to take over the government." He pictured a distraught Nasser telling him that he was no longer in control of the country:

> I am worried . . . My dear Anwar, the country is being ruled by a gang of thieves . . . and I can't carry on like this. I cannot continue to be President, to hold such a serious responsibility, while it is Amer who actually rules the country and does precisely what he wants.

It is likely that the portrayal is exaggerated, since it was useful for both Nasser and Sadat to stress Amer's power and therefore his responsibility for the chain of events that led to the 1967 disaster. Still, it can be independently confirmed that Nasser in the mid-sixties was to find his efforts to reorient Egypt's domestic development strategy severely strained by opposition from the military center of power.[8]

THE POLITICAL SOLUTION CONSIDERED

By the early sixties Gamal Abdul Nasser had learned from the experiences of a decade of rule an important distinction. It was one thing to gain and hold power; it was quite another to use that power creatively and constructively to revolutionize society. In the face of the daunting domestic and foreign policy difficulties of that era, Nasser gave serious consideration to the left political alternative as a means to accomplish that demanding task. "It is time," as Nasser was later to put it, "to depend on political action rather than administrative action."[9]

For a political solution, Nasser realized, the key instrument was an effective party. The Arab Socialist Union, the third of his political structures, was to be such a party. Nasser expressed his new enthusiasm for the potential of a party as an instrument for modernization in numerous passages of the 1963 unity negotiations with the Syrians and Iraqis. In the spring of 1964 Haikal reported that Nasser had concluded that the construction of an effective political party had priority over everything, up to and including the presidency of the republic. Haikal wrote that Nasser had come to view the creation of such a popular political organization as the natural and desired outcome of his role as a charismatic leader. Finally, in a speech to the National Assembly in January 1965, Nasser made public his reflections on the central role of an effective political party as "the guarantee for the perpetual continuation of the revolution and its ever-driving force."[10]

If Nasser had at this point reached such conclusions concerning the importance of a political party, why did he not devote his full energies and personal authority to the exacting task of strengthening the Arab Socialist Union?

Nasser's Hesitations

There was by the mid-sixties already an established gap between the rhetoric of intention and the paucity of constructive action on the issue of an effective political party. While Nasser over the years spoke frequently of the imperative need to mobilize mass energies through such a party, a genuine effort along those lines was never made. During the first decade of Free Officer rule Egypt, to be sure, had had two political organizations. But they were administrative structures, intended to meet quite different needs.

The Liberation Rally, founded soon after the revolution, was in fact an instrument for depoliticizing Egyptian public life. Of the rally Aly Sabry baldly stated: "Its primary and basic goal was the destruction of the political organizations opposing the revolution. The rally was successful in achieving this."[11] The rally, then, was the instrument whereby deeply ingrained Free Officer suspicion of autonomous political forces was translated into administrative action for the elimination of such forces. This destruction of potentially threatening political life was really the first and last role played by the rally. Its own political ineffectiveness was not in the early years of the regime a cause for official lament.

The formation of the National Union, announced in the constitution of January 1956, responded to yet another need—to reinforce national unity in a time of peril. As the pressures that were to explode in the tripartite invasion of Egypt in 1956 mounted, Nasser groped for means to shore up his domestic position. Looking back some years later, he identified the National Union as one expression of "the great and mighty unity with which we defeated aggression." After this national goal had been achieved, the National Union lingered—to what purpose no one was ever quite sure.[12]

In contrast to these earlier efforts, the Arab Socialist Union for a time was seriously considered for a genuine mobilization effort. Beyond the usual formal and often meaningless official rhetoric assigning the ASU a key place in Egyptian public life were more persuasive signs; it appeared that Nasser, in the context of a general "left orientation," was considering making the ASU the key vehicle for mobilization of the Egyptian people to meet the tasks of economic modernization. In January of 1965 Nasser publicly raised the possibility of not standing for the pro forma election to the presidency scheduled for that year. Instead, he would devote himself to building an effective Arab Socialist Union:

> It has crossed my mind sometimes that the time has come for me to give over the coming stage to the task of completing the structure of the political organization of the working powers of the people allied in the Socialist Union.[13]

Then Nasser hesitated. He retained the presidency, and the effort to make the ASU into a party capable of galvanizing mass energies failed. This time it was a genuine failure, the failure of an intended effort. And from it much can be learned of the political dynamics of Nasser's Egypt.

On the most immediate level it was power considerations that deterred Nasser from making the required commitment of time and energies to the ASU. To leave the presidency to assume active control over the ASU would have entailed the risk, M. H. Haikal explained, of "handing over the levers of command to the elements which had formed the 'centers of power.' " The most influential such center was the military, which since 1962 had enjoyed an increasingly independent position. Given Nasser's towering prestige and his personal ties with Amer, a genuine military coup against him was unlikely. On the other hand, a gentler process of "kicking him upstairs" into some purely honorific position did appear to be a real possibility. By abandoning the presidency and identifying his fate with that of the Arab Socialist Union, Nasser would have risked himself producing that very result. Sadat later claimed to have warned Nasser at the time against just such an eventuality: "It would be unreasonable for you, Gamal, to quit the presidency and concentrate on the Socialist Union. Amer and his assistants would be in sole control of Egypt."[14]

It is true that with Nasser at its head and firmly committed to its revitalization, the ASU would have been a difficult force to contain. In any case, Nasser's willingness to make such a bold move was weakened by some ultimately disabling, deep-seated doubts.

To begin with, Nasser had no illusions about the actual strength of the ASU in the mid-sixties, despite an alleged membership of some five million and an organizational structure that theoretically reached down into the villages. In March 1965 Nasser flatly remarked: "The fact is that we have no actual organization, except on the books." A year later Haikal could still make virtually the same observation: "In the area of political organization the result up to now has been negative."[15]

Given the institutional weakness of the ASU, its success both as a modernizing instrument and as a primary power base would depend on whatever infusion of strength Nasser's personal magnetism could provide. Nasser was willing to believe, as Haikal points out, that "the political authority of any government is its influence on the masses and ability to make them act."[16] Nasser knew to his early amazement that he did enjoy a charismatic hold over the Egyptian people, which transcended direct dependence on the military/police complex. Yet he lacked confidence that this influence could be exploited effectively to guarantee his own political survival and Egypt's modernization.

The kind of response Nasser could evoke from the Egyptian masses without doubt could have released a forceful political spontaneity that might have provided the dynamism and drive for a genuine political movement. For such mass spontaneity Nasser had no taste. He simply did not trust the impulses of the Egyptian people. So, although he realized that a more active popular participation was essential for Egypt's development, Nasser was afraid that mass impulses if released would lead Egypt away from modernity and perhaps to disaster.

The Leninist Model

It was the distrust of mass spontaneity coupled with an appreciation of the potential importance of the mobilization of popular energies that attracted Nasser to the Leninist model of a vanguard party of professional revolutionaries. Lenin had evinced a similar abhorrence of political spontaneity and had relied on a tightly organized and disciplined party—"a small core, consisting of the most reliable, experienced, and hardened workers"—in order to control and direct it. With the party as an organizational weapon Lenin had thus provided one way to channel and control the mass participation that Nasser had come to perceive as integral to a modernization effort having a left orientation. The people in the Leninist vision were to be mobilized under the strict guidance of the professional revolutionaries. Nasser was understandably attracted.[17]

Such a vanguard party, operating within the Arab Socialist Union, might just have provided it with the needed organizational backbone. Nasser could then safely shift to the party and infuse it with the emotional force of his personal charisma—without fear of losing control of the direction of Egypt's revolutionary experience. Accordingly, in 1964 the Nasser regime announced the intention to form a "political apparatus" or cadre of militants within the Arab Socialist Union. Almost immediately the problems of applying the Leninist model became apparent.

An Egyptian leftist, Muhammad Sid Ahmed, provided a convenient framework for the discussion of those problems in *al-Tali'ah*. Sid Ahmed dealt with the formation of the political cadres as it had been achieved in the socialist experiments of other countries. In his treatment of Lenin he identified three basic characteristics of the Bolshevik movement as crucial for its success in Russia:

(1) *A tradition of revolutionary struggle.* "Through daily work in revolutionary struggle, the devoted cadre was developing its revolutionary skill and its theoretical and practical experiences. The cadre led the hot battles against Czarism."

(2) *Revolutionary professionalism.* "The cadre in that party was made up of a small group of revolutionary professionals who were totally devoted to the revolutionary activities of that party."

(3) *Clarity of revolutionary ideas.* "The most important characteristic of this party was that it was concerned with quality before quantity. Its program and revolutionary ideas were clear."[18]

By implication these same characteristics may be considered as the essential prerequisites for the application of the Leninist model to other experiences; on all three counts, it soon became clear, the newly announced Egyptian vanguard party fell desperately short.

The rapid collapse of the ancien régime and the absolute curtailment of the popular role in the 1952 coup d'état effectively deprived the mass of Egyptians of any real sense of participation in revolutionary struggle. And once the coup was launched the Free Officers succeeded, in the words of leftist analyst Michel Kamel, "in rallying all the nationalist forces behind it with no or very little effort, propaganda, or organization."[19] Outside the narrow and restrictive Free Officer elite, it was therefore difficult to develop a sense of significant involvement even in the efforts to consolidate power. Egypt's successive mass parties launched mobilization campaigns and rallies designed to stimulate mass participation in a struggle against Egypt's backwardness. But no one was fooled. The Liberation Rally and the National Union were recognized as administrative creatures of a regime in power. They had no revolutionary aura of their own.

The central idea in the Leninist model of the political party was the imperative of reliance only on those who were professionally engaged in revolutionary activity and bound together in a seasoned and stable revolutionary organization. It is instructive that by 1964 M. H. Haikal was openly regretting the fact that Egypt's revolution was spearheaded by a band of military conspirators rather than by revolutionaries experienced in political struggle. From the standpoint of creating a new political order for Egypt, Haikal argued in *al-Ahram* at the end of 1964 that the army was "the last place" the revolution should have broken out. He states bluntly that "the revolutionary command which had succeeded . . . in overthrowing the ancien régime was not prepared to construct the new." Haikal argues that the course of Egypt's development since the 1952 coup would have been much simpler if the vanguard that took power had been a political organization. Reflecting Nasser's growing disenchantment with the military and bureaucratic elite on which he had been forced to rely, Haikal opines that such an organization would have provided a ready-made solution to the cadre problem: "the political organization has cadres, that is political elements capable of overseeing its plans and programs conforming to its objectives." In contrast, the officers and former officers who exercised authority were far from "revolutionary professionals" and their loyalties depended on various forms of material inducement.[20]

Egypt does have a history of leftist factions and groups with a proud tradition of active opposition to the British and the ancien régime. But the members of such groups, who might have staffed the revolution in a time of left orientation, have not fared well in the new Egypt. It should not be forgotten that among the first acts of official violence by the Free Officers was the execution of the leftist labor leaders Mastapha Khamis and Muhammad Hassan el-Bakary for organizing a strike in August of 1952. This first attempt at popular political action with popular leadership was crushed by terror. In the consolidation period of 1954 and 1955 many leftists, who earlier along with the Moslem Brothers had earned their nationalist credentials in resistance to the British, were jailed as potential threats to the new July order. Despite this early repression, the Egyptian left remained appreciative of Nasser's progressive, anti-imperialist stance in global politics. Thus, when Nasser was preparing to leave for the great Third World conference at Bandung, he was startled to find on his desk a telegram from the recently arrested communists: "Long live our militant in the anti-imperialist struggle! We salute you."[21]

The 1956 Suez crisis, with its attendant rallying cry of national unity, brought relief to the left. Many were released from prison. Reconciliation was short-lived, this time disturbed by events outside Egypt's borders. Massive arrests took place in 1959. Nasser was angered by the left's response to General Kassem of Iraq, whose coup had overthrown the reactionary monarchy. The Egyptian left—and the Russians—were delighted that Kassem gave a much freer reign to the Iraqi communists, even to the point of including some in his coalition government. From 1959 to 1964 the left suffered horribly in Egypt's concentration camps. The brutally murdered included Shohdi Attia el-Shafei, a brilliant Marxist historian and theoretician. One could claim with justification that the best intellectual circles in Egypt were found in prisons like Abou Zaabal and concentration camps like Kharga. Joined by persecuted elements of the right (especially the Moslem Brothers), the prisoners constituted a virtual countersociety.[22]

In 1964 the regime once again released the militants of the left who, as a result of the "socialist" conversion of the regime and in the context of the left alternative, were then useful for information and propaganda functions. In 1965 the Egyptian Communist Party officially dissolved and the communist left joined the ASU. Although wary and distrustful, the left once again responded to the regime's call. Several prominent Marxists, including Lutfy el-Kholy, Mahmoud el-Alem, and Khaled Muhieddin, attained posts of second-level importance in the information sphere as well as in several branches of the ASU. However, after the 1967 defeat the regime once more turned against the left.[23]

This record of repression, despite the intermittent relaxations, meant that talk of an official left orientation was filled with irony for Egypt's genuine leftists. Furthermore, the persecution of the left was only the overt manifestation of a much more widespread repressiveness characteristic of Nasser's Egypt. The heavy-handedness of the secret police and military security forces was widely felt. No one dared to debate political questions in public; a pervasive fearfulness limited such discussion to only the closest and most trusted of friends and relatives. Such a general atmosphere was hardly conducive to that release of popular energies for which Nasser's political solution called.

For their part, Egypt's official leftists gravitated to the successive mass political organizations that functioned as one more administrative apparatus in a bureaucratized regime. With their memberships comprising the bulk of the adult male population, there could be no question of "revolutionary professionalism." The primary motives for joining the mass parties were the nonideological—even conservative—ones of protecting existing rights, maintaining social prestige, securing redress of specific grievances, and possibly attaining minimal qualifications for cooption into the higher echelons of the state. Even the activists among the official leftists, Aly Sabry has explained, engaged in political work primarily on a volunteer or part-time basis. Their regular official or administrative work took priority. Faced with the severe limitations of the official party activists, Nasser in 1964 announced his intention of selecting a new vanguard or cadre of militants to strengthen the ASU. From the beginning the effort was plagued with problems. It was ultimately abandoned.[24]

Nasser had no illusions that the search for a cadre of militants would be an easy task. As early as 1962, in the course of the unity talks with Iraq and Syria, Nasser revealed that he had given serious consideration to the idea of establishing the ASU as a vanguard party of approximately three hundred thousand instead of a mass organization of some five million. He then dropped the idea because of the difficulty anticipated in making the choice of who should or should not be accepted for membership in the new political elite.[25]

When the idea was revived in 1964 in the form of the intended creation of a vanguard within the ASU, the task of selecting the cadres did in fact present a real problem. Since it had been decided that the identity of the new vanguard would be kept secret, an analysis of these difficulties must rely on indirect evidence. Most insightful of the published commentaries on the subject is a series of articles by Aly Sabry that appeared daily in *al-Jumhuriyyah* from January through June of 1967.[26] Sabry was actually concerned with the more limited task of selecting members for the Central Committee of the ASU. Still, the problems encountered with that task reflect in concentrated form those experienced in selecting the vanguard generally.

In his wide-ranging discussion Sabry argued that the important cadres should not be chosen either by popular choice or by merely coopting individuals already holding high executive, legislative, or political positions. He reasoned that popular activity under a socialist aegis was something new for Egypt and that the masses would not have the necessary political maturity to make suitable choices. The method of cooption of high-ranking officials, Sabry explained, afforded no protection against the many opportunists who held such posts and who would be able to infiltrate the upper levels of the union and exploit it for their own selfish ends. In the light of these considerations, Sabry concluded that the healthiest method of selection was individual and personal evaluation by the top leadership elements of the ASU.

In the spring of 1965 Vice-President Kamal Rifaat had indicated that the selection process for the vanguard was underway in just such a personal manner, one that emphasized "direct contacts" and "personal acquaintances." Sabry in a lengthy interview in the fall of 1966 attempted to give the process an air of precision with the observation that "we select the suitable elements on the basis of their work experience and their pursuit of the struggle and this reduces our chance of error." Intentions aside, neither Rifaat nor Sabry offered any real criteria for the selections other than vague and platitudinous injunctions that only the most devoted and most positive elements be allowed to join the vanguard. The danger of such an approach was that it inevitably reinforced the personalization of power that has been identified as characteristic of Egyptian politics.[27]

Nasser's awareness that Egypt did not in fact possess revolutionary cadres to make up a real political vanguard, and his anticipation of the problems of training them, was undoubtedly a strong factor in his decision not to leave the presidency in 1965. He would remain and concentrate his energies on strengthening the ASU. During 1966 comments by ASU officials on the vanguard or political apparatus within the ASU grew ever more vague. It was emphasized that the process of selection would be a slow one. Two years later it was acknowledged that not only had little been accomplished, but that the whole effort had been abandoned.

In *What Is To Be Done* Lenin stressed the critical importance of ideology to his conception of the party. Moreover, he emphasized that it was the intellectuals who were the bearers of theory:

> The theory of socialism . . . grew out of the philosophic, historical, and economic theories that were elaborated by the educated representatives of the propertied classes, the intellectuals.[28]

Many of the problems experienced by Egypt's new rulers stemmed from the fact that in a fundamental way the study of Nasser's Egypt is the story of a regime come to power without an ideology.

The Free Officers did not share an ideology at even the most elemental level. They had no action program that would have provided some conception of the society their revolution aimed at creating. It does not follow that self-interest filled the void. Rather, as demonstrated earlier, a compelling if operationally unclear dream of an independent and strong Egypt provided the motive force for the 1952 coup. But were dreams enough to launch a revolution? After more than a decade at the center of power, M. H. Haikal thought not: "That group [the Free Officers] caressed numerous hopes but the authority of the state cannot content itself with vague hopes in order to set in motion its giant wheels; it has need of plans and programs."[29] The harsh experiences of rule had taught Egypt's new elite that a true political community could not rest on a vague dream alone; power without ideology was of limited effectiveness.

THEORY AND PRACTICE

In a 1961 address Nasser remarked:

I was not asked on July 23rd to stage the revolution with a printed book including my theory. This is impossible. If we had stopped to write such a book before July 23rd, we would never have succeeded in carrying out two operations at the same time. Those who ask for a theory are greatly complicating matters. This is torture.

In place of ideology in the early years Nasser offered the simple but compelling demand for radical change. He spoke of an imperative for two revolutions, political and social, and expressed that imperative succinctly in the sloganeering form of the famous Six Principles. To be sure, these goals were all eminently desirable. But they did not provide a real guide for action or even suggest the outlines of the social system within which such objectives could be achieved. Ten years after the revolution, Nasser quite frankly acknowledged in the charter: "Those principles were only banners for the Revolution and not a method of revolutionary action nor a program for fundamental change." Early habits of exclusive concentration on securing power were carried over by the Free Officers into the post-1952 period, in the form of an equally overriding concern with problems of holding power. A testament to the skill with which this concern was exercised was the unusual stability that marked the years of Nasser's rule. The cost was the totally inadequate resolution of the problem of how power would be used to revolutionize Egypt.[30]

M. H. Haikal has suggested that in its early years the regime had completely lacked an appreciation of the centrality and complexity of that problem: "This movement, although it had principles . . . did not really have an exact vision of the import and the profundity of the enterprise which it had undertaken." Haikal makes a case for the naiveté of the Free Officers, arguing that they believed that once the king and the British had been removed the answers to the question of what to do with power would be self-evident.

Once the shallowness of this view had been exposed, Nasser had no choice but to confront the realities of ruling power on a pragmatic, ad hoc basis. Later Nasser explained:

Our circumstances were that the revolutionary application, our revolutionary application, may be prior to the theory. Then what is the theory? The theory is the evidence of the action.[31]

In 1962, in the wake of the nationalizations and the Syrian secession, Nasser announced the birth of the theory that codified Egypt's revolutionary practice. The *Charter of National Action* begins with a schematic and didactic survey of Egyptian and Arab history (chapters 1 to 4), continues with a rather detailed program of action that describes the coming decade as the period of socialist conversion leading to an inevitable "scientific socialism" (chapters 5 to 8), and concludes with discussions of Arab unity and foreign policy (chapters 9 and 10).

The idea fundamental to the charter is that "political democracy cannot be separated from social democracy." For Nasser social democracy was necessarily grounded in a far-reaching economic structuring that would make it possible to attain the status of an economically developed country. Such a restructuring would constitute socialism in that (1) the basic economic infrastructure (including major transportation and communication networks) would be publicly owned; (2) the bulk of heavy, medium, and small industries would be under public ownership, while whatever independent industrial private sector did exist would be under the general control of the public sector; (3) all import and three-quarters of export trade would be in the public realm; (4) banks and insurance companies were likewise to be in public hands; and (5) private ownership of land was to continue within prescribed limits, although a clear distinction was to be made between "exploiting" and "nonexploiting" land ownership.

Within and outside Egypt the charter has been the subject of endless critical commentary. Of particular relevance to the analysis here is the record of Nasser's own changing evaluation of the utility of the charter as a guide to revolutionary action. In the period immediately following its promulgation Nasser apparently believed that he had provided Egypt with a working ideology. In his July 1962 speech commemorating the tenth anniversary of the revolution the president acclaimed the charter as "a guide to revolutionary action" and the definitive repository of the doctrinal assumptions on which that guide was based—"the principles . . . concerning socialism, democracy, social justice and political freedom." Disillusionment was not long in coming. Within two years Nasser's enthusiasm for the charter's utility had notably cooled. He would then refer to the document simply as a summing up of past experience. In a 1964 address, for example, Nasser observed: "In the *Charter,* we outlined our experience and fixed our aspirations." Several years later Haikal illustrated more fully the nature of the shift in thinking. The Free Officers, he explained, had acted in 1952 on the basis of a set of first principles although the movement had "no general theoretical view embracing the multiple transformations which it desired to make." The charter later "supplied the necessary definitions." But Haikal's enthusiasm was limited since, in his words, "these definitions were once again the fruit of experience and did not precede it as is the rule."[32]

The charter was indeed the result of a decade of experience with ruling power; in the realm of theory it crystallized the three main trends of Egypt's ideological development: positive neutralism, pan-Arabism, and socialism. The problem with the charter was precisely its accuracy in reflecting past experience, for by the mid-sixties Nasser was becoming more aware of the inadequacies of that experience as a guide for Egypt's future development. As Nasser paid closer attention to the problems of Egypt's domestic development, he became better informed about the severe limitations of the newly created military-bureaucratic elite. For a time Nasser looked to the ASU as a more suitable vehicle for Egypt's modernization. Nevertheless, to serve that function the union required an ideology to both educate and motivate its own activists. Nasser had come to regard this as crucial for the realization of his development aims. To his chagrin, Nasser soon discovered that on both counts the official ideology codified in the charter was grossly inadequate.

The complex vision that had initially propelled Egypt's revolution gave way in the sixties to an official ideology. In the early years Nasser's vision had proved sufficient to generate diffuse popular support and legitimate elite autonomy; it had not provided a vehicle for popular participation. At that time Nasser thought that the independence and greatness of Egypt was to be attained through the actions of the elite; the mass of Egyptians were cast in the role of grateful spectators. In contrast, the official ideology pieced together by the early sixties was intended to have a mobilization function. Yet the three main components of that ideology (positive neutrality, pan-Arabism, and socialism) had been developed in response to the rhythms of foreign policy on the one hand and the exigencies of power maintenance on the other. Nasser had first learned that even an elaborated elite vision could not provide ideological cement for a viable political community. By the mid-sixties he was forced to another realization: Egypt's official ideology—the product of his regime's manipulative needs—did not respond to the essential needs of his people.

Gamal Abdul Nasser assuredly had contributed greatly on the nationalist plane to the liberation of Egypt. In hard strategic and political terms he had responded to the challenge to negate Egypt's colonial or semicolonial status and achieve for Egypt an autonomous place in the modern world. Yet on the domestic plane, for the mass of Egyptians, the goal of political community seemed as remote as ever. In the realm of self-transformation, the transformation of values and beliefs, little of significance had been achieved. "The old scale of values," observed Mirsky, "has gone together with the old order, and a new scale has not yet asserted itself."[33]

Preoccupied with questions of power and foreign policy, President Nasser had never really responded to this essential challenge. Islam, so intricately involved in the political and social order, was either ignored or exploited. One searches in vain for a sensitive treatment of the problems of adjusting Islamic traditional beliefs to the pressing demands of the modern world. Rather one sees a frequent tapping of the emotional force of the Islamic attachment to win support for the regime's policies (for example, pan-Arabism) or to buttress it in times of danger. (In the wake of the 1956 and 1967 attacks on Egypt there was a striking increase in the volume of official Islamic exhortation.) The relation between reason and revelation—which had been the touchstone of the West's own adjustment of its religious heritage to the demands of modernity—was ignored. On the other hand, the alternative of a total rejection of the Islamic heritage in favor of a secular faith on the communist model was also explicitly rejected. The regime merely temporized and pretended that there was no problem.

Typical of the official attitude is the following Nasser observation:

> Ours is a scientific socialism based on science not on chaos. It is not at all a material socialism. We have never said that it was, nor have we said that we were opposed to religion. What we have said was that our religion is a socialist one and that in the Middle Ages Islam had successfully applied the first socialist experiment in the world.

The difficulties dissolve in the assertion that Islam had in fact anticipated modernity in its socialist guise by several centuries. The same facility and superficiality has characterized the official pronouncements of the relationship between revelation and reason. The rector of al-Azhar provides an example of the approach encountered: "Furthermore, there is no conflict between science and religion . . . Religion never has and never will contradict science, because good never stands in the way of good." Thus there has been little evidence to suggest any grappling with the ideological problem on the basic level—that is, a serious rethinking or reformulation in order to ground the official ideology in a set of doctrinal assumptions and a belief system that would make sense of the challenges Egyptians are now facing.[34]

In the mid-sixties there were signs that Nasser at least recognized the critical importance of a resolution of the ideological problem if he were to succeed in establishing a viable political community. As Nasser focused on the problems of developing Egypt in terms of its own resources, he could not but perceive that the official ideology had little to offer. Originating as a response to quite other considerations, that ideology simply did not deal with the real questions—those of basic beliefs, habits of work, sense of duty—in the right way.

In more recent years, especially after the shock of the 1967 defeat, Egyptian intellectuals have struggled to formulate an ideology in these terms, in language accessible to the mass of Egyptians. The distinguished novelist and political commentator Fathy Ghanem, for example, has argued that Egypt's official ideological theorizing has suffered because it has not attempted to shape the beliefs and habits of the men and women who are to perform the practical tasks involved in modernizing Egypt: "In reality the market of ideas in our society is full. However, the majority are, regrettably, thoughts not connected with reality.'' Ghanem commented that an accomplishment far more important than the High Dam would be the training of a hundred thousand people ''whose sound socialist thought is connected to sound behavior and the capability to work in various projects.''[35]

The irrelevance of the official ideology was emphasized to Nasser as he discovered that it proved incapable of engendering more than self-serving, opportunistic lip service. That this negative result is not simply the reflection of an endemic passivity of the Egyptian populace is demonstrated by the continuous success of the Moslem Brotherhood in eliciting fervid support in the most unfavorable of circumstances. The astute Egyptian publicist Ihsan Abdul Kudus, writing in *Rose al-Yusuf,* provides a more sophisticated explanation for the regime's dilemma. Kudus argues that it is much easier to spread an ideology before coming to power than to preach it after power is attained. From the Egyptian experience Kudus concludes that after the spokesmen for new ideas about society come to power, their ideas become mere slogans of government.

> People are liable to argue: Now the ideologists are in power, what do they want of us? Why do they need our faith and struggle if they can make laws as they like? Ideology has become reality, not a hope and a faith. In this situation people tend to adopt a passive attitude and to become spectators towards the government and its laws.

In such a situation, Kudus concludes,

> the ideology leans more on the laws than on persuasion—and this is dangerous since the law cannot achieve its aim unless it is carried out by people conscious of their tasks. Since the construction of a new society requires sacrifice and suffering for an extended period, at the expense of immediate gains, the public cannot pass through this period unless it is armed with a strong faith.[36]

This is a persuasive yet not totally adequate analysis of the regime's failure in gaining converts to its official ideology. It is helpful in explaining why the regime has not been able to win over a hard core of militants, which could then be charged with propagation of the ideology. And yet, by not considering the substantive content of the ideology and inadequacies on that score (and, given the censorship, this would have been all but impossible for an Egyptian journalist to do), the explanation is ultimately unacceptable.

The Moslem Brotherhood, whatever may have been the particular shortcomings of its answer, was at least responding to this challenge; therein lay the source of its appeal. Mirsky argues that part of the youth of Egypt was drawn to the brotherhood not because of its vague ideas of a theocratic state, but rather because of ''the puritanism and self-denial it propounds, its fanatical devotion to an idea and its exhortations to moral purification and return to the original virtues of Islam."[37]

The objection might be raised that it is unreasonable to look to the official ideology to formulate an adequate response to this basic challenge of modernity. This point is strengthened when one realizes that the ideology has essentially been the product of one man—Gamal Abdul Nasser. But since Nasser himself assumed that burden and prevented others from contributing to it, he must take responsibility for its success or failure.

During his first years in power Nasser was wont to ridicule the role of ideas in social change and to underestimate both the intellectuals and the ideological problems with which they were concerned. With time, however, Nasser came to see that the issues raised by the intellectuals were indeed crucial to the modernization of Egypt. In a speech to the National Assembly in 1964 Nasser admitted that the official ideology, despite the considerable material changes wrought during the years of his rule, had not yet provided Egypt with the moral basis for a modern society:

> As far as the moral texture is concerned, we cannot change it overnight. So far, we have not been able to create a model for the new relationships that should prevail . . . The values that existed still exist . . . Our social relationships have not changed.[38]

To be sure, this discussion was concerned with the problems of the conversion to socialism—socialism conceived as merely the particular guise for the modern society to which Egypt aspires.

Nowhere is Nasser's growing awareness of the inadequacies of the official ideology crystallized in the charter more fully demonstrated than in a lengthy speech to the National Assembly on January 20, 1965. The president began his discussion with the exhortation: "It is imperative upon us, in the forthcoming stage, to consolidate the values of the socialist society so that they may gain stability and permanence, and their roots grow deep into our life." In a later passage he committed himself to undertake that ideological formulation, which he then realized to be essential:

> If I am right in appraising this . . . objective of the forthcoming stage, it would be my pride and honour to contribute my share in consolidating the moral values of the socialist society, especially that the *Charter of National Action* shall be the object of new study in a national convention which will be held, God willing, in 1970 in accordance with the terms of the *Charter* itself.

That commitment was never fulfilled. Almost four years later, in an extended analysis of the regime's shortcomings, Haikal gave primary emphasis to the alienation of the intellectuals and the failure to resolve the ideological problem. "The state," Haikal explained, "broke contact with the intellectuals and underestimated their role under the pretext that they could only contribute words and more words." In the mid-sixties Nasser turned away from the political solution and the concern with ideology that it entailed.[39]

FAILURE OF THE POLITICAL SOLUTION

In 1965 Nasser accepted another term as president and abandoned any plans to devote his energies to the ASU. Aly Sabry became secretary general of the party. Deprived of Nasser's charisma, the ASU performed indifferently until the disaster of June 1967. In the postwar period Nasser did in fact assume the position of secretary general of the union and in his March program called for a complete restructuring and revitalization of the ASU. By then his real concerns were the continuing conflict with Israel and the burdens of national reconstruction; the political alternative, considered in the sixties as a way out of Egypt's difficulties, had collapsed. The fate of the ASU, once Nasser withdrew his personal energies and prestige, reveals a great deal about the dynamics of power and ideology in Nasser's Egypt.

From its inception the ASU was not exempt from the consequences of the essential methods of Nasser's rule. The party was popularly perceived as but one more administrative extension of Nasser's power. Nasser, in fact, treated it as such. Top-level ASU appointments were made by the mandate system. A presidential decree of 1962 allotted the key positions to trusted and reliable appointees, who were grouped in the Superior Executive Committee under Hussein el-Shafei as secretary general. Of the twenty members of the second-level General Secretariat of the ASU, there were twelve Free Officers.[40]

In familiar fashion these high-level appointees rapidly moved to consolidate functional "fiefdoms" within the structure of the ASU. The General Secretariat was carved up into fifteen branches, each headed by an appointee who promptly surrounded himself with a responsive "family" of retainees. This strict personalism was made more complex by a process of double-bonding, whereby clusters were reinforced by crude ideological convergences. Leftists, for example, tended to gravitate to the branch responsible for ideology, which was headed by Kamal Rifaat, or to the branch responsible for the press, which was headed by Khaled Muhieddin. Elements further to the right were drawn into the circle of Sayid Marei, who was responsible for national capitalism, or that of Ahmed Toeima, who was responsible for the liberal professions. Confidence in the functional rationality of the ASU organizational structure naturally eroded as its "feudalization" proceeded apace.

Equally damaging was a concomitant bureaucratization which, again in familiar fashion, sapped the vitality of the union. Each member of the General Secretariat enjoyed ministerial status and had little difficulty in attracting hordes of government bureaucrats to his staff. The endless, self-serving swirl of bureaucratic movement supplanted the orientation and direction the ASU was to have provided the country.

An unsettling ambiguity developed around the functions of the ASU and that ambiguity, by generating political fears, further diminished the effectiveness of the party. In a high-level debate over the shortcomings of the ASU, published in March 1965, a prominent trade union leader observed: "I think that there are many people who believe in the purposes and goals of the Socialist Union, but these people have to be given a certain function to perform and a certain responsibility."[41] Quite clearly the role of the ASU had not yet been defined. One is inescapably reminded of the exasperation playwright Aly Salem described when no one was quite sure what the Well of Wheat project was all about!

In the published debate, dissatisfaction with the performance of the union was most evident on the part of Field Marshal Amer. In a strange and unprecedented remark Amer attacked the basic principle of a one-party mobilization system:

> Even after the questions of selection and revitalization are solved, the Socialist Union will suffer of lack of overt opposition. The Socialist Union will continue to display vigor and dynamism only if it is given a permanent job to do and responsibility to hold.

In context it appeared at the time that Amer was simply calling the attention of the participants in the debate to the necessity, in the absence of opposition, of a sharp definition of function—and not suggesting that an opposition should be created. More may have been involved. Sadat later claimed that Amer in his rivalry with Nasser since the early sixties frequently resorted to appeals to democracy that he knew would anger Nasser. At any rate, Nasser did take Amer's remarks seriously and responded sharply to them:

> Commenting on Field Marshal Amer's statement, I would like to say that the main problem stems not from the lack of overt opposition but from the existence of active opposition elements within the Socialist Union.[42]

Amer's remark seemed to give expression to a certain uneasiness within the military establishment at the thrust of the political solution. The ambiguity of the ASU's role undoubtedly stirred fears that the full formal potential of that role would be asserted, thereby challenging the preeminent position of the military. Such worries were not calmed by the fact that Nasser, at the high point of his enthusiasm for the political solution, was prone to talk of the ASU, rather than the military, as the vanguard and shield of the revolution.[43]

The sensitivity of the military burst into ill-considered action in the fall of 1966. Military intelligence claimed to have uncovered a vast network of communist infiltrators in the ASU youth affiliate. Over seventy-five were arrested, and the military used the incident as a pretext to close the Socialist Institute. Prominent leftists associated with the institute, including its director, Ibrahim Assad ed-Din, and the editor of *al-Tali'ah*, Lutfy el-Kholy, were accused of being in contact with the alleged communist network. Nasser ordered the minister of the interior to investigate the charges independently. When assured of the innocence of the principals, Nasser ordered them reinstated, to the consternation of the military intelligence apparatus.[44]

Reactions of the technocratic elite to the ASU were quite similar to those of the military. In *al-Jumhuriyyah* of June 19, 1969, Fathy Ghanem summarized the attitude of the technicians and administrators toward the attempts to use the ASU to mobilize mass participation in the tasks of modernizing Egypt. Describing "the fear of the technicians and the administrators of the authority designated for the people," Ghanem presented the rationale for the opposition of these bureaucratic and technocratic elements to the ASU in the following terms:

> It appeared to them as if those who have expertise in technical and administrative affairs are the only ones with the right to perform those jobs without caring for the experience of others.

Ghanem suggested that opposition to the ASU on these grounds was active and organized. He claimed that those opposed to an active ASU in production sought to discredit the Union

> by looking for peculiar examples or through using words spoken by the members of the Socialist Union Committees to establish that unreasonable forces wished to dominate production—thus leading to a real catastrophe.[45]

The ASU had been formally assigned a preeminent role which, without Nasser's direct involvement, it could not carry out. In such a situation the vagueness of the ASU's actual role served to activate the distrust and misgivings of key established elements in the Egyptian political system. The technocrats would clearly have preferred a right orientation, which would have constrained the ASU and given the technocratic elite a more central role. They also feared, with good cause, the hostility of Egypt's leftists. Elements within the military apparently shared these feelings. Accounts of the failure of the union typically make too much of popular indifference and passivity and too little of this overt opposition on the part of the technocratic and military elites.

The opposition of these elites was particularly keen to the secret vanguard party organized within the ASU under President Nasser's orders in 1964. Once again distrust was heightened and opposition stimulated as a result of the lack of a clear definition of the precise role of the vanguard. Before long the impression was created that the party militants constituted a "spy system" designed to infiltrate the various hierarchies of the state and to report deviations. The impression may not have been totally inaccurate. The text of the *al-Tali'ah* debate on the revitalization of the union contains a strong suggestion that Nasser himself conceived the union's role at least partly along the lines of an information gathering agency. During a discussion of the halting of profit distribution by an Egyptian company, Nasser remarked:

> What is the real role of the Socialist Union? Tell us how we can know what happened concerning the distribution and then halting of profits. I have heard about this question through the Minister of the Interior, while the Socialist Union said nothing about it.[46]

Nasser was clearly suggesting that by not reporting on this incident (as the police had done), the union was derelict in its duties.

To be sure, union officials heartily denied that the vanguard apparatus had such a spy function. In a 1966 *Rose al-Yusuf* article Aly Sabry, then secretary general of the ASU, was asked to describe the function of the political apparatus. Sabry began with a typically vague formulation: "The political apparatus can fulfill a creative, positive role in the operation of building the socialist community, with a membership possessing an enlightened ideological unity." Then, in clear response to the widespread apprehension stirred by the vanguard, he added: "Some have imagined that the work of the political apparatus is the gathering of information . . . This is an erroneous idea and far from the truth."[47] His felt need to make such a public defense is an interesting measure of the opposition aroused by the political apparatus.

After Nasser had made the decision early in 1965 not to assume the position of ASU secretary general, he appointed a strong personality, Aly Sabry, to the post. The peculiar logic of the mandate system soon asserted itself. Before long there were signs of wariness on Nasser's part of Sabry's successful use of the ASU as a personal power base. The uneasiness provoked by Sabry's rapid consolidation of his hold on the ASU paralled closely the tensions Nasser had experienced with Field Marshal Amer and the military establishment since 1962. In 1965 and 1966 Nasser began to speak out pointedly against the dangers that such personalized power rivalries posed for Egypt's development. In a speech to the National Assembly in the autumn of 1965, Nasser spoke of the sovereignty of the law, which must affirm itself as superior to "centers of power and the particular will of individuals."[48]

Nasser's developing perception of the ASU as one such dangerous center of power is reflected in the changed official descriptions of the rightful role of the ASU. A high point of enthusiasm for the union and a most generous definition of its role is registered in a 1964 article in *al-Ahram* by M. H. Haikal. Written before the structure of the union had solidified and before the appointment of Aly Sabry as secretary general, the article describes the union as "the receptacle of all the hopes and of all the potentialities of the people." Politically, the union is seen as governing "above all the administrative apparatus, directing it instead of being directed by it." Haikal continues:

> It is also from that organization that the elected National Assembly surges . . . *Above both of them,* that is the government and the Assembly, is the Political Organization which imposes its will and its authority.

He also makes it clear that the position of the political organization is to be dominant in relation to the technical cadres: "To the experts and specialists it will impose service to the patrie and will compel them to give proof of their loyalty."[49]

The first real sign of Nasser's departure from such a positive view of the ASU came with his handling of the notorious Kamchiche affair. Using the murder of a minor ASU official as a pretext, Aly Sabry in the spring of 1966 launched an immensely popular attack against remaining "rural feudalists." Sabry succeeded in uncovering some dramatic examples of continuing exploitation of the Egyptian peasantry by old landowning families; in the process he reaped considerable political capital for the ASU. President Nasser acted quickly to undercut Sabry's drive. He established a special commission to investigate the rural feudalists and appointed Field Marshal Amer to head it. Thus the prestige and popularity accruing to Sabry was deflected to the military establishment and the drive against rural feudalists was contained. One center of power was played against another to protect Nasser's own position. Amer of course simply exploited the Kamchiche affair to his own ends.

By 1967 Nasser's official descriptions of the union reflected his concern over its use as a power base by Sabry. Once again Haikal was the mouthpiece. In an *al-Ahram* article of August 1967 Haikal bitterly attacked the ASU as a center of power that "dared" to place itself above the government:

There is first of all the fact that the Socialist Union has often developed into one or two centers of power. Thus, it has sometimes seemed to wish to be a government above or at the side of the government—and this is an error, *its proper place being in fact behind the government,* which is in reality the executive organ of the avant-garde.[50]

After the 1967 defeat Nasser anticipated an overt challenge from the ASU. That danger was delayed but not defused, as Anwar es-Sadat learned in 1970.

DISTORTION OF THE IDEOLOGICAL PROBLEM

If Nasser was successful in containing the threat of the ASU as a center of power, that success had its costs. By not identifying himself completely with the ASU, Nasser weakened the union's announced role as guardian and repository of the regime's ideology. Before long, the tensions between Nasser and the ASU were reflected on the ideological plane.

As early as 1966 Nasser's veiled apprehension at the emerging independent position of Sabry in the union was expressed in ideological terms. When Haikal in February of 1966 charged that "frankly, the political organization in Egypt leaves much to be desired," he proceeded to concretize that judgment with reference to ideological distortions. Leftist ASU slogans, directed against the technocrats and the state bureaucrats, were denounced by Haikal as "inappropriate" and "ideas peculiar to their authors." Quite explicitly, Haikal sought to remove the mantle of Nasser's prestige and authority from the ideological pronouncements of the ASU. Haikal charged that ASU slogans distorted Nasser's meaning by quotations that were misinterpreted and out of context.[51] The delay in developing a coherent ideology for Egypt was extended, as ideology was subordinated to the exigencies of personal power rivalries. The ultimate failure of the ASU to establish itself as an effective voice lay in the distrust Nasser came to have for the whole enterprise.

Nasser's response was to retreat from ideological speculation. Signs of his dissatisfaction with the ASU theorizing were especially pronounced in the period following the 1967 war. Haikal then explained the popularity of Nasser with the Egyptian masses—so recently confirmed by their support for him in the wake of the June disaster—by the fact that "he never addressed them with the intention of developing an ideological philosophy." In other columns Haikal gave vent to sharp criticism of particular ideological formulations advanced by leftists centered in the ASU. He decried "false interpretations of the *National Charter.*" He mentioned first "that heresy according to which there exists an incompatibility between socialism and economic freedom," then provided a brief catalogue of ideological deviation:

> Furthermore, it is not true to say that profit—if it is legitimate—is a crime; that the sovereignty of the law is a limit to revolutionary activity; that the private sector must be absorbed by the public sector.

Interestingly, in each specific case the line of argument prepared the way for a turn to the right orientation that Nasser's successor was eventually to implement.[52]

As Egypt moved into the second half of the sixties, its ideological development remained problematic. On the one hand, Nasser regarded himself (and was widely accepted) as the fountainhead for the regime's official ideology. On the other hand, the ASU with its expanding propaganda apparatus was officially charged with disseminating Egypt's socialist ideology. Ideological confusion was heightened as the differences between Nasser and the union leadership surfaced. It is noteworthy that this ideological conflict was but one manifestation of more fundamental misgivings on Nasser's part that the ASU was being exploited as a base for rival political power.[53] So despite Nasser's late-developing appreciation of the importance of ideology for the development of Egypt, political circumstances encouraged him to revert to his earlier view of ideology as a threat to rather than an instrument of political power.

President Nasser by the mid-sixties had come to understand that the real battleground for modernity lay within—in the challenge of ideas, values, and beliefs. In a 1964 speech he had exhorted his people accordingly:

> We need to struggle against ourselves and to realize our responsibilities. Fighting against ourselves is naturally much more difficult than fighting against an outside enemy. The question is not simple.[54]

The demands of foreign policy and domestic power considerations continued to intervene. When Gamal Abdul Nasser died in the fall of 1970, there were few signs that the struggle for which he called was seriously underway.

5. From Despair to Exultation

There, on the Gezira bank, a murmur arose. The clamor mounted, until the furious march of the military band seemed suddenly to fall silent. An oblong object hovered over the crowd, draped with the national flag, whose white stripe alone was visible—it was Gamal's coffin. The cry became clearer: "You live, O Abu Khaled."[1]

Gamal Abdul Nasser died on September 28, 1970. Thousands of the common people of Egypt streamed into Cairo. With their public outpouring of grief, they claimed their dead ruler and prevented a staid, official funeral. To his people the man known to the world as Nasser had become Abu Khaled—the father of Khaled, Nasser's virtually unknown eldest son. With that traditional Arab form of address, which asserts familial continuity, the people of Egypt sought assurance that the man who had ruled them for eighteen years had left an enduring legacy.

As a nationalist, Nasser's preeminent position in the history of his country is secure. Egyptians take just pride that their revolution is perhaps the classic model of nationalist revolution in the Third World. Nasser embodied that Egyptian triumph; his charisma derived from it.

But beyond the end of semicolonial dependency, beyond charisma, what—Egyptians asked themselves—had become of Nasser's promise and Egypt's need of radical social reconstruction? From the beginning Nasser recognized that Egypt's domestic development was unavoidably tied to its regional and international position, largely because of the paucity of domestic resources. Although the Free Officers pursued a strategy for development that recognized this dependency on foreign resources, they were not always sufficiently aware of the costs of that strategy, nor of the measures that might be taken to minimize those costs. In consequence, a regime ill formed for the tasks of generating far-reaching social change took shape.

The power of Nasser's personality had masked the full measure of the difficulties confronting an Egypt of slender resources and growing population. Consequently, Nasser was able to avoid a decisive choice between alternative forms of social organization and the regional and international orientations that each required. Initially at least, his successor was seen as a man of lesser stature. Yet, ironically, a brief and dangerous period of transition from 1970 to 1973 made it clear that to rule an Egypt facing steadily worsening underdevelopment would require making the hard decisions Nasser had deferred.

NASSER'S LAST YEARS

Ruling Egypt had been a heavy burden in Nasser's last years. Economic development ground to a virtual standstill and foreign policy appeared paralyzed in the face of Israeli power. Still, in those years Nasser did evolve the broad outlines of a strategy that gave promise of rescue from Egypt's stalemate. Domestically and internationally, Nasser began a move to the right, aimed at both an economic retrenchment and an upset of the Israeli-imposed regional status quo.

In domestic affairs hard economic indicators told a depressing story. The impressive growth rate registered in the seven or eight years after the 1956 Suez War began to decline after 1963. Gross domestic product fell from 8.7 percent in 1963-64 to -1 percent in 1967-68. A short recovery was registered in 1968-69 and 1969-70, but available evidence indicates that the general performance of the economy was erratic in Nasser's last years.[2]

With the downward trend already established by 1967, the June War with Israel cost Egypt dearly. In addition to most of its air force, Egypt lost much of its armor and artillery. Major sources of revenue were completely gone or seriously disrupted. The Suez Canal was closed until 1975 and tourism declined precipitously. The Israeli occupation of Sinai also meant the loss of approximately half of Egypt's oil production. After 1967, defense outlays were enormous; the average was at least $1.61 billion yearly (national income in 1970, to put that figure in perspective, stood at $5.77 billion). Public capital to implement the military budget drained public sector development. The only cautious expansion was of the High Dam and the Helwan Iron and Steel Complex. The policy of economic retrenchment announced in the mid-sixties was accelerated. Significant concessions were made by Nasser to the private sector of Egypt's economy. Between 1966 and 1969 the value of private sector imports, to cite one indicator, increased five times.[3]

The burdens of the June War, then, contributed to a trend already under way to abandon earlier expansionist economic policies and to move toward economic orthodoxy. But to move in any direction, Nasser realized, Egypt would first have to upset the unfavorable regional status quo imposed by Israel after its 1967 victory. At this point in Egypt's history, regional and global factors were decisive in shaping the domestic political scene.

In the post-1967 period Nasser focused his primary efforts on development of a foreign policy that would overcome the devastating effects of the June War. Central to any such strategy was the proposition that, for Egypt, the status quo was intolerable and the only way to alter it was renewed conflict with Israel. In *al-Ahram* Haikal pounded away at the theme that a situation of "no war, no peace," such as prevailed after 1967, benefited everyone—except Egypt: the USSR had its "protector of the Arabs" role, which assured its coveted Middle East entrée; Israel held onto its 1967 conquests; and the United States was guaranteed that minimum of order necessary to protect American interests in the area, notably access to oil. Meanwhile, occupied Egypt faced Israel with only the impotent "three no's" of the 1967 Khartoum summit of Arab states—no peace, no negotiations, no recognition—and stagnated.

Nasser was determined to upset this situation. Slowly he pieced together a strategy that, in essence, called for the exchange of a myth for a reality: the myth of Egypt's militancy vis-à-vis Israel in the name of the Palestinian cause (which had buoyed Nasserist visions of pan-Arab unity) was to be supplanted by a realistic policy based on Egypt's national interest. This would allow for moderation, which in turn would allow for a modicum of genuine Arab solidarity. And that solidarity could be used to support the effort to keep the conflict with Israel open.

In response to the exigencies of regional and global politics, Nasser's commitment to Arab unity already had been transformed several times. In the nationalist phase of the fifties it was articulated as a call for "unity from above" and found expression in the Egyptian-Syrian union in 1958. When that state-level merger failed in the sixties, Nasser issued his call for "unity from below"—or at least for unity only of states that had undergone an Egyptian-style social revolution. In the post-1967 period Nasser spoke once again in the less demanding terms of a new solidarity of all Arabs to face the Israeli threat. It was a return to a milder variant of the original vision.

In the wake of Israel's overwhelming victory in 1967 its military superiority on the regional level was starkly revealed to the world. Somehow Nasser survived the revelation of Egypt's weakness vis-à-vis Israel. After 1967 it was no longer necessary to cloak Egypt's moderation on the issue of Palestine in the rhetoric of confrontation, which called for a grand clash of Arab and Israeli destinies. More modest and more real Egyptian national interests were now directly involved.

That Nasser's policy toward Israel had in fact been a moderate one in the context of inter-Arab politics is clear from the historical record, as are the reasons for that moderation. Yet since the myth of Egyptian militancy was fostered by both the Egyptians and the Israelis—each for their own reasons—it has persisted. Nasser's actual policy of "militant inaction" was predicated on his long-standing appreciation for the strength of the Zionist state. In the West it tends to be forgotten that in the first Arab-Israeli conflict of 1948 the Jews had more men and women mobilized than the Arab countries, despite the fact that they numbered only seven hundred thousand, while the population of the Arab states was forty times as large.[4] Nasser, who fought in Palestine, had seen the Jews maintain and increase this numerical superiority; from the beginning he had no illusions about Israeli capabilities.

It is instructive that Nasser's decision to nationalize the Suez Canal in 1956 was based in part on his judgment that Israel would not intervene. An attack from the French and the British was expected, but Nasser was startled by Israel's cooperation with the two former colonial powers. For that miscalculation the Egyptians paid dearly: estimates of Egyptians killed in the Sinai range from two to three thousand. In the West it is rarely understood that the quiet on the Egyptian-Israeli border from 1956 to 1967 resulted from the presence of United Nations troops stationed on Egyptian soil. Nasser's moderation toward Israel, exemplified by those UN troops, resulted from the rational calculation of hard military facts.[5]

The inflammatory rhetoric of Radio Cairo was intended to mask this moderation of Nasser's. War with Israel would come, Nasser argued in Arab diplomatic circles, but only when the Arabs could marshal superior military power, engineer the diplomatic isolation of Israel, and secure real Arab unity.[6] The strains generated by the formation of the UAR, the rivalry with Kassem's Iraq, and the Yemen War had led to a reconsideration of the benefits of an activist foreign policy. Between 1959 and 1963 Nasser studiously worked to tone down the confrontation with Israel and the alienation of Egypt from the West. But in 1964-1965 Egyptian relations with the United States deteriorated, and in the winter of 1965 Nasser broke off diplomatic relations with West Germany for its sale of weapons to Israel. Late in 1965, however, Egypt's president returned to his earlier policy of conciliating the West and moderating tensions with Israel. Syria, Jordan, and Saudi Arabia, all alienated from Egypt at the time, joined in mocking attacks. Nasser was accused of hiding behind the UN forces on Egypt's border with Israel and of allowing the Israelis to violate collective Arab rights by diverting Jordan River waters for irrigation.

Behind the scenes in the Arab summit conferences of the sixties, Nasser counseled restraint. With particular vehemence he argued against the repeated Syrian proposals to launch large-scale guerrilla warfare against Israel and used his control over any united Arab military command (and over the Palestinian groups reliant on Egypt) to forestall such confrontation.

In 1967 Nasser's policy of moderation collapsed and he chose to act out his militant public rhetoric. In 1966 Palestinian commando incursions into Israel, launched from Jordan, Lebanon, and especially Syria, grew in number and intensity. The radical Syrian regime, brought to power by a coup in 1966, supported the Palestinians. In a press conference the Syrian prime minister announced "We are not sentinels over Israel's security and are not the leash that restrains the revolution of the displaced and persecuted Palestinian people." Containing the Syrians and Palestinians became a real problem as the violence of the Israeli reaction mounted. The well-established Israeli policy of massive retaliation was applied with devastating effect. Jordan was the target, and the Israeli raid of November 13 left eighteen Jordanians dead and fifty-four wounded. Charles W. Yost has commented that "the consequences in and out of the region, of this disproportionate and misplaced retaliation were considerable."[7]

Under the weight of Syrian threats and Palestinian incursions with the resultant Israeli response, Nasser's policy of militant inaction failed. By the mid-sixties he no longer had the prestige necessary not to act. Although Nasser felt no great affection for the Syrian regime, a Russian warning of impending Israeli attack on Syria compelled a response. Nasser requested the UN secretary general to withdraw UN forces from the Sinai. The request was interpreted to include those troops stationed at Sharm al-Shaikh at the mouth of the Gulf of Aqaba. Israel had made it clear that a closing of the gulf would be a cause for war.

On June 5, 1967, Israel attacked. All seventeen of Egypt's airfields were struck, and most of Egypt's air force was destroyed on the ground. In the Sinai, Egypt's forces were rapidly defeated and put to flight. An estimated ten thousand Egyptian soldiers were killed or died of thirst in the desert.[8] Israeli forces reached the canal on June 9. Egypt was crushed. Nasser resigned.

Nasser resigned, but that resignation was not accepted. A popular outpouring of support in massive demonstrations, only partly manipulated, called on Nasser to stay in office. On June 10 he announced his agreement to the unanimous demand of the National Assembly that he remain as president. Nasser has described his mood on the morrow of defeat: he was, he said, like "a man walking in a desert surrounded by moving sands not knowing whether, if he moved, he would be swallowed up by the sands or he would find the right path."[9]

The Final Strategy

Once recovered from the shock of defeat, Nasser began to realize that the Israeli victory had created conditions favorable to an openly moderate Egyptian strategy. Such a policy would require new initiatives on the regional and global levels. It would be necessary to win Arab support for a more limited but real confrontation with Israel, to extract the maximum support from the Soviets, and to remind the Americans that Israel was not their only interest in the Middle East. Nasser strove to foster the most supportive regional and global conditions for Egyptian refusal to accept the verdict of June 1967. This included Egyptian determination to keep the conflict with Israel open, but on a manageable scale. Within Israel a "paralysis of historical imagination" apparently born of the euphoria of victory, left the diplomatic field to Nasser.[10]

Nasser was able to exploit the fact that the radius of Israeli power had been sharply extended in 1967. The Israeli threat was felt to be more immediate and more direct to a wider circle of Arab states.[11] Furthermore, the leadership of an openly defeated Nasser was preferable to the conservative Arab regimes. Earlier they had feared the revolutionary impact of Nasser's charisma on their own peoples. However, the display of overwhelming power by Israel in the June War alarmed the conservative states and they moved closer to Egypt. Reconciliation with the oil-rich Arab states of Kuwait, Saudi Arabia, and prerevolutionary Libya was already in the offing. At the Khartoum Conference in August 1967 a bargain was struck whereby pressure on the oil producers to continue their boycott of Britain and the United States was eased in return for an annual subsidy. Egypt was to receive approximately $350 million annually to compensate for its losses of canal and tourist revenues. The Yemen War was ended. These were impressive beginnings for the building of a post-1967 Arab solidarity on a moderate platform.

On the global level Nasser had little choice but to plunge deeper into debt to the Soviets. He had never been comfortable in his relationship with the Russians, and occasionally (as in 1958-1959 over the Iraqi issue) their disputes were aired openly. This time Egypt had no alternative. Its military capacity had to be restored and, with the United States now Israel's major supplier, only the Soviet Union could act to offset the fundamental power imbalance. Nasser strained to draw the Soviets as deeply as possible into the task of rebuilding Egypt.

Finally, Nasser's strategy called for a new initiative toward the Americans. Despite the evident hostility of Lyndon Johnson's administration, Nasser worked to involve the United States in his plan to break the Middle East deadlock. Every effort was to be made to drive even the slightest wedge between the Israelis and the Americans. The United States, after all, had supported Resolution 242 voted by the UN Security Council in 1967. That resolution called for the withdrawal of Israel from territories occupied in the war in return for the right to live in peace within secure and recognized boundaries. American tacit support for the Israeli de facto annexationist policy after 1967 was deeply disturbing to the Egyptians. The election of Richard Nixon and announcement of his intention to develop a more "even-handed policy" raised hopes that the crucial

American factor might yet be made part of a strategy to recover the conquered territories. Nasser realized that, given the general satisfaction of the Israelis, the Americans, and even the Soviets with the status quo, Egypt would have to demonstrate the latent dangers in the stalemated situation.

The War of Attrition

It was with these considerations in mind that Nasser launched the War of Attrition in March 1969. The war was enormously costly in Egyptian lives (perhaps as costly as the June War itself) and must ultimately be judged a failure for Egypt. Yet it did accomplish one aim: the Arab-Israeli conflict was placed once again on the global crisis agenda.

Egyptian artillery barrages across the canal provoked the expected Israeli response. The Bar Lev defense line to hold Sinai was completed, and Israeli artillery effectively answered Egyptian attacks. The Israelis went one step further: devastating air raids, which gradually mounted in range and intensity, were launched. Deep-penetration bombing peaked with the attacks of December 25, 1969: massive raids were begun on the Canal Zone followed in January by in-depth raids on Egyptian industrial sites in the Nile Valley itself.

This escalation of violence did attract American attention, ultimately producing the Rogers Plan, which called for a settlement on a modified version of UN Resolution 242. The Soviets had demonstrated no great enthusiasm for the War of Attrition and had pressed for a political settlement when Nasser visited Moscow in early July. But the ferocity of the Israeli raids—notably the attack on a major factory at Abu Zaabal near Cairo—may have convinced the Russians that the Israelis were planning to systematically destroy the Egyptian industrial base.[12] In January 1970 an already ill Nasser flew to Moscow to argue for Soviet assistance to protect Egypt from Israeli raids.

When the Soviets balked, Nasser claimed that they were evidently unwilling to support their allies in the same way that America backed Israel. To Brezhnev's objections, Nasser responded:

> I am a leader who is bombed every day in his own country, whose army is exposed and whose people are naked. I have the courage to tell our people the unfortunate truth—that, whether they like it or not, the Americans are masters of the world. I am not going to be the one who surrenders to the Americans. Someone else will come in my place who will have to do it.

The argument proved effective. The Egyptians received the surface-to-air missiles (SAM-3s) that they had been requesting, and the Soviet crews to operate them.[13]

Such direct Soviet involvement further alarmed the Americans, and they began to perceive American interest in a negotiated settlement more clearly. The Soviets, too, were fearful of further escalation. The stage was set for Nasser to bring the moderate strategy to fruition. He announced that Egypt would accept an American-sponsored ceasefire and indicated his willingness to proceed to a settlement on the basis of the Rogers Plan.

Anwar es-Sadat, interestingly enough, opposed the ceasefire as premature. In actuality, it was to have no lasting effect. The Egyptians used the first hours of the ceasefire to cheat on the deployment of missiles. The Israelis responded with delaying tactics on the negotiations. They did so with evident relief, since they had feared the U.S. pressure that might accompany a moderate solution. The Palestinians, for their part, had correctly understood that Egypt's acceptance of the Rogers Plan meant at best a minimal solution for their nationalist aspirations—that is, a dependent and vulnerable enclave state composed of the Gaza Strip and the West Bank of the Jordan. Palestinian disruptive activities aimed to prevent such a negotiated settlement. Flamboyant plane hijackings eventually provoked King Hussein's Black September suppression in Jordan in 1970. The ailing Nasser mediated between Hussein and the Palestinians, an effort that finally exhausted him. By the end of the month Nasser was dead and hope for the Rogers Plan seemed to die with him.[14]

THE END OF AN ERA

The seventies seemed to hold little promise for Egyptians: part of their land was occupied; their revolution, which had already lost momentum, now had lost its leader. As the national grief subsided, a popular mood of apprehension crystallized. It found expression in a flood of "noktas," or anecdotes. One reserve strength of the Egyptians as a people is their subtle humor, which they turn to greatest effect against themselves and their leaders. To laugh for the Egyptian is to illuminate—and to endure. The uncertainties of the period of transition from the charismatic Nasser to the unprepossessing Sadat surfaced in the anecdotes of the period. Somehow it did not seem that Sadat—a figure who had left little imprint on the popular consciousness—could possibly fill the void left by Nasser's death.

The Docile Heir

Who, after all, was Anwar es-Sadat? Popular stories asked that question in a hundred ways and also managed to convey condescension and disbelief that Sadat was a man of sufficient stature ever to play Nasser's role:

Shortly after Nasser's death a Cairo taxi driver took his cousin visiting from a village on his first tour of the city. Stopping at a café in a popular section of the city, the cousin noticed a prominently displayed picture of Nasser shaking hands with Sadat.

Ah, said the cousin, our beloved Abu Khaled, our beloved Nasser! God rest his soul. But who is that with him? The taxi driver, eager to demonstrate his sophistication, pointed to Sadat whom he did not recognize and replied with assurance: He's the owner of this café!

Anwar es-Sadat, despite his status as a Free Officer, was an unknown quantity in Egypt.

Knowledgeable Egyptians for years had not taken Sadat seriously despite the fact that his nationalist credentials were impeccable. In the prerevolutionary period Sadat had been involved with several resistance groups and had used his position in the military to supply them with munitions and equipment. Such resistance activities had led to his imprisonment on several occasions. Through these difficult times Sadat was steeled by a good-humored resilience and confidence that his would be an important role.

Mohammed Anwar es-Sadat was born on December 25, 1918, in Mit Abul Kom, a small village in the Nile Delta between Cairo and Alexandria. When Sadat was six, the family moved to Cairo where his father worked as a clerk in a military hospital. Sadat's big chance, like Nasser's, came in 1936 when the Royal Military Academy was thrown open to cadets of modest backgrounds, and he began his military—and his revolutionary—career. For his role in the Free Officers' movement Sadat was made a member of the Revolutionary Command Council. But Nasser most frequently used Sadat (with his status as a Free Officer) to give a pseudosignificance and false luster to positions actually far from the real centers of power in Egypt. It was a clever strategy, and Sadat appeared to fill the role amiably. He was first editor of *al-Jumhuriyyah,* the government newspaper, then secretary general of the Islamic Congress. The congress, grandiloquently charged to rally 400 million moslems to Egypt's vanguard flag, actually accomplished little. Later Sadat was secretary general of the National Union, the second of Egypt's three successive political parties, then speaker of the National Assembly before being appointed vice-president by Nasser in December 1969.

The role of speaker of Egypt's parliament seemed ideally suited to Sadat. Within the framework of an authoritarian presidential system, the provisional constitution of 1964 theoretically accorded the assembly a number of supervisory functions vis-à-vis the executive branch. The assembly also had the power to nominate the president and then refer the nomination to the people for a plebiscite. Basically, though, Egypt under Nasser was ruled by presidential decree in all vital domestic and foreign areas. The assembly did strain, at times impressively, to exploit its investigatory and supervisory powers on more marginal but not unimportant issues. As speaker, Sadat functioned to legitimate the criticisms and complaints of the assembly, at the same time containing them at acceptable levels. It was Sadat who would suggest that perhaps the assembly had been a bit "unfair" in some criticism of the government; it was Sadat who pointed out that "the responsibility of the Assembly is not to fish for the mistakes of the Government."[15]

Sadat's mild career thus left great uncertainties both as to his abilities (generally thought to be modest) and his political leanings (thought to place him on the Nasserist right because of his Islamic Congress and National Assembly connections). A popular story conveys these impressions:

> When the chauffeur of the presidential car reached an important intersection, he asked Anwar es-Sadat for direction.
> "But which way did Nasser usually go?" asked Sadat.
> "At such times he usually went left, your excellency."
> "Ah," replied Sadat. "Well, signal that we're going left and then turn sharply to the right."

Egyptians waited anxiously to learn just how durable their new president would be and how much change—and continuity—his rule would bring. As Anwar es-Sadat moved to consolidate his power, he was severely burdened by two handicaps. Not only did he come to power with an unheroic reputation, but he was to take charge of a stalled revolution. That combination gave Egypt's people little comfort.

The Coup Manqué

It was in his survival of a coup attempt that Sadat first showed unsuspected qualities of shrewdness and toughness. The move against him came in the spring of 1971, little more than six months after Nasser's death. Sadat demonstrated his complete understanding of the fundamental patterns of power in Nasser's Egypt by eliminating his opponents in the abortive May coup. Having won the support of the military, he was able to contain his major rivals despite the opposition of the Arab Socialist Union and without recourse to popular support. His role as an original Free Officer (shared by none of his leading opponents) and his status as Nasser's vice-president provided his consolidation of power with a sense of revolutionary and constitutional legitimacy. Sadat called his May 1971 success the Corrective Revolution.

The initial though short-lived smoothness of Sadat's assumption of power had been possible because key personalities such as Aly Sabry regarded him as the man least likely to disturb their privileged positions. Furthermore, as a veteran Free Officer placed by Nasser in the formal, constitutional position to succeed him, he would be an effective symbol of continuity. Sadat's public demeanor at first had reinforced the impression that he would be an unthreatening successor to Nasser. The new president seemed slightly stunned to find himself in such an exalted office. "You have invested me," Sadat confided to his people, "with an honor which, God knows, has never crossed my mind throughout my life; nor have I striven for it."[16]

Gradually the self-effacing Sadat began to signal strength and self-confidence by acting independently on key issues. He took new initiatives aimed at improving relations with the United States in order to bring American pressure to bear on Israel; and he gave the full weight of his support to the Arab Federation with Syria and Libya. It seems to have been the unilateral character of Sadat's actions on these issues that provoked the conspiracy. At the conspiracy trial in Cairo later, Ahmed Kamel (former chief of intelligence) stressed in his testimony that vice-premier Sabry and interior minister Gomaa had thought that they could control Sadat and were enraged when he refused to play the figurehead role. Sabry is quoted as saying: "We either let him ride on our backs or we send him to prison."[17] Sadat's subsequent show of independence was read as a threat to the entire system of rule by mandate.

It was the issue of federation with Syria and Libya that the conspirators used as a pretext for their confrontation with Sadat. The major figures who coalesced in opposition to Sadat were Aly Sabry, vice-premier; Sami Sharaf, Nasser's primary aide; Muhammed Fayek, minister of information; Muhsin Aboul Nur, first secretary of the Central Committee of the Arab Socialist Union; Labib Shukair, speaker of the National Assembly; General Muhammad Fawzi, minister of defense; and Sharawi Gomaa, minister of the interior. A first showdown came in the spring of 1971, at a meeting of the Executive Committee of the ASU. Sadat found his federation proposal sharply attacked by Sabry, Aboul Nur, Shukair, and Gomaa. He was able to prevail only by referring the matter to the party central committee.

In retrospect it is puzzling that, having fully alerted Sadat to their opposition, the conspirators failed to move against him immediately. Sadat seized the initiative. In his May Day speech the president openly and threateningly spoke of individuals and groups

> concealing themselves behind slogans and maneuvers in order to establish centers of power so as to impose their control over the people after the people acting with Gamal Abdel Nasser had overthrown all the centers of power in order that the people themselves might remain the sole masters of their destiny.[18]

Responding to the scarcely veiled warning in the speech, Sabry and the others resigned en masse, most likely intending thereby to embarrass

Sadat. Efforts were also made to organize mass demonstrations drawn from the ASU and the police apparatus. But there was no strong unity among the powerful men who opposed Sadat. Entrenched in their respective centers of power, they were highly suspicious of one another and found it impossible to act together effectively to defeat the president. Sadat moved rapidly. On May 14th the entire group of conspirators was arrested. Their trial ended in December 1971 with ninety-one former officials and leaders sentenced.[19]

Sadat's success in suppressing his rivals showed his grasp on the core political principle in Nasser's Egypt: ultimate power rested with the military. His May Day speech had signaled support for the military, whose reputation had been severely tarnished since the 1967 debacle: "Before concluding," the president soothed, "I would like to tell you that you must be proud of your armed forces." In that same speech Sadat alluded to extensive meetings just concluded with military commanders. Sadat later revealed that Muhammed Ahmed Sadek, army chief of staff, had assured him of the army's loyalty in the face of the challenge to his power:

> He contacted me on May 13th and told me: "Everything is going well, Mr. President. The armed forces are healthy and uninvolved in this childplay."

Sadat apparently won this support of the military, despite defection of the minister of defense, with promises of a refurbishment of the military image and a reinstatement of the officers purged by Nasser after 1967. Lingering military resentment of the ASU challenge in the post-1967 period was probably also a factor in swaying the military against the conspirators. Nasser's confidant M. H. Haikal lifts no veils in his *Road to Ramadan,* where he reports only that Sadat did succeed in maintaining the allegiance of both the commander of the presidential guard and the chief of staff of the army. Given their crucial role in preserving Sadat's position, the senior officers' corps in post-Nasser Egypt clearly had lost none of its fundamental importance.[20]

The October War

Anwar es-Sadat had found it relatively easy to consolidate his domestic power by eliminating his rivals after the coup attempt of 1971. The task inherited from Nasser of thawing the regional status quo imposed by Israel and backed by the United States proved more daunting. Until that foreign policy challenge was met, Sadat—whatever the success of his Corrective Revolution—could make no persuasive claim to Nasser's legacy. To be sure, the War of Attrition had achieved some gains, although at frightening cost to Egypt in lives lost and Canal Zone cities destroyed.

With Russian help the Egyptians had rebuilt their armies and secured sophisticated military hardware and the training to use it. The conservative Arab regimes, with their oil potential, had drawn closer to a moderate Egypt. (The 1969 coups in Libya and Sudan also held promise of strengthening the Egyptian position.) Finally, some progress had been made in reminding the Americans that they had interests in the Middle East other than Israel.

Despite these gains, the situation as seen from Cairo in the early seventies remained bleak. Israel refused to budge from the conquered territories, and the United States gave tacit support to Israel's policy of "creating facts," Moishe Dayan's euphemism for annexation. Equally alarming was the apparent convergence of U.S.-Soviet interest in freezing the Middle East stalemate. Finally, in Egypt itself the new regime's apparent inaction was producing signs of popular revolt.

The Israeli failure to come forward with a genuine and sweeping peace initiative after the overwhelming military victory of June 1967 requires more of an explanation than reference to the ingrained rigidity of official policy toward the Arabs. The mid-sixties had been a time of multiple domestic struggles for Israel on the economic, social, and ideological planes. The external crisis of the June War of 1967 then imposed an end to the mounting divisiveness within Israel: competition on the basic issues that had divided Israelis was suspended. As a result of this self-imposed political immobility, the Israeli government responded to the external challenges and diplomatic opportunities after the June War primarily by military initiatives. This trend within Israel was reinforced by the nature of the American-Israeli relationship in the wake of the June 1967 victory. By the late sixties and early seventies Israel was viewed by the United States as a regional extension of American power, potentially useful both to help contain the Soviets and to parry any threats to U.S. access to Middle East oil. The stunning victory in the Six-Day War was a powerful reinforcement of this view. Israeli and U.S. satisfaction with Israeli dominance was such that there were few pressures to generate a spirit of compromise in relations with the Arabs.[21]

From an Egyptian perspective the intolerableness of Israeli inflexibility was heightened by growing evidence of Soviet acquiescence in the already established American interest in perpetuation of the status quo in the Middle East. Most distressing was the continuing problem of Soviet delays on military resupply questions. On numerous occasions Sadat described the Soviet style, so much in contrast to its public rhetoric of all-out support:

The problem was that our Soviet friends would begin by refusing whenever we asked for a new weapon. Then, after pleading and disputes—and my steady pressure—they would agree. They would then inform us of the numbers we were to receive and specify the time span for delivery, along with the stipulation of a very long training period.

By 1975, when the strain in Soviet-Egyptian relations was again public, Sadat was even to maintain that his inability to strike against Israel sooner—particularly during 1971, which he had called the year of decision—resulted from Soviet pressure exerted through delays in arms deliveries:

> They refused to deliver the military matériel we need. That's how it was in 1971—the year I said would be decisive—they kept me from unleashing hostilities by a very simple means: they refrained from honoring the arms contracts that had been made.[22]

Such Soviet behavior fed the Egyptian conviction that the emerging United States-Soviet détente would be translated in the Middle East into a permanent freezing of the post-1967 situation. Sadat consistently maintained that he inherited from Nasser the determination for a military strike against Israel to prevent just that. Such a strike, he was convinced by Soviet delaying tactics, was not part of Soviet strategy. Still, Sadat was determined to wring maximum assistance from the Soviets. In this aim both Nasser and Sadat were quite successful: in the years before 1973 they secured from the Soviet Union at least $4 billion and possibly as high as $6 or even $7 billion worth of weapons and equipment. For all the emphasis on the difficulties with the Soviets over military supplies, it should not be forgotten that in February 1973 the Egyptians did conclude a massive new arms deal. It was apparently linked to an extension by Sadat of the maritime facilities arrangement for the Soviet Mediterranean fleet that Nasser had concluded in 1968. Sadat has described the February agreement with the Soviets as "the biggest arms deal ever to be concluded (either with Nasser or myself)."[23]

Given this determination to secure as much Soviet aid as possible, it should not be surprising that Sadat, in the wake of his elimination of the ostensibly pro-Soviet coterie around Aly Sabry, signed the Soviet-Egyptian Treaty of Friendship and Cooperation on May 27, 1971. Sadat was willing to bow to Soviet pressure for the treaty, even though he thought its timing ill-advised. The treaty had no real operational significance, and Sadat later revealed that at the time of the signing he was already giving serious thought to a break with the Soviets.[24]

It was after the Nixon-Brezhnev summit in May 1972 that Sadat did make that decision. To a confidential briefing of Cairo editors, Sadat reported:

It was clear to me that in Moscow the two superpowers had agreed that there was to be no war in the Middle East area. There was to be nothing for us but surrender.

Two months later, on July 23, 1972, in a speech on the twentieth anniversary of the revolution, Sadat announced that the Russian advisers and personnel (estimated by Western analysts to number about six thousand) were to be repatriated and all Soviet-manned bases in Egypt were to revert to Egyptian control. Whenever Sadat had articulated his plans for a military strike, the Soviets had countered that war needed long preparation and the buildup of morale. Ironically, one morale problem Sadat had confronted was disquiet over the large Soviet presence in Egypt. Following the publication earlier in 1972 of an *al-Ahram* colloquium dealing with Egyptian-Soviet relations, a delegation of prominent Egyptians, including a number of former Free Officers, petitioned the president to indicate their alarm at the scope of the Soviet role in the country. With his expulsion of the Russians in July, Sadat significantly improved public confidence in his regime: Egyptians felt they had recovered their sovereignty from a Soviet threat.[25]

The petition to the president was only one sign of mounting unrest in the country. It was most in evidence among the students, who demanded both domestic reform and action against Israel. But student opinion was by no means isolated. *Al-Ahram* of January 25, 1972, to cite one example, reports that the Association of Engineers issued a report in which "it endorsed the student movement. It stated that the student movement was not only an expression of anxiety for the future in which they are not alone but indeed a universal expression in the breast of every Egyptian." Since 1967 there had been enough student unrest to speak meaningfully of a "student movement" that pressed for domestic reform and a redemption of national honor by military action against Israel. The history of that movement, and its sporadic suppression by both Nasser and Sadat, has yet to be written.

In a series of articles appearing in *Rose al-Yusuf* Abdul Rahman el-Sharkawy, novelist and social commentator, eloquently sided with the students. Sharkawy identified "the demands of the student movement . . . with the demands of the nation, as well as its desires." The movement, Sharkawy revealed, had its martyrs: "The youth movement erupted in 1967. It was hit by bullets. The prison camps were filled with young people who knew the horrors of torture." President Sadat had repeatedly spoken of the year 1971 as the year of decision for action against Israel. When that year ended quietly, the students once more revolted, dramatizing Sadat's credibility gap. There were strikes and demonstrations. Once again Sharkawy lent his prestige as a well-known novelist and man of letters to support the students. He began his article of February 14, 1972, by remarking: "Discussing the student movement today is like walking on spikes." He then took up the defense of the students. The young people of Egypt, Sharkawy argued, are not in opposition to the national authority but simply demand that "everything be subject to the needs of the battle" and not delayed by "historical necessity."[26]

When President Sadat gave the order to launch the October War in 1973, knowing full well that Israeli military superiority was overwhelming and that the loss of life would be terrible, he did so with the moral approval of Egypt's youth. Sharkawy again has most cogently expressed the Egyptian position and the rationale for war:

> Stagnation can spell more danger to life and the future than anything else. The rigid situation being imposed on us is an intolerable burden on our national pride. This state of affairs also exhausts efforts, funds, and potential beyond endurance and patience. There is no course other than the battle and, in this battle, there can be no alternative to victory.

For Egypt a continuation of the situation of "no war, no peace" meant economic ruin. The country was being drained by yearly defense expenditures that made real development impossible, and there had been no advance toward recovering the occupied territories. The national humiliation was worsening. Sadat himself gave expression to Egyptian pain as the Israelis proceeded with their policy of annexation by building settlements and even incipient cities in Egyptian territory; referring to the Israeli project for building a port city called Yamit in the Egyptian Sinai, Sadat said:

> Every word spoken about Yamit is a knife pointing at me personally and at my self-respect.

Nasser had accepted the 1970 ceasefire with few illusions:

> I am going to accept it just because it has an American flag. We must have a breathing space so that we can finish our missile sites. We need to give our army a break, and to cut down our civilian casualties. We need a ceasefire, and the only ceasefire the Israelis will accept is one proposed by the Americans. But I don't think the initiative stands any chance of success. I wouldn't rate its chances at more than a half percent.[27]

The peace initiative did fail, and—to the astonishment of the world— Sadat launched the October War. At 2 P.M. on October 6, 1973, Egypt's forces attacked. Within two days two armies, hundreds of tanks, and a forward air-defense screen of SAM-6 surface-to-air missiles had crossed the Suez Canal, plunging into the Egyptian territory that Israel had occupied since 1967. Tawfik el-Hakim, perhaps Egypt's most distinguished intellectual, wrote:

> The profound meaning of October 6 is not merely a military victory or a material crossing, as much as it is a spiritual crossing to a new stage in our history . . . and that stage is the reconstruction of [our] civilization.[28]

For a while at least, it was a time for Egyptians to exult.

6. Sadat's Egypt Takes Form

In his inaugural address in 1970 Anwar es-Sadat said to his people: "There is an edifice we shall continue to build as we catch up with progress."[1] But it was only with the momentum provided by the 1973 October War that Sadat's project for Egypt in the seventies took definite form. Hailed after the fighting as the "Hero of the Crossing," Sadat gave authoritative expression for the first time to his vision of Egypt's future.

The shape of that future, Sadat had learned, was constrained by the past. Inescapable were the limitations imposed by a history of exploitation, sharply limited resources, and a burgeoning population. Unavoidable was the burden of dependency on foreign powers for the means to progress. Yet October did bring a rekindling of political will. In a sense Sadat returned Egypt to the crossroads of the mid-sixties, when multiple crises had first revealed the stark alternatives confronting the country. Sadat took the measure of Nasser's failed political solution. There would be no intensification of the revolution and no deepening of the ties to the Soviet Union. Egypt would turn right, to liberalization and to the West. Sadat's would be the era of the economic solution. With confidence renewed by the experience of October, Egypt would swing wide an "open door" to Western and Arab investment. A liberalized Egyptian economy would be revitalized by the investment of private Egyptian capital and, more importantly, by Western and Arab capital. The most oppressive features of Nasserist authoritarianism would be softened, as Egypt began restructuring the socialist economic mechanisms developed under Nasser. Such was the initial promise of Sadat's rule.

That Sadat would be granted the time to redeem this promise was not at all clear. Western and Arab response to Egypt's open-door economic policy was disappointing in its slowness and caution. At the same time, disengagement from the Soviets had its costs. Egypt after 1973 was also plagued by recurrent fears of diplomatic isolation in the Arab arena as a result of its new moderation. Moreover, there were few immediate signs of progress toward a general settlement with Israel until Sadat's own dramatic and dangerous visit to Jerusalem in November 1977 initiated an Egyptian peace offensive. At home Sadat's rule did bring some liberalization, but in a freer environment social pressures mounted. Already by January 1975, and again on an even larger scale in January 1977, angry crowds of workers and students surged through the cities of Egypt demanding: "Hero of the Crossing, where is our breakfast?"

THE MEANING OF OCTOBER

Egypt did not "win" the October War in any conventional sense. Once Israel recovered from the shock of initial Arab gains and once the United States abandoned its early equivocations and rallied to Israel's side with massive supplies, the Israelis (as universally expected) were able to demonstrate their military superiority. By October 14th, after eight days of fighting, the Israeli counterstrike was well under way: an armored task force struck back across the canal, destroying missile sites and disrupting supplies to the soon encircled Egyptian Third Army trapped on the east bank of the canal. There is no doubt that without outside intervention, Israeli forces could have crushed the Third Army. Sixteen days of extremely hard fighting and enormous losses secured for Israel a partial military victory.[2] But it was a war with political and psychological objectives that Anwar es-Sadat launched in October 1973, and in those areas the Egyptians registered important gains on both the global and regional levels.

From Nasser, Sadat had inherited a deep-seated distrust of what superpower détente would mean for Egypt. In his *Road to Ramadan* dealing with the October War of 1973, M. H. Haikal recalled the following warning he had given Sadat: "I'm afraid it looks as though the détente is going to become a reality and impose itself on us before we can impose ourselves on it." Sadat replied: "Maybe we will just be able to catch the last part of the tail of détente."[3] The October War accomplished just that.

Above all else, Egyptian political analysts have stressed the global strategic advantages that accrued to Egypt as a result of October. Sadat, they reason, demonstrated that Egypt had a last-resort capability to seize the initiative in pursuit of its own interests. Illustrative is the thinking of Ahmed Bahaeddin, the respected *al-Ahram* political commentator. In April 1974 Bahaeddin celebrated the fact that Egypt had "upset the scales," which had been frozen since 1967. It had succeeded in blocking the local and international "crisis managers" who had worked to "put the fire out and transform the fact of Israel's new expansion into a permanent fact which the Arabs would confront by capitulating in everything except words." President Sadat stressed that the October initiative was a "100% Egyptian decision against the will of the two superpowers.'' (In the years after 1973 Egypt frequently used the experience of the October military strike to illustrate its determination to act independently in its own interest.)[4]

Despite an unfavorable military balance, Egypt survived its ''suicidal'' strike in October 1973 and significantly improved its regional as well as its global position. Egypt at that point had no illusions about its military capabilities vis-à-vis Israel. The October War was launched not to regain a maximum of Arab territory, but with the limited objective of demonstrating to the Israelis just how high a price they would have to pay to hold on to the territories occupied in 1967. How much security, Egyptians argued, had expanded territory brought Israel in 1973? One striking indicator of the unexpected price Israel paid on the battlefield was the alarm the Israelis experienced as a result of U.S. delays in the airlift of supplies to the Israeli forces. After the first several days of fierce fighting, Israeli Premier Golda Meir suggested going herself to the United States to explain the seriousness of the military situation. Israel may also have warned at that time that its known nuclear option would be used if U.S. military supplies were not forthcoming in time to save the battlefield situation.[5] The October War, it was hoped by Egyptian analysts, would undermine the exorbitant faith in Israeli power born of the 1967 June War. Not even the daring and technical virtuosity of the Israeli commando rescue of hostages held at Entebbe in June of 1976 could erase the memory that in October 1973 casualties had been too high and resources too clearly overstrained.

It is true that the American commitment to Israel had held in October 1973 and Israel had ultimately triumphed. But Egypt had not failed to notice the strains in the American-Israeli connection. American diplomacy had used its impressive resources, control of the massive supplies essential to Israel, and its détente coordination with the Soviets, to ensure an Israeli victory—but a limited and costly one aimed at softening Israel's hard-line regional position. Egypt recognized its own potential advantage in this evidence of renewed subtlety in American support for Israel.

For Egyptians, and for Arabs everywhere, the sweetest fruit gathered in October was undoubtedly the surge of Arab solidarity the war evoked. Never mind how short-lived: in October Arabs acted together and to great effect. ''The Arab solidarity in this war was supreme,'' wrote Muhammad Ahmed Mahgoub, former prime minister of the Sudan. ''Almost every Arab state sent a fighting unit to the battle zone.'' Mahgoub, an Arab moderate with no great love for the Syrian or the Egyptian regime, could not but exult in the Arab oil weapon used to support the confrontation states. He reminded the world that the oil boycott was the work of King Faisal of Saudi Arabia, not of Arab radicals and extremists.[6] In the pre-1973 period Faisal had been the very symbol of a pro-American orientation. The moderate guise of the new Arab solidarity was to make it a still greater asset for Egypt. Sadat lost little time in attempting to translate the global and regional advantages brought by the October War into resources for Egypt's development. In doing so, Egypt's new president both claimed Nasser's legacy and adapted it to his own understanding of the challenges and opportunities of the seventies.

AMENDING NASSER'S VISION

The October War initially made Sadat a truly popular leader—but not a demigod in the Nasser mold. In many ways, after the high drama—and the disasters—of the Nasser era, Egyptians were ready for the lowering of sights that their new ruler seemed to bring. In the *October Paper* of 1974, where Sadat presented his first programmatic statement, he voiced his intention to build on Nasser's legacy in meeting the demands of the seventies: "When we speak of new responsibilities in our lives after October, we should record that we are not starting from a void. We have a rich experience behind us." And the essential components of Nasser's vision were reaffirmed in the *October Paper*: the commitment to build a strong Egypt, the continuing task of confronting Israel, the call for Arab unity with Egypt as "the heart of the Arab nation," and the insistence that Egypt play an important world role.[7]

If the Nasserist themes did not vanish, they were stated by Sadat more guardedly and without the old éclat. Development, Sadat acknowledged, had suffered from "the battle against aggression"; confronting Israel was openly described as a heavy, if unavoidable, "burden"; Arab unity moved from "the framework of enthusiastic slogans" to "possible practical measures . . . particularly in the field of economic cooperation." As an ultimate aim "political unity . . . has not lost value, but . . . the road to that political unity . . . may be long." Sadat, in building on the strength brought by the October War, promised to bring a new moderation to Egypt's affairs.[8]

"The burden of progress and construction," Sadat explained in the *October Paper,* "must fall principally on the shoulders of the Egyptian people." Yet, he realistically continued, "we still have a great need for foreign resources." Egypt's changed global and regional situation, Sadat added, "would make it possible to obtain these resources in a way to strengthen our economy and speed up development. Hence the call for an outward-looking economic policy."[9] Sadat's much trumpeted program of "Economic Opening" was to provide the foundations for Egypt's new progress. In the wake of October, the moderation of Sadat's strategy was to be the moderation of hope and not of despair.

The basic formula was impressive in its simplicity: Arab (as well as Western) capital would be wed to Western technology and lured to an emerging market economy in Egypt. That formula contained great promise: an inflow of foreign capital, improved access to advanced technology, a role for indigenous capital in an expanded private sector, and vast new employment possibilities for Egyptian labor. The implications of the "opening" strategy for Egypt and its place in the world were far-reaching. Nasser had prepared the way. The origins of the policy can be traced to Nasser's economic retrenchment of the mid-sixties and his post-1967 moves (especially the acceptance of the Rogers Plan) to draw the United States back into the Middle East area. Sadat carried the logic of Nasser's strategy further when in 1971 he inaugurated discussion of an expanded liberalization of the Egyptian economy, which would eventually reintegrate Egypt into the Western world market.

Dr. Abdul Aziz Higazi, former dean of the Faculty of Commerce at Cairo's Ain Shams University, presided over Sadat's liberalization of the economy. By reputation Higazi was a man of the right, Western in orientation, and reputedly hostile to Egypt's socialism. Nasser had appointed Higazi minister of finance in 1968, and under Sadat he became a key economic adviser. As deputy prime minister for economy and finance, he initiated the opening. After the October War, Higazi was made prime minister, and the opening received fullest official backing. The new prime minister made it clear immediately that Egypt's revised economic policy was based on a cold calculation of its desperate economic condition, strained by continuing military expenditures and massive external debt. Higazi explained that an underlying financial crisis had crippled Egypt's development and isolated the country from the world economy and technological advances. As a long-term goal Higazi announced his government's intention to restore the Egyptian pound to its status, lost more than twenty years ago, as a convertible currency traded on the world market.

Both the seriousness and the causes of Egypt's financial problems were already apparent to Nasser in the mid-sixties. There were three major drains on Egypt's hard currency reserves: the failure of the import substitution program, the matériel needs for the disastrous Yemen War, and the necessity to buy wheat when the United States stopped its aid program in the mid-sixties. Egypt had been forced to turn to the Soviet bloc with barter arrangements. The cost of such dependence, Higazi pointed out, was a parallel dependence on inferior Soviet technology.[10]

Prime Minister Higazi was also quite explicit that the confrontation with Israel was an impossible strain on Egypt's resources, especially in the period since 1967. Egypt's military expenditures in 1967-68 were about $690 million. By 1973-74 they had swollen to $2.56 billion: "We spend," Higazi complained, "33 percent of our national income on the armed forces."[11] In addition, the 1967 June War affected Egypt's hard currency situation with the closing of the canal (reopened only in June of 1975) and the damage done to the tourist industry in Egypt. These hard currency losses were only partially offset by the subsidies paid to Egypt by Saudi Arabia, Kuwait, and Libya as a result of the 1967 Khartoum agreement.

Sadat and his new minister for the economy also stressed the intolerable level of the Egyptian national debt. Even though estimates of the total debt vary, the conservative figures of an American Universities Field Staff analyst writing in June 1975 are alarming enough: $2.56 billion for nonmilitary goods owed to the socialist countries; about $5.11 billion for military goods owed to the Soviet Union; and approximately $2.56 billion for military and nonmilitary goods owed to the West.[12]

If Sadat's strategy of "peace and reconstruction" was impelled by a sober appraisal of Egypt's dire economic situation, it was at the same time responsive to an international balance of power clearly in flux as a result of two factors: U.S.-Soviet détente and the new Arab petro-dollar power. In the early years Nasser had been successful in exploiting the Cold War for Egypt's benefit. Sadat was determined to preserve Egypt's maneuverability in order to secure its national interests in an era of superpower détente. Moreover, the October War had revealed divergences of interest between the United States and Israel and stimulated the vast flow of wealth to the Arab oil producers. Sadat aimed to harness these developments in the service of his open-door policy.

Sadat realized that a market orientation necessitated stability in the Middle East area and that stability meant some form of negotiated settlement with Israel. An agreement with Israel was one important part of Sadat's broader post-October plans to guarantee the success of the opening. Those plans imposed certain diplomatic imperatives and entailed certain risks. The Soviet connection fostered by Nasser had to be loosened in order to make way for the American and Western role Sadat envisioned. In the wake of the inevitable Soviet hostility, Sadat held firm. But he did make every effort to avoid, or at least delay, a complete break —which, in his words, "would go against the interests of Egypt and the Arab world in general."[13] Sadat had also to convince the Americans of the advantages of closer ties with Egypt, such as the prospect of increased regional stability resulting from negotiations with the Israelis, and an enhanced Western diplomatic and economic presence in the Middle East. In return, Sadat could expect Western technology and aid. Finally, that ever-fragile Arab solidarity, strengthened by the October War, had to be kept at a level sufficient to maintain and accelerate the flow of Arab capital into Egypt.

The October War made possible for Egypt the negotiations with Israel that Sadat needed. In *al-Ahram* of December 1973 Ahmed Bahaeddin explained:

> Before the war the Arabs had no cards to play in negotiations . . . They had only their memoranda, and talk of legitimate rights, things that have no weight in international life. They were not fighting; moreover, it had become fixed in the world's mind that they would never fight. They talked of using oil as a weapon, but it was unconvincing. And their differences seemed more important than their shared interests. After the War all that changed.[14]

Sadat's "gamble on the future," as he baptized his post-October strategy, called for active American involvement in the search for agreement with Israel. Like Nasser, Sadat had come to believe that only an agreement stamped "made in the U.S.A." would be acceptable to the Israelis. Consequently, to the chagrin of the Soviets, Sadat opted initially for step-by-step negotiations under the auspices of Secretary of State Henry Kissinger in preference to negotiations conducted in the Geneva Conference forum. (The Geneva Conference, presided over jointly by the United States and Russia, met briefly in December 1973 after the fighting between Israel and Egypt had ceased and adjourned shortly thereafter.)

Egyptian-Israeli negotiations proved extraordinarily difficult, and Kissinger's efforts were dubbed "shuttle diplomacy" as he flew between Cairo and Tel Aviv. A complete breakdown occurred in March 1975. While not openly blaming Israel for the breakdown, the United States combined pressure on Israel (notably arms shipment delays and a not very subtle call for "a reassessment" of U.S. Middle East policy) with promises of increased aid in order to revive the negotiation process.[15]

Finally, on September 1, 1975, an Egyptian-Israeli interim agreement was signed. It called for a partial pullback of Israeli troops in the Sinai and the return of the Abu Rudeis oil fields to Egypt in exchange for a mutual pledge to refrain from the threat or use of force or military blockade. Nonmilitary cargoes destined for or coming from Israel were to be allowed through the Suez Canal, which Sadat had decided to reopen in March 1975 despite the initial failure of the talks with Israel. There was also provision for an early-warning system, under American supervision and staffed by a small contingent of American civilians. The signing of this second Egyptian-Israeli disengagement agreement represented some limited progress toward that regional stability so essential to Sadat's overall strategy.[16]

Even in barest outline Sadat's "gamble on the future" of pursuing an Israeli settlement through a Western connection was a complex policy requiring considerable diplomatic agility and involving heavy risk, especially with regard to the Soviets. In the post-October War period Sadat managed his relations with the Soviets cleverly. He alternated just the right show of firmness to win Western support with just enough reasonableness to avoid a complete break with the Russians. In March of 1976 Sadat abrogated the 1971 Soviet-Egyptian Treaty of Friendship and Cooperation that he had signed shortly after coming to power. The following month he canceled the Soviet right to use Egypt's ports. By then Egypt's president, having recognized that little more was to be gained by step-by-step diplomacy, was issuing periodic conciliatory statements affirming that the Soviets must be a party to a general peace effort for the Middle East, preferably in the Geneva forum.

The costs to Egypt of alienating the Soviets were considerable. Despite Sadat's exploratory efforts in 1974 and 1975 to obtain arms from the West and thereby end Egypt's almost total reliance on Soviet arms, Western defense analysts stressed the great difficulties in a full-scale switch from Soviet to Western arms. Sadat was aware that the massive introduction of Western arms into a military establishment trained by the Soviets for Soviet-made weapons and equipment would produce a logistics nightmare. Equally to be feared from Soviet alienation was continued Soviet intransigence on the Egyptian debt. In 1975 Sadat reported to the ASU Congress a balance of payments deficit of $3 billion. In 1976 it was estimated that the balance of payments deficit for that year would be as high as $5 billion. President Sadat in 1975 publicly condemned Soviet "pressure" on the debt repayment issue (an issue with unpleasant historical memories for the Egyptians). He asked for a ten-year moratorium similar to that already granted the Syrians. The Soviets refused. By the end of 1976, an *al-Ahram* editorial complained, the Soviets still refused to budge. Finally, in 1977 an exasperated Sadat declared a unilateral ten-year moratorium on Egypt's debt repayment to the Soviets.[17]

In some autobiographical reminiscences published first in Cairo in early 1977 and in 1978 as *In Search of Identity,* Sadat was particularly frank in his criticisms of the Soviet relationship with Egypt. Specifically, he complained that Soviet weapons supplies before the October War were scanty and obsolete. The Soviets registered official outrage at these charges in a long *Pravda* editorial, accusing Sadat of "political libel" and "historical falsification." Sadat, the February 1977 editorial concluded, in his unfriendly attitude toward the Soviet Union had gone "far beyond the limits of elementary propriety and norms generally accepted in relations among states." It was against this background that the Soviets reacted with expected hostility to Egypt's fall 1977 peace initiative.[18]

Meanwhile, Sadat had stepped up his efforts to enlist the Western powers as military suppliers. The United States broke its long-standing arms embargo with the sale in March 1976 of six C-130 military transport planes. A year later, during his visit to Washington to confer with the new American president, Sadat urged that the United States open a significant military supply relationship with Egypt, including the sale of about two hundred F-5E fighter aircraft as well as antitank weapons and other equipment.

In the spring of 1976 Sadat had explored a variety of other arms sources. With Britain and Italy he discussed rearming and getting new engines for a thousand Soviet tanks. China was contacted for spare aircraft engines and parts. From France Sadat received promises of one hundred Alpha jet trainers and ground attack planes as well as forty Mirage F-1s. Britain and France entered into discussions concerning the joint establishment in Egypt of an aircraft industry for French jets and British helicopters.

For all the violence of the Soviet-Egyptian polemics and the frantic quality to Sadat's efforts to strengthen the Western connection, a complete break with the Soviets was avoided in these difficult years. In April of 1976 a trade agreement was signed for exchanges totaling $802 million, so that Russia's position as Egypt's largest trading partner was preserved. Furthermore, both American and Israeli intelligence analysts have claimed that the Soviet Union continued to supply some weapons, ammunitions, and spare parts to the Egyptians through third countries, although there are sharp disagreements over the volume of such shipments. The years 1977 and 1978, though, did bring a cold public confrontation. Sadat somewhat disingenuously bemoaned the fact that he could apparently do nothing to please the Soviets; the Soviets charged that in his November 1977 peace initiative Sadat had sacrificed the interests of the Arab states as a whole.

If there were such immediate and grave problems in Sadat's loosening of the Soviet connection, there were also risks in his decision to turn to the United States. First of all, there were limits to projected U.S. involvement in Egypt—or at least an American intention to proceed slowly. On his visit to the United States in the fall of 1975 Sadat raised an exploratory plan for the purchase of American arms to be paid for by Saudi Arabia and other Persian Gulf countries. A promise for further study of the matter was the American response, with the decision to sell Egypt only the six C-130 transport planes coming in March of 1976. Furthermore, Secretary of State Kissinger, wary of congressional opposition, made it clear that "we can't be the principal arms supplier to Egypt." The Ford administration announced plans for supplying Egypt gradually with a range of other military equipment such as radios and mine detectors, none of it weaponry. Sadat won an initial pledge from the Americans of $1 billion in aid—$750 million in economic assistance (subject to congressional approval) and $250 million in food aid. That was four times the aid Egypt was then receiving and an astounding amount when it is recalled that for the previous eight years U.S. aid to Egypt had stopped altogether. During Sadat's 1975 visit to Washington preliminary provisions were also worked out for the sale to Egypt of two nuclear reactors (with unique safeguard arrangements); the reactors are believed to have been earmarked for such uses as providing electricity for desalinization plants. By fiscal year 1977 the billion-dollar American aid program to Egypt was greater than to the rest of Africa and Latin America combined. In October U.S. treasury secretary W. Michael Blumenthal ended a two-day visit to Cairo with the pronouncement that "we feel we are getting our money's worth in providing assistance that enables Egypt to deal not only with its immediate problems but in setting in motion longer-term development projects." Massive aid to the "Egyptian powderkeg" would continue for a long time, declared administrators of the U.S. Agency for International Development. "Investment in foreign policy"—Sadat style—was paying impressive dividends.[19]

Yet without arms sales Sadat could not regard his efforts as a complete success. The military parade in Cairo on the third anniversary of the October War spotlighted Sadat's dilemma: aging Soviet-made weapons with a limited supply of Western-made arms and virtually no American equipment moved past the reviewing stands. In the spring of 1977 Sadat, again in the United States, lobbied extensively for arms sales. This time the Egyptian president sought to capitalize on American fears. Sadat argued that Egypt needed arms to counter a growing pattern of Soviet and Cuban involvement in Africa, which had begun in Angola but which threatened Egypt, the Sudan, and Zaire as well. Again the Americans temporized; Sadat's hopes that an arms deal would be concluded during his visit were dashed. In the spring of 1978 Sadat was still waiting.

While the benefits of Sadat's American connection were delayed, its dangers for Egypt were soon abundantly clear, especially in the inter-Arab arena. The Syrians, and even more particularly the Palestinians, greeted the September 1975 Egyptian-Israeli Interim Agreement with grave suspicion. Radical forces in the Arab world felt that the logic of the American connection would eventually lead to Egypt's isolation from the Arabs. By December 1975 President Assad of Syria was publicly denouncing Sadat's agreement with Israel as a sellout of the Arab cause. In private, or so reported Arnaud de Borchgrave in *Newsweek,* Assad broadened the charge to include "war-time treachery." Hussein of Jordan showed signs of sharing Assad's suspicions of Sadat. Meanwhile, relations with the volatile President Qaddafi of Libya also deteriorated. Syria in 1975 launched a diplomatic initiative to consolidate a northern front of Iraq, Jordan, and the Palestine Liberation Organization (PLO) on the assumption that Egypt had been "taken out of the battle."[20]

Sadat could not afford to let such charges stick. While in the United States in the fall of 1975, on virtually every occasion (including his address to a joint session of Congress) he pleaded the cause of the Palestinians. The president also made it clear that he regarded Egypt's fate as linked to that of Syria. In his address to the United Nations on October 29, 1975, Sadat announced: "We do not hold any part of Arab territory to be less dear to us than occupied Egyptian territory." He then went on to describe the interim accord with Israel as "only limited in scope and effect." The accord, Sadat explained, was "merely a move envisaging the establishment of a proper climate for progress." The Egyptian president concluded his discussion with an appeal for a reconvening of the Geneva Conference, "with the participation of all the parties concerned with the Palestinian question."

Sadat has not been willing to risk complete isolation in the Arab arena. There have been signs of a greater emphasis on Egyptian nationalism in Sadat's Egypt. On occasion, and to select audiences, Sadat has gone out of his way to emphasize that he is an "Egyptian nationalist" who wants to "solve Egypt's problems." After the Sinai accord of September 1975 the mood in Egypt seemed to be reflected in two billboards: one, at Cairo radio station, showed a woman symbolizing "Mother Egypt" and proclaimed "Egypt First." The other, at an army camp near Alexandria, said "Egypt First, Second, and Last." Nevertheless, such mood indicators hardly signaled a withdrawal into the Nile Valley and out of the Arab arena. Egypt needs its Arab position: isolation from the Arab world would mean economic disaster. Egypt's requirements for food and other vital goods, since 1967, have been met partially by grants from the Arab states. And for the future, the policy of the opening is built on attracting Arab capital to Egypt. While the flow of Arab capital to Egypt has been disappointing in volume, it is hard to see how an Egypt that had openly abandoned Arabism would be a greater magnet.[21]

Ironically, Sadat's emergence from dangerous isolation in the Arab world was linked to the devastating Lebanese civil war that began in the spring of 1975. A Syria threatened by the growing radical Palestinian presence in Lebanon intervened actively to tame the Palestinians. In the process the Syrian position was both moderated and strengthened. By the time Saudi King Khalid arranged the ceasefire of October 1976 that ended the civil war, the Egyptians and Syrians had begun a process of rapprochement. Egypt sanctioned the Syrian show of strength in Lebanon, while Syria recognized Egypt's president as the leading diplomatic spokesman for the Arab confrontation states. In December of 1976 Egypt and Syria announced the formation of a united political leadership. By January of 1977 the reconciliation had been extended to Hussein of Jordan. Egypt, no longer isolated, was a key element of a new moderate bloc of Arab states, along with Saudi Arabia, Syria, and Jordan, with the PLO apparently in tow. Meanwhile, the radical camp that opposed any negotiation for a Middle East settlement was reduced to Libya, Iraq, and Algeria, along with dissident elements in the PLO. This so-called rejectionist front for the time being had lost decisive power to shape Arab strategy.

Thus, as 1977 began, Sadat had won significantly broader support for his American connection, now aimed at negotiation in Geneva for an overall settlement of the conflict with Israel. To Sadat's distress, the path to Geneva was littered with obstacles. May of 1977 brought changes of earthquake proportions in Israel: in a stunning electoral upset, the right-wing opposition under Menachem Begin won the mandate to form a government. There were further settlements in the occupied territories, massive retaliatory raids into southern Lebanon, and an adamant Israeli refusal to deal with the PLO in the Geneva forum. Meanwhile, Egypt's domestic situation deteriorated and its military strength relative to Israel declined. Sadat was virtually driven to seek an agreement, in order to bolster his open-door policy. Risking Egypt's improved position in the Arab world by his November 1977 trip to Israel, Sadat presented the Arab case to the world from that most dramatic of platforms, the Israeli Knesset. Egypt's president was hailed as the "Master of Decision" and the "Hero of Peace." Egyptians rallied to their president, as the predictable attacks from the Syrians and "Arab rejectionists" mounted in intensity.

Events in the spring of 1978 led to further deterioration. A Palestinian raid on Israel that was launched from Lebanon in March ended with over thirty Israeli civilians killed. Sadat promptly broke once again with the Arab world in a public condemnation of the attack on civilians. Within days came the Israeli response to the Palestinian raid: the invasion and occupation of southern Lebanon, with hundreds of lives lost. The Egyptians denounced the Israeli invasion as organized genocide; the Israelis argued their right of self-defense against terrorism. For all this, Sadat announced his intention to continue the peace drive, calling on the Americans with ever more urgency to intervene actively in the peace process. For the Egyptian people these devastating complications meant further delays in concrete results from Sadat's initiatives. As Sadat explained, in the last analysis all the complex international maneuvering was aimed at improving the life of the people of Egypt.

THE OPENING: PROMISE AND PERFORMANCE

The "opening," at least in the short run, had not brought such improvement. In the several years following the 1973 war, the mass of Egyptians welcomed an influx of Western businessmen with "gold rush" excitement, heard rumors of fabulous Arab investments, and witnessed the new prosperity enjoyed by resurgent bourgeois elements. Yet their own already precarious standard of living steadily eroded. *Al-Tali'ah* estimated in the spring of 1976 that the purchasing power of 80 percent of the population had declined since the October War. In a somber speech to the People's Assembly that year, Premier Mamdouh Salem starkly revealed the depth of Egypt's continuing financial crisis and the hardships it would entail. Egypt's annual balance-of-payments deficits were enormous. In such circumstances, the prime minister announced, there could be no further general wage increases without a corresponding rise in production. Even the more privileged elements of the population would suffer. With inflation spiraling, real wages for government employees and workers in public sector industries would continue to fall.[22]

The pain of these new deprivations was heightened by the high expectations that Sadat's economic program had raised. The potential for Egypt's development was there, and the regime had taken steps to realize it. The respected Western weekly, *Business International,* stated flatly that Egypt in the seventies had the best growth prospects of any country in the world. To entice a Western and an Arab response, Egypt's investment advantages were loudly advertised: its strategic location, the size of the domestic market, the existent industrial infrastructure, the relatively high level of its trained manpower resources, the extensiveness of its communication and transport networks.[23]

Nor were these advantages left to speak for themselves. In a typical interview with *Business Week* four months after the October War, Abdul Aziz Higazi, then a deputy prime minister, announced: "My policy is maximum flexibility. We need foreign money and technology to develop, and we will get it as best we can." Crucial, Higazi realized, would be reassurances to prospective investors that Egypt's age of nationalization presided over by Nasser was over. "We have to give ironclad guarantees that this sort of thing will not happen again," observed Higazi. "Without them, people will not come back, and I do not really blame them."[24]

The guarantees, as well as a host of special privileges, came with Law 43 of 1974 "Concerning the Investment of Arab and Foreign Capital and Free Zones." All foreign investments in Egypt proper and the Free Zones (in Port Said and elsewhere) were to be approved by the General Authority for Arab and Foreign Investment and Free Zones (GAAFIFZ). Project acceptance by GAAFIFZ brought an array of incentives. The profits of new companies set up in Egypt proper were exempted from taxes for the first five years of operation, a privileged status extendable for an additional three years. Projects in the Free Zones were made totally exempt from Egyptian profit taxes and their foreign employees were not required to pay income tax to Egypt.

Law 43 also excluded foreign companies from the 25 percent profit-sharing requirements that apply to Egyptian concerns. Greater foreign exchange freedom was accorded to companies operating in Egypt proper, while companies in the Free Zones were subject to no foreign exchange controls. Furthermore, the new investment law freed companies from the requirement that they have majority local ownership; wholly foreign-owned projects are now allowed. Important labor relations concessions were included as well: Egyptian labor law requirements were significantly eased for companies outside the Free Zones and removed for companies in the Free Zones. Finally, Article 7 of Law 43 provided explicit protection to the new investors: "Projects may not be nationalized or expropriated, nor may invested capital be confiscated, seized or sequestered except through lawful process."[25]

Despite the potential, the incentives, and the guarantees, the heralded open door initially led only to disappointment. The stream of Western company representatives and Arab delegations in and out of Cairo yielded projects surprisingly few in number and relatively unattractive in developmental import. The first comprehensive report on foreign investment projects for the period September 1971 to December 1974 revealed the approval of 196 investment plans. However, by June 1975 only ten modest projects had actually gotten under way, with three of them in the Free Zones. Furthermore, 65 percent of all planned investment went into tourism and hotel facilities, housing and construction. Slightly less than half the capital for internal (as opposed to Free Zone) projects would be raised locally, so that hard currency transfers were not involved. Capital in this early period gravitated toward middle- and high-income-level housing construction, especially in Cairo. Western private interests, this first complete report indicated, were not eager to invest their own capital in Egypt. There was instead a marked preference to sell management expertise and equipment.[26]

Especially resented by Egyptians was the slowness with which petrodollars found their way to Egypt. From October 1973 to October 1975 an estimated $4.45 billion in investments did flow into Egypt from the Arab oil-rich states and Iran. Of this $1.14 billion was from Saudi Arabia, $848 million from Kuwait, and $680 million from Iran. But Egyptian expectations, both official and popular, had been for a much larger share of the billions of surplus funds held by the oil-rich states. There were sharp disappointments: *Akhbar al-Yaum* on one occasion generated great excitement with headlines of a billion-dollar Saudi grant to Egypt. The actual agreement, in a pattern that proved typical, provided only $300 million in commitments for specific purposes.[27]

In 1975 the return of the Abu Rudeis oilfield in the Sinai as a result of the second Egyptian-Israeli disengagement, the reopening of the Suez

Canal, and extensive Canal Zone reconstruction projects should have been encouraging signs to potential foreign investors. Still, by the summer of 1976 it was clear that only the international oil companies and banks were responding with any enthusiasm to opportunities in Egypt. Some thirty oil exploration groups invested about $650 million over a seven-year period. They planned forty-one exploratory wells—twenty-one offshore, with the Gulf of Suez judged the most productive field. By 1980, it was estimated, Egypt would be producing one million barrels a day, which would bring in $1.20 billion to $1.50 billion in foreign earnings.[28]

Banking, as one Western financial observer has put it, is also "an area where the wind of change in Egypt is beginning to rustle some dead leaves." By 1975 a number of joint-venture banks were gradually beginning operations, with U.S. and European banks partnering the main Egyptian ones. Other banks from the United States, Europe, and the Middle East were opening local branches.[29]

Despite this substantial activity in banking and oil exploration, foreign companies remained reluctant to move into Egypt. In July of 1976 it was reported that 181 foreign investment projects worth $769 million had been approved by the Egyptian government. Of that number only a handful had actually gotten under way. The lack of investor confidence was further reflected in the fact that with the exception of the Michelin car tire plant—which was a heavily political decision—no major international group had yet invested in Egypt. One source recorded that by the end of 1976 only $75 million in investment capital had actually come into the country. That figure meant that Sadat's opening was in serious trouble.[30]

The extreme caution of foreign investors resulted in part from fears of persistent regional instability coupled with the expected wariness born of memories of the Nasser era nationalizations. Even those investors who overcame their hesitancies were confronted by a formidable array of shortcomings in Law 43, the legal backbone of the "open door." In addition, there were general institutional and structural impediments to successful operations in Egypt. Most vexing for many potential investors was the continued existence of the multiple-currency exchange rate system explained in Chapter 2 (see note 4). There were also flaws in Law 43 that reflected official uncertainty on proper public-private sector relations. In the drive to bolster the private sector Sadat and his economic advisers had to tread cautiously in order to minimize the inevitable opposition of supporters of Nasser's socialism. Economic minister Higazi has explained that the open door is not a repudiation of Nasser's emphasis on the public sector, but rather an attempt to build in a new situation on the foundations Nasser erected:

We needed nationalization to build up our infra-structure and give work to people. Now we have moved into a new stage. Those state companies have to start being profitable. And now there is a place for foreign investment.

But Law 43 did not specify clearly the modalities of public-private sector interaction, aside from a general pronouncement that "investment of Arab and foreign funds in the Arab Republic of Egypt shall be for the realization of the economic and social development goals within the framework of the general policy of the State and its national plan." Egyptian officials, in the spirit of this provision, have sought to require that all foreign investments do in fact promote the planned development goals of the country.[31]

That effort has been hampered by a series of technical problems unresolved by Law 43.[32] On the most general level, the new investment law does not define with sufficient clarity Egypt's investment priorities nor integrate them into the development plans. Consequently, there is no effective mechanism to harmonize expanded private investment with planned development. GAAFIFZ, the General Authority for Arab and Foreign Investment and Free Zones, which might have performed that task, was not given enough decision-making authority to coordinate and manage the work of other agencies. As a result, explained one Western management specialist:

> Foreign investors are faced with an overwhelming maze of government offices, complicated rules, and a confusing hierarchy of bureaucrats. While officials recognize this problem, the Open Door may add another bureaucratic barrier facing investors.

Reports filed from the field have confirmed these fears. The representative of one leading American bank told this story:

> I tried to get in my own furniture as a start, but customs said I had to pay for it. When I told them I was exempt according to the investment law, they told me to get a signed paper from the Investment Authority. I have not been able to get anybody to sign such a paper so far. Instead I signed the paper myself, pledging to pay customs, if it turns out that I had to pay them.

In operation a number of more specific omissions in Law 43 have also hindered investment activities. The investment law does not, for example, state clearly the precise nature of the required foreign-Egyptian partnership; the requirements for the repatriation of profits are ambiguously stated; and the future exchange rate to be used between the Egyptian pound and convertible currency is not specified. Some foreign investors have also objected to the requirement that the repatriation of foreign capital can only be done over a ten-year period. Finally, several provisions of the law raise prospects for conflicts over the long term. The law does not state the requirements and incentives for local private investment, and this may generate hostility between Egyptian and foreign investors. In addition, the preferential treatment accorded Arab investors in the areas of housing, landownership, and agriculture is likely to produce friction between Arab and non-Arab investors.

Difficult as these technical problems have been, they do not exhaust the challenges for the foreign investor in Egypt. The trials of dealing with Egypt's notoriously overblown bureaucracy have been exacerbated by the corrupt antics of an expanding class of "middlemen" who—for a fee—act as expediters for the bewildered foreigner. The laissez-faire climate of the opening has allowed for the vast expansion of the scope of operations of Egypt's middlemen. Impressionistic evidence suggests that their partially institutionalized corruption has reached alarming proportions. The consequences of such a situation are damaging: one deal, for example, related to the building of a manufacturing plant collapsed when the Egyptian agent telexed the European bank involved in the deal and demanded several million dollars to be placed in a Swiss bank account![33]

Investment enthusiasm has also been dampened by more mundane but still depressing economic problems that can only be briefly catalogued here. The migration of technically skilled workers to Arab countries where they receive higher wages has created serious labor shortages in critical categories. Estimates of trained manpower abroad range as high as four hundred fifty thousand. Egypt's communication and transportation infrastructure is so overburdened that Dr. Samir Radwan of Oxford's Institute of Economics and Statistics warned in 1975: "Basic services, telephones, transport, water, sewerage, are near complete collapse." For foreign businessmen transactions by telephone are barely feasible:

> Phoning in Cairo is an adventure. The procedure is to lift the receiver and wait. Anything can happen, from getting President Sadat on the line to finding that the line does not work because it is overoccupied. International telephone calls have to be requested two or three days ahead of time. Businessmen who can afford it regularly fly to Athens to do their phoning.

The pressure on transportation facilities is, if anything, greater. *Al-Tali'ah* estimated in 1976 that there were in Cairo only twelve hundred buses for its eight million inhabitants.[34]

Business activity in Egypt is further hampered by the lack of internal credit facilities, the absence of quality controls in most domestic industries, and the complicated and costly pattern of linkages between public and private firms. Finally, Egypt's post-October War inflation rate has been running at an estimated 30 percent annually.[35]

For the mass of Egyptians such arcane analysis of the technical and broader social reasons for the limited success of the opening has little meaning. What is clear is that expectations raised by Sadat's economic solution have not been fulfilled. Heightened class conflict has been the result. The hardships for Egypt's people implicit in the limited results of the program have not been borne equally. Social cleavages have widened as a result of the differential impact, and social violence reminiscent of the 1940s has surfaced.

The lines of the emerging class conflict cannot yet be drawn with any great precision. Social stratification is very much in flux, especially for the critical middle strata. But a broad-stroke characterization of three distinct middle-class elements—all objects of heightened mass resentment—can be sketched. In Sadat's Egypt the old liberal bourgeoisie has revived, Nasserist state or bureaucratic strata have consolidated their position of relative privilege, and a "new class" of middlemen and profiteers has thrived.

Gamal Abdul Nasser, confronted with the harsh development alternatives of the sixties, had halted before the prospects of a real political intensification of his revolution. As a result, although Egypt's traditional bourgeoisie was cowed, it was not eliminated nor even really bled for the sake of the development effort. Nasser argued that there was a place for all Egyptians in the new Egypt. Che Guevara, for one, found this aspect of the Egyptian revolution anomalous. When Guevara learned that Egypt's social transformation had not produced a massive exodus of middle-class elements, he concluded in conversation with Nasser:

> That means that nothing much happened in your revolution. I measure the depth of social transformation by the number of people who are affected by it and feel that they have no place in the new society.

Egypt's prerevolutionary elite, despite the assaults of Nasserist nationalizations and sequestrations on its privileged position, managed to survive and to preserve some elements of its material base. Sadat's various liberalization measures, especially his desequestration actions and call for a revival of the private sector, improved the condition of the former elite substantially. In the era of the open door, the old bourgeoisie of Egypt's liberal age once again raised its head.

In *In Search for Identity* Sadat celebrated the revival of the most important of the liberal professionals, the lawyers:

> As I restored the rule of law, lawyers today are in great demand to fight social injustices. The demand for lawyers has risen even higher with the adoption of our open-door policy as foreign businessmen need legal representation in Egypt. The legal business has thus regained its earlier vitality in every respect.

He also went out of his way to praise the old liberal party, the Wafd, as "a symbol of the struggle of the entire Egyptian people against the British."[36]

In Sadat's Egypt the state or bureaucratic bourgeoisie managed to add to the gains it had made since the revolution, although access to real power continued to elude it. In the Nasser years, the traditional administration had been vastly expanded as middle-class elements, many with technological and managerial training, moved into key positions in the newly created public sector. The approximately two thousand public sector managers were only the most visible and prosperous of the more than two and a half million Egyptians with the privileged status of public sector employees. Earlier, Nasser's mass welfare commitment, symbolized by the food subsidies program, and his socialist rhetoric had to some degree screened the special advantages of the state bourgeoisie. In the seventies those relative advantages have been quite obvious, although the political clout of the state bourgeoisie should not be overestimated. Despite the reliance by the state on their modern skills, this new technocracy of the public sector has been kept politically subservient, not to say impotent. Advancement, as in the Nasser years, results from political docility as much as from technical competence. Moreover, the view that key decisions have been made by technical criteria is erroneous; the technocrats participate in decision making only to the degree to which they have passed political muster as individuals.[37]

But Sadat has not, despite the new emphasis on the private sector, been blind to the value of the state bourgeoisie as a pliant prop for authoritarian rule. The open door is designed in part to revitalize the public sector through competition from a strengthened private sphere. However, the public sector will continue to play the major role in the economy. In fact, one informed Western observer has noted: "In all likelihood the public sector will be the major beneficiary of the open-door policy."[38]

The old liberal elite and the state bureaucracy have been joined as middle-class strata, especially since 1967, by a variety of colorful arriviste elements (the "parasitic bourgeoisie," in the parlance of the Egyptian left) who have flourished as Egypt has moved to the right and to a reemphasis on market activity. "You have seen how many new cars there are in Cairo," observed M. H. Haikal in October 1975. "A new class is emerging . . . a parasite class . . . creating a very high pattern of consumption, vulgar consumption." These new elements have made the interstices between the public and the private sectors the domain of their operations, notably in subcontracting and the black market. Their origins are even more diverse than those of the state bourgeoisie: they range from middle-level rural landowners enriched by a variety of black-market speculations to urban building contractors and real estate manipulators.[39]

The survivors of the old liberal bourgeoisie, the inherited state bourgeoisie, and the newly emergent parasitic bourgeoisie do not yet form a cohesive class with shared consciousness. But they are middle-class elements who have thrived in the years of the open door. It is the new liberalization that has created the climate especially conducive to their relative prosperity. And that flaunted but narrowly shared prosperity has angered the mass of the Egyptian people.

NASSERISM WITH A LIBERAL FACE

Anwar es-Sadat has sought to offset the disappointments occasioned by Egypt's flawed economic performance by pushing ahead with political liberalization. For Egyptians of all political leanings the most welcome of Sadat's changes has been the relative enhancement of democratic freedoms and the overall increased sense of personal security. In the *October Paper* Sadat stated that the aim of his "Corrective Revolution" was "withdrawing all forms of exceptional measures, and ensuring stability of laws, rules, institutions, and relations within a clearcut framework." Egypt, Sadat averred, was to be a "state of institutions."[40]

The repressive side of Nasser's regime has now been acknowledged by even so loyal a Nasserite as M. H. Haikal, the journalist who was Nasser's closest confidant. Over the years reports on the brutality of Egypt's police and military intelligence networks had come from their victims in a steady stream. Outside observers, notably Amnesty International, called the world's attention to the fact that under Nasser "the maltreatment and torture of political prisoners was said to have been almost a matter of routine." Especially after the revolution began to lose momentum in the sixties, the numbers of political prisoners and detainees mounted sharply, with estimates ranging as high as twenty thousand. Political opponents received harsh treatment in Nasser's Egypt: a number of leaders of the Moslem Brotherhood were hanged, and communist militants beaten and tortured to death. Nasser's name also bears the stain of the arrest of five hundred loyal and baffled Egyptian Jews, spitefully detained in the wake of the 1967 disaster; nearly all of them eventually were forced to emigrate. The most courageous of Egypt's intellectuals had sought to expose and condemn these reprehensible actions committed in the shadow of the charismatic leader. Through their art men like Tewfik Salah, the film director, and Aly Salem, the playwright, eluded the censors to present trenchant criticisms of the abuses of the Nasser era. After Nasser's death the veils were partially lifted: Nasser's Egypt, while far from a totalitarian state, was revealed as a repressive, authoritarian country.[41]

Among Sadat's first liberalization measures was the freeing of political prisoners. As far as can be determined, during the first years of Sadat's rule virtually all political prisoners were released (notable exceptions included Aly Sabry and Sharawi Gomaa, who were found guilty of engineering the May 1971 coup attempt against Sadat).[42]

In the *October Paper* Sadat had announced the lifting of the censorship of the press, and Egyptians with gusto availed themselves of their new opportunities. To follow the course of debate on major issues, one could for a while read (rather than decipher) the press. The range of opinions and the boldness of the revelations and exposés were sometimes startling in the first years of Sadat's rule, until official uniformity was reimposed after the January 1977 riots. Whereas in the Nasser years it was the left-wing press that was most revealing in its social and political commentary, under Sadat the right-wing seized the initiative. The right-wing press tends to combine criticisms of the past with panegyrics to President Sadat. Clustered primarily in *al-Akhbar, Akhbar al-Yaum, Akher Saa,* and *al-Musawwar,* the right has above all stressed the violations of legality in the Nasser years.

Most scandalous of the right-wing assaults, and most damaging to the Nasserists, has been *The First Year in Prison,* by Mustapha Amin, published in Cairo in 1974. Amin was pardoned by Sadat after having served nine years in prison on charges of spying for the United States. His book describes in shattering detail the brutal torture to which he and others were subjected. Amin forthrightly charges that Nasser had ordered his arrest and must have known of the treatment he received. Amin's brother, Aly Amin, who had returned from political exile abroad, replaced Haikal as editor in chief of *al-Ahram* when Haikal's disagreements with Sadat on foreign policy became apparent. Subsequently, Aly and Mustapha Amin were made editors of *al-Akhbar* and *al-Akhbar al-Yaum,* the newspapers they had founded in 1944. Aly Amin has made his regular column in *al-Akhbar* an important outlet for sentiments especially reassuring to Egypt's middle-class strata. He commented in one column: "I can hear people say 'no' without looking over their shoulders now." In another he wryly observed on the October victory: "After having spent long years killing each other, we turned our cannon against the enemy."[43]

Even more virulent and bitter in their attacks on the "violations of the past" have been the two conservative editors of the weekly *al-Musawwar,* Fikri Abaza and Salah Jawdat. In an amazing article, which provoked widespread rebuttal and perhaps reached the outermost limits of what could be tolerated, Jawdat assailed the Nasserist legacy in its entirety. While far from typical, the column does suggest the bitterness of the debate that raged only three and a half years after Nasser's death.

With heavy irony, Jawdat begins:

> The facade was magnificent, destroying capitalism, feudalism, and exploitation; fighting imperialism; strengthening the army;

justice for the workers and peasants; achieving social justice generally; industrializing the country; and uniting the Arab nation from
the Ocean to the Gulf. It was a brilliant facade which dazzled us . . .

This is the facade. But application was a completely different
thing . . . It did not contain any of the qualities of the facade.

Jawdat then continues with an extensive catalogue of abuses and failures:
domestic affairs—eminent scholars "silenced for their dissidence";
skilled workers and scientists who emigrated to "get away from this sub-
jugation"; the army, handed over to "weak, corrupt, and dissolute commanders" so that it suffered "the worst defeat without a battle"; the
Israeli occupation—"The British left . . . so that the Jews could enter our
country and occupy our canal and all our Sinai and so that this dear part
of our homeland could remain for seven lean years under the yoke of the
most humiliating colonialism in the history of Egypt"; Arab unity—
"This past . . . let its tongue loose with searing and slander against Arab
kings and presidents . . . accusing this one of treachery, that one of mad-
ness"; foreign relations—"Our relations with all the states deteriorated
and many of these relations reached the extreme of total alienation."[44]

In contrast to such assaults on the past, the expressed attitude of the
right toward Sadat has ranged from general satisfaction to extreme adulation. The audience for the right-wing press has been a mixed one and
includes the aristocratic and bourgeois survivals of the ancien régime, the
more successful middlemen (the parasitic bourgeoisie, in the terminology
of the left), members of the liberal professions in great numbers as well
as the religious right (the last rather by default, although the Amin
brothers have used their papers to raise questions about the brutality of
the assault on the Moslem Brothers). Nasser's socialism did not mean
physical elimination of the aristocrats and the bourgeoisie, although he
sharply curtailed their previous political and economic dominance.
Egypt's social structure, as Soviet analysts in particular have stressed, is
too much in flux to speak with any confidence of classes or even of
sharply defined constituencies. But it is clear that the right could command a sufficient audience for its views and a fluctuating constituency
for the policies it advocated.

The left in Sadat's Egypt has been on the defensive. Such a total negation of Nasser's rule as can be found in the more extreme right-wing articles is intolerable to the left, although certain aspects of the rightist critique—notably the revelations concerning the Nasserist violations of
legality—have evoked approval in left circles. *Rose al-Yusuf,* under Abdul Rahman el-Sharkawy, articulated the left view for the widest audience. Aside from the inevitable coteries of intellectuals, the audience for
the left has been drawn primarily from Egypt's burgeoning student population. The left has also appealed to the interests of the working class and
has garnered some support in professional circles.

Essentially, the left has argued that Nasser's principles and basic orientations ("socialism at home" and "anti-imperialism abroad") were sound, although at times violated disastrously in practice. For the left, Nasser did not go far enough, did not create a truly revolutionary party and ideology to galvanize the masses. Furthermore, the left has argued, Nasser allowed the growth of a parasitic and dangerous middle class; that class, aligned with foreign capitalists, now threatens to dismantle the revolutionary gains Nasser was able to register, restore capitalism, and compromise with Israel. Writing in *Rose al-Yusuf,* Sharkawy remarked that "the intellectual and ideological vacuum from which our life suffers" could prepare the way for "a new fascism."[45]

In addition to warning against the dangers of an alliance of the "new class" and international "reaction," the left has also insisted that Sadat's Corrective Revolution of May 1971 was not a repudiation of the past. Sharkawy argued that Sadat had secured his hold on power in May in order "to protect Nasserism from those who distorted it, and to protect the stage of socialist change from those who squandered its socialist, humane, and democratic values."[46] The left has been transparently alarmed that the rightist critique of the abuses of the Nasser era would be used as a platform for a call that Sadat move toward the creation of a regime of parliamentary rule with competing political parties dominated by the middle-class strata. Thus, for the left, it has been important to "protect" Nasserism from deviation (past and present) and not to dismantle it.

Rose al-Yusuf, of the various Egyptian newspapers and journals, has most consistently used the new liberalization for criticisms of the Sadat era. For example, when New Year's Day disturbances in 1975 were blamed by the government on "communists and leftist adventurers," the major Cairo papers echoed that interpretation—with one exception. Sharkawy rebutted the charge, declaring that no leftist organization would so disrupt national unity and attack a government which had shown that it could fight Israel. Bluntly, Sharkawy stated the real causes of the disturbances: "Everybody knows that we are suffering from high costs and that life has become difficult to bear."[47] Sharkawy then went on to urge the government to face Egypt's difficulties honestly and not to search for scapegoats.

The pattern was repeated after the January 1977 price riots. *Rose al-Yusuf* alone dissented from the official claim that the riots were leftist inspired. The American Central Intelligence Agency, the journal asserted, was more likely to be responsible than the communists. More pointedly, *Rose al-Yusuf* took issue with government reports that two of its editors had been arrested while engaged in rioting. The arrests came while one man was at home and the other in his office, the journal explained. Sadat, after a short period of equivocation, early in 1977 moved to sack Sharkawy and other outspoken journalists, replacing them with spokesmen for the regime.[48]

A further indicator of the improved but still controlled climate of public debate came when Kamal el-Din Hussein, a Free Officer and former Egyptian vice-president, accused Sadat of "dereliction" in creating the conditions that led to the January price riots. Hussein also labeled "unconstitutional" Sadat's punitive law-and-order measures taken in the wake of the riots. Sadat had called for a public referendum on the new measures, which would make strikes, demonstrations, and other disturbances punishable by hard labor. Similarly defiant was Khaled Muhieddin's official "left" party, which urged its members to vote against the referendum. *Al-Ahram* denounced Hussein and refused to publish his telegram, which did appear in *al-Jumhuriyyah* and *al-Akhbar*. Egypt's largest newspaper called Hussein "impudent" and explained that his views were not published "out of respect for the sense of morality of the readers." Hussein was later expelled as a delegate from the People's Assembly by a vote of 281 to 28 for his action. The law-and-order referendum was approved by 99.4 percent of the voters, according to the government.[49]

Salah Jaheen, Egypt's leading political cartoonist, in his own idiom has been as bold and consistent as Sharkawy of *Rose al-Yusuf* in probing the limits of acceptable criticism of the Sadat regime. Sadat himself has not escaped Jaheen's scathing wit. In a cartoon published in *al-Ahram* in 1974 Jaheen depicts an oversized and overbearing Sadat lecturing at an Arab Socialist Union meeting from an elevated platform to a sea of upturned, indistinguishable faces. Sadat is proclaiming: "Among the negative features of the experience with the ASU is that all ideas come from above."[50] Egyptians did not miss the point: Sadat's "liberalism" has not meant the end of basically authoritarian patterns of rule.

For the most part Sadat held himself aloof from the turmoil and excitement generated by the press debates. He has presented himself as too preoccupied with the grave regional and global dangers confronting Egypt to participate in domestic squabbles.[51] Obviously, the debate rages with his implied blessing, yet he has refused to take sides other than to set certain limits. In 1973 Sadat had responded to trenchant left-wing criticism with a suspension from the ASU of over a hundred intellectuals, mainly journalists, when they appeared to be destroying public confidence in his regime. But the left was allowed to bounce back. Similarly, in 1976 and 1977 Sadat periodically stepped in when the right pushed attacks on Nasser too far. For example, charges made in the right-wing press of embezzlement by Nasser were staunchly denied by the president, who apparently felt that to allow such charges to stand would question the overall legitimacy of Free Officer rule. Finally in 1977, apparently angered by the defiant tone of the leftist rebuttal to the official version of the causes of the January riots, Sadat acted to remove the management of both *Rose al Yusuf* and *al-Tali'ah*. For a while, at least, the left was to be muzzled.

Sadat's actions have been aimed at giving the right a deserved but contained outlet for its grievances after years of enforced silence, while at the same time not completely alienating the left. Sadat has offered himself as a symbol of "continuity with a difference" with the Nasser era, which is sufficiently ambiguous to make him acceptable to both right and left. In that same way he has also sought to reassure the Egyptian center, based in the great civil and military bureaucracies.

Also important to the strengthening of liberal rights under Sadat's rule have been the guarantees of freedom of movement. Such guarantees are especially important to Egyptian intellectuals and other financially comfortable segments of the population. Egyptian citizens, the regime has announced, would no longer require exit visas to go abroad. Concerned about a continuing brain drain, President Sadat has also promised students and recent graduates living abroad that, if they come home, they will be free to leave again at any time. (As always, however, caution is in order in accepting the official version of the changes. There have, for example, been reports that attached clauses dilute the meaning of the measures. Egyptians desirous of leaving the country have been informed that they must have "releasing" statements from their employers, which may not be so easily obtainable if their skills are in demand.) The draft age for graduate and professional students has been raised to thirty-five.

If the classic liberal values of the rule of law and freedom of speech and movement have received great emphasis, it should not be surprising that the question of property rights has also been raised. Almost immediately on coming to power, Sadat ended a practice that Nasser had used to discipline and punish the Egyptian middle class: punitive sequestration. During the Nasser years it is estimated that at least six hundred families suffered from such confiscations. In December of 1970 Sadat ordered a complete review of all past sequestrations and the return of seized properties. An estimated two thousand individual Egyptians benefited from these measures. In March of 1972 Egypt's parliament sponsored hearings on the issue, and since then the press has periodically carried reports on the "injustices" involved in the sequestrations.[52]

In a 1974 interview in *al-Hawadith* of Beirut, Dr. Higazi, architect of the opening, made some remarks that help illuminate official thinking on the property rights issue. In an obvious move to protect the regime's vulnerable left flank, Higazi cited the authority of none other than the former Soviet ruler Nikita Khrushchev:

When Nikita Krushchev . . . visited Cairo in 1964, the subject of sequestrations that had been imposed on the properties of a number of Egyptians came up, and he said: "I am surprised that you have begun to outdo us in socialist application, although with a poor method. Does anyone imagine that sequestration is a socialist measure? The greatest mistake we were ever involved in was that we nationalized petty industries even though we steadily affirmed that one of the basic goals of socialism was to prevent the domination of people's resources by exploitative capital. The goal was never to consolidate all the national resources in the hands of the regime."

Higazi then noted that Anwar es-Sadat shared these views. Especially significant was the comment in reference to "petty industries," which may have indicated an intention to divest the public sector of small industrial holdings over time. It is instructive that several days later Egypt's highest court of appeals, in the first judgment of its kind, ruled in a test case that confiscation of the private property of citizens during the Nasser years was illegal and must be rescinded. To underscore the importance of the ruling, all Cairo papers gave it great prominence, with *al-Ahram* running the story under a three-column front-page headline. Although there was no mention of the legality of over five hundred nationalizations of factories and companies during the Nasser period, there were immediate rumors and speculations in Cairo that the confiscation ruling in fact was a harbinger of the eventual dismantling of the public sector.[53]

Higazi moved to squelch such an interpretation of the regime's intentions with a lengthy interview published the same year in *al-Ahram*; in it Higazi went out of his way to convey "his deep faith in the public sector concept." However, he had problems making a convincing case. In an interview published earlier that year in *al-Iqtisad wa al-Muhasib,* he had spoken openly of public sector enterprises that "suffer losses and require continual state support, and therefore constitute a burden on our resources." Higazi went on to disparage "rigid theories" and to raise the prospect of "eliminating" such enterprises.[54] It was clearly not an easy act to juggle: to reassure foreign (and domestic) capital on the one hand; to preserve confidence in the future of the public sector on the other. In the Sadat era progress in liberalization did not come without ambiguities and equivocations, but it did come.

CONTINUITIES WITH THE NASSERIST PAST

Nasser's death undeniably opened a new and in some ways a more enlightened era in Egypt's history. But for all the gains in freedom and security during the Sadat years, some basic institutional characteristics of Nasser's authoritarian system of rule have endured. Sadat has remained the interpreter of the official ideology, despite an evident distaste for ideological politics. The shape of the economy and the conduct of foreign affairs have been determined by presidential decision. Key appointments in all the bureaucracies have been made by Sadat and the bureaucratic feudalism of the Nasser years has not been dismantled. Constitutional structures, it will be seen, have expanded their scope of activities, although they do not yet define the channels through which real power flows. Early in his regime Sadat emptied the jails, but he did not eliminate the powerful security apparatus or dilute his control over it. And dominance of the armed forces has remained the key to power: in the face of the January 1977 riots Sadat's position was preserved when the military loyally dispersed the protestors.

In the Egypt of Sadat, as of Nasser, real power has rested with the military/police complex, not with civilian institutions. If anything, Sadat has enhanced the power and prestige of Egypt's officer corps. It is no accident that as Egypt entered the second half of the seventies, the regime of Anwar es-Sadat had as its prime minister Mamdouh Salem, a man who made his career in the security apparatus and who was rewarded by Sadat for his support during the 1971 Corrective Revolution with the post of minister of the interior. The vice-president was Husni Mubarak, an air force general who had distinguished himself in the October War. Sadat's solicitude for the military and its special caste privileges has been manifested in countless ways. Officers purged in political cases before May 1971 and in the failed coup against Sadat have been fully reinstated. Sadat has exploited Egypt's performance in the October War to restore the prestige of the army, disgraced by the 1967 defeat, and consolidate his support within it. (The Egyptian public still has not received an accurate account of the limitations of the military's performance in 1973.) In the wake of October, Sadat promoted a whole series of front-line commanders. The Second and Third armies, for example, in 1975 were commanded by the officers who led them during the actual fighting in 1973. Their predecessors, with less reason for gratitude to Sadat, have been moved into honorific but innocuous positions as "advisers" in the War Ministry. Military salaries and other privileges have been increased.[55]

Also extremely important has been Sadat's restoration of the public luster of a military career. Shortly after the war, Sadat summoned the entire military command to a commemorative session of the People's Assembly, in which leading officers were decorated and the dead honored. Sadat, wearing a field marshal's uniform, then called forward the commander of the Third Army and questioned him before the assembly:

PRESIDENT SADAT: "The enemy claimed that he occupied Suez. Was Suez occupied?"

GENERAL BADAWI: "The enemy could not occupy Suez."
PRESIDENT SADAT: "At one moment the enemy imagined he had encircled you. Did you protect my sons, the soldiers and officers?"
GENERAL BADAWI: "I protected all soldiers and officers and we remained steadfast."

Sadat thus invited the military to bask in the adoration of the Egyptian
people grateful for October. The president has also acted to remove re-
troactively the stigma of 1967. In a series of articles, prominent military
spokesmen have argued (obviously with official approval) that the disaster of the June War was completely the result of the failure of the political authorities. One such article sums up: "The gist of the matter is that
Egyptian forces did not have the opportunity to fight in 1967." Finally, it
deserves mention that in October of 1974 the Egyptian armed forces
staged a massive military parade, the first since 1967. Clearly, Sadat has
taken important steps to restore to the military the privileged position
enjoyed in the early Nasser years.[56]

Nevertheless, Sadat has not simply recreated the pattern of regime-
military relationships that Nasser had established. For one thing, the
military itself in the decades since 1952 has undergone a major transformation. The police force of the prerevolutionary period has grown, for
all its limitations vis-à-vis Israel, into the most powerful and modernized
armed force in the Arab world. Large and internally diversified, the
Egyptian armed forces "probably represent in microcosm all the political
trends that one finds in Egyptian society as a whole."[57] At the same time
the original core group of conspiratorial Free Officers had completely
dissolved by the seventies. Dominant in the affairs of state in the 1950s,
the sometimes independent-minded members of Nasser's Revolutionary
Command Council (RCC) had gradually given way in the 1960s to docile
technical and managerial personnel.

June 1967 was very much a turning point in regime-military relations.
Before then Abdul Hakim Amer had made of the military a key "center
of power," bound to his person by the loyalties of the officer corps. His
loyalty despite important qualifications ultimately went in turn to Nasser. Since the June defeat and Amer's alleged suicide, the situation has
been muddied. Army officers in the highest government posts became
rare, limited essentially to the ministries of war, war production, and
supply. The Egyptian military was called on less frequently to play a political role; under a call for a real return to the barracks, primary emphasis was to be placed on the task of confronting Israel.

However, there have been two important qualifications to this general
pattern during the Sadat years: Egypt's vice-president has remained a
military man (that has been true since 1952), and key decisions appear to
require, at a minimum, high-level military acquiescence. Two events

illustrate the pattern. In the tense spring of 1975 Sadat replaced Hussein el-Shafei, the last of the RCC members other than Sadat still in power, with air force commander Husni Mubarak. There had been intense speculation that the post would go to the civilian Sayid Marei, closely linked to Sadat. The president, though, chose to respect precedent and accord the post to a leading military figure.

Deference to the military was similarly in evidence in the critical autumn of 1977. In November of that year, when Sadat made his daring visit to Israel, great prominence was given to support of that decision by Minister of War and Commander in Chief Muhammad Gamassy, who was pictured in the forefront of the officials seeing Sadat off. The general's message to the president was widely quoted:

> The armed forces are aware of the dimensions and responsibilities of the present situation and are closely watching your courageous step toward a just peace. So, march ahead, Mr. President, with the blessings of God, and you have, from all members of the armed forces, greetings, esteem, and prayers for success.

Sadat in power had proved himself to be a "Man of Decision." Still, for each of his initiatives, and especially the boldest, he has sought and won overt displays of military support. Even though the precise mechanisms whereby that support is obtained remain elusive, Sadat's actions leave no doubt that he has understood that in extremis the army will remain the final arbiter in Egyptian political life.[58]

That understanding, though, has not meant the elimination of all signs of strain in Sadat's relations with the military. Consider the removal of General Muhammed Ahmed Sadek in the fall of 1972. Sadek, it will be recalled, had thrown his support to Sadat in the crucial May 1971 period. Sadat had rewarded the then chief of staff with the post of minister of defense. The president explained his subsequent dismissal of the general from that position by claiming that Sadek had failed to carry out "orders to prepare for the battle." It seems likely that more was involved. Possibly Sadat, like Khrushchev after a similar reliance on Marshal Zhukov to outmaneuver his political rival, feared Sadek's potential power. Such an interpretation finds some support in the persistent rumors that Sadek had been nettled by the presence of so many Soviet advisers in Egypt before their expulsion in July of 1972. That expulsion measure was very popular in Egypt and it is possible that Sadek was receiving credit for it, at least within the military. In addition, Sadat may have used the firing of Sadek, with his known Soviet antipathies, in order to secure resumption of Soviet military shipments. Whatever the complete story, the regime's interest in discrediting the general culminated in a December 1976 trial at which Sadek was convicted and given a one-year suspended sentence for torturing members of the armed forces. The nature of the charge, as well as the suspension of the sentence, suggests that the intent may have been to disarm a potential power threat by undercutting his support in the military, simultaneously avoiding a punishment so vindictive as to outrage the general's supporters. Despite the unknowns, the incident suggests that Sadat does not yet have a reliable formula to stabilize fully his relation to the military. The gap is an important one.[59]

A major impediment to effective political institutionalization in the Nasser years was the understood reality that power did not flow through the formal civilian channels, that military and security officials (aided by docile technocrats) held the key positions and made the critical decisions. That essential reality has not changed in Sadat's Egypt. Moreover, the personalization of power so characteristic of the Nasser era shows few signs of abatement. Patterns are still too recent to be as clearly discernible as those of the Nasser years; still, Sadat himself has drawn criticism for his close links, including familial ties, with prominent middle-class figures, such as Speaker of the People's Assembly Sayid Marei. Some fear the emergence of a Nasser-style "center of power" around the presidency, others see in these personal linkages a reflection of Sadat's more fundamental ties to an emerging, composite middle class, newly prosperous as a result of open-door liberalization. It is too soon for definitive judgments, apart from the realization that power in Sadat's Egypt retains its very personal face.

Sadat's "State of Institutions"

President Sadat (like Nasser before him) has spoken repeatedly of the sovereignty of the law and his aim to create a "state of institutions." But a close look at Egypt's major civilian institutions (the presidency, the parliament, the press, and the Arab Socialist Union) reveals that the undoubted liberalization during the Sadat years has not been grounded in such a state.

The presidency. Egypt's president is constitutionally a strong one who appoints vice presidents, a prime minister, his cabinet, and the governors of Egypt's twenty-four governorates or provinces. He is popularly elected after nomination by the parliament. Sadat has been elected twice in unopposed elections, with the people asked to vote yes or no on his candidacy. In addition to a veto power, the president has emergency powers to issue binding decrees when the parliament, by a two-thirds majority, delegates such authority.

In practice, virtually all important decisions in domestic and foreign affairs are made by the president and his staff. Furthermore, constitutional myths notwithstanding, the power of the president rests ultimately on his support in the military.

The parliament. It is true that the parliament, the unicameral People's Assembly, has played a larger role in the Sadat years than before. Particularly important has been the assembly's investigatory role. As controversial as its hearings on sequestration abuses have been its reports on Egypt's land reclamation program. An assembly subcommittee issued a report published in *al-Akhbar,* which concluded that despite the millions of pounds spent, one-fourth of the lands reclaimed from the Western Desert (in the so-called New Valley) were once again reverting to desert sand. The committee revealed that a drastic reduction of the irrigation budget for the area was responsible. In 1974 the assembly expanded its land-reclamation activities, sending specialists to all major land-reclamation areas. Spectacular press headlines resulted: in spite of the increased water from the High Dam, not one feddan had actually been added to Egypt's total agricultural land area. A closer look at the findings reveals that, under the pressure of Egypt's alarming population growth, agricultural land was being used for housing and commercial purposes. In addition, the investigating committee regaled the reading public with reports on corruption: *al-Akhbar* blamed the former centers of power; *al-Iqtisad* drew attention to planning and administrative deficiencies.[60]

The acerbity of parliamentary discussion and debate even of extremely sensitive issues has at times been surprising. Roughly ten months before the October War *al-Ahram* reported the comment of one Assembly member that "people have heard so much about preparation for the battle that they are fed up with slogans uttered here and there without result." The member went on to complain "about the problem of the youth who are in a state of anxiety over the lack of clarity in our basic problem, the liberation of our territory." Among other signs of the increased vitality of the parliament under Sadat is the fact that government ministers who report to the assembly at times have been subjected to harsh questioning and outspoken attacks on their performance.[61]

Despite these gains, it is still true that the parliament has no role in major policy decisions. John Waterbury of the American Universities Field Staff in Cairo, a close and reliable observer of the Egyptian scene, has summarized the method of the parliament's deliberations:

> The normal pattern . . . has been to tear a given policy to pieces in committee . . ., to give ample newspaper . . . coverage to the findings, and then to have the Assembly as a whole approve the policy with marginal modifications.[62]

In the fall of 1976 the legalization of a limited version of a multiparty system for the elections to the assembly held promise of making Egypt's parliament a more significant political forum. (That important development will be analyzed shortly as part of a review of the role of the Arab

Socialist Union.) So far in crucial policy areas, however, the assembly has been largely irrelevant.

The press. Alarmed by the riots of January 1977 and the defiant coverage of those events by the leftist press, Anwar es-Sadat moved to sharply circumscribe journalistic freedom. The press of the Sadat era became if anything even more conformist than during Nasser's years.

The initial liveliness of the press in the seventies obscured the fact that discussion of sensitive issues took place within fairly well defined boundaries. The Egyptian press since 1960 has been owned by Egypt's unique political party. Every journalist today has to be a member of the ASU, and all discussion in the press is to take place within the context of the "basic documents of the revolution": in practice, this has meant that the role of the press has been largely explanation and advocacy of government positions. Granted, Sadat has officially abolished censorship and it was possible, at least until January 1977, to identify with ease competing positions on as important an issue as the meaning of Nasser's legacy. Nevertheless, Sadat has set limits to the national dialogue on Egypt's recent past: on numerous occasions the president has stated categorically that he shared responsibility for every decision made in Egypt since the July revolution. By clearly identifying himself with the past, Sadat has set boundaries for the critical review of Nasser's legacy. Also instructive about the actual degree of autonomy of the press is the fate of M. H. Haikal, the most powerful journalist in Egypt during the Nasser era. When Haikal persisted in criticizing Sadat's American connection and in describing the result of the October War as "no victory, no defeat," Sadat in early 1974 removed him from the editorship of *al-Ahram*.[63]

The ASU. There remains the Arab Socialist Union, Egypt's sole political party during the Nasser era and the first years of Sadat's rule. At first Sadat showed no real interest in reviving the ASU after the failure of the "political solution" under Nasser. The subsequent attempt to use the ASU as one base for the coup attempt against him in 1971 did not endear the ASU to Sadat. The new president looked instead toward establishment of a market economy to develop Egypt. The ASU was thereby deprived of what was to have been its major role—that is, to constitute the driving force for Egypt's economic modernization. When Sadat's statement of evaluation and guidelines for the future of the ASU was published on August 9, 1974, it was clear that the organization, at least for the time being, was to play no major role in Sadat's Egypt. Ihsan Abdul Kudus, the journalist closest to Sadat, wrote in *al-Ahram*:

> In reality the ASU is an official organization, like any other governmental unit, and it could have been called the Ministry for Political and Popular Affairs.[64]

In the fall of 1974 Sadat revealed his real thinking about the ASU for the first time: he raised the issue of moving away from a one-party system. A parliamentary committee was appointed to consider the question of a return to multiparty politics in Egypt. During the first days of public debate, urban middle-class elements (represented by the professionals and intellectuals of Cairo and Alexandria) called for expanded political liberties and a restoration of party competition. Their voices were overwhelmed by the opposition of the members of Egypt's official "popular" organizations representing farmers, workers, women, and students. They rejected the political license of a multiparty system that would undermine the gains of the revolution. Sadat concluded from the debates that Egypt was not ready for a democratization of its political structure, and the issue was put aside for fifteen months.

In January 1976 Sadat reopened the debate. A new and more powerful commission was ordered by the president to consider once again the question of parties. This time Sadat identified himself with a moderate position between the advocates of continued one-party rule and those who called for the formation of additional parties. He warned of the dangers of excessive political fragmentation and took sharp exception to any possibility of the military being drawn into active political participation in any parties formed. But Sadat did argue that Egypt would benefit from a more active political life. He suggested that political "groupings" around right, left, and center platforms be formed within the ASU and allowed to compete in the fall elections to the People's Assembly.

In September of 1976 President Sadat, running unopposed in a referendum, was reelected to a second six-year term with 99.94 percent of the vote. Elections to the People's Assembly were held in October. The three political groupings engaged in a relatively free political contest, the first in Egypt since the party system was dismantled shortly after Nasser's revolution.

The right grouping, headed by a wealthy cotton broker, Mustapha Kamal Murad, called for a return to a capitalist system. The right platform advocated further liberalization of import policies, permission to open private banks, reform of the currency system, and a return of light industry to private hands.

The left grouping, headed by former Free Officer Khaled Muhieddin, warned against erosion of the socialist gains made by the Nasserist revolution. While defending the democratization of political life by Sadat, the left warned against a dismantling of the public sector.

The center grouping had official backing, represented in the leadership of that faction by Prime Minister Mamdouh Salem. Predictably, the center backed Sadat's "opening" strategy with its mixed economy of socialism and expanded private enterprise. Foreign policy was not an issue in the elections, with all three groupings reserving that domain exclusively to the president.

The election results gave the right group 12 seats, the left 2 seats, and the center 280 seats, with the remainder going to independents. Sadat, not surprisingly, declared the experiment a success. In November of 1976 he announced: "We are starting out on a new democratic experience." Sadat reinstituted a limited version of the prerevolutionary, multiparty political system. The left, right, and center groupings were henceforth to be called political parties. The ASU, however, was not to be dismantled. Rather it was to remain "far above" the new parties and in control of their budgets. The ASU would also continue to exercise its supervisory role over the press and organizations of women and youths.[65]

The president went on to explain that the parties were to respect certain further restrictions. They were to observe "national unity," with Sadat presumably acting as arbiter of the integrity of that vague concept. In addition, a provision reflecting concern over possible Moslem Brotherhood infiltration cautioned that the parties were not to function as religious groups. Finally, Egypt's new parties were not to undertake any actions that would deprive the masses of the social gains they had registered since the revolution. Again, the power to define the nature of those gains was reserved to the president. For all the reservations, Egyptians felt that Sadat's liberalization was bringing real gains. But the precariousness of those gains was revealed when the country was shaken by popular disturbances in January of 1977.

The January 1977 Riots

On January 18 and 19 massive demonstrations, the most destructive since the revolution, erupted in Egypt's major cities. Before order was restored an estimated 79 had been killed, 1,000 wounded, and 1,250 jailed.[66] The immediate cause of the rioting was the reduction of government price subsidies on such basic commodities as rice, sugar, and cooking gas. More fundamentally, the disturbances originated with the social strains generated by Sadat's open-door policy.

The official explanation attributed the rioting to leftist agitators. The country's chief prosecutor triumphantly announced in *al-Ahram* of January 26 that no less than four underground communist groups had been discovered. Three days later Prime Minister Mamdouh Salem extended the indictment of the Egyptian left by attacking the official left party headed by Khaled Muhieddin for its "shameful involvement" in the disturbances. "Many communist elements," the prime minister alleged, had infiltrated the new party and tried to use it to "overthrow the government and install a communist regime."[67]

For the regime the explanation was undoubtedly a useful one. Blame for what was from all indications a spontaneous and massive social protest could be deflected to the small and vulnerable left. Furthermore, attacks on communists and leftist radicals could be counted on to mask for the United States and conservative Arab states the incongruity of Sadat's public pledge on January 29, 1977. Even as massive arrests were made of those who had protested, he promised not to renege on his democratization policies.

The grand sheik of al Azhar, Egypt's ancient Islamic university, issued "a serious warning" on January 21, 1977, that Saudi Arabia, Kuwait, and United Arab emirates must come to Egypt's help. Dr. Abdul Halim Mahmoud sounded the warning in a sermon broadcast via Radio Cairo, which can be heard throughout the Arab world. By January 22 the conservative Arab states had rallied with a billion-dollar aid pledge aimed at keeping Sadat in power. By February 1 the United States announced that it would transfer $190 million in allocated aid funds for immediate use to meet the crisis.

Whatever the profitability of the official explanation, it obscures a revealing lesson of the January disturbances. For in those two days of protest thousands of Egyptians offered the judgment that the social costs of Sadat's opening were too high. At the height of the demonstrations some thirty thousand protestors battled the police in Cairo alone. The social content of their protest was reflected both in the slogans chanted and in the targets of their anger. Sadat's market strategy had widened the social cleavages in Egypt, producing (it was commonly believed) several hundred new millionaires at the expense of Egypt's poor. The demonstrators, most of them young men, shouted "Down with Sadat!" and "Nasser, Nasser, Nasser!" On Cairo's streets Nasser's welfare concessions of price controls and direct subsidies had not been forgotten. One of the most popular chants was: "With blood and lives we will bring prices down." Favorite targets were symbols of the new wealth in Egypt, such as the large American and German cars that were stoned and burned. Despite the reticence of the regime on the issue (for fear of offending conservative Arabs), it also seems plausible that elements of the Moslem Brotherhood were involved. Several night clubs on the "golden strip" leading to the pyramids—anathema to the religious right—were ransacked.

The failure to foresee that subsidy price cuts would push Egypt's urban poor to revolt confirmed early impressions that Sadat, for all the adroitness of his political and diplomatic maneuvering, was a man with a shallow understanding of social issues and little taste for the tasks of day-to-day governance. In pursuing his narrow economic strategy, he had taken the advice of foreign economic experts and ignored impressive evidence of growing domestic political unrest. The decision to remove the price subsidies was taken in response to the pressures of the experts of the International Monetary Fund (IMF), the U.S. government, American private banks, and the governments of Saudi Arabia and Kuwait—pressures Nasser in his day had denounced as "collective colonialism." Egypt, the foreign experts argued, simply could not afford such socialist welfare measures.

The first indication that Sadat was finding the bankers' arguments persuasive came in November 1976. Sadat rearranged the cabinet to create a powerful new post of deputy prime minister for financial and economic affairs and selected Dr. Abdul Moneim el-Kaissouny, chairman of the Arab International Bank for the position. Dr. Kaissouny, respected in Western economic circles as an advocate of fiscal restraint, was placed in charge of four cabinet ministers all dealing with economic matters.

The new economic team made the decision to cut the subsidies on narrow economic grounds. One minister explained:

Last year we had a budget deficit of over $2 billion. When we came into the Cabinet, we decided this must be reduced. Of the four key budget items—military, investment, subsidies, and debt service—it was decided that the subsidies were the only expendable item.[68]

Overlooked was the use of the subsidy program as a form of material incentive to secure mass loyalty to the regime. And such incentives were especially critical in the troubled years after 1967. Costs of the program had skyrocketed from $175 million in 1972 to $1.7 billion in 1976. The cuts enacted in January were intended to contribute $600 million toward reducing a projected budget deficit of $3.250 billion, according to an interview by Dr. Kaissouny in *Akhbar al-Yaum* immediately after the riots. The new ministers hoped that such belt tightening would induce the IMF, private Western banks, and other potential donors to supply the remainder to meet the deficit in low-interest loans. It was also felt that foreign investors might be favorably impressed by these signs of Egyptian financial responsibility. And so the ministers acted swiftly and without concern for political consequences. Later one minister explained: "The problem was it was a bad strategy. We are not trained politicians. We did not anticipate trouble."[69]

There had in fact been ample signs of political discontent with Sadat's economic orientation. In January of 1975, workers had smashed stalled commuter trains and marched through Cairo taunting and ridiculing Sadat for the inflation, food shortages, and corruption that had dimmed his reputation as the Hero of the Crossing. In March 1975, forty thousand textile workers struck in the delta town of Mahalla. Clashes with the police resulted in one death, a score of injuries, and over thirty arrests. In

September of 1976, striking bus drivers in Cairo battled army strike-breakers with stones and clubs until police armed with machine guns cordoned off the bus terminal area. In November 1976, five hundred left-wing students demonstrated in Cairo to demand that they be allowed to form parties in addition to the three official ones allowed by Sadat. Student leaders argued that the formation of parties "should not be imposed from above."[70]

The indications were there, but Sadat and his ministers were heeding other voices. Grand economic strategy was made by presidential decree and was attuned, as in the Nasser years, to global and regional opportunities. Sadat was determined to pursue his open door despite the opposition and despite the disappointing results the policy had achieved. He continued to pin his hopes—and Egypt's—on a regional settlement that would bring stability, which would in turn bring foreign investors to Egypt. Sadat's economic advisers indicated that the subsidy cut, rescinded when the poor revolted, would be reinstated gradually. In his 1977 May Day address to Egyptian workers and union leaders, Sadat responded to their pleas "to relieve the workers of the pressures of life and living conditions" with the reply: "Wait until 1980." By 1980, Sadat reasoned, he would have secured his agreement with Israel and the "market solution" would begin to bring relief. In the meantime, to contain and placate the masses, there were to be foreign policy successes, continued domestic liberalization—and repression, if necessary. Sadat had used the police and the army in January 1977: he would do so again.[71]

Nasser's death did mark the end of an era, and Sadat did bring changes to Egypt's political life. But to stress change is not to deny continuity. The move to the right, begun by Nasser himself, was consolidated both domestically and internationally by Sadat. As a development strategy, the open door promised rescue from economic ruin. That promise has been slow of fulfillment. But the adoption of a right strategy was a reflection of more than Sadat's personal political predilections. It was conditioned by an international configuration of power changed by superpower détente and Arab petro-dollars.

An Egypt of limited resources and exploding population, whoever its leader, was constrained to respond. For Egypt can develop neither on its own nor unmoved by the poles of attraction created by the superpowers. The October War did demonstrate that Egypt had some scope for independent action. Ultimately that independence could be used only to give particular form and content to Egypt's global dependency. An Egypt on the verge of collapse could no longer afford the equivocations of the Nasser era. In the seventies Sadat made a series of hard choices: for the Nasserist right orientation over the left; for the Americans over the Soviets;

for the market solution and foreign investment over an intensification of the revolution; for incentives to middle-class elements over the immediate welfare of the masses; and finally in the fall of 1977 for a dramatic peace initiative over another war or continued stalemate with Israel. Domestically, Sadat with his "gamble on the future" has only begun to dismantle the basic institutional legacy of Nasser. He has set in motion pressures, especially class pressures, that one day may in fact bring more fundamental changes.

PART TWO

TRANSFORMING EGYPT

The long years of Free Officer rule brought more than order and relative stability to Egypt: they brought the promise of thoroughgoing social revolution. Egypt, freed of colonial dependency, was to be remade.

No society, least of all an authoritarian one, is unconstrained in its critiques of its fundamental myths. But by the late sixties the collective voice of Egyptian literature in the whispers of its metaphors and allusions had delivered an indictment of the revolution: Free Officer rule had not fulfilled its promise of a renewed political community.

In his 1968 play, *The Buffet,* Aly Salem subtly portrayed the dilemma of Egyptians enmeshed in the oppressive social structures of Egypt's stalled revolution. (The play is available in an English translation by John Waterbury, from which the quotations below are taken.) Salem's work has three players: a theater manager, an author, and a waiter from the snack bar or buffet of the theater. The controlling force is a "contract" that binds the players. The main action takes place in the manager's office, which is furnished with two chairs: one behind an impressive desk for the manager and another for the author who comes to talk to the manager about producing his play. The contract provides that whoever sits in the manager's chair gives orders, whoever sits in the visitor's chair is forced by the waiter to obey them. The actual coercion takes place in the buffet.

The plot of *The Buffet* is simple: the manager orders the author to revise his play and thereby compromise his art. When the author refuses, the expressionless waiter is bound by the contract to enforce the order. For Egyptians, subject to the endless tyrannies of bureaucrats both powerful and petty, the meaning of Salem's work is clear and moving. Lives are regulated by the logic of the contract. Symbolic of the social mechanisms of the bureaucratic feudalism of Free Officer rule, the contract is brutal and corrupting in its violation of the creative striving for liberation represented by the author.

In the course of the play the author, after a beating by the waiter in the buffet, succeeds in gaining the manager's chair and the power that goes with it. To no avail. For now the author finds himself caught in the manager's repressive role: *the contract cannot be broken.* Dispirited, the author remarks to the manager (p. 18):

> Neither you nor I know how to close the buffet, nor how to change the contract. The owner of the buffet is still on top coming up with a contract like that.

Salem ends the play with the author, damaged in body and spirit, giving the manager back his chair and accepting payment for acquiescence in the violation of his art (pp. 18-19):

> (The manager sits down again in his chair and the author begins to do the revisions)
>
> AUTHOR: We take out the second act (he tears up Act II and throws it in the waste basket). The hero becomes a woman . . . the woman becomes a man . . . we'll put some dancing in here . . . and some songs in here . . . and we'll change this . . . and condense that . . . and make nonsense of this . . . and take out you son of a bitch . . . and put in you son of heaven . . . the actors will be in the theatre and the spectators on the stage . . . anyone can sit any place . . . any place can sit on anyone . . . anyone can say anything . . . anything can say anyone. O.K., here's the play. Give me the loot.
>
> (the manager gives him a big wad of bills)
>
> AUTHOR: (feeling the money) It'll be great, it'll go a long way.
>
> MANAGER: It'll be fantastic!
>
> AUTHOR: What are you talking about?
>
> MANAGER: About the play.
>
> AUTHOR: I'm talking about the money.

The causes of the deficiencies of Free Officer rule have already been made apparent on the national plane. The original lack of ideological coherence, the disadvantages of the secretive and conspiratorial organizational structure, the quickness of the 1952 revolution, the failure to forge popular ties, the alienation of the intellectuals—all these factors and more limited the initial competence of the Free Officers for the tasks they had assumed. Yet out of the immediate demands of the struggle to gain and keep power, and out of the experience of the flawed attempts to launch an effective strategy of socioeconomic development, the regime of bureaucratic feudalism took shape.

The case studies that follow give as concrete a sense as possible of the more immediate social and institutional situations confronted by Egyptians working in industry, agriculture, and rural health. Primary attention is given to the crystallization during the Nasser years of the essential character of these environments, although important subsequent changes are considered. In these chapters will be seen the ways in which the center of power, personalized and bureaucratic, became the prototypic mechanism of social control in the new Egypt. The pattern was replicated throughout Egyptian society with devastating results. Egyptians working in all spheres have found themselves trapped, like the characters in Aly Salem's play, in a network of repressive social structures, their creative energies and generosity of spirit dissipated and subverted.

7. Managers and
the New Industrial Order

Of the many transformations undergone since 1952 none has been more decisive in determining the character of Egypt's present and the shape of its future than the drive to industrialize. In Egypt, as everywhere, industrialization has placed a premium on the managerial skills necessary to organize the human and material resources for the creation of an industrial order; commitment to an industrial revolution unavoidably entailed the creation of a managerial elite. Although the Free Officers were able to absorb the managers into their system of rule without diluting their own supreme authority, the control mechanisms to ensure political subservience of the managers complicated the regime's industrial relations. Ambiguities in both the institutional and ideological expressions of Egypt's socialism made it difficult to achieve an effective, working environment for top-level industrial personnel.

INDUSTRIALIZATION UNDER NASSER

During the years of Nasser's rule Egypt did make considerable industrial progress. In 1950, industry contributed 21 percent of total national output; by 1970, that figure had increased to 38 percent. Furthermore, the products of Egyptian industry were more diversified and complex. Unfortunately, the achievements of Nasser's industrialization drive were undercut by rapid population growth and the mounting costs of the confrontation with Israel. Furthermore, there were inherent limitations to the system of industrial relations established by the revolutionary regime. In important part the flawed character of the regime's industrial performance resulted from the lack of clarity of its socialist orientation.[1]

Nasser changed Egypt's economy from a basically free-enterprise system in 1952 to one where key production decisions and nearly all investment decisions were made by the state; and this arrangement he officially described as socialist. But for Nasser socialism really meant only two things: the most rapid, state-directed modernization possible and a measure of social welfare for the people of Egypt. Egypt's economic transformation was not the result of planned adherence to a clearly defined socialist ideology. Instead, the public sector was created by a series of political decisions important for consolidation of the regime's power. The early agrarian reforms involved the government in agricultural planning. The nationalization of the Suez Canal Company in 1956 set the precedent that led to the Egyptianization of the banks in 1957 and their nationalization in 1960. By the early sixties the government owned and operated all large-scale industries. In the Charter of 1962 the demise of market capitalism was consecrated. However, Egypt's socialism was described as providing for a mixed economy, with a private sector concentrated in light industry, land holdings, and domestic trade coexisting with the powerful new public sector.[2]

In theory, the activities of the public sector were to be regulated by a tight organizational structure and the relation of the public sector to the private sector was to be controlled by a system of central planning. The administration of the public sector was plugged directly into the ministerial system, immediately subordinate to the president. Public sector functions were divided into five major categories: industry, finance, trade, marketing, and communications. Responsibility for each category was delegated to an appropriate minister, who was to exercise that responsibility through public corporations (similar to holding companies) that grouped related industries.

In the industrial sphere nine corporations were set up for mining, foodstuffs, textiles, chemicals, building materials and refractories, metals, engineering, petroleum, and small industries. All industrial manufacturing companies were grouped under these nine corporations in product-related clusters. In the public sector generally, a four-step authority flow has thus been established: from president to minister to corporation chairman of the board to company chairman of the board.

Coordination of economic affairs both within the public sector and between the public and private sectors was to be achieved by comprehensive economic planning. Desultory attempts at overall planning had been made prior to the nationalization decrees of the early sixties. In August of 1961 a new Ministry of Planning was set up, which absorbed all previous planning agencies. Two ten-year plans subsequently were announced for the periods 1960 to 1970 and 1973 to 1982.[3]

In operation the organizational and planning structures have proved far less efficient than this schematic presentation might suggest. The essentially political character of the motivations that prompted the nationalizations and the creation of the public sector has meant that there is no central economic theory underlying the administrative arrangement of the economy. Furthermore, while the first five-year segment (1960 to 1965) of the first ten-year plan was carefully executed, that achievement was eroded by the political and security difficulties later in the sixties as Egypt's revolution stalled and confrontation with Israel produced disaster. The Planning Ministry was unable to insulate itself from these pressures. It had never become an independent locus of economic power, despite the fact that 90 percent of investment decisions were in the hands of the government. The ministry functioned rather as a kind of statistical bureau. Actual investment decisions appear to have been made within the planning services of the individual ministries to which corporations and their enterprises were attached. The second five-year segment of the plan was vaguely formulated, poorly executed, and eventually overwhelmed by the disruptions of the 1967 war. Until Sadat's announcement of the beginning of the second ten-year plan on January 1, 1973, Egypt was really without a comprehensive economic program.

Officially, the regime has described Egypt's economic system as one that combines socialism with the best elements of capitalism. The ad hoc character of the emergence of the public sector is explained as part of the leadership's pragmatic approach to the economy. Disruptions of the planning process are explained as resulting from bureaucratic inefficiencies and the crush of external events. Such a description is misleading if it is understood to mean that Egypt's rulers have made the critical decisions affecting the economy essentially on their economic merits. Egypt's rulers have been pragmatic, but their pragmatism has been a response to the exigencies of power consolidation and the demands of foreign policy with the aim of creating a strong and independent Egypt. This fact has had curious results. In the Egypt of the Nasser era one found socialism without socialists and without a coherent socialist theory to guide the organization of the economy. In the Sadat era one finds the persistence of the socialist label for a development strategy that looks to an open-market arrangement.

These anomalies have not resulted, as might be thought, primarily from deficiencies in political vision of the leadership. Rather, Nasser was acutely sensitive to the necessity of preserving his hold on power and using that power to shape his regime in a way that would allow for the maximum extraction of resources from outside Egypt. Underlying the radical shifts in the nature of Egyptian "socialism" and the developmental strategies embodied in them was a creative response to the changed character of the external environment. Nasser early realized that Egypt's domestic resource base was so meager that the prospects for economic development were inextricably linked to Egypt's position in the world. It is this linkage that explains the regime's ambiguous and changing conception of socialism. For example, as the global configuration of power shifted in the sixties from the sharp bipolar Cold War confrontation to the era of superpower cooperation and détente, Nasser and then his successor adjusted the economic form of Egypt's revolution in order to continue to derive advantages from an external environment they could not control. A move to the right, initiated by Nasser and consolidated by Sadat, signaled the end of the period of competitive superpower bidding and a closer identification with the United States. From such an identification, it was judged, Egypt in the seventies would draw greater benefit. Sadat's leading economic advisers were therefore given the task of reopening the Egyptian economy. The major corporations nationalized by Nasser were not returned to the private sector. But movement toward a more market-oriented economy was begun in June 1974 with the passage of parliamentary laws encouraging the formation of new private sector firms to compete with the state sector enterprises and set standards for price and quality.[4]

THE ROLE OF THE MANAGERS

The radical shifts in the regime's approach to structuring the industrial order resulted from rational choices made by the leadership in the international realm. To recognize them as such is not to minimize the problems such changes have created in the domestic arena. If, as Sadat has affirmed, "Egypt's future depends on industrialization," then the regime in turn depends on the industrial managers.[5] In the Egyptian case the political leadership must not simply deal with the classic problems of securing the loyalty of the managers while guaranteeing their efficiency; it must do so in a setting without stable ideological or structural moorings.

Egypt's industrial managers are a hand-picked group. From the beginning assignment of personnel to fill the leading roles in the public sector has been the direct concern of the highest political authorities. Nasser set the pattern by his personal choice of Aziz Sidki in 1956 as Egypt's first minister of industry. (Later, after the nationalizations of 1961-63, selection of the chairmen of the boards of public sector corporations and enterprises was centralized in the Higher Supervision Committee presided over by Nasser's friend Abdul Hakim Amer, who was then first vice-president.) Aziz Sidki, with a doctorate from Harvard, had attracted Nasser's attention a year before his appointment by his professional competence when acting as a guide for the president in one of the agencies Nasser was visiting. The appointment of an unknown, unconnected with the Free Officers, to such a key position was a departure from Nasser's usual practice. It was an early indication that in the formation of the managerial corps for public sector enterprises considerations of technical expertise would rank high. Profiles of the managerial personnel actually selected for thirty-seven of the thirty-eight public corporations confirmed that impression. *Al-Ahram* of May 25, 1962 described the pool of 301 new managers as including 57 engineers and scientists and 57 holders of doctorates. The remaining 187 were divided between high state officials, army officers, and former company officials who were typically trained in law and business. More recent studies of the industrial managers suggest that the patterns of a generally high educational level, a new prominence of engineering backgrounds, and a comparatively low military profile have endured.[6]

The Manager as Technocrat

The strong representation of engineers among the public sector directors has led to the frequent characterization of Egypt's managers as the technocratic partners of the ruling military elite. Substantiating such a view is the fact that the financial rewards and opportunities for advancement offered the public sector managers tend to be more generous than in the civil service or even in the military. Leftist Egyptians have been particularly disturbed by the huge wage differentials prevalent in the public sector, which set the managers apart as a privileged segment of Egyptian society.[7]

Still, "partners" is a far too expansive term to describe the relationship of the regime with the managers. Furthermore, fears voiced by the leftists over the potential emergence of a technocratic class with a capacity to subvert the revolution are exaggerated. The managers have not been able to secure an independent base within the industrial system. They serve completely at the discretion of the highest political authorities. If Nasser's choice of the unknown Sidki represented a concession to considerations of efficiency, it by no means signaled an abdication of control. Before making his selection, Nasser had given himself a full year to determine Sidki's political loyalty. Haikal reported that Nasser had implied as much to Sidki: "I have selected you without knowing you. We talked only one time . . . Since that time I have followed you." Still more explicit was Nasser's observation on the ultimate limit to the latitude Sidki would enjoy: "I will leave you considerable freedom but will ask for an account later."[8]

The managers of the individual enterprises similarly are held directly accountable to the Higher Supervision Committee, which not only makes initial selections but plays a continuing watchdog role. And from the decisions of the political elite the managers have no recognized means of redress. During an interview with an *al-Jumhuriyyah* correspondent, a leading public sector manager pointed to a delivery man standing in his office and complained:

I cannot fire this man, while the responsible minister could fire me, if I would not for one reason or another make him happy . . . In case

I was unfair to this deliveryman, he would go to the workers' court and press charges, while the law does not make it clear where I should go to defend myself if anything of that nature happened.

The surveillance of the political authorities is given an additional cutting edge because the financial rewards enjoyed by the managers are directly controlled and manipulated by top-level appointees. Article 28 of the Statute on Employees of the Public Sector provided that the amount of the all-important expense allowances granted to the factory manager shall be determined by presidential decree.[9]

This direct political control indicates that loyalty has been as significant as efficiency in appointing Egypt's managers. Relatively well endowed with highly skilled personnel, Egypt's leaders have enjoyed a latitude uncommon in the Third World to choose carefully among qualified people. But there have been ample signs that if Egypt's leaders could not have both loyalty and efficiency, loyalty was the preferred commodity. This general pattern was set as early as 1954 when, during the Nasser-Naguib power struggle, the educated classes had sided predominantly with Naguib. From that experience Nasser deduced this lesson: priority was to be given to political reliability over both experience and know-how.[10]

Considerations of political loyalty helped produce diversity in the managerial corps. For although the engineers have occupied a strong position, other groups with secure ties to the political elite are represented as well. The presence of such nontechnical elements has not gone unremarked by Egyptian commentators. Hossam Issa, an instructor of the Faculty of Law at the University of Assiut, has forcefully argued that considerations of political loyalty have considerably weakened the technocratic complexion of the managerial corps: "The public enterprises are peopled with newcomers of the revolution, without technical competence in the precise sense (officers, jurists, etc.)"[11]

One major group of these nontechnocratic newcomers has been the bureaucrats from the various government agencies. Haikal has written colorfully of "a large number of leaders of the traditional government apparatus which have broken with it in order to sail in the new ocean." More prosaically, Haikal suggested that the higher salaries in the public sector industries have provided the motivation for the shift.[12]

The Manager as Bureaucrat

The presence of a large number of bureaucrats among the managers has led some commentators to view the managerial corps as just one more offshoot of the Egyptian bureaucracy.[13] The strong position of the engineers (which would not be characteristic of the traditional state apparatus) suggests the limitations of such a view. Nevertheless, the bureaucrats are present in the industrial managerial corps, and they have made their presence felt by transferring bureaucratic attitudes and methods into the new industrial domain.

In his interview with Aziz Sidki, the first minister of industry, Nasser at the outset made explicit his intention to rescue the institutional structure in industry from traditional bureaucratic influences: "I would like you to create a new administrative organ for this task without being bound by what already exists."[14] That effort failed.

A flood of material from the Egyptian press indicates that the nationalized enterprises have functioned like government agencies and their staffs like civil servants. A preoccupation with statistics and reports designed to please the higher authorities has become characteristic of Egypt's managers. Haikal has offered the persuasive judgment that such concern with paperwork has led the managers to "ignore the large questions which determine the march of production."[15]

The contamination of the enterprises by bureaucratic methods was reinforced by specific measures taken by the regime on social welfare grounds. Productivity was adversely affected by the government's employment drive of 1961-62, which compelled managers to overstaff their enterprises. A graded system of salary levels was first introduced in 1963. With that system came mechanical procedures for the determination of wages and advancement, which have guaranteed employee remuneration largely independent of productivity. Strong disincentive effects have been the result throughout industry. Other reforms instituted in 1963 made it extremely difficult to dismiss employees, so that problems of factory discipline were heightened. Such political measures, whatever their justifications, have seriously weakened the authority of managerial staffs within the factories.[16]

The Illusion of Cohesiveness

The diversity of the recruitment sources for industrial managers, their dependent political status, and the sharp limitations on their authority within the industrial enterprise suggest caution in viewing the managers as a strong and cohesive elite. There is, for example, a clear difference in outlook between those managers with technical training and those recruited from the government agencies. While such distinctions cannot be established with great precision, Haikal has conveyed the flavor of managerial diversity by focusing on their varying responses to incipient bureaucratization. While some directors have resisted the encroachment of bureaucratic methods, others, according to Haikal, have welcomed it as the proper method of proceeding. Thus, he wrote of the "tendency of certain directors to believe that the new units of production are only hiring agencies for workers, to which the socialist laws apply, and that this is the desired goal." Such a view, Haikal suggested, "relieves the units of production of their primary reason for being, that is, production." He also reported on the evasion of responsibility of managers with such views by their deferral of all decisions to higher authorities on the pattern so typical of the Egyptian state bureaucracy. By contrast, Haikal found other directors engaged in an active struggle to preserve their freedom of initiative against incipient bureaucratization. These men complained to the political authorities of the restrictions placed upon them and were critical of fellow managers who fostered paper-shuffling behavior.[17]

In March of 1967 President Nasser met with the heads of public sector companies to discuss their problems in a so-called Production Congress. The extensive transcripts of the ensuing debates, published the same month in *al-Jumhuriyyah,* contain revealing evidence of the resentments and antagonisms within the managerial corps. The manager of the Nasr Company for Foreign Trade, Muhammed Ahmed Ghanem, made an eloquent plea for expansion of the scope of initiative of the managers and curtailment of nonproductive paperwork:

> There is, Mr. President, the question of reports. Planning requires reports. But I regret to tell Your Excellency that too many reports actually are made . . . Every service is entitled to request reports and you can be sure that most of those reports are useless. They may sometimes serve some purpose, but that is a constant routine work which involves loss of time and energy. The time which I may spend writing a report is wasted, whereas I might usefully spend the same time doing something else for production.

Ghanem had been stung by the criticism and punishment handed out to managers who demonstrated initiative in contrast to the success of managers who adopted a "do-nothing, play it safe" attitude. In an open attack on such managers, he urged Nasser:

> However, we might change that situation; just as we try those who have made some mistake, we might also try those who just do nothing at all. We must be active and such inaction might contribute to hinder people . . . We hope that those who are afraid to go ahead or slip should also be subject to legal regulation.

Ghanem concludes with an allusion to the poisoned nature of relations among the managers with a criticism of the practice of "some of our brothers to inform against their colleagues."[18]

In response Nasser acknowledged the difficulties and suspicions among the managers, attributing them to the fact that Egypt was going through a period of transition. There were as yet no regularized patterns of human relations in industry, Nasser argued; consequently, there were bound to be struggles for power and privilege among the managerial personnel. Nasser is unquestionably correct in his view that the conflicts among the managers were symptomatic of the broader problems of a society in transition. There is a self-serving facileness to his explanation, for he ignores the question of what measures the regime has taken to ameliorate the inevitable problems of a society undergoing industrialization. Still, from such discussions the minimal conclusion can be drawn that the frequently presumed group cohesiveness of the managers is much more a figment of the imagination of interpreters of Egyptian developments than a reflection of the actual character of the relationships among managers. The fears of the Egyptian leftists who see the managers as the spearhead of a technocratic elite, or the hopes of Western commentators prone to view the managers as the organized spokesmen for rational economic policies, are equally exaggerated.[19]

A close study of the actual functioning of the system of industrial relations created by the revolutionary regime reveals a pervasive sense of insecurity and even fear as the outstanding characteristic of the managers. Egyptian commentators write openly of the "complex of fear," or "frightened management," as the primary enemy of increased productivity. Haikal stated bluntly that, despite a manager's apparent security at the apex of industrial arrangements, "he does not feel himself to be in an atmosphere of security. He feels that the more he strives to serve the less are his chances of surviving." The managers' lack of a strong sense of unity has undoubtedly been one contributing factor to this sense of insecurity. Its roots lie much deeper, however: ideologically and institutionally, the functional role of the manager has been systematically undermined.[20]

The Problem of Ideology

In a fundamental way it might be more accurate to say that ideologically there simply has been no provision for the managers' role. Arab socialism was articulated essentially as a response to power considerations and was affected much more by developments in international affairs than by domestic social circumstances. While the functional importance of the manager was realized on a practical level, the official ideology assigned the manager no clear-cut status. Furthermore, vague aspirations for improvement of the condition of the Egyptian masses were expressed by Nasser in terms of a desire to close the gap between classes. This formulation proved difficult to reconcile with the very considerable rewards offered to the industrial managers and in fact lent those perquisites an aura of ideological illegitimacy.

Thus exposed, the managers have consistently been the targets of virulent attacks in the Egyptian press. Leftists have led the assault, apparently finding the theme a popular one. Aly Sabry, head of the Arab Socialist Union, expressed a harsh leftist view of the managerial elite in a series of articles that appeared daily in *al-Jumhuriyyah* in the months prior to the June 1967 war. Sabry's basic theme was the abuse of privileges by key public sector personnel; he articulated leftist fears that such elements constituted the spearhead of a new class that threatened the revolution.[21]

By the time of the 1967 Production Congress, Nasser had become alarmed at the unsettling effect such attacks were having on the managers and, indirectly, on production. In his prefatory remarks to the congress he rose to the managers' defense. Nasser spoke warmly of the managers as a select and capable elite, an essential vanguard that directed the work of a growing industrial network of 48 corporations and 384 companies with an annual production amounting to $3.12 billion. Given the background of the leftist ideological attacks on the managers, identified especially with Aly Sabry and the ASU, Nasser's stout and public defense of their interests was the occasion for an unusual and dramatic public airing of the ideological debate and confusion prevailing at top government levels. And the exchange was taking place openly in the press. Thus, on February 28, 1967, Sabry asserted:

> However, it appears that in fact many of those who hold the levers of command in the nationalized enterprises and corporations of the public sector have carried out devious procedures for exploiting that sector while striving to maintain their positions for the longest possible time.

At the Production Congress (which met in mid-March), in what can only be read as a direct response, Nasser commented:

> What annoys me more than whatever may be written about deviations is the way they describe the top executives and the public sector, picturing the top executives as profiteers! Are all our top executives profiteers?

For all the extravagance of the rhetoric, the ideological issues raised by Sabry and the leftists could not be taken lightly. If there did exist considerable doubt about the accuracy of labeling the managers technocrats or bureaucrats, one thing was clear to everyone: they were not socialists. Given Nasser's stated commitment to the "inevitability" of the socialist solution for Egypt, the privileged material position accorded the managers created a sensitive situation. That sensitivity was played upon by the leftists with considerable skill and enthusiasm.[22]

At the Production Congress Nasser responded to implicit charges that the regime in its treatment of the managers had abandoned its socialist commitment. Nasser's comments are revealing both as a reflection of the ideological differences undermining the coherence of the top leadership groups (notably the increasing alienation of Sabry and the leftists concentrated in the Arab Socialist Union) and as an exposition of Nasser's own views as Egypt entered the late sixties. Nasser began by accepting the obvious: there were managers who were not socialists. However, he went on to argue that although a socialist order was being created in Egypt, "those who are building socialism are not necessarily socialists."[23] The reason for the employment of such nonsocialists, Nasser stated simply, was the necessity of exploiting their technical competence for industrialization.

The leftist response to this argument was not long in coming. In a particularly biting *al-Jumhuriyyah* article in April 1967, Sabry attacked "reactionary elements" who had infiltrated the public sector, justifying themselves by creating "a deceitful aureole around themselves inducing belief in their capacity and incomparable experience." Sabry stated flatly that "the experience, the knowledge and the capacity of these individuals is devoted essentially to exploitation, domination, and arbitrariness." This forceful response constituted a ringing indictment of public sector malpractices. In fact, the preceding summer Nasser had already announced that the state would take over much of the construction industry in order to restrict the potential scope for such deviations in the interstice between the public and private sectors. Sabry, though, was apparently dissatisfied and was spreading the corruption indictment more widely to undermine the managers of the public sector.[24]

Nasser was unwilling to go that far. Nor was he impressed by the implicit assumptions of the leftists that they could do a better job of managing Egypt's public sector. At the Production Congress Nasser went to considerable lengths to make it clear that he was not naive concerning the dangers of assigning a key role to nonsocialists in the socialist transformations. He insisted that, on the other hand, simply believing in socialism was not enough to make one an effective operative in industry: "other people may be socialists, but that does not necessarily mean that they are technicians." While this consideration provided the ultimate rationale for Nasser's support of the managers, the leftists were unimpressed. Dr. Fuad Mursi, a noted economist and former professor of the Faculty of Law of Alexandria University, presented the leftist position most cogently in the course of a round-table discussion published in *al-Katib*. Mursi spoke of the need to harness popular energies so "human investments . . . can replace financial investments.'' He argued that the masses would ''perform miracles and offer any sacrifice'' provided that complete responsibility was placed in their hands. Nasser responded that he could never accept such a strategy based on the miracles of popular enthusiasm as an alternative to reliance on the technical expertise of the managers. If the rejection of such a strategy meant that Egypt's development had to be purchased at the price of large wage differentials and even the rise of a new class, that cost would have to be paid:

> Some people may say that there exists a new class. You must have heard that. Let me tell you that there actually exist many new classes, but I see nothing wrong in that as far as our society—or the socialist society which we are building—is concerned. On the contrary. Without this new class—managers and directors—we would not be able to effect . . . any socialist change. The difference between ourselves and other countries which are unable to effect any socialist change and follow the path of socialism to self-sufficiency and justice, is that they have no competent cadres—such as we have here. We are privileged to have technical cadres. They must therefore receive salaries and enjoy special privileges, because they provide knowledge and experience—and they make production run. Without this new class—managers and directors—we would not be able to effect any socialist change.[25]

And so debate raged, with the managers paying the cost of this ideological confusion. They obviously could not feel secure—no matter how privileged and despite Nasser's support—as long as such influential elements as the leftists in the ASU regarded their position as fundamentally illegitimate.

The Deficiencies of the Institutional Framework

These ideological ambiguities were not the only factors that accounted for the general lack of confidence at the upper levels of management. The institutional arrangements of the public sector industries were also far from satisfactory from the perspective of the manager.

Located at the bottom of the four-step hierarchy from president to minister to corporation head to enterprise head, the manager found his authority considerably diluted by a plethora of administrative control agencies, including the Central Agency for Audit, the Central Agency for Administration and Organization, and the Legal Department. Moreover, investigations by these agencies were to be carried out, according to President Nasser, ''without the knowledge of the chairmen of the board of the company or institution.'' The problems of operating under such multiple surveillance were increased by the fact that the manager had, to begin with, no clear definition of the scope of his authority within the administrative hierarchy and particularly vis-à-vis the corporation to which his company was attached.[26]

During the years immediately following the nationalizations and up to 1966, there was a strong tendency toward centralization. All important decisions made by a manager had to be ratified by the corporation to which his enterprise was attached before they could be implemented; the ratification procedure had to take place within a thirty-day limit. Given the uncertainties of his position and the penalties for mistakes, the manager's behavior tended to reinforce this centralization as he pushed as much responsibility as possible on the higher levels.[27]

In 1966 an attempt was made to reduce centralization and to strengthen the position of the enterprise manager in the industrial hierarchy. The areas of decision that required ratification by the corporation were reduced to the annual budget, the financial statements, and the procedural regulations and organizational structure. The corporation's role was restricted to a general supervisory one, while the industrial manager, responsible for achieving the objectives of the economic unit, was granted the necessary authority to enable him to fulfill his obligations. But the actual provisions of the 1966 statute defining the respective spheres of authority were vague. The key article provided:

> The general organization shall specialize in supervision and control, in arranging and steering performance with regard to the economic units that are subordinated to the organization but with no interference in their executive matters.

There were soon signs in the press that such formulations had had little impact on the established pattern of corporation interference in enterprise affairs. Typical was the commentary of Muhammad Aly Shita, chairman of the board of the Egyptian General Organization for Foodstuff Commodities, who charged that the corporations did not restrict their activities to planning and coordination among units under them, general supervision of their activities, and evaluation of their overall results—as intended by the new statute. Rather, Shita charged, they attempted a broader, in fact stifling, dominance.[28]

While the tendency of the corporations to extend their authority seems natural enough, the inability of the managers to resist infringement of their sphere is at first puzzling. To understand the managers' behavior it is necessary to reflect further on the attitude of the regime toward the managerial corps. Nasser did defend the managers against the attacks of the leftists, primarily in the interest of the efficient operation of the public sector industries. However, there were limits to his support. For while Nasser justified the privileges accorded to the managers as a kind of tribute paid for their technical skills, he signaled clearly that as nonsocialists they were not to be trusted. That attitude undermined the resolve of the managers and made them vulnerable to the pressures of the corporations.

Noninstitutional Control from Above

This lack of trust on Nasser's part manifested itself in concern lest the managers translate their important functional roles and high status into an independent base within the industrial system. To be sure, that system was, in terms of its ambiguous distribution of authority (which encouraged centralization) and multiplicity of control mechanisms, already stacked against this eventuality. Nevertheless, the regime provided additional measures to ensure that the institutions of the industrial order did not shield the managers from control by the highest political authorities. Privilege was one thing, independence another. Mention has already been made of the role of the Higher Control Committee. In Nasser's words, that committee was established specifically to "examine questions concerning top executives." The committee did not operate through the regular administrative or judicial channels. Its process of decision making and the criteria for its decisions had no regularized basis; from those decisions there was no institutionalized means of redress. Nasser so hinted in his own description of the committee: "I believe that this is more important than a mere tribunal, because the examination of the cases will be human and social, as well as material and political."[29]

Similarly, reservation of a great many prerogatives to the office of the presidency allowed Nasser to bring to bear the full weight of his authority on individual managers. In Statute 32, which dealt with the corporations and companies of the public sector, Article 64 directly empowered the president to determine the percentage and utilization of company profits to be distributed to employees without reference to the manager or consideration of his views. Presidential Decree 3309, which dealt with workers' regulations in the public sector, provided in Article 4 a listing of required qualifications for appointments to the board of directors of the public sector companies; those qualifications necessitated the passing of an examination by the administrative board. However, the final sentence of the article allowed the president to waive any or all of the requirements in any specific case. Article 12 of the same decree provided that all appointments above the second level were to be by presidential decree.[30]

By these and similar measures Nasser was able to maintain considerable initiative in industrial affairs. The regular procedures of the industrial system could be bypassed or undermined whenever they threatened to provide the managers with any degree of independence from the political elite.

Popular Controls from Within

To supplement controls from above, the regime acted to guarantee the loyalty of the managers by injecting surveillance mechanisms directly into the individual factory. At the 1967 Production Congress, the president remarked of the managers: "I must say that we have to resort to such people's help on account of their competence and technical skill, but we cannot entrust them with responsibility for political action." Since the president conceived the problem as having a political dimension, not unexpectedly a political solution suggested itself.[31]

Nasser's dilemma was not without obvious historical precedent. The Soviet Union, confronted in the early years of its development with the necessity of employing "bourgeois specialists" in industry, had resolved the difficulty by introducing politically reliable cadres of the Communist Party directly into the factory system to perform a watchdog function. On the surface, Nasser appeared to adopt a similar arrangement for Egypt. Committees of the Arab Socialist Union were formed within the industrial enterprises. Despite official contention that their role was to be political education of the workers and support for production, it soon became apparent that the committees were to be engaged in information gathering and general surveillance. Leftists of course denied that ASU political activity in the industrial sphere aimed "to create a new apparatus for acting as a watchdog." However, in the wake of the 1967 war, after Sabry had been removed as head of the ASU and Nasser had assumed that position, Haikal charged that the ASU had in fact functioned primarily as a spy system.[32]

In the Egyptian case, this use of the Arab Socialist Union for surveillance of the managers was not the whole story. Nasser was wary of assigning the ASU a monopoly on such a crucial task, since the party appeared to be emerging as a potential challenger to his own position. Willing to exploit the antipathy of the ASU to the managers, Nasser nevertheless feared that the position of the union committees would become too powerful. His approach to the task of keeping the managers in check went beyond the Soviet model in a way very much in character with early established patterns of Nasser's rule. Rather than rely solely or even primarily on the ASU, Nasser fostered several popular organizations within each industrial establishment and assigned the watchdog function to them all in various and ambiguous degrees. In each large factory there existed: a labor union, a joint labor-management consultative committee, worker members of the board of directors, and the Arab Socialist Union Committee. All four groups acted as "popular" restraints on the managers, while their mutual rivalry prevented any one of them from assuming a too powerful position in the institutional framework.[33]

The worker members of the board of directors illustrate the general point of the competing watchdog function of the four formations. Presidential Decree 114 of July 19, 1961, provided that the administration of the public sector enterprises was to be consigned to a board of directors, not to exceed seven members, of whom two were to be elected from the employees of the enterprise and the remainder to be appointed by presidential decree. The inclusion of workers in the boards was much heralded as an expression of the special character of Egypt's socialism. Nasser proclaimed that Egypt's was a humane socialism that had faith in the individual worker and his capacity to play an important role in industrial production. Workers, according to Nasser, were not to be considered mere cogs in a machine, but were to be actively responsible for the running of the factory in which they worked. Later rationales for the inclusion of workers have typically added that the measure "aimed to effect a revolutionary change which endows the workers not only with rights but also with obligations." These new obligations were to be discharged in the form of increased concern with production.[34]

In 1963 the original presidential decree was amended: five members (including the manager) were to be appointed by the president of the republic, and four elected from among the employees of the company. The manager would have only limited influence on both the elected and appointed members of his board of directors, since their selection did not lie in his hands. Conversely, the board members were not to elect or choose their chairman. Statute 32 of 1966 provided in Article 55: "The administration board resolutions will be passed by a simple majority vote of members attending, and in case of a tie the chairman will have the determining vote."[35]

President Nasser and other high officials have repeatedly stressed that "it is the chairman of the board of every unit who is primarily responsible for the direction of the work performed in that unit and he has to be perfectly aware that he is the one to be judged—to be rewarded or punished in case of success or failure."[36] Given the diffusion of administrative authority among eight other board members over whom he has little control, the manager's attempts to escape responsibility by deferring judgments to higher authorities become much more comprehensible.

The presence of workers on the boards, the managers have argued, both diluted managerial authority and introduced confusion into industrial relations. What precisely, they have asked, is the role of such workers to be? The regime has given no clear-cut answer.[37]

Available information on the group characteristics of the worker members of the boards provides considerable insight into the causes of the peculiar difficulties experienced by the enterprise managers in working with them. Voting for membership in the boards takes place through direct secret ballots under the supervision of the Ministry of Labor. Under present law candidates are required to be members of the ASU and to secure a certificate from the union indicating approval of their candidacy for the board and attesting to their good character.[38]

The first elections of worker board members for 432 companies began in April 1962 and were held over a period of eight months. In *al-Ahram* of January 19, 1963, the results were summarized. A total of 429 white-collar and 383 blue-collar workers were chosen for the boards of 432 companies. A total of 285,973 persons took part in the elections, including 58,750 white-collar and 227,223 regular workers. Of the 432 companies, 226 were located in Cairo and 111 in Alexandria.

The election results showed that the more educated white-collar workers enjoyed the greatest success. Furthermore, even when white-collar and blue-collar workers are combined, over 40 percent of those elected to serve on the management boards can be described as well educated. Consequently, while there was an educational gap between the elected and the appointed board members (the latter virtually all had higher education), that gap is by no means as large as one might expect. The degree of education of the worker members of the boards has aided in making them a constant source of irritation for the managers—an irritation that was to influence Sadat's decision in 1974 to drop the provision for their mandatory inclusion.[39] On the one hand, the educational gap remained to hinder an identification of the elected with the appointed members; on the other hand, the workers were sufficiently well educated to defend their viewpoints and interests effectively.

On the ideological level, there has been considerable confusion over just what those interests should be. On the one hand, the inclusion of workers on the boards has been trumpeted as a socialist gain, since they would in some sense represent labor interests at the board level. But there have been frequent denials that such is the official intent. Rather, it is argued:

> Representatives of the personnel are part of the Board of Directors and they cooperate with the other members of the Board in planning the programs . . . there is no difference between these representatives and other members of the Board. They perform their duties as one team with mutual aims and interests.

According to this version, the worker members are intended to play a supporting role in the battle for production. In practice, it appears (from impressionistic evidence in the press) that the worker members have at least attempted to represent the interests of the workers. In doing so, they have aroused considerable opposition from the managers. Haikal, summarizing the complaints of the managers of the public sector, wrote of those worker members of the boards who "were interested only in salaries and other pretended rights claimed by the workers who elected them." Similarly, in an analytic study of the role of the workers in the boards of companies, Ibrahim Ghubashy remarked: "Because they belong to the workers the elected members are not yet able to escape their influence so as to have the interest of the producing unit in mind."[40]

In addition to inciting the antipathy of the managers, the activities of the worker members on behalf of the workers have been interpreted by the other popular formations in the factories as a direct threat to their functional roles. Amin Ezz ed-Din, a former professor at the Institute for Socialist Studies, has argued that the lack of a clear official description of the role of the worker members of the board has greatly exacerbated this rivalry with other popular organizations. He notes, for example, that some labor union elements considered that the "admission of workers in the boards of directors menaced their position." They did everything possible, therefore, to "shake the confidence the workers had in them."[41]

The results of a public opinion survey published in the January 1966 issue of *al-Tali'ah* points to a similar rivalry between the ASU committees and the workers in the boards. This study openly discusses that rivalry—attributing it to insufficiently developed consciousness on the part of the ASU committees:

> Instead of competing with them [the workers in the boards] the Socialist Union committees should guide them and help them to exercise their responsibilities.[42]

From the manager's perspective, the inclusion of workers on the board of directors served to introduce dissension at the highest administrative level within the factory and to engender confusing and disruptive rivalries with the other popular formations with which the manager must contend. Both results undoubtedly detracted from the manager's already frail sense of security.

In the interest of preserving his own position of power from any possible challenge, Nasser acted to dissipate all potential aggregations of power—managerial, political, or even bureaucratic—within the industrial context. Writing in *al-Ahram,* Haikal described the results by stating that power in the units of production was "lost between the diverse administrative and popular organizations."[43] The economic costs to Egypt of Nasser's political success were high.

THE MANAGERS AND SADAT'S OPENING

With insecurity already the outstanding characteristic of Egypt's public sector managers under Nasser, the initial effect of the era of the opening was to create new trauma. Sadat's orientation threw into question the shaky intellectual and institutional foundations of Egypt's system of industrial relations: a more market-oriented system, designed to attract Western technology and Western and Arab capital, would be introduced in Egypt.

Sadat and his key economic advisers strove to provide assurances that the commitment to the public sector remained intact. The opening would mean that the Nasserist drift to further socialist measures would be halted. However, the core of the public sector—the major corporations in banking, finance, international trade, transportation, and manufacturing—would not be returned to the private sector. In October of 1974 Sadat announced:

> No one should fear for the public sector or the workers, for [in] all of this are but seeds of doubt . . . When we wish to change something, we will change it openly and not in secret.

The calming effect of assurances from Sadat was diluted by his tendency to combine soothing reassurances with critical assessments of the public sector performance record. Furthermore, Sadat spoke openly of the need to amend Nasser's Charter of 1962, which delineated the relation between public and private sectors in the Egypt of the Free Officers. He came closest to doing so in the 1974 *October Paper.*[44]

The president was careful to reassure Egyptians that he was not dismantling Egypt's socialism. He explained that the nationalized industries assured that "the general direction of Egypt's development will be subject to official determination . . . for it is only the public sector that can be directly committed by the plan."[45] But planning in Egypt has had such a checkered history that those with a stake in the nationalized industrial sphere could not have been overly impressed with a defense of the public sector that linked its continued existence to the planning function.

An attitude more in keeping with the rightist orientation of Sadat's opening was the tendency to view the public sector as a means of support for the new private sector enterprises and for foreign investors:

> The public sector—especially in developing countries—also provides the private sector and foreign investments with essential services that they cannot do without. Investments are not guided towards countries which lack the necessary components of an investment environment; they proceed to those countries where this environment is available and constituted of sufficient production frameworks, vital utilities, a reasonable standard of industrialization, local technical expertise and skilled manpower. The public sector in Egypt has played a vital role in creating and providing these factors on a level not available in many other developing countries.[46]

The managers did not fail to note that this characterization was a far cry from the leading role envisioned for the public sector in Nasser's Charter.

The worst suspicions of the industrial managers seemed confirmed in late 1974 and throughout 1975, as officially inspired criticism of the public sector mounted. Illustrative is an *al-Ahram* article of November in which a member of Parliament charged that "cost accounting in the public sector is forged for the purpose of showing false profits." The most comprehensive critical review of the public sector in the first years after the announcement of the "opening" was that made by a committee of the People's Assembly and reported widely in the press in the spring of 1975. This report charged that the return on investment in public sector enterprises had averaged a meager 2.4 percent per year. The committee report went on to recommend the sale of shares in certain public sector companies and the total divestiture of others. Even more alarming to those with a stake in the public sector were measures taken a year later. Some small department stores were sold outright from public sector holdings, and plans were made to sell shares in other public sector firms both to their workers and to the public at large. Apparently Sadat hoped to use criticism and limited tampering in this way to reform the public sector operation. This aim was really part of the basic "opening" strategy: competition from the invigorated private sector, it was anticipated, would act as a spur to the public sector companies. Yet if we consider the overall history of the managers, it is hard to be optimistic that one more spur is what they needed to operate more effectively.[47]

The managers in general have felt threatened by Sadat's new orientation. But their group cohesiveness is low, and it should not be overlooked that individual managers stand to benefit handsomely from the economic turn to the right. In his *October Paper* Sadat went out of his way to pacify "the public sector's personnel shaped by experience into hundreds of thousands of directors, experts, technicians, and workers, who are now considered a national wealth of which the country is proud and an immense resource for the construction of its future."[48] Sadat's domestic move to the right (especially with the resultant silencing of the Nasserist left represented by Aly Sabry in the ASU) has made life more pleasant for Egypt's managers as members of an emerging technocratic elite. At least the ideological ambiguities in their role have been muted.

Furthermore, for individual managers the opening has offered striking opportunities for advancement. One difficulty that has resulted from Sadat's liberalization policies is the greater facility with which skilled manpower on all levels has left Egypt to participate in the boom economies of the oil-rich Arab states. For Egypt's industrial managers the prospect of an expanded private sector affords opportunities potentially as rewarding as going to the Arab states, through "internal migration" to a private sector perhaps enriched by foreign capital. Foreign capital will easily be able to outbid the public sector in order to attract managerial talent, so that there will be considerable incentive for individual managers to move to the private sector. At present, there are maximum salary laws that curtail the play of the market, but those laws have produced anomalous situations. For example, when the question of licensing a joint Chase-National Bank was worked out, it was agreed that the bank president would be an Egyptian, the second in command to be appointed by Chase. By law the Egyptian bank president can receive no more than $10,000 per annum, whereas the salary for the Chase appointee was rumored in 1975 to be in the neighborhood of $100,000. It is not hard to see that the private sector, if it takes off in the manner envisioned by Sadat, will be an irresistible magnet for managerial talent.[49]

Leftist commentators have reported that this consequence of the opening might in fact be part of a long-range plan to undermine and then eliminate the public sector by eventually depriving it of its most vital human resources. An initial situation of a dual economy will "naturally" evolve, they fear, into a free-enterprise system built around foreign capital and linked to the international banking and market systems. The managers will, in this leftist vision, come into their own as the vanguard of the new parasitic class that grew up and exploited the public sector during the Nasser years. Earlier it was pointed out that Aly Sabry had warned against such an eventuality in his *al-Jumhuriyyah* series of the spring of 1967. Leftists of the seventies, such as Fuad Mursi writing in *al-Tali'ah* of February 1974, have argued that the opening was in the process of creating just such a reality.

Predictably, the managers of the public sector have responded to the new ambiguities of the Sadat era with a blend of increased caution and cynicism. Press reports of an increase in red tape have risen sharply in number, and Egyptian analysts have pointed to the basic uncertainty of top-level orientation as a root cause. High-level personnel are eager, reported *al-Ahram,* to provide themselves with maximum bureaucratic protection:

Scientific studies have shown that there is a segment of officials in Egypt all of whom have private archives which they keep for themselves in the form of letters and documents for which they are afraid they may be responsible someday. Also, there are officials who keep for themselves at their office, or sometimes at home, some originals of documents by which they can defend themselves were an accusation directed at them someday because of them . . . Such is the pattern of the Egyptian official whose behavior is guided by the principle of fear of responsibility.

Press studies in the seventies, frequently with minister-level documentation, have also given extensive coverage to studies of public sector corruption.[50]

CONCLUSION

The tidy images of Egypt's managers as the spearhead of a new technocratic class or alternatively as yet another edition of the ageless Egyptian bureaucrat have not withstood the test of a close look at managerial backgrounds, group characteristics, and functional roles in Egypt's industrial system. The managers are an assorted group drawn heavily from the ''new men'' with technical training, but containing a generous share of bureaucrats and others as well. They are a transitional group without fundamental cohesiveness. Their outstanding characteristic is insecurity.

In the Nasser era the managers were buffeted by the ideological challenge of the Egyptian left, which regarded their privileges as fundamentally illegitimate. They were hamstrung by the institutional and noninstitutional controls of a regime that needed but did not trust them. By implicitly calling into question the survival of the public sector, Sadat's opening strategy has added immensely to the uncertainties of the managerial elite. Until the fundamental ideological and institutional ambiguities of the Sadat transition are resolved, the already flawed performance of the industrial managers can only worsen.

8. Agricultural Cooperatives

For Egypt's peasants there has been no real revolution. For all the investment in agriculture, expansion of cultivatable land, and alteration of landholding patterns by the regime of the Free Officers, the essential social and production relations of the countryside have been reformed but not revolutionized. The agricultural cooperative movement, along with land reform efforts, was charged by the new government to bring the revolution to rural Egypt. In the sharp limitations on the achievements of the cooperative effort are reflected the broader limitations both of vision and of institutional capability of Free Officer rule.

THE DEVELOPMENT OF AGRICULTURAL POLICY

The agricultural policy of the new regime was shaped by three fundamental decisions. While industry was assigned top priority in the development program, the agricultural sphere was not to be neglected. Moreover, it was decided that in contrast to patterns elsewhere, the drive to industrialize was not to be financed initially by a repressive tax on agriculture. Finally, there was to be an effort to raise both production and peasant living standards by strengthening and reforming the agricultural cooperative movement inherited from the ancien régime. The cooperatives would increase government control over the agricultural sphere. That control might later be used to skim off an assumed agricultural surplus, which could then be diverted to industry.

Given the spiraling population and very limited land area available for cultivation (approximately 3.5 percent of the total area after completion of the High Dam), the decision to emphasize industry was a sound one. Moreover, agriculture was not left to stagnate, and there was a respectable rate of investment in that sphere. For the years 1960-61 through 1968-69 investments totaled $1.60 billion, or an annual rate of $180.64 million. If by the mid-sixties Egypt was no longer an overwhelmingly agricultural country, agriculture was still vital to the national economy as the biggest earner of foreign currency and the source of half the country's total employment. Approximately 28 percent of the national income was derived from it.[1]

The regime's concern with agriculture resulted in an approximately 33 percent expansion of the cultivatable area between the years 1952 and 1964. In the period 1959-60 to 1964-65 agricultural production developed at a respectable annual rate of 3.3 percent. While modest in comparison to the 8.5 percent for Egyptian industry in the same period, the increase appears substantial when measured against the record of other developing countries. This is especially true if one considers the difficulties of expanding crop area in Egypt.[2]

The investments of the regime were directed to an agricultural sphere essentially in private hands. A policy of nationalization of the land that would have given control over production comparable to that exercised over "socialized" industry was vetoed by Nasser as unworkable. In place of nationalization the regime adopted an approach of land reform plus cooperatives. It was possible to do this because the strategy of the regime for Egypt's development through industrialization had consciously rejected the pattern of capital formation through mass deprivation (particularly of the peasantry) that had characterized the European industrial revolution and the Stalinist industrial drive in the U.S.S.R. The Charter of 1962 charged that these earlier models for development "realized their objectives at the expense of increasing the misery of the working people, whether to serve the interests of capital or under pressure of ideological applications which went to the extent of sacrificing whole living generations for the sake of others still unborn." Nasser believed that the Egyptian peasantry would never accept nationalization: "The fellah is too individualistic, too attached to his secular dream of owning a piece of land to ever rally to such a measure." Whatever the weight of the moral scruples that might have colored the regime's attitude toward the peasants, it did eschew a policy of wringing a capital surplus from the peasant masses to fund a forced industrialization program. Instead, it based its primary strategy of capital formation on windfall financing from sequestrations and foreign aid.[3]

This is not to say that agriculture went completely untaxed. Some form of agricultural taxation has existed in Egypt from time immemorial. Under the ancien régime, though, that system was clearly loaded to favor the rich landowning class. A land assessment in 1899 established an average rental value of land and then set the tax rate at 29 percent of the rent. For the next forty years that rate remained unchanged despite the fact that the rental value of land increased many times over. Finally, in 1939 a new assessment raised the rental value about 37 percent (yielding a figure still much lower than the prevailing rates), but then reduced the rate of taxation to 16 percent. Between 1942 and 1945 small landowners were granted considerable remission, and in 1949 the rate was further reduced to 14 percent. In 1951-52 income taxes and fees accounted for approximately 29 percent of total government revenue, whereas the indirect taxes, which fall heavily on the lower classes, provided about 49 percent.[4]

Since the revolution some minor adjustments have been made to the income tax, but there has been no thorough reform of the taxation system as a whole. The most important source of revenue remains customs and excise duties. A considerable surplus in agriculture continues to exist, one that could be mobilized for the regime's industrialization program. While in strict economic terms a case can be made for heavier taxation in agriculture, the regime has shied away from such an approach. Probably the political risks of a heavy taxation of the peasants were judged too high and the administrative task too daunting.[5]

Reliance on agricultural cooperatives was central to the regime's cautious approach to the administrative problem of dealing with millions of individual peasant households. The peasants' right of ownership was to be exercised within an ever expanding framework of cooperatives which, while short of nationalization, nevertheless held out the promise of providing a mechanism for increased government control over production. Ideologically, cooperation evoked a favorable response among the ruling elite who characterized Egyptian socialism as cooperative and democratic—unlike Marxism. The land reform measures undertaken by the regime soon after the revolution were intimately bound up with the cooperative movement.

The Charter declared that "the revolutionary solution to the problem of land in Egypt is by increasing the number of landowners." Through a series of land reforms the regime has undertaken to implement that solution: immediately after the revolution in 1952 agricultural holdings were limited to 200 feddans; in 1961 the maximum was reduced to 100 feddans; in 1962, in order to prevent evasions of this limit, it was stipulated that the 100 feddans would be the maximum holding for a family (the family being taken as husband, wife, and minor children); finally, in 1969 it was decreed that individual holdings would be reduced to 50 feddans, with the limit for a family to remain at 100 feddans. Politically, land reform was perhaps the regime's earliest success, since it marked the political demise on the national level of the large landowners who had dominated Egyptian politics. Socially and economically, the various measures were reformist rather than revolutionary. The land reforms produced a redistribution of 17 percent of the cultivatable land to benefit some 250,000 families, or about 8 percent of the fellahin. Recipients of land under the various agrarian reform measures were required to join newly created agrarian reform cooperatives, over which the state exercised a high degree of control.[6]

The possible use of the network of cooperatives as a mechanism for skimming off the surplus in agriculture was given more attention as flaws and limitations in the strategy for capital formation adopted by the regime became apparent. Egypt's new rulers soon realized that the range of sequestrations could not be expanded without fear of provoking serious opposition. Furthermore, by the mid-sixties Nasser had become acutely aware of the dangers of relying heavily on foreign aid to finance Egypt's industrialization.

The regime's case for a cooperative agriculture rested on its positive interpretation of the performance record of the agrarian reform cooperatives in raising production. Based on that assumption of success, the thrust of official agricultural policy has been to spread throughout rural Egypt the new type of cooperative. The implementation of this long-term strategy has encountered sharp and revealing obstacles. These are rooted in both an overestimation of the successes achieved by the new cooperatives and an underestimation of the problems of replacing the inherited traditional cooperatives with the more tightly regulated variety.

The Cooperative Movement before 1952

The Egyptian cooperative movement had its historical roots in the early years of the twentieth century. Following an economic crisis in 1907 that was disastrous for the farming population, a private philanthropist named Omar Lutfy took the lead in calling for the formation of "agricultural syndicates" to help the farmers meet their supply and marketing needs. A committee of agricultural specialists also recommended that the government create a special banking fund to arrange for loans to farmers and pass a law for formation of cooperatives. Although the government refused to take these steps, the cooperative movement did slowly take hold and by 1911 seventeen agricultural cooperatives had been founded, along with a General Central Syndicate to coordinate their efforts. These first societies were concerned with credit, supplies, and marketing.

Official support for the nascent movement came with Law 27/1923, at a time when the rising cost of living and extensive profiteering accentuated the importance of the cooperatives for the farmers. The law provided that any ten farmers could form an agricultural cooperative company to be managed by a board of directors and a supervisory committee, both bodies to be elected by the general assembly of cooperative members. A Department of Cooperation was established in the Ministry of Agriculture. With official sanction, the movement expanded more rapidly and by 1925 the cooperatives numbered 135. One important factor still limiting their growth was the establishment of the value of a cooperative share just high enough to preclude participation by those with low incomes.

In addition to their primary marketing function, cooperatives were looked to by reformers during the interwar years to provide the organizational framework for a system of social security throughout the countryside. To this end the stipulation was made that a part of the profits realized by the societies had to be set aside for social service. Official acceptance of this view of the cooperative's potential is reflected in the 1939 decision to shift supervision of the cooperatives from the Ministry of Agriculture to the Ministry of Social Affairs.

World War II provided the next impetus. During that crisis period the government made use of the cooperative societies for the distribution of fertilizers and other supplies. Law 58/1944 provided for the extension of government control and supervision over the cooperatives. Thus, although the cooperatives were "voluntary" in the sense that members were encouraged and not compelled to join them, the organizations themselves were subject to a tutelary relationship with the central government. Registration with the Ministry of Social Affairs was required and cooperative accounts were subject to official review. Ministerial decree could also override decisions made by the elected cooperative boards. Law 58 allowed capital share contributions to be paid in installments, thereby opening the movement to less prosperous farmers.

Even more vital to the expansion of the cooperative movement was the conversion in 1949 of the Egyptian Agricultural Credit Bank (founded in 1930) into the Agricultural Cooperative Bank. The credit of the bank was expanded by about $2 million, to be contributed equally by the government and the cooperative societies represented on its board of directors. Cheap credit was available from the bank, and it became the chief inducement for farmers to join the cooperatives. In 1925, there were 139 cooperatives with a membership of 20,673. By 1952, cooperatives numbered 2,103 and claimed a membership of 746,836.[7]

Model Land Reform Cooperatives

The leadership of the Nasserist revolution of 1952 immediately embraced the flourishing cooperative movement as its own. And before long the Free Officers sought to turn the inherited movement in a new direction. Once the regime's first agrarian reform law (limiting land ownership to 200 feddans) had been launched in September 1952, it became apparent that the cooperatives would have economic as well as administrative utility. Economically, the cooperative could help offset the potentially disruptive impact on production of land parcelization brought about by the redistribution program; administratively, the cooperative greatly enhanced the regime's ability to exert influence on the peasants who received land as a result of the reforms. In fact, the regime's experience with the reform cooperatives had a profound impact on the conception of cooperation in agriculture as it was to be practiced in revolutionary Egypt. The land reform cooperatives provided a model for cooperatives of a new type, which claimed increased productivity and allowed for greater state control.

The land reform cooperatives differed in both form and function from those before 1952. To begin with, they were in no sense voluntary organizations. Membership was required of all those benefiting from the land reform laws. Although nominally run by a board of directors elected by the members, an appointed supervisor directly responsible to the Ministry of Agrarian Reform held effective power. Formally, private ownership was maintained; in practice, a system of strong government tutelage was instituted.

In addition, the functions of the new agrarian reform cooperatives went considerably beyond those of supply and marketing, which still characterized the traditional cooperative movement. The new organizations, concerned primarily with preventing a drop in output, were heavily production oriented. So the agronomist appointed by the Ministry of Agrarian Reform to manage the land reform cooperative could in the last resort compel the farmers to adopt any cultivation methods thought advisable by the ministry. The cooperatives were empowered to advance agricultural loans of all kinds to members of the society according to the needs of their land. Farmers were also provided with seeds, fertilizers, livestock, machinery, and storage and transport for their crops. Expert assistance was given in such matters as seed selection, pest control, and irrigation methods. Finally, the cooperatives were charged with selling the principal crops on behalf of the members. In that way the government could directly deduct payments on the land acquired, government taxes, and fees for cooperative social services.[8] The broad function of the cooperatives and the key role of appointed managers has meant firm control of agricultural production on land reform cooperatives by the central authorities.

The regime has argued that such control resulted in a dramatic increase of production on the land reform cooperatives, and it has invoked that "success" as justification for its policy of spreading the state-controlled type of cooperative throughout Egyptian agriculture. On the basis of the available evidence, it is hard to evaluate the validity of that claim. While there have been indications of improved production on agrarian reform lands, the statistical evidence is by no means as conclusive as official publications suggest. Figures available for cotton and sugar cane production do point to an impressive production increase. For example, between 1952 and 1959 total cotton output by supervised cooperatives in sixteen districts increased by 45 percent, compared to an average increase of 15 percent for the rest of the country.[9] It is pointless, however, to report these results in detail, since it is impossible to know how representative they are.

Official spokesmen did not hesitate to interpret such data as proof of the increased efficiency of the production methods of the new cooperatives. True, some official doubts are probably reflected in the caution with which the government moved in transforming the bulk of general cooperatives. Although the decision to extend the system of agrarian-reform-type cooperatives was taken early in 1960, it was not until 1963 that implementation really got under way. In that year the changes in production methods characteristic of these cooperatives (notably the consolidation of fragmented holdings) were introduced in the general cooperatives of two governorates—Beni Suef in Upper Egypt and Kafr el-Sheikh in the Delta. Aly Sabry explained in a 1963 article that this step was regarded as a pioneering experiment from which "we shall be able to glimpse . . . the general outlines of a socialist agricultural society."[10]

There were clear precedents to legitimate the government's leading role in such social experimentation. The prerevolutionary cooperative movement had developed with strong state encouragement right from the start. And extensive financial assistance from the state guaranteed a measure of control.

The task of strengthening government control over the movement was facilitated by the steady erosion of some of the voluntary aspects of the inherited cooperatives. The primary element of volition had come from the fact that farmers were induced and not compelled to join. The attractiveness of the inducements (notably cheap, and after 1961 free, agricultural credits) is reflected in the fact that by 1960 nearly all farmers had become members.[11] So by the end of 1962, when the regime did finally compel those remaining outside the cooperatives to join, the coercion could be smoothly implemented.

This eventual disappearance of the farmer's option to join the new groups or not is an important landmark in the regime's transformation of the supervised cooperatives into compulsory ones. In functional terms, an important (though fading) distinction still earmarked the reform cooperatives. From their inception they were minutely concerned with production; in contrast, the vast majority of other cooperatives were concerned only with bulk purchase of inputs and marketing. By and large, the actual mode of exploitation of the land remained in the hands of the individual landowners. Having achieved compulsory membership of the farmers, the government since 1962 has directed its efforts to expansion of the role of the cooperatives in production, along the lines suggested by the agrarian reform cooperatives. Egyptian agriculture since that time has largely been a function of these efforts and the obstacles they have encountered.

IMPLEMENTING THE NEW COOPERATIVE STRATEGY

The burden of managing the agrarian reform cooperatives was lightened by two important factors. First, the peasants on the new cooperatives, as beneficiaries of the land reform distributions, were all of approximately the same socioeconomic category and were all indebted to the government alone for their newly acquired land holdings. Secondly, because of the limited scope of the land reform programs, staffs of a relatively high quality could be mobilized to represent the government's interest. The fact that neither of these two conditions was duplicated for the majority of the supervised cooperatives greatly complicated the government's tasks.

Land Reform and the Shape of Rural Egypt

Unlike the situation on the controlled agrarian reform cooperatives, officials dealing with the other supervised cooperatives were faced with a highly stratified peasant population. The new regime's successive land reform measures did eliminate the largest landowners. Nevertheless, in 1964 there were still an estimated ten thousand landowners who owned more than 50 feddans and as a group controlled about 13 percent of the land area. Presumably it was this group that Nasser had in mind when he commented: "Feudalists still exist . . . They are hostile to the socialist revolution . . . They are not found in museums or concentration camps."[12]

The intermediate group of peasants having from 5 to 50 feddans continued throughout the entire period from 1943 to 1964 to hold roughly 30 percent of the land. However, the number of such landowners increased and the average size of their holdings diminished. This indicates that the intermediate group was enlarged by smaller landowners who were able to purchase additional holdings as a result of the reforms.

Small landowners with less than 5 feddans constitute the vast majority of those with landholdings in the Egyptian countryside. In 1964 they accounted for fully 94 percent of landowners and controlled 55 percent of the land. The increase in the percentage of total land area controlled by this group is striking, since before the reform the figure was only about 35 percent. This increase has apparently resulted much more from the growth in size of very small plots (from an average of 0.8 feddan in 1952 to 1.1 in 1964) than from the growth in number of landowners. Land reform served to increase slightly the size of the plots of the small landowners rather than to turn landless peasants into landowners on a scale large enough to be reflected in statistical tables. The size of the group of landless peasants, estimated in 1965 to be fourteen million or approximately three-fourths of the rural population, thus has not been reduced by the successive land reform measures. Moreover, since the increase in population has been more rapid than the growth in the number of land-owners, the proportion of landless peasants in the rural population has actually increased.

Clearly, then, Egyptian land reform has primarily benefited those who already had a stake, however small, in village society. Aside from elimination of the largest landowners, the agrarian reforms consolidated and did not change existing traditional village relationships. Muhammad Abdul Nabi described the situation:

> The social structure of the rural areas remained as it was before the revolution. The village is headed by the umdah [mayor] assisted by a number of elders and regular guards. These form the privileged class in the village. If we thoroughly examine this social structure, we find that the umdah is either a very rich man or the son of the largest family in the village.

The fact that the intermediate groups have been able to maintain their position is of cardinal importance. By tradition these farmers have played a key role in the countryside; their independence and relatively more secure financial status make them less intimidated by authority and less amenable to control. The attitude of these more prosperous peasants toward the cooperative movement has been not so much one of opposition but one of subverting the services offered by the cooperative to their own exclusive use. With their social and economic influence, they have succeeded in dominating the administration of the cooperatives and taking full advantage of them. An intensive study of one village in Beheira province stressed the success of the umdah in preserving his traditional power a full seven years after the revolution. He ran the village cooperative society virtually as a private business, the preserve of friends and relatives. Press reports suggest that these observations do point to a general trend.[13]

The Pattern of Abuses

Records of the corruption of the cooperatives by the more prosperous and influential peasants have appeared intermittently over the last decade. The most dramatic revelations came in the wake of the murder of Salah Hussein, an activist of the Arab Socialist Union in the village of Kamchiche (about fifty miles north of Cairo) on May 1, 1966, allegedly by members of the large landowning family that dominated the village. The government organized a Committee for the Liquidation of Feudalism, which launched an attack on "agrarian feudalists." The committee uncovered some startling evidence of abuses by the remaining large landowners. One family was revealed to have succeeded in retaining 2,320 feddans, while another was discovered to hold 1,200 feddans. As a result of the committee's activity, the capital and possessions of eighty-eight large landowners from seventeen provinces were sequestered; the landowners themselves were required to leave their villages and live in the cities. Twenty-five thousand feddans of illegally held land were uncovered, and by June of 1966, 239 village umdahs had been removed for their complicity with the large landowners.[14]

A comprehensive survey of the problems of the cooperatives appeared in *al-Ahram al-Iqtisadi* of May 15, 1968. It was reported that through 1968 approximately three hundred boards of directors were dissolved by the Ministry of Agriculture for "causes ranging from misuse of influence and embezzlement to dealing on the black market."[15]

Taking the province of al-Manufiyyah as a case study, the *al-Ahram al-Iqtisadi* report provided a detailed view of the nature of the corruption in the cooperatives:

The cooperative society of Mit Khalaf village, the report revealed, was turned into a family affair. One of its officials appointed five members of his immediate family to positions in the cooperative: three as watchmen, one as a mechanic, and a fifth as a cooperative treasurer.

In the cooperative society at Mit Mas'us one of the members of the board of directors had taken $1,570 from the cooperative fund without appropriate justification: he used the funds for investment in trade. When asked to return it, he is reported to have delayed doing so for months.

Similarly, embezzlements were reported from the cooperative societies at Kafr al-Batanun ($415) and Mit Khaqan ($460).

On a much larger scale, an investigation at the office of the largest town in al-Manufiyyah showed that members of the board of directors had misappropriated about $11,500 for use in trade, the purchase of livestock, and other forms of business.

Other investigations established the fact that members of the boards of directors of some cooperative societies in the province sold insecticides on the black market, divided the profits among themselves, and then sprayed the peasants' fields with diluted insecticides.

These examples reveal the nature of the general trend: many members of the boards of directors gain possession of the profits of the cooperatives and use them in trade for their own benefit. The offense is compounded by the fact that by so doing they naturally deprive the peasants of the legitimate and intended use of those funds.

Poor Peasants and the Curbing of Abuses

The possibility of such abuses in the cooperative movement was not unanticipated. Aware of the dominant position in the countryside of the more prosperous peasants, the regime naturally viewed them as the most likely sources of corruption and from the beginning sought ways to curb them. The first overt sign of this attitude toward the "kulak peasants" came with the debate at the Congress of Popular Forces in 1962 over the definition of a peasant. Some delegates wanted to restrict the term to those owning less than 5 feddans. Although the definition eventually adopted expanded the peasant group to include all those owning less than 25 feddans, an early clue to the regime's own more stringent preference came with a suggestion by Abdul Latif Mandur, director general of the Organization for Cooperatives. He proposed that four-fifths of the members of the boards of directors of the cooperatives be composed of peasants owning less than 5 feddans. Despite the published opposition of members of parliament, a law to that effect was passed in 1962. The regime felt that by turning to the poor peasants—those it repeatedly described as having a natural interest in socialism—it could lessen the domination and attendant abuses of the prosperous peasants. The attempt failed and the most ingenious exploitation of the cooperatives by the richer peasants has continued.

The causes for the failure of the government's plan to rely on the poor peasant to control such abuses are complex; they reveal a great deal about the broader problems confronting any effort to transform the countryside.

First of all, and perhaps least surprisingly, the one-fifth limitation has hardly been successful in weakening the large landowners' exploitative appetites. Their end runs around the restrictions have been clever and resourceful. The *al-Ahram al-Iqtisadi* article reported, for example, that "a certain class has infiltrated the boards of directors and ruined the situation. They are large landowners who have changed their holdings to less than five feddans. Most members of the boards of directors belong to this group."[16] Given the close family relations predominant in the villages, it is not difficult to visualize a landowner formally transferring his holdings to a trusted relative, so that he could qualify for board membership. The rewards of office would then be shared with his family. More directly, there is the simple fact that legally the landowners of up to 25 (later revised to 10) feddans were still entitled to one-fifth of the positions. This proportion frequently proved more than adequate for effective domination of the board.

A field study of ten Egyptian villages by the research department of *al-Jumhuriyyah* (reported in the editions of June 13 and 20, 1968) provided persuasive documentation of this ascendancy of the more affluent members of the boards. In their representative sample of villages the *al-Jumhuriyyah* researchers found that invariably it was not the board of directors that controlled or led the cooperative association, but "usually one or two individuals, with the supervisor or the secretary a rich peasant." The board of directors was most often found to be a mere rubber stamp. The following examples of patterns are provided:

In the village of al-Aziziyah, in spite of a majority of poor peasants in an administrative council composed of ten people, actual power is concentrated in the hands of the president of the council, who owns 18 feddans, and the secretary, who is one of the rich peasants owning more than 5 feddans.

In Taha al-Bish, the president of the council is dominant; he owns 11 feddans and is an in-law of the umdah.

In Mit Suway the president of the council, who owns 18 feddans, is in control.

In Musha, the secretary of the association, the former secretary of the umdah, dominates.

Of even greater interest in the study are its findings concerning the role of poor peasants in the cooperative boards. In an attempt to determine what had become of the four-fifths majorities of the poor peasants on whom the regime had counted to prevent such domination of the cooperatives by the richer elements, the *al-Jumhuriyyah* staff interviewed peasant board members in the ten villages surveyed. The following important points emerged from those interviews:

Most of the peasant members were not "invited" regularly to attend board meetings called by the dominant figures. Instead, they were called on once a month or once every several months in order to sign or stamp some of the council reports.

As a result of their poverty most of the peasants are thoroughly preoccupied with subsistence. For them there is no incentive to go to the association except at times when fertilizer or insecticides are to be distributed.

A control function is still more untenable for the poor peasant board members inasmuch as most of them either rent from or work for some of the rich peasants and medium landowners and therefore are inclined to their interests. The involvement of the poorer peasants in cooperative administration might have provided an arena for the practical education of the peasantry in administrative and organizational skills. Undoubtedly, some limited progress in this direction was achieved. But the reforms of the Free Officers had not altered traditional village relations sufficiently to allow such reforms to succeed.

The effectiveness of the more affluent peasants in successfully exploiting the cooperatives is a reflection of their continued dominance of Egyptian village life. The pattern is not confined to the cooperatives. In an illuminating series of articles on "national capitalism" in agriculture by Aly Sabry in *al-Jumhuriyyah* during January 1967, attention was focused on the continuing strength of the larger landowners. Drawing on materials discovered by the Committee for the Liquidation of Feudalism, Sabry pointed out how certain landed proprietors belonging to the category of national capitalism (that is, owning more than 25 feddans) "managed to establish links with the administrative, technical, and cultural organizations in the village with the aim of exploiting them uniquely for personal aims."[17]

A specific example of these networks of the more prosperous elements combining to secure their own interests to the detriment of the smaller farmers is provided by Michel Kamel, an editor of *al-Tali'ah*. Writing in *Démocratie nouvelle* of February 1968, he described a family in one village whose members held the following posts: in the administration—the mayor, his alternate, and his four assistants, the chief of police and his assistants; in the Arab Socialist Union—the secretary of the committee, the vice-secretary, and eighteen out of a total of twenty members; in the village council—the chairman, the secretary, and ten members; in the village cooperative— the president, the secretary, and another member of the board of directors. Commenting on such domination of the villages by influential families, Sabry comments that "these links resemble in more than one way those which previously linked the feudalists and the public administration entirely subservient to their authority." This statement makes clear Sabry's view that much of the touted change and reform in the countryside has been imaginary.[18]

Still, this control asserted by the large landowners through their network of connections in the villages does not completely explain the deviations in the cooperatives. There is evidence that poor peasant members of the cooperative boards also have indulged in freewheeling corruption. The 1968 *al-Ahram al-Iqtisadi* study concluded that they help themselves to the "funds, fodder, insecticides, and fertilizers of the cooperatives."[19] The regime's erstwhile "natural allies" have demonstrated no immunity from the deviations that have wracked the cooperative movement. It has become apparent that the problem of finding reliable cadres remains to be solved.

Appointed Officials and the Curbing of Abuses

Disillusioned with the performance of the poor peasants, the regime turned to centrally appointed experts rather than elected boards of directors to run the agricultural cooperatives. However, the condition of agricultural education did not encourage an optimistic view of the workability of such an approach. Programs of training for work in cooperatives have had a long but disappointing history in the UAR. The first cooperative educational center was established by the Cooperative Federation in Cairo, with a course of study of one year. In 1956 the Agricultural Cooperative Institute was established, and the curriculum of universities throughout the UAR included advanced studies for the graduation of cooperative leaders. The very limited quantitative and qualitative results of these early efforts was indicated by a conference called by the Socialist Union for Farmers at the University of Cairo in 1967. Ignoring the efforts of the previous ten years, the conference issued a declaration calling for the "spread of technical cooperative education throughout the country and the preparation of trained experts for the future"—much as if that goal had just been discovered.[20] Consequently, in actual practice the burden of an administrative approach that relied on centrally appointed experts would fall on those with secondary and even below secondary-level training.

The record of officials with such minimal training already working in the field is not impressive. Studies of corruption in the cooperatives make it clear that the centrally appointed personnel have been directly and fully implicated. Focusing on the agricultural specialists, the 1968 *al-Ahram al-Iqtisadi* study reported that they were often compelled to work in the countryside "despite lack of knowledge and experience, and lack of understanding of the requirements and nature of work among the masses." The attitudes of government workers compelled to work in the villages have been ably described by an American specialist:

> A director at one of the agricultural training centers told me of his difficulties with Egyptian teachers and government workers who were supposed to be undergoing training for rural construction work. To begin with, his students resist even the idea of visiting nearby villages during their training period. They prefer to listen to lectures on rural problems rather than observing them in the raw. Once they are "forced" into the villages, they insist on maintaining their "dignity"—which means they refuse to wear work clothes, open-necked shirts and overalls or khaki trousers. Instead, they must wear their business or office suits and sport a necktie and jacket so as to maintain the proper distance from the peasants. "They are afraid," he said, "to get their hands down into their native soil . . . They are ashamed of dirt and disease and of the peasants among whom they will work in the future."

Not unexpectedly, the performance of the agricultural officials has been less than satisfactory. The findings of a study of the inspectors in the province of Beni Suwayf are typical. The criteria used for evaluation were the leadership ability of the supervisor and his grasp of village problems. Out of a group of 140 surveyed, 75 were declared politically aware and performing excellently, 45 were described as preeminently concerned with office work and the keeping of records and lacking completely in any political understanding of their task, and the final 20 were declared to be both negligent and corrupt.[21]

The demands on the agricultural inspectors are considerable, especially with their modest training. Most are the holders simply of a middle-school certificate. Yet inspectors typically are responsible for about 7,000 feddans and the supervision of three cooperative societies. The vulnerability of these inspectors to the pressures and blandishments of the large landowners is also a problem. The 1968 *al-Jumhuriyyah* field study stressed that in most of the villages examined the inspectors had little to do with the peasants, but essentially confined their relations to the village notables and officials:

> In Taha al-Bish the agricultural supervisor holds his meetings daily in the house of the umdah. In many other villages the supervisor hardly knows or does business with anyone except the secretary or president of the association.[22]

Another key figure in the cooperative system is the bank credit clerk assigned to each village by the credit banks. Given the critical importance of the interest-free credit that he administers, the post is a significant one in the village sphere. As a result, in the words of the *al-Ahram al-Iqtisadi* study, the clerk "is able to do as he likes with the cooperative society and its board of directors." This state of affairs is serious; the study reports that of 3,240 clerks recently examined 966 were designated totally unqualified for the performance of their tasks, in addition to 346 who stood in ill repute.[23]

The publication of such sharply critical reports has not adversely affected the position of the bank credit clerks. Calls for their removal have been countered by reports of their probity and efficiency obtained from the boards of directors. Since the clerks are in such a strong position vis-à-vis the boards, the support of board members can be easily secured. Even the most venal of clerks thus are afforded an almost automatic protective device.

The extensive funds made available by the government since August 10, 1961, without interest charges have provided an appealing target for the corrupt elements in the countryside—a target clearly not made less attractive by the low caliber and apparent corruptibility of many of the administrative clerks.

A 1967 article by Aly Sabry treated in detail those abuses of the credit system. Stressing the idealism of President Nasser in formulating the interest-free credit program as a means of stimulating production in the agricultural field, and above all as an expression of the president's faith in the honesty of the Egyptian peasant, Sabry painted a rather dismal portrait of the results of the experiment. The large landowners emerge as prime villains. Sabry contended that the majority of outstanding loans are due from the major landowners, whose delinquency record he contrasted with the general tendency of the small proprietors to pay back their debts on time. Of the large landowners Sabry reported:

> Their greed rose to such a point that certain of them instead of paying back the money, invested it in commercial enterprises. Instead of honoring their previous commitments . . . they then requested further funds. Due to the weakness of certain elements or to their own powerful personal influence, they were able to obtain them.[24]

Michel Kamel gave figures to support Sabry's general charges in *Démocratie nouvelle* of February 1968:

> The sum total owed by farmers owning more than 25 feddans (who comprise only 2.5 percent of all of those who have received agricultural credit) is 60 million Egyptian pounds [$138 million]—that is, 75 percent of the total owed which rises to 80 million pounds [$184 million].

Drawing on Arab sources, a Soviet specialist provided the following specific example of the use of credit in one Egyptian village. Of the $46,000 made available, half went to five large landowners controlling among them 492 feddans; the remaining $23,000 was divided up among 795 peasants who together controlled 800 feddans. The majority of the peasants received no credit at all. As a result of this monopolization of credit by the large landowners, the poorer peasants were forced to resort to that traditional exploiter, the village money lender. An earlier study (in 1963) conducted by the weekly *Rose al-Yusuf* uncovered examples of the peasants paying as much as 10 percent a week interest on such loans.[25]

Nasser's Final Initiative

Nasser in his final years was aware of the depressing limitations of the "cooperative revolution" in rural Egypt. In 1969, just a year before his death, he inaugurated a last reform effort that reflected both his diagnosis of the ills of the cooperative movement and his ideas for reform.

On August 16, 1969, Law 51 on Agricultural Cooperatives was promulgated. It provided a revised legal framework for the cooperative movement, which confirmed the intention to extend further administrative control.[26] Two articles are particularly important. Article 31 required that each society have a responsible manager chosen by the board of directors from among those recommended by the competent administrative authority. The responsibility of the manager and his relationship with the board of directors is only vaguely defined. Bearing in mind the example of the reform cooperatives, the door was at least left open for the managers to assume effective control. Article 29 of the law provided that "in application of the penal code and of penalties specified in other laws, the resources of the societies shall be regarded as public property and [cooperative] society workers, [who are] members of their boards of directors, shall be regarded as public employees." Making the resources of the cooperatives public property and their administrators public employees should significantly enhance central control.

The provision that four-fifths of the members of the boards of directors must own less than 5 feddans was modified in the new law, which provides simply that four-fifths of the members of the boards must be peasants as defined by the ASU. At the Congress of Popular Forces in 1962, peasants were first defined as those who owned less than 25 feddans. (Since then the definition has been revised to those with less than 10 feddans.) Confirming the regime's reliance on centrally appointed managers to direct the cooperatives, the new law thus also reflected disillusionment with the poor peasants. To help lessen the temptation for corruption, the law provided that the peasant board members must be paid:

> Such an amount as is decided on by the general assembly is to be paid as stipends to members of the board for specific work undertaken; the total amount of these stipends is not to exceed ten percent of the net surplus for each fiscal year.

Support of the "natural allies," the regime apparently felt in 1969, could be secured only with the threat of punishment for corruption combined with a material incentive.

The requirements for membership on the board of directors enumerated in Article 32 of the new law reflected the lessons learned about past abuses. The article specified that members must have paid all outstanding debts to the society or to the Egyptian General Organization for Agricultural and Cooperative Credit and affiliated banks; members may not be those who gain financially from projects falling within the scope of the society, or who are involved in enterprises that conflict with the interests of the society; and members must not be connected with governmental administration—which includes mayors, heads of guard or police units, or their immediate subordinates. The article also provided that members must not be employed in any branch connected with administration, supervision, finance, or supply of the agricultural cooperative societies; that members must not be involved in contracts with the society for sale, rental, supply, or development in connection with society property, or under contract for any other dealings with the society; and finally that members of the same family or persons with kinship closer than the fourth degree are not permitted to be on the same board of directors.

Given the untransformed nature of village social relations and the non-availability of competent central officials, these various provisions had a primarily hortatory character with virtually no prospect of implementation, even if Nasser had lived. They do accurately reveal, however, some of the more serious ills of the cooperative movement.

Cooperatives under Sadat

Anwar es-Sadat inherited few illusions about the achievements of the Free Officers' revolution in rural Egypt. While the Egyptian left in the seventies has continued to argue that the remedy for revolutionary failures in the countryside was more revolution, Sadat's "move to the right" put them more than ever out of touch with political realities. There was a bitter tone to the left's acknowledgment of how little had been accomplished toward making "the cooperative, democratic society" slogan a reality in Egypt's rural areas. Its members felt that they were charged by the right with the failures of the Nasser regime—failures that they themselves had so brilliantly and boldly denounced. Now, with the right in the ascendancy, renunciation of the Nasserist past seemed to mean a renunciation of any left strategy at all. Illustrative of the bitterness of the left position is the appraisal of Fathy Abdul Fattah:

> Our Egyptian peasant, who still represents more than 50 percent of working forces in our country, is that man who works and toils on the land with his own hands and who squeezes a living, his sustenance and the sustenance of his children from the soil of the earth and who at the same time is subjected to the pressures of material, social and educational circumstances which overwhelm him and limit his resources and capabilities.

Summing up the achievements to date in altering that status of the peasant, Fattah concludes:

> This is how the peasant was before the issuance of the agricultural ownership decrees around the end of the 19th century. This is how the peasant has been after the issuance of these decrees and throughout the first half of the 20th century, and this is how the peasant has continued to be despite the reforms and laws enacted by the July Revolution.[27]

To the poor mass of Egypt's peasants, the left argues, the Free Officers had brought no real advance.

The Egyptian right, for its part, wrote with gusto of the shortcomings not only of the cooperative structure but of the very principles on which it rested. Intimations were made that by interfering with the "market" the cooperatives had in fact slowed Egypt's agricultural development. The one "asset" they brought to the countryside, right-wing analysts seemed to suggest, was bureaucratization. Writing in *al-Musawwar,* Yusuf al-Qaid observed that Egypt's peasants were faced "with a new disease, red tape." Qaid then went on to regale his readers with an account of the bureaucratic morass in the village cooperative where his father had property: it was the familiar tale of endless papers, stamps, and seals.[28]

More solid, but equally in keeping with the rightist tone of the Sadat era, have been the economic studies aimed at demonstrating that the "market distortions" wrought by the government through its manipulation of the cooperative networks have meant a loss in agricultural income. The prices of crucial commodities—land, credit, water, pesticides, seeds—are set arbitrarily by the government. Consequently, it is argued, they do not reflect scarcity values and produce distortions that lead to important income loss. While this right-wing position has been given considerable play in the Sadat years, it overstates the case against the cooperatives. For all their considerable faults, the cooperatives have complemented the regime's increased investments in agriculture by providing a means to bring expanded credit, improved agricultural inputs, and new farming techniques to the countryside. There is evidence that the peasants have regarded the cooperatives as a force for progress and as a tangible sign of the regime's commitment to reform, if not revolution, in the countryside. Moreover, overall production levels have undoubtedly been raised as a result of the cooperative efforts, even if the benefits were largely siphoned off to the more privileged groups in rural Egypt. Despite their failures, the cooperatives have brought more than red tape to Egypt's peasants.[29]

CONCLUSION

By 1969 the Nasser regime had a full understanding of the nature and extent of corruption in the cooperative movement. Stopping short of a full revolution in the countryside, it stood by essentially powerless as the much heralded benefits of cooperation were preempted by the traditionally dominant elements in the villages, with the active connivance of cooperative officials. The poor peasants, looked to hopefully as allies with "a natural interest in socialism," had proven themselves weak reeds if not supported by political cadres from the outside. Efforts to bring forth new, ideologically motivated cadres—above corruption and willing to work in the villages—had produced only meager and disappointing results. Given the weakness and disarray of the ASU, exhortatory appeals for it to play a role in curbing abuses had little practical effect. The cooperatives did make it possible to improve production by rationalizing agriculture with the introduction of large-scale farming techniques adapted to an agriculture of small, private plots. The condition of the cultivators was also improved by increased protection from moneylenders and merchant middlemen. But the cooperatives were not forged into a strong national movement with roots in the villages that could have provided the institutional mechanism for the establishment of firm government control over agricultural production. Consequently, the regime was denied the means to tap the surplus in agriculture effectively.

In its early years, M. H. Haikal has explained, "the revolutionary movement was not yet comfortably enough established in power to allow it to analyze national reality in depth."[30] Later, with its power consolidated, the regime through its efforts with the cooperative movement came to understand the "reality" of the problems. Tragically, understanding does not automatically bring with it solutions or the means to effect solutions. The manner in which the Free Officers had consolidated power and the regime produced by that consolidation had not provided the leaders with the means—neither the cadres nor the ideology—to deal effectively with the problems of developing rural Egypt. The failure of the political solution under Nasser meant the end of the possibility of a radical political solution by his regime to the transformation of the Egyptian countryside.

Anwar es-Sadat's economic solution in practice has had a dampening effect on the cooperative movement. Nasser's successor thus far has shown little real interest in the cooperatives; he has not made any major contributions to the debate over their role in rural Egypt nor has he promulgated any substantive innovations. He seems unlikely to do so. In his major program statement, the *October Paper of 1974,* Sadat described the Egyptian economy as comprising three national sectors: the public sector, the private sector, and the cooperative sector. Yet the lengthy and critical discussions of the public sector, and the detailed and enthusiastic statement of his hopes for the private sector, contrast sharply with his treatment of the cooperative sector, which comes in one brief and perfunctory statement:

> The cooperative sector in agriculture and crafts is also in need of a strong drive so as to keep pace with the sought rates of development.

There have been no signs of such a drive. For Nasser's successor has concluded that

> the main hope for providing our increasing millions of people with food lies in Egypt's ability to export enough of its industrial products in return for the needed food supplies.

Sadat's economic advisers appear to be convinced that there is no optimization plan for land use or for crop allocation, and no structural reform in the agricultural sphere, that will solve Egypt's production problems and feed its people. To survive, they conclude, Egypt must industrialize. Sadat expects no "miracle" from the agricultural cooperatives; accordingly, he gives them no great attention.[31]

9. Rural Health Care

Nowhere are the goals of Egypt's revolution more appealingly embodied than in its program for the provision of adequate health care to the people of Egypt. Like other revolutionaries before them, the Free Officers saw themselves as agents chosen to oversee a major effort at social reconstruction. The power they amassed was viewed as having a moral sanction because it would be used to secure social justice for Egypt's masses. Whatever their preoccupation with maintaining power and conducting foreign policy, Egypt's revolutionary leaders never stopped speaking of the new Egypt as a strong state able to provide an improved standard of well-being for all Egyptians. The 1962 Charter proclaimed:

> The first right of all citizens is health care—not the bare treatment and drugs like goods bought and sold, but rather the unconditional guarantee of this care to every citizen in every corner of the country under conditions of comfort and service.[1]

The effort to redeem this pledge for the millions of inhabitants of rural Egypt thus far has failed.

This is not to say that no progress has been made. There was a surge in the development of rural health care facilities shortly after the revolution. But before long the competing demands of development and defense undercut that effort. In the period up to 1965, during which the regime's policy in health care took shape, there was continuous but slow progress. In practice, it proved difficult for the regime to sustain a high-level commitment to a rural welfare "revolution from above" when the support of the intended peasant beneficiaries meant little or nothing in the calculus of power.

Still, the analysis of rural health care under the new regime reveals more than an unintended and undesired moderation of revolutionary welfare goals. Such an analysis also demonstrates the insufficiencies of vision and organizational means that the Free Officers brought to their task. Egypt's rulers showed that they could build rural health facilities in fair if still not adequate numbers. But they were unable to create the intricate interplay of motivational, institutional, and social supports that would make it possible for Egyptians to work effectively in those facilities to bring modern medicine to the peasants.

THE CHALLENGE AND THE RESPONSE

The nature of the health problems confronting the rural Egyptian population is determined by the effects of poverty and the prevalence of debilitating parasitic diseases. The major threat no longer comes from the epidemic diseases such as typhoid and malaria, but rather from the parasites that infect the majority of the population. It is generally estimated that more than half of the Egyptian people suffer from bilharziasis, ankylostomiasis, and ophthalmia. Forty percent are estimated to suffer from anemia, and the blind and nearly blind constitute roughly 6 percent of the population. It is a revealing fact that 80 percent of the fellahin are regularly judged unsuitable for military service because of the state of their health.[2]

A close study of the health conditions in one Egyptian village in Lower Egypt at the time of the revolution depicts in microcosm the situation inherited by the Free Officers. In the village 95 percent of the males suffered from bilharziasis, while over 90 percent were afflicted with trachoma. The general health of the villagers was described in these terms:

> The burden of disease carried by the population is heavy. Nutritional deficiencies, epidemic and chronic eye diseases, enteric fevers and dysenteries, tuberculosis, syphilis, and bilharzia are all found at extremely high levels in the village population.[3]

The ancien régime had taken only the most halting steps to relieve this misery. In 1942, a program for the construction of medical centers with in-patient facilities was inaugurated. The original plan called for the building of 840 centers; by the time of the revolution only 222 had actually been completed. In 1946, a second program called for the building of rural social centers, which combined other services for the local population with medical facilities. In 1952, 160 such social service centers were in operation. A dramatic reflection of the inadequacy of these early efforts is the fact that on the eve of the revolution only about six hundred doctors (of an estimated forty-five hundred) were working in rural areas, where an estimated 80 percent of the people lived. For all practical purposes, the vast majority of the rural population was deprived of the benefits of modern medicine.[4]

Set against such a background, the record of the new regime is impressive, especially in the period up to 1965 before Nasser's revolution stalled. The degree of improvement is registered in the fact that the total amount spent in the seventy years prior to the revolution for health care was matched by the Nasser regime in just the years 1961 to 1964. The budget for health care in 1951-52 was $19.35 million; by 1963-64 it had increased almost four times to $71.94 million. In the period from 1959 through 1965 the number of health care units had doubled to a total of 1,525, compared to the 382 or so that functioned on the eve of the revolution. By 1966 the number of doctors working in the rural areas had risen to 1,775.[5]

While the achievement represented by these statistics is not to be underrated, it falls far short of the goals the revolutionary regime had adopted for itself. A careful look at the institutional framework for rural health care delivery will reveal the limitations more precisely. Rural health care is provided in four major institutional forms: health centers, social service centers, combination units, and rural units. Each offers a different range of health services; each has had a distinctive history.

Health Centers

Initiated in 1942, the Health Centers Program represented the first serious attempt by the Egyptian government to attack the problems of rural health care. As originally conceived, the program called for the building of 840 centers, each serving an estimated fifteen thousand inhabitants. The units included out-patient clinics and in-patient wards designed for the treatment of contagious as well as indigenous parasitic and malnutritional diseases. Programs of preventive health, maternity care, and in-school treatment also were operated by the centers. Implementation of the program proceeded slowly, with 222 units functioning on the eve of the revolution. The Nasser regime sustained the operation of the centers and even expanded the program slightly. By 1965, 37 new units had been created to bring the total to 259.[6] However, the regime preferred to create new institutional forms to carry the brunt of its own efforts for the improvement of rural health care.

Social Service Centers

With the intention of making available in one building the combined services of doctors, teachers, agronomists, and social workers, the government in 1946 launched a program of social service centers. The original plan called for the building of such a unit in every village, but at the time of the revolution there were only 160 in operation.

After the revolution the basic combined services idea of the social service centers was incorporated in the revolutionary government's own program for combined units to be discussed below. These combined units were to be built on a more elaborate scale, with each of them serving several villages. Some of the larger social service centers were upgraded to combined units. But the social service center program itself was not dismantled. In fact, the first five-year plan called for the building of 194 units of that type. In 1965, though, it was reported that only 20 units were actually built, or 10 percent of the projected goal. In 1964-65 109 units were in operation.[7]

Combined Units

In July of 1955 Gamal Abdul Nasser himself presided over the opening of the first combined unit. Trumpeted as the revolutionary regime's answer to the problems of rural health care, the original program called for the construction of 864 units. Each unit was to be equipped with health, social welfare, agricultural, and cottage industry facilities—all designed to serve the needs of fifteen thousand rural inhabitants.

By early 1956 the program was already in serious trouble. A ranking public welfare official acknowledged at a press conference in August that lack of funds and "politics" necessitated a drastic scaling down of the expansion plans. In the appropriations crunch rural health care had already lost its priority. The original plan to construct 600 units within three years was shelved, and by 1959-60 there were only 213 combined units in operation. Over the next five years the number of combined units climbed slowly to reach 300 by 1965.[8]

Rural Units

In the program of rural units was reflected the scaling down of the regime's goals for the provision of rural health care. Having lost its early priority claim on appropriations, the ambitious combined units program by 1965 had yielded not even half of the 864 units originally estimated to be necessary to service the countryside. The rural units were designed to fill in the gaps on a much more modest scale.

Referred to as semihealth units, they contained no in-patient facilities and had a very limited staff of one doctor, one or two nurses, and aides. An estimated 2,500 units were planned, each intended to serve about five thousand persons (a village in most locales). By the beginning of 1965 581 rural units were functioning.[9]

Review of the four major health care programs in the period from 1952 to 1965 shows concretely that the regime's early commitment to a full-scale attack on the problems of rural health care was not long sustained. In the absence of supportive pressures from below (for which Nasser's system of rule provided no means of expression) the government found it easy, if regrettable, to lower its sights in order to meet other demands either judged more important or more strongly defended. Concern for rural health care was not abandoned, but emphasis was shifted from the ambitious combined units to the more modest rural units, which do not have in-patient facilities. The regime's achievement was also diluted by the fact that the 1,525 rural health care units of all types were very unevenly distributed geographically, with the more remote areas poorly represented. In addition, the operational efficiency of these units was undercut by frequent staffing and supply problems, with deficiencies again most severely felt in the remote provinces of Egypt.[10]

THE OFFICIAL REASONS FOR THE FAILURE

Official explanations for the regime's failure to realize its goals in rural health care have focused on the insufficiency of two critical inputs: appropriations for the health care programs, and medical personnel willing to work in the rural areas. Stressing Egypt's heavy financial burdens for defense, official spokesmen recognize that appropriations have been insufficient to realize stated health care objectives. But they are quick to add (and with justification) that the record still represents a dramatic improvement over the prerevolutionary situation.

The government has been even more comfortable in stressing the second point—that is, the shortage of medical personnel for the rural areas. A 1965 article in *al-Ahram,* discussing the failure to meet the health care goals of the first five-year plan, emphasized the question of cadres; the list of difficulties experienced began with "the lack of completion of some of the work teams as a result of . . . the lack of persons willing to work in the rural areas and remote regions."[11]

This official interpretation of the problems encountered in the health care program directly reflects the regime's fundamental assumptions about the process of social modernization. The Free Officers tended to view the challenge of modernization as an engineering task. Not unexpectedly, when the rural health program suffered from an insufficiency of both funds and technicians, the shortage of these two inputs was regarded as an adequate explanation for failure.

The policy implications are important here. Viewing the problems encountered in the project as essentially a "not enough" phenomenon, the regime has charted a "more of the same" course for overcoming the difficulties. Such an approach is a dangerously simplistic one. To begin with, it leaves questions of the functional efficiency of the units now in operation largely unexamined. Aside from the problem of understaffing, the units are viewed—in the official and widely accepted version—as "in general effective and popular."[12] In actuality, there is ample evidence in the Egyptian press and from foreign observers to suggest that many of the problems in the rural health units are related to the motivations of the medical personnel and to the administrative, political, and social systems within which they function. Of course, there is a self-serving reason for the regime's preference for the simplistic interpretation. By focusing attention on the unwillingness of medical personnel to work in the rural areas, Egypt's leaders have been able to use the doctors as scapegoats.

During the revolutionary period, the number of doctors serving the total population (rural and urban) improved considerably. It is estimated that by 1964 there was one doctor for every two thousand people, as opposed to one for every four thousand in 1952. This increase in the number of doctors has manifested itself in a growth from an estimated 600 doctors working in rural Egypt in 1952 to 1,775 in 1966. Yet the rural areas remain drastically undersupplied, with the overwhelming majority of doctors continuing to work in the urban areas. (Statistics for 1960, for example, indicate that of the ten thousand doctors then practicing in Egypt, fully 60 percent were located in Cairo and Alexandria.) The percentage of doctors working in the rural areas hardly changed from 1952 to 1966, remaining at about 14 percent.[13]

The failure of the government to increase the percentage of doctors working in outlying regions is a clear indication that the ideological inducements that the revolutionary leaders presumably could offer had little appeal among the medical personnel. Just to maintain the pre-1952 percentage, the regime has had to resort to coercion, supplemented later with some attempts at material persuasion. The regime has acquired a two-year period of service in the villages after internship in order to force the doctors into practice in the rural areas. The same *al-Ahram* article, in dealing with the social service centers, mentions a new program to provide personnel with free lodging on the premises of the social unit in order to induce the cadres to remain in the villages.[14]

The refusal of Egypt's physicians to respond to the call for "socialist service" in the villages has provoked virulent attacks on the "feudalism" of the medical profession. In a series of six articles in *al-Jumhuriyyah* of February 1967 Aly Sabry, then secretary-general of the ASU, sounded a ringing indictment of the medical profession as dominated by reactionaries and opportunists tainted with crass materialism. Sabry seemed to be particularly incensed by the lack of ideologically motivated response to the country's call for service on the part of the young doctors and medical students. This he blamed on the example of the older reactionary elements entrenched in the medical profession, who demonstrated to their younger colleagues "what could be gained dishonestly."[15]

The policy implication of Sabry's arguments was clearly the increased regimentation of the medical profession by Egypt's rulers, with stronger coercive measures to compel further compliance with official goals. Western observers, impressed with the patent reluctance of professionals to work in the rural areas, in general have been inclined to go along with such an approach.[16] As far as it goes, the argument is not unreasonable. Obviously, there can be little improvement in rural health care without an increase of trained cadres working in the villages and supported by an adequate program of investment in health services. But a critical review of the actual operation of the health care units from 1952 to 1965 reveals problems that go beyond the inadequacies of investment funds and the shortage of medical personnel. Additional shortcomings in the regime's approach to rural health care show up in the accumulated experience of those years.

A CRITICAL VIEW OF THE FAILURE

Grave flaws in the government's performance in its rural health care program have resulted from a complex pattern of obstacles compounded of ideological and institutional factors. Experience suggests that these problems will not be resolved merely by compelling the physical presence of medical personnel in the rural areas and maximizing rural health care appropriations.

The operation of the rural health units has been adversely affected by the fact that the backbone of their present staffing is a group of two-year conscripts fresh from the medical schools of the UAR. These recruits, who are to carry so much of the burden of rural health care, frequently come from urban backgrounds—or at least have enjoyed an urban setting for the long duration of their medical studies. Their encounter with the rural milieu is pregnant with insight into the broader problem of urban-trained cadres working in rural Egypt.

The drama of this encounter is best told in specific human terms. An American student of rural Egyptian social development has recorded the story of one young doctor in a remote village of Suhag province.[17] From a well-to-do family of Alexandria and used to a comfortable European standard of living, this doctor had never lived in a village before. After graduation from medical school he was assigned to the general hospital of Suhag for a seven-week orientation period to prepare him for a village assignment. At the end of that course "his" village was pointed out to him on a map, and the young doctor began his adventure equipped with his little black bag and a large trunk. After a long and difficult journey he arrived at his remote destination, only to find the village health unit "a filthy mess unfit for my dog to live in," and the village itself "dirtier than I had ever dreamed."

My room was even dirtier than the reception portion of the health
unit. There was no food in the health unit and I didn't dare eat the
"baladi" food offered by the 'umdah . . . For the next three days it
was like a nightmare—finally exhausted, nearly famished and completely defeated, I left the village.[18]

Although the director of health subsequently assigned the young doctor
to a village with a combined unit, any altruistic feelings that he may have
entertained as a student were clearly dissipated; he spent the remainder of
his assignment longing for his return to Alexandria.

Clearly unequipped for the hardships that awaited him, this young
doctor also lacked the strong commitment that might have spurred him
to at least attempt to overcome them. While hardly the villain of Aly
Sabry's scenario, he will contribute little to alleviation of the health problems that burden the rural population.

Evidence from the Egyptian press indicates that this case points to a
general pattern. In 1968 the research staff of the Egyptian daily *al-Jumhuriyyah* conducted a detailed field study of ten Egyptian villages, six of
which had a health unit. One major conclusion reported was the following:

Most of the physicians working in these units look on their work in
the village as an exile; they exert all their efforts to be transferred to
the city, and this is of course reflected in their work.[19]

So compulsion, while it may secure the doctors' physical presence in
the countryside (and thereby help provide impressive statistics that attest
to the regime's progress), does not ensure that once there the doctors can
or will perform effectively. And perhaps one should not even take that
physical presence too much for granted. Lacking a sense of identification
with the national goals for rural health care—or more accurately, a willingness to make personal sacrifices for these goals—the doctors tend to
view their assignments as part of the workings of an authoritarian system. They are more than willing to match their considerable wits to elude
that system. Finagling and influence peddling to secure the most favorable assignments are phenomena hard to quantify, but impossible not to
notice. Once a "good" position has been secured—that is, a village located near Cairo, Alexandria, or a provincial urban center—a doctor's
task can become one of reducing to an absolute minimum the time actually spent in the village. The stratagems are ingenious, but all basically
variations on a familiar pattern of behavior.

For example, among the portraits in Tawfik el-Hakim's classic novel
of prerevolutionary Egypt, *The Maze of Justice,* is that of an unforget-
table judge. Arriving in his village like a whirlwind in the early morning,

he races nonstop through his cases in order to catch the eleven o'clock train back to Cairo. Nothing, certainly not justice for the peasants he judges, is allowed to block his escape from the village. Echoes of that brand of irresponsibility remain in the rural Egypt of the socialist era.[20]

An American field researcher has reported the case of a woman doctor assigned to work in a health unit located forty minutes by train from Cairo. Averaging two or three visits to the unit each week, she rarely remained in the village more than a few hours. If by chance her absence were recorded by a government inspector, the doctor then would make it a point to be at the unit every day for a week or two. Her absences were made possible by an orderly who operated the clinic largely on his own. Such willingness of an orderly to cover for his physician results from the profitability of the task of distributing medical supplies, which then falls into his hands.[21]

Of course, reports of efficient and devoted medical personnel working in the rural areas do appear in the press. What is striking about these accounts, though, is the invariable implication that they are rather singular exceptions from the normal, depressing pattern. An *al-Tali'ah* study, for example, praises one village health unit and attributes its success to "the faithfulness and sincerity of the doctor who believes in his mission and responsibility." The report goes on to make it clear that the performance of the doctor was not typical of specialists working in the village: other government officials are accused of bureaucratic methods and exploitation of the peasants. One village veterinarian, for example, is charged with refusing to treat a sick water buffalo unless he received a gratuity. The findings of the *al-Jumhuriyyah* team give a similar impression. The only health unit singled out for its efficiency is the one in Musha, a village in Upper Egypt: "This is due to the presence of a resident and energetic woman physician who is a member of the young people's organization and works with sincerity and political awareness." The limitations of a conscription program for forcing medical personnel to work in the villages is quite obvious. Even in those cases where a professional and humanitarian commitment does exist, doctors brought to the villages may still be unable to help the peasants significantly.[22]

The health programs of the peasant population are often aggravated by traditional practices and activities that have become an integral part of rural life. The doctors, frequently of urban backgrounds, are not always sufficiently sensitive to this fact. While the resistance to change of the peasants can be overemphasized, when it involves matters they consider basic to their most essential selves, it does constitute a serious obstacle.

These hazards of communication, which plague the doctor's relationship with the peasants, again can best be understood by a case study.[23]

Bilharziasis, a ravaging parasitic disease, was the target of one doctor's campaign in his village. Working overtime to implement a complex twelve-injection treatment program, the doctor succeeded in breaking the life cycle of the parasite and curing the peasants. Yet within three months all had been reinfected and the effects of his victory were wiped out. The explanation for this failure elucidates the complexity of the problems facing the country doctor. The doctor first had to spend long hours convincing the peasants of the nature of the disease that afflicted them and of the fact that he could cure it. Next came the investment of time and energies in the inoculation program itself. A still greater problem, unrealized initially by the doctor, still lay ahead: to convince the peasants to avoid reinfection. Since the peasants had already agreed to undergo the treatment, one might think that this demand would present no hardship. It did, however, for the simple reason that the precautions necessary to prevent reinfection would require a profound change in the life style of the peasants.

First, since canals were the source of the infections, they had to be avoided. But to the youths of the village, it was too hot *not* to swim in the canals (and given the summer heat of Upper Egypt, it was an argument with some force). Furthermore, the men of the village complained of the tastelessness of the well water and preferred the "richer" Nile water. The cause for this preference was also linked to a matter more basic than taste, since Nile water was reputed to increase a man's virility. Given the social emphasis placed on sexual prowess for men, this too was a consideration not to be taken lightly. Moreover, since the farmers' irrigation duties compelled them to wade in the canal waters anyway, it was probably much more satisfactory for the peasants simply to reject the doctor's explanations for the source of their ailments and consign themselves to the will of God. Confronted with such barriers, even a doctor with a strong personal sense of mission would be subject to disillusionment.

Support from the official administrative structures could be an important factor in the face of such inevitable discouragements. The record from Egyptian sources indicates that such support for the doctors has not been forthcoming. In fact, there is a noticeable tendency on the part of the central authorities to value statistics and reports—that is, the traditional trappings of correct bureaucratic behavior—more than actual medical care. In an interview with an American specialist in the field, a young doctor expressed just this criticism:

The central government does not really care about my medical work—all they want is that I perform my administrative responsibilities. I have so many administrative duties that if I did them properly I would have no time for my medical practice.[24]

One need not rely on the testimony of the doctors alone. In 1966 three Egyptian experts in administrative matters conducted an extensive survey of the administrative structure in the UAR, which contained invaluable data on rural health administration. Focusing attention first on the small rural health unit, the report vividly substantiated the complaint of the young doctor concerning the heavy burden of administrative duties: "In the rural unit we find that the physician who provides medical treatment is also frequently the responsible administrative official, while he has to examine the patients and supervise the care given to mothers and children, health care in schools and health inspection." Stressing the over-burdening of the unit doctor, the report continued: "He is the one person to take care of recording deaths and births and to distribute drugs." The almost total absence of pharmacists in the rural areas further complicated the doctor's role: "At the same time—and most important of all—he is responsible for taking care of the drug supplies and delivering prescriptions to the patients." Since the rural health units are similarly devoid of dentists, the physician's paramedical functions often included dentistry as well. This compounding of the doctor's role is all the more harrowing when one recalls that in some of the more remote provinces one doctor must serve several health units.[25]

The same study pointed out that the performance of these multiple duties is not made any easier for the doctor by the complex bureaucratic procedures involved. The following incredible example was given, followed by an admirably restrained conclusion:

> With reference to the measures required to justify the expense involved by the maintenance and purchase of basic supplies such as gas, table salt, and so forth, we note that the following documents are required:
>   Request for a specific item;
>   Evidence that this particular item is not already in stock;
>   Authorization from the head of the health department to obtain that item from a larger store;
>   Special entry form concerning the deposit of the item in question in the store . . .
> If we just think how far the unit is from the health department and consider that the value of the corresponding credit may not exceed 15 pounds, we find that this single unit—which covers such a small area—has to cope with excessive complications and measures which finally affect the medical service itself.[26]

Egyptian public administration experts recognize the duplication of effort in rural health care programs, especially between the health unit and the combined service centers. In speaking of the combined centers, the administrative study reported on the problems caused by lack of coordination within the unit because the various sections are under the jurisdiction of different central ministries. The outlines of this administrative nightmare sharpen when one realizes that the education section actually is controlled by the Ministry of Education, while the social section is placed under the Ministry of Social Affairs, the agricultural section under the Ministry of Agriculture, and the medical health section under the Ministry of Health.

Further complications are ensured by the local administrative unit—the village council if there is one, the mayor or police chief if there is not. The medical section of the combined units (according to the official description) depends on the Ministry of Health technically, but on the head of the village council administratively. The meaning to the doctor of this nebulous formulation is that while he remains subject to the bureaucratic harassment of the central authorities, he is also at the mercy of the local head of the village council. His dependence on the village council stems from the inclusion of the budget for the medical section in the budget for the council. Assessing the meaning of this budgetary control, the study reported that it "always causes conflicts concerning the requirements of the medical section in drugs and services—especially when the head of the village council is not a technician."[27] Since the heads of the councils are most often schoolteachers, one concludes that conflict must be the order of the day.

This dual supervision of the doctor by the central health department and the local village council is rendered still more bewildering by the fact that coordination between the two bodies is practically nonexistent. The precise nature of their authority is unclear, and they apparently do not cooperate. For example, the administrative study reports that the inspection and evaluation reports on the medical section of the combined units are not made available to the village council, despite the fact that it is the village council that controls the section's budget. Since the council lacks medical expertise itself and is denied the reports of the medical inspectors, it is hardly surprising that its decisions frequently appear arbitrary and technically unworkable to the doctor.

To complete the picture of the doctor's tour of service in the countryside, the role of the local Arab Socialist Union members must not be overlooked. Grandiloquently but vaguely charged with acting as the vanguard of the people and the protector of their interests, the ASU official out to prove his zealousness can make life still more difficult for the rural doctor. The problem is illustrated by the case of a recent graduate from the University of Cairo medical school:

The doctor was assigned to a village boasting a health unit adequately housed in a two-story building.[28] The doctor's responsibility included the distribution of United States medical aid supplies, and on a day when he was supervising this distribution, the ASU local leader paid him a visit. At the moment of the leader's arrival, however, the doctor's orderly had taken over the task to allow the doctor time for a cup of tea in his apartment over the clinic.

The ASU man, incensed at what he took to be a dereliction of duty, rushed into the doctor's apartment and ordered him back to work. Enraged by the unjustness of the attack and the presumptuousness of the political worker, the doctor retorted that he would return to work when he was good and ready.

Two weeks later the doctor was relieved of his position in the village and assigned to a new one in Qena. While his first village was only about a two-hour train ride from Cairo, Qena in Upper Egypt is referred to as the Siberia of the UAR. The charge levied against the doctor was substantiated by five witnesses—all members of the village ASU organization; they charged the doctor with requiring gratuities for his services and with spending the greater part of his afternoons and evenings caring for the rich landowners of the village and neglecting his clinical duties.

Acquaintance with the pattern of abuses in the rural health centers suggests that these charges are not beyond belief. Whatever the guilt or innocence of this particular doctor, it is enough for our purposes to note the potential for conflict with the ASU local officials.

To complete the analysis of factors that have hampered the functioning of the rural health units, we must examine the broader social context within which they operate. Despite the efforts of the Nasser revolution (particularly the successive land reform laws), the Egyptian countryside has remained under the dominance of the larger and more powerful landowning families. The relevance of this social situation to the health units is that the richer peasants and landlords often succeed in preempting the services offered. Aly Sabry has provided an example of the process, including a description of "how one proprietor made the village doctor his personal physician."[29]

This cooption of the medical personnel by the leading social strata in the village is by no means a coercive process. The professionals tend to feel a natural affinity for such elements, the members of which are usually literate and enjoy sanitary health conditions. One 1966 study notes that "government workers look down on the villagers and only associate with the wealthy and educated individuals in the village." Consequently, the potential positive impact of their presence in a village is minimized. Furthermore, in cases where ethical commitment is lacking on the part of the medical professionals, considerations of financial gain must not be excluded. Salaries for village work are low, and the temptation to supplement incomes strong. According to the *al-Tali'ah* study, the wealthier elements in the villages are willing to pay for special service and consideration: "the larger landowners in the village are ever willing to offer him financial and material assistance so that he will provide his services to them."[30]

This attraction of the professionals to the well-to-do elements in the village society has its obverse side in a recorded disdain for the illiterate villager. A 1961 article in *al-Jumhuriyyah* described these conditions:

> In the combined unit there is not enough medicine, the nurses are rude to patients. Of the fourteen in-patient facilities, only one is actually available; the rest are occupied by the employees of the unit who use the rooms as a dormitory.[31]

Precise quantification of such highhandedness is not available; but impressions from the Egyptian press suggest that the phenomenon is an important factor in limiting the effectiveness of the rural units. At any rate, it appears that purely statistical study of the rural health units can be seriously misleading.

There is indeed a shortage of health professionals in the villages of Egypt, as the official view of the regime's shortcomings in rural health care argues. But a close study of the actual operation of the units reveals the problems encountered to be infinitely more complex and calling for a great deal more than simply increased numbers of medical personnel. Motivation as well as the administrative, political, and social conditions under which the doctors work must be improved.

There have been some signs of a more productive approach. The excellent 1966 *al-Ishtiraki* study referred to earlier is a prime example of a clear perception of the problems and the obstacles that must be overcome if effective medical care is to be provided Egypt's people. It is noteworthy that the study concludes by making the peasants' attitudes toward the health program the acid test of its efficiency:

> The peasant does not even know those terms (bureaucracy, routine, etc.) and how to use this language. All he knows is that there is a service which is not given to him as it should be; that there is a physician who does not do his work as he should; that there are drugs which are not given to him; and that there are nurses who tried to get money from him. The peasant says nothing about causes and he only realizes the results. He is aware of the shortcomings of the rural unit and accordingly resorts to the central hospital. He may even go as far as Cairo to look for some better treatment and some better service. Consequently, the peasant is the radar which we may use to evaluate the situation.[32]

It is very difficult to estimate the percentage of the rural population that actually benefits from the various rural health programs. A Soviet source records that in 1964 a total of 3.30 million people in Egypt received medical treatment. Out of an estimated rural population of 17 million that suggests a figure of 18 percent. The problem with such estimates is that they are based on the records of the Egyptian health establishments; a tendency to inflate the figures as evidence of hard work is built into them. When this causation is taken into account, the 18 percent official figure seems a tragic reflection of the inadequacies of the results achieved by the mid-sixties.[33]

From Nasser to Sadat

In Nasser's demanding last years modest additions were made to the rural health care network. In 1970-71 health care units in the villages totaled 1,827, with 263 health centers, 43 social service units, 324 combination units, and 1,197 rural units. Expenditures continued to grow at a steady if uninspiring pace. Between 1952-53 and 1969-70, the Nasser era, they increased an average of 11 percent per year. Yet when Nasser died in the fall of 1970 the pledge of his regime to provide health care "to every citizen in every corner of the country under conditions of comfort and service" obviously remained unfulfilled. In the 1974 *October Paper* Nasser's successor reaffirmed that Free Officer pledge. Sadat wrote, "The progress of nations is measured not by the standard of those few at the top, but rather by that of the broad masses at the base." Health care for Egypt's peasantry, Sadat averred, must be an indispensable part of such progress.[34]

In recent years there have been efforts to deal with the obstacles inherited from the Nasser era in a manner consonant with the rightist tone of Sadat's rule. The thinking of the new regime was outlined in a major policy statement of Dr. Ahmed Said Darwish, the minister of health. Darwish addressed head-on the problem of the shortage of medical personnel, especially doctors, for the rural areas. That problem, he announced, had reached critical proportions with a personnel shortage of approximately 30 percent for the rural program. He proposed a variety of ways in which to reward doctors who remained at their posts in the countryside. Supplemental income, up to 50 percent of base salary, would be offered to doctors who agreed to work in two health units (one in the morning and one in the evening). The minister pledged to provide them with more adequate professional support services in the countryside. Medical magazines and professional journals were to be distributed free. The minister also reported a project under study to provide rural doctors with specialized training programs and refresher courses, prepared by eminent professors of medicine and broadcast to the rural areas. Mention was also made of a plan to expand the opportunities for doctors working in the rural sector to take advanced training abroad in relevant specialties. There was no trace in all of this of the earlier leftist charges of "medical feudalism" and the left strategy to compel the doctors to serve the peasantry. Doctors in Sadat's Egypt were to be wooed and lured into rural work with capitalist and professional inducements. Young doctors were to be made more susceptible to such blandishments by subtly making their medical training itself more "society oriented."[35]

The moribund state of the ASU in the Sadat era presumably has eliminated or at least sharply curtailed the harassing potential of ASU militants. The bureaucratic dragon, however, enjoys health as lusty as ever, although it has been made the target of a series of journalistic attacks. *Al-Ahram* in April 1973 provides the details of one illustrative horror story, which attests to the continuing bureaucratic ensnarement of the rural doctors. This particular doctor's ordeal began in 1965 when he petitioned for a pay raise differential resulting from a promotion from grade 6 to grade 7, civil service fashion. The *al-Ahram* researcher tracked down thirty-two documents bearing on the case in various offices of the Ministry of Health, as the case dragged on into the 1970s. Those eventually involved in the matter included three undersecretaries of the Ministry of Health, five directors of fiscal and administrative affairs, five directors of staff affairs, three directors of accounts, and nine directors of hospitals! All in all, the thirty-two documents for the case bore 111 signatures. Presumably, as a result of the *al-Ahram* exposé, the doctor has been paid.[36]

Although it is too early for any definitive judgments, existing trends make it hard to be optimistic for any great improvement in rural health care in the near future. The Sadat efforts toward reform simply have been too modest to generate much enthusiasm. Capitalist incentives are much more likely to carry young Egyptian doctors abroad—to the West or to the oil-rich Arab states—than into the villages of the Nile Valley. As long as the gap between village and urban life remains the chasm it is today, the regime simply will not have the resources to attract doctors with material incentives. And there have been indications, although no precise figures, that the brain drain of medical personnel has sharply accelerated as a result of Sadat's liberalization measures.

Not unexpectedly, a new minister of health, Dr. M. Mahfuz, announced a return in the seventies to the earlier coercive policy: five hundred doctors from central hospitals were to be transferred to the various rural health units. Mahfuz also announced that 25 percent of each medical school graduating class would be trained for rural work.[37] Even so, there is no reason to expect results more positive now than those attained in the Nasser years by such methods. There is not even the rhetoric of ideological inducement, the bureaucratic hindrances are as virulent as ever, and village social relations are basically unchanged. Newspaper exposés are no substitute for streamlining reforms, and by the mid-seventies there were no signs of such reforms in Egypt's rural health care program.

CONCLUSION

To take a broad view, it can be seen that the regime of the Free Officers was able to expand appreciably if not adequately both the network of rural health care facilities and the absolute numbers of medical personnel to staff them. But it failed to stimulate a sense of mission and dedication sufficient to persuade those doctors to practice their skills where they were most needed—in rural Egypt. Egypt's doctors proved unwilling to sacrifice their self-interest in order to provide Egyptian socialism with a genuine welfare content. The resort to coercion by the government produced a statistical rise in the absolute number of doctors working in the villages; it is much less clear that a corresponding rise in health care for the rural masses has resulted. In place of strong official support, administrative confusion, political harassment, and excessive bureaucratization have added to the already staggering burdens of understaffed, poorly supplied, and frequently unmotivated doctors. Through the medium of power the regime in the Nasser years was able to achieve the physical presence of medical personnel in the villages. But with a power based on coercion and largely devoid of the dimension of ideological inducement, it was not able to produce enough doctors with a genuine commitment to the regime's goal of raising the health standards of rural Egypt.

There has been a need for bold, new initiatives in the Sadat era, based on the lessons learned from the obstacles Nasser's programs encountered. To date there have been no such initiatives. The lack of direction of the present regime's health care program is reflected in top-level instability; during the six months from September 1971 to January 1972 there were five different ministers of health. The possibility of an effective health care program for rural Egypt depends on increased investments coupled with a system of workable incentives. Material and intellectual resources must be found to expand the training of medical personnel for village work, to imbue them with a spirit of service, and to create supportive institutional, political, and social structures in the villages. Until then, the peasants will continue to suffer.

10. The Regime and the Revolution

For Egyptians it was startling when Tawfik el-Hakim, the respected dean of Egyptian letters, in the fall of 1974 called openly for a critical review of the entire Nasserist experience. "The dossier [on the Nasser years]," wrote Hakim, "must be opened."[1] The liberalization of the Sadat era has made it possible for Egyptians to begin a meaningful assessment of their revolution. The historical judgment undoubtedly will be a mixed one.

NASSER'S EGYPT IN RETROSPECT

Originating in conspiracy in the unpromising Egyptian military, the regime of Gamal Abdul Nasser and the Free Officers was propelled by a nationalist dream of a strong Egypt purified of its legacy of colonial dependency. These aspirations for national greatness and independence remained as constants in the years after 1952. However, it was soon realized that a strong Egypt in the environment of the twentieth century would have to be a modernized Egypt. By any objective criteria social and economic conditions there rank among the most onerous of any country in the world. Painfully the young and inexperienced army officers learned the magnitude of the tasks that the imperative of modernization imposed, and they groped for a way to deal with them.

Of the lessons subsequently learned, the most difficult was undoubtedly the realization that Egyptians had escaped from their colonial past only to experience new forms of international and domestic dependency. An overpopulated Egypt with slender resources had to have outside help to develop. Thus, foreign and domestic affairs were inextricably linked. By the authoritarian exercise of political will, the Free Officers determined the country's broad development strategy. But any such strategy required foreign assistance to realize its goals. Moreover, authoritarian patterns of rule left the mass of Egyptians dependent on the successful maneuverings of their new elite. Whether the rulers wrested aid from the superpowers in the competitive bidding of a Cold War climate, or secured it as part of a special relationship with either the Soviet Union or the United States, the form of Egypt's revolution was inevitably distorted by foreign influence and elite manipulation.

In the Nasser years the meaning of the link between foreign and domestic affairs was obscured by simplistic but powerful views of what modernization meant. During the nationalist phase of the fifties an engineering view of how modernity would be brought to Egypt prevailed: modernity could be grafted on from the outside with the help of imported capital and technical skills bestowed on a neutralist Egypt in a Cold War age.

The new rulers were denied the critique of such views that Egypt's intellectuals might have provided. Lost was the legacy of serious reflection by intellectuals across the political spectrum on the fundamental questions of the ideological and institutional bases of political life. In the formative years the Free Officers feared the divisive impact of social ideas and ideologies. Egypt's intellectuals were alienated from the plebian military regime. That alienation, Nasser later realized, was a profound loss.

In the early years, though, the limitations of the views of what modernity would mean and how it might be achieved were obscured by brilliant successes in foreign policy. Those accomplishments yielded a diffuse but enduring pool of popular support. By the mid-fifties an elaborated vision had taken shape, which promised to give greater coherence and direction to Nasser's regime. Domestic and foreign considerations were interwoven and the vague yearnings for Egypt's greatness coalesced around more concrete goals. The Free Officers saw themselves as the chosen agents of history. Their preoccupation with power was justified by a vision of the new Egypt they would create. Under their rule a developed Egypt would take its rightful place as the head of the Arab world and leader in the struggle against Israel. The activism of its foreign policy would raise Egypt's global prestige and earn the foreign aid needed for domestic development.

By the mid-sixties the shortcomings of Free Officer conduct of Egypt's domestic and foreign affairs were evident. Foreign commitments brought Egypt to the brink of disaster; the domestic revolution was mired in bureaucracy and military patterns of rule. By binding together Egypt's multiple aspirations domestically and internationally, Nasser gave his regime the tactical flexibility that became its hallmark. With a multitude of ways to serve his goals, he could shift emphasis from one goal to another according to the opportunities of time and place. But there was a fateful precariousness to Nasser's perception. A decisive setback in the pursuit of one of these goals could have ruinous consequences for all. Just such an eventuality was realized in the sixties.

In 1961 Nasser's efforts to advance Arab unity suffered a major reversal with the secession of Syria from the United Arab Republic. To regain the initiative in Arab affairs, Nasser in 1962 precipitously rushed into "revolutionary war" in Yemen. That intervention provoked conflict with Saudi Arabia and eventually poisoned relations with the United States, which backed the Saudi regime. American aid was cut off in the mid-sixties, with inevitable harm to Egyptian development. This chain reaction of reversals created the mood of despair and desperation which was one factor that caused Nasser to abandon his policy of "militant inaction" toward Israel and to act out his rhetoric of confrontation in June 1967. For Egypt devastating defeat at the hands of the Israelis meant dependency on the Soviet Union.

The results of the June War prompted an internal questioning of the revolution on all levels. Even before 1967 Nasser had been forced to face the limitations of his achievement in ruling Egypt. In order to pursue his activist foreign policy he required a radical independence from societal constraints. That independence and the resulting maneuverability were gained by basing his regime firmly on dependent administrative structures. The character of the official ideology belatedly pieced together was similarly shaped by the exigencies of foreign policy.

As foreign aid resources became strained in the mid-sixties, Nasser was made fully aware of the problems of the instruments of rule he had created for Egypt. Faced with the task of developing Egypt increasingly in terms of its own resources, Nasser realized that he had not created the political tools—neither the ideology nor the organized and motivated cadres—that would be necessary. More damaging still was the realization that the political system shaped under Nasser's aegis worked actively against the creation of these tools. The nonparticipation of the masses, the isolation of the intellectuals, the prominence of bureaucratic and military figures, with the resultant ascendancy of bureaucratic methods and inflation of defense spending, and above all the channelling of political energies into personalized struggles for power, characterized that system. The impact of these flaws was crippling to Nasser's efforts in the mid-sixties to build a political party and fashion an ideology geared to the demands of transforming Egypt through a strategy involving mass participation. Such a "political solution" had to be abandoned.

The story of Nasser's Egypt, broadly speaking, is the story of the attempted reshaping of a military coup d'état into a social revolution managed and controlled from above. Nasser's legacy contained constructive as well as negative aspects. Above all, the Nasser regime did expel the British. It also implemented permanent if limited socioeconomic change, which raised the status of Egyptians in their own eyes and in the eyes of the world. In a long-range view of Egyptian internal history, the single most important development—despite its flaws—is surely the continuing commitment and drive to remake Egypt from an overwhelmingly agricultural into an industrialized nation. Less tangible but no less real is the increased national pride that has accompanied accomplishments in this direction.

Nasser was acutely aware that his revolution had not gone far enough. By the mid-sixties he understood that a truly modernizing revolution for Egypt would entail self-confrontation at the profoundest levels of values and beliefs. Egyptians, Nasser realized, had themselves been damaged by their legacy of bondage to tradition and colonial dependency. He called for "a struggle against ourselves" and warned his people that such a struggle would be far more arduous than the fight against the outside enemy. Bitterly, he admitted that his regime had not fashioned the political weapons for such a contest. Once again, however, he was diverted in 1967 by the demands of foreign policy. Nasser died in 1970 still preoccupied by the results of his foreign policy miscalculations.[2]

Still, the Nasserist legacy does contain the articulated call for total revolution—revolution that weds power and ideas in a process of purposeful social change:

> It must be a living revolution, a continuous revolution, an effective revolution. It must produce this effect in the field, in the wilderness, in the factory, the school, the university, the service centres, in any place which promotes human endeavor.

Seeking to go beyond his revolution from above, Nasser looked increasingly to political rather than administrative means: "It is time to depend on political action rather than administrative action." He was forced to consider the nature and potential uses of his own political power. A beginning exploration of Egypt's potential for definitive change is part of the Nasser experience—whatever the limitations of the results actually achieved.[3]

Nasser had repeatedly justified his own intense preoccupation with the maintenance of power and the preservation of his regime in terms of the modernizing uses to which that power could be put:

> Some of these nationalist movements forget that coming to power is not an end of the revolution but is the beginning action for the revolution through the medium of power.[4]

Power for Nasser had become, at least theoretically, a medium for transformation. Yet Nasser's very conception of the nature of power, while adequate to ensure his own position and the stability of his regime, was inadequate to manage the socioeconomic changes necessary to modernize Egypt.

From the outset Nasser evinced a marked and enduring suspicion of the ideological dimension of power. During the conspiratorial phase of the Free Officers movement he was conditioned to see ideology as a divisive threat. Later, even after he had become aware of the importance of ideology as an instrument for heightening political power, his distrust of it was revived as debate over ideological formulations threatened to provide a platform for challenging his own preeminent political position. Fundamental was Nasser's demand for a flexibility and mobility that would tolerate no restraint and no delay. An elaborated ideology, especially if embodied institutionally in a political party with its motivated cadres, would have brought just such restraint and delay.

Publicist Ihsan Abdul Kudus has spoken of the need of the Egyptian people for "a strong faith" if they are to pass through the sacrifice and suffering required for the construction of a new society. Sociologist Abbas Ammar has spoken of the "missionary spirit" necessary to sustain those heavily charged in the effort to modernize Egypt. Nasser's regime provided neither that faith nor that spirit—nor the institutions in which they could be embodied. And still worse, the repressive dimension of Nasser's rule left a bitter legacy of fear. "The revolution," Sadat wrote, "was reduced to a huge, dark, and terrible pit, inspiring fear and hatred but allowing no escape."[5]

THE PROBLEMS AND PROSPECTS OF SADAT'S EGYPT

In the liberalized climate of the Sadat era, Egyptians have begun to deal openly with the inadequacies of the political structures produced by the 1952 revolution. Tawfik el-Hakim has illuminated one debilitating aspect of Nasser's political legacy:

> Little by little, voices that were accustomed to debate became faint, and the beloved ruler himself became accustomed to rule without debate. The iron curtain slowly began to descend between the people and the conduct of the absolute ruler. We loved him, yet we did not know his inner thoughts nor the real motives for his conduct. Our hearts pierced the curtain between us, but our faculties of reason were totally isolated, never grasping what went on behind the veil. We never knew of our own affairs, or of foreign affairs except what he told us from on high, during holidays and on other occasions.[6]

Nasser had cast the Egyptian people in the passive role of witnesses to the drama of their national liberation. With the Suez War of 1956, Egypt—so it seemed—had been freed. The colonial bonds were finally broken. There was at last an opportunity for the building of a genuine political community. But for this second task Nasser's rule proved flawed. Hakim conveys the hard-gained knowledge that the total revolution that alone could create such a community could not be realized by elite manipulation, no matter how bold. Such a revolution could only mean the self-transformation of a people. Such self-transformation in turn necessitated supportive institutional and intellectual structures. Judged by this standard, the rule of Anwar es-Sadat so far has been as disappointing as that of his predecessor.

Although there has been an enhancement of political freedom and personal security in Sadat's Egypt, he has done little to alter the basic intellectual and institutional constructs of Nasserist rule. It is true that Sadat's liberalization has meant an expanded social role for a variety of middle-class elements. But the new prominence of middle-class strata to date has rested on either a carefully monitored and highly individualized technological input into decision making, a consolidation of the relative privilege of the public sector employees, or an unofficial toleration of the new "middlemen" or "expediters" who have multiplied and flourished in the Sadat years. The advance of the technocrats has been most impressive. In the seventies the composition of Egypt's cabinets has registered a decline in military and a rise in technocratic figures (though the docile technocrat was already a fixture in Nasser's Egypt). Furthermore, Sadat's liberalization measures are too recent, and Egypt's social structure is too fluid, to speak of a new middle-class foundation for Sadat's rule. The artificial military/bureaucratic caste inherited from the Nasser years is still the major social prop of the regime. Real power has continued to be lodged with the military/security complex. Elite energies have remained focused, however unavoidably, on foreign policy considerations. Increased debate and criticism has not yet meant the emergence of a more meaningful realm of social action for Egyptians.

There has been the promise of the "opening." Sadat's strategy, while bold in conception, built wisely both on lessons learned in the Nasser years and on an appreciation for the new demands of the seventies. Sadat understood that Egypt had to draw on its external environment for the resources to develop. Yet he also realized that "investment in foreign policy" was as dangerous as it was unavoidable. Consequently, he insisted that Egypt in the seventies would play a regional and global role, but a role with lowered sights. Sadat explained that Egypt would still remain at the head of the movement for Arab unity and of the Arab struggle against Israel. But the drive to unify the Arabs would be conceived in cautious and pragmatic terms, the confrontation with Israel linked to an openly proclaimed moderate strategy.

Sadat with good reason called this moderate orientation a "gamble on the future." A shadow was cast over the strategy because of the accompanying costs of alienating the Soviets and potentially of isolating Egypt in the Arab arena. And there could be no assurance that Egypt's American-backed moderation would in fact yield the Israeli reciprocation necessary to bring regional stabilization.

Significant internal reform was also demanded by Sadat's strategy. Investment Law 43, with its incentives and guarantees to foreign investors, was only a beginning. Above all, the deadening bureaucratization of Egyptian society somehow had to be reversed and the new forms of corruption curbed. That, Sadat realized, would take time. In his important speech to the nation during the October War, Sadat remarked that in some ways Egypt's most dangerous enemy was the internal one: a whole generation, the president warned, might be required to alter the ingrained, self-seeking habits that poisoned Egyptian public life.[7]

By 1977 much of the initial optimism generated by the open-door policy had been dampened. Response by Western and Arab capital to the new investment opportunities in Egypt was too meager to fuel the hoped-for economic miracle. Foreign investors saw an Egypt burdened with the threat of war with Israel, mired in bureaucracy and corruption, nearly overwhelmed by the crush of its population growth—and they stayed away.

Periodically Sadat renewed his call for the very difficult reforms that alone could make the opening work on the domestic plane. There were authoritative attacks on bureaucratism, calls for solidarity and patience, and denunciations of those "millionaires" whose exploitative actions were destroying the spirit of the open door. But Sadat himself seemed always more preoccupied with Egypt's external affairs, unavoidably driven from stratagem to stratagem to secure the regional stabilization that would reassure the foreign investor in Egypt.

If a revitalized and dynamic private sector had resulted from a successful opening, spontaneous social forces might have been unloosed to reinforce the structural and value changes Sadat anticipated. In the absence of that success, official exhortations were as ineffective as in the Nasser years. There could be no translation into an intellectual resource, a mode of thinking, that the mass of Egyptians could adopt in their efforts at massive social reconstruction. Sadat's difficulties stemmed in part from the fact that the reorientation and readjustments necessary to make the opening strategy work could not be hurried. As Abdul Aziz Higazi, the architect of economic liberalization, wrote in *al-Ahram:* "Even economic miracles require time to bear their fruits."[8]

However, mounting social strain suggested that there were limits to popular patience. In 1972 and 1973 a number of incidents of conflict occurred between Egyptian Moslems and Christians. In the spring of 1974 right-wing religious groups allegedly attacked the army's engineering academy in a suburb of Cairo. Eleven were killed and twenty-seven wounded in ensuing clashes with the police. The year 1975 began with an eruption of social discontent: more than a thousand industrial workers rioted to protest inflation and growing social inequalities.

Sadat, while loosening the repressive grip of Nasserism, had not provided an institutional framework to absorb constructively the social energies inevitably released. Nasser's repressiveness combined with a mass welfare commitment had guaranteed stability. Political order was threatened by Sadat's liberalization measures, unaccompanied by effective institutional reform. Should the market solution succeed, its fruits would filter to ever wider segments of the population and thereby strengthen Sadat's support. Denied that success and faced with mounting social pressure, Sadat's response was to accelerate the move to the right. The president was convinced that Egypt's desperate situation called for extreme measures. The country would have an even stronger dose of the liberal/capitalist remedy for its ills.

First Sadat acted to shore up his position. In a forceful reaction to these initial setbacks, a thorough governmental shakeup in the spring of 1975 was accompanied by a major policy statement on Egypt's domestic and international situation. Sadat reaffirmed his revolutionary commitments as a Free Officer and gave assurances that the policies of his regime would not be conducted at the expense of the poor. Sadat condemned profiteering and pledged that Egypt would not become a society of millionaires. Premier Higazi was also removed amid rumors that he had opposed various welfare supports for the poor.

At the same time, the new government was given a more pronounced military coloration, with both the vice-president and the premier having military/security career patterns. Clearly, Sadat was working to refurbish his tarnished "revolutionary image," simultaneously solidifying the military support for his regime and strengthening the repressive apparatus. With his power base reinforced, Sadat in the fall of 1976 renewed the push to the right. A new economic team headed by Dr. Kaissouny was installed, which promptly reduced costly government price subsidies and thereby precipitated the January 1977 riots. Army loyalty kept Sadat in power; but the level of violence, both popular and official, was chilling. Still, a hard-pressed Sadat stood firm. Cabinet shifts announced in October 1977 further strengthened the hand of Kaissouny by adding the Ministry of Planning to his portfolio. At the same time an American-educated economist, Aly Abdul Meguid, replaced a Marxist, Ismail Sabry Abdullah, as head of the Institute of Planning. Meguid was expected to overcome an alleged socialist bias of the planning staff and orient the work of the institute more toward mixed market planning. There would be no retreat from the open-door policy.

In such a climate, inevitably, there were expectations of further mass unrest that would lead to a military coup, a war with Israel, or both. But in November 1977, in a stunning preemption, Anwar es Sadat announced that in search of peace he would go to Jerusalem to address the Israeli parliament. Sadat told the Israelis and the world:

> The people of the world have known us twice: the first time in October 6, 1973, when the entire world knew that . . . we are fighters who would give our blood and lives in defense of our land and the dignity of man; the second time was when the world as a whole today recognized the fact that we are the people who would forge ahead, storm ahead for peace and freedom, for the happiness of man.

Sadat explained that in the Arab cause Egypt's efforts had been unstinting:

> We have sacrificed the greatest share of our national revenue. We have sacrificed part of our everyday food so that we might buy sophisticated weapons while we are in dire need of the smallest revenue no matter how minute it is. We have waged war when we have exhausted every peace initiative.

Now, however, Sadat made the case for peace and reconciliation. In Jerusalem he told the Israelis:

> In all sincerity I tell you we welcome you among us with full security and safety.

Back in Cairo several days later Sadat explained to his own people the motivations for his momentous journey:

> I wanted to see the greenery instead of the skull. I wanted to see water running instead of blood. I wanted men to live instead of seeing that weapons were destroying everything.

Sadat had risked his office and his life in an attempt to bring that peace to the Middle East without which the opening would fail.[9]

In February 1978 Sadat came up with another surprise, this time at home. The pre-Nasser Wafd, the nationalist party that had dominated political life before the Free Officer coup, was revived. There were now to be four recognized political parties. The new faction was led by Fuad Serag ed-Din, former Wafd secretary-general and minister of the interior, who called for endorsement of Sadat's peace initiatives and extension of domestic liberalization.

The boldness of Sadat's foreign and domestic policy initiatives was, of course, no guarantee that they would succeed. By the spring of 1978 serious criticism in the press and in the People's Assembly gave the first signs that the pace of the peace drive, which by then had slowed, was taking a domestic toll. Popular anger over surging prices also resurfaced. Sadat responded that Israel had not yet found the courage to make the necessary decisions for peace. Although he admitted that not enough had been achieved at home, he warned that slander of his government would not be tolerated.

With that warning and the president's subsequent actions in the spring and summer of 1978 came forceful reminders of the repressive potential built into Sadat's "Nasserism with a liberal face." For all the promise of liberalization, the market solution anticipated by Nasser and pursued by Sadat connoted not only an American connection and technocratic control of a retrenched economy but also social discipline enforced by the president through the security apparatus and ultimately the army.

In May 1978 Sadat charged prime minister Mamdouh Salem with direction of yet another cabinet shuffle. Sadat called for dynamic and energetic leadership, but introduced profound uncertainties about the fate of his open-door policy by accepting the resignation of his chief economic strategist, Dr. Abdul Moneim el-Kaissouny. Immediately came new evidence of fundamental continuities with the Nasserist past, however shaded with the moderation of Sadat's style. The president denounced the intellectual terrorism of his critics, now identified with the New Wafd Party of Serag ed-Din, the left party of Khaled Muhieddin, and various, largely left-leaning Nasserist elements. A nationwide referendum produced the expected overwhelming support for Sadat's demand for a mandate from the people to "protect the home front and social peace." The New Wafd disbanded, and the left party suspended activities in protest over restrictive legislation that put new curbs on political activity. After the Jerusalem initiative there could be no doubt of the depth of Sadat's own determination to lead Egypt to peace and prosperity. But in the spring and summer of 1978 Egyptians were reminded that Sadat himself would define both the strategy for dealing with Israel and the content and limits of liberalization.

CONCLUSION

Preoccupation with the short-term considerations of Egypt's future is inevitable, given the precariousness of its situation at the present moment. Yet it is important for both Egyptians and those who would understand Egyptian political evolution to step back and assess the long-term meaning of the experience of two decades of Free Officer rule.

It is perhaps not surprising that an American social scientist learned in the sixties that to Egypt's peasantry the outstanding achievement of the regime of the Free Officers was the eviction of the British.[10] But to rid Egypt of the occupiers was only to begin the task of building a political order worthy of a free people.

Nasser took halting steps toward that objective. With all its flaws, the

Free Officers movement did call for the revolutionary reconstruction of Egypt. To Anwar es-Sadat, Nasser bequeathed a complex vision of Egypt's destiny—which was to animate revolution from above. Formulating that vision was an act of genuine creativity, for in it were linked disparate ideas about Egypt's domestic and international situation. Nasser offered a comprehensive (or seemingly comprehensive) and adequate (or seemingly adequate) understanding of the world and Egypt's place in it. To find inconsistencies in components of the vision, to dismiss it as "reactive" rather than creative, does not alter the central fact of its enormous power to move the people of Egypt.

Yet the power to move is not the power to transform or the power to organize. A brief passage in the novel *Egyptian Earth* by Abdul Rahman el-Sharkawy summarizes this fundamental limitation of Free Officer rule. After hearing a tale of adroit maneuvering, a character in the novel comments: "If only he could use such trickery for the right cause, Egypt would be free." The Nasserist vision, while apparently adequate to Egypt's situation, ultimately was dependent on a kind of "trickery," of diplomatic manipulation, to make Egypt free. Sadat has amended the vision and altered the strategy. Nonetheless, Egyptians as a people have escaped a situation of colonial dependency only by a new dependency on the cleverness of their authoritarian rulers.

Nasser eloquently wrote: "Building factories is easy, building hospitals and schools is possible, but building a nation of men is a hard and difficult task."[11]

The failure of Nasser and Sadat that stands out in sharpest relief is precisely the inability to fashion an institutional and intellectual context in which "new men and women" in critical functional roles can work effectively. The industrial manager has been plagued by fear and insecurity in a fluctuating system of industrial relations without firm institutional or ideological anchors. The cooperative official, part of a relatively unchanged pattern of rural life, has been a witness or even a contributor to a perversion of the effort to bring the revolution to the countryside. The rural doctor, faced with awesome responsibilities, has suffered from the lack of a sense of mission in a social, political, and administrative environment that multiplies burdens and offers little support.

For all the braveness and all the promise of Sadat's trip to Israel in search of peace, it was but another of the spectacular, solitary initiatives of the two men who have ruled revolutionary Egypt. Seeing the massive crowds that welcomed Sadat back to Cairo and hearing their chants for their Hero of Peace brought inescapably to mind the sad observation of Egypt's most prominent literary figure that "the larynx became the mind" for the mass of Egyptians from 1952 on. Once again, in 1977, the revolution cast Egypt's people in a role, passive and applauding, that had become customary:

> I shall assume that all the gains of the Revolution are genuine . . . But there is one loss, no doubt about it, which no other gain can replace, and that is the loss of consciousness . . . Egypt has become like a man with a weak personality . . . ignorant of the meaning of responsibility because he has not experienced it by himself throughout a whole generation.[12]

Egypt's experience is a reminder that a free nation does not necessarily mean a free people. While the self-transformation of Egypt has been placed on the historic agenda, the rule of the Free Officers thus far has failed to provide the intellectual and institutional resources essential to the search for political community. Egyptians have remained spectators to the unfolding of their national destiny.

Notes

INTRODUCTION. COLONIALISM AND NATIONALISM

1. Safran, *Egypt in Search of Political Community,* chap. 4; Wallerstein, *Social Change,* intro.

2. These comments on the particularities of the Egyptian experience with outside domination draw on a critique of an earlier version of this book by L. Carl Brown of Princeton University (private communication, Dec. 16, 1975).

3. Memmi, *Portrait du colonisé;* Safran, *Egypt,* p. 57; the Earl of Cromer, *Modern Egypt,* vol. 2, pp. 154-155, 159, 163.

4. The problem for the researcher here is to describe the colonization of Egypt from the point of view of the nationalist revolutionary. The method used is that of situational analysis, as distinguished from that of "sympathetic" or "empathetic" understanding through reenactment. For clarification of this methodological distinction see Popper, *Objective Knowledge,* pp. 186-190.

5. The position here is by no means one of the "relativity of history." Rather, the point is that there can be no history without a point of view, and every historian should make his or her point of view explicit. To write the history that interests one is not to distort or misuse history. To quote Popper:

> The only way out of this difficulty is, I believe, consciously to introduce a *preconceived selective point of view* into one's history; that is, to write *that history which interests us.* This does not mean that we may twist the facts until they fit into a framework of preconceived ideas, or that we may neglect the facts that do not fit. On the contrary, all available evidence which has a bearing on our point of view should be considered carefully and objectively . . . but it means that we need not worry about all those facts and aspects which have no bearing upon our point of view and which therefore do not interest us. (*The Poverty of Historicism,* p. 150; emphasis added.)

6. Cromer, *Modern Egypt,* vol. 1, p. 326 (emphasis added).

7. While the attempt at such a reconstruction might be a perfectly plausible historical project for those in a colonial situation, its existence as such a project cannot simply be assumed, nor does it have any special logical or moral status. For this reason Western "strain" theories, which conceptualize the problems of social change in developing areas in terms of the disequilibrium provoked when a static traditional culture is disrupted by the dynamic culture of the West, are of

limited use in understanding the nationalist revolutionary. Such approaches focus research efforts first on an elegant reconstruction of the traditional culture, and second on the presumed theoretical task of adapting that culture to the demands of the modern world as represented by the West. Both efforts overlook the colonial situation itself and the formative actions of people in that situation. Such approaches, then, do not illuminate the meaning of social change to those actually undergoing it.

8. Mansfield, *The British in Egypt*, p. 49.

9. See Berque's *Egypt*, especially pt. 2; an excellent brief account, differing in several important respects from Berque's analysis, is to be found in Gabriel Baer, "Social Change in Egypt: 1800-1914," in Holt, *Political and Social Change in Modern Egypt*, pp. 135-161.

10. Issawi, *Egypt in Revolution*, p. 77; Safran, *Egypt*, pp. 196-197.

11. P. K. O'Brien, "Nasser's Economic Legacy," *The New Middle East*, Sept. 1971, p. 20; Charles Issawi, "Egypt Since 1800: A Study in Lopsided Development," *Journal of Economic History*, 21 (1950): 1-25; Mansfield, *Nasser's Egypt*, p. 30; Issawi, *Egypt in Revolution*, p. 172; O'Brien, *The Revolution in Egypt's Economic System*, p. 12.

12. The interpretation of the Moslem Brotherhood presented here is based primarily on Mitchell, *Society of the Muslim Brothers*. For quotations and evidence to support the views summarized here, see especially pt. 3, pp. ix, 218, 229, 313, 328. See also *Memoirs of Hasan al-Banna*, vol. 1, pp. 4-5 (cited in Harris, *Nationalism and Revolution in Egypt*, p. 146).

13. Dekmejian, *Egypt under Nasir*, pp. 34-35.

14. Ulam, *The Unfinished Revolution*, pp. 7, 284-285.

15. Mitchell, *Society*, pp. 35-79, 226.

16. The discussion here draws on the analytical concept of "situation" developed by Parsons and Shils in their book, *Toward a General Theory of Action*. They define a situation as "that part of the external world which means something to the actor whose behavior is being analyzed. It is only part of the whole realm of objects that might be seen. Specifically, it is that part to which the actor is oriented and in which the actor acts. The situation thus consists of objects of orientation." For a discussion of the meaning of the concept of "expression" see Dilthey, *Pattern and Meaning in History*; on the methodological problems involved in the reconstruction of a life situation see Popper, *Objective Knowledge*, esp. pp. 179-190. The final phrases are from Berque's *Egypt*, where these themes are developed.

17. Compare Johannes Fabian, "Ideology and Content," *Sociologus* 16: 1-18. If Egypt's momentous search for political community and for a respected place among the nations of the world is to be understood, analysis must avoid the twin pitfalls of psychologism and logicism. The tremendous power of Nasser's personality, for example, must not be allowed to mask the shallowness of interpretations of Egypt's history in crudely psychologistic terms, whether of the sympathetic "search for dignity" or the hostile "drive for power and empire" variety. Equally to be resisted are the temptations for arid logical dissection of the ideas that animated Egypt's revolutionaries without precise and concrete references to the situation in which those revolutionaries acted. Apologistic attempts

to discern an underlying logic to Nasser's theoretical revolution, or critical attacks on the incoherence of the ideological whole, are equally limited in their contribution to an understanding of Egypt's actual political evolution if they do not relate ideas to actions, theory to practice. Power is a social category and cannot be made the psychological motive for action without reference to the environment for action. Ideas—both of one's situation and the means to transform it— are of crucial importance to understanding social change. The concern with questions of power and ideology that distinguishes this book is grounded in the study of ongoing social change.

1. THE MILITARY CONSPIRATORS

1. Excellent journalistic accounts of the origins of the regime are contained in political biographies of Nasser, which naturally tend to structure the political events of contemporary Egyptian history in the continuum of Nasser's life; all sense of alternatives to Free Officer rule is lost. In the academic literature the July coup is variously understood as but one more case of an endemic military praetorianism embedded in Egyptian history, or as yet another example of that perennial predisposition for authoritarian rule somehow etched in the Arab mind, or as fresh confirmation of the military as the necessary surrogate for a modernizing middle class in a developing country. Despite the diversity of interpretations, the sense of the inevitability of rule by the military conspirators is reinforced throughout.

2. Ghanem, *The Man Who Lost His Shadow,* p. 191.

3. Quoted in Jean Lacouture, "Nasserism in Uniform," *New Outlook* 4 (1961): 3.

4. Be'eri, *Army Officers in Arab Politics and Society,* pp. 313-314; Zaki Murad, *al-Tali'ah,* Nov. 1966, pp. 40-48. (Arabic-language articles are not listed again in the bibliography. Complete page numbers for articles cited therefore will be given in the notes.)

5. UAR Information Department, *President Gamal Abdel Nasser's Speeches and Press Interviews, January-December, 1962* (Cairo, n.d.), p. 92; Murad, *al-Tali'ah,* Nov. 1966, pp. 40-48.

6. Lacouture, "Nasserism in Uniform," pp. 6-9.

7. Naguib, *Egypt's Destiny,* p. 43.

8. Quoted in Mansfield, *Nasser,* pp. 21-22.

9. Sadat, *Revolt on the Nile,* pp. 76-77; UAR Information Department, *Nasser's Speeches, 1962,* pp. 89 (emphasis added), 92; Mansfield, *Nasser,* p. 27.

10. Khaled Mohy Ed-Din, "The Course of the Egyptian Revolution and its Future," *World Marxist Review* 9 (1966): 35; *al-Ahram,* Dec. 18, 1964, and Nov. 15, 1968.

11. Quoted in Mansfield, *Nasser,* p. 29; Be'eri, *Army Officers,* p. 316.

12. UAR Information Department, *Nasser's Speeches, 1962,* p. 93.

13. See Manfred Halpern, "Middle East Armies and the New Middle Class," in Johnson, The *Role of the Military in Underdeveloped Countries,* pp. 246-247; the quotation is from Mansfield, *Nasser,* pp. 30-31; Sadat, *In Search of Identity,* p. 21; Stephens, *Nasser,* p. 49.

14. Mahfouz, *Socialisme et pouvoir en Égypte,* pp. 64-66.

15. Mitchell, *Society of the Muslim Brothers,* p. 97; Mahfouz, *Socialisme,* pp. 64-65.

16. Cited in Lacouture, *Nasser,* p. 95.

17. See Naguib Iskander, *al-Tali'ah,* Dec. 25, 1965, pp. 27-34; Nutting, *Nasser,* pp. 32-33.

18. *Al-Ahram,* Nov. 15, 1968; Nutting, *Nasser,* p. 303; Sadat, *In Search of Identity,* pp. 90, 101, 155.

19. Quoted in St. John, *The Boss,* p. 36.

20. Nasser, *The Philosophy of the Revolution,* pp. 42, 50-51.

21. Sadat, *Revolt,* p. 13; Mirskii, *Armiya i Politika v Stranakh Azii i Afriki* [*The Army and Politics in the Countries of Asia and Africa*], p. 28.

22. Be'eri, *Army Officers,* p. 106.

23. Nasser, *Philosophy,* pp. 33-34; St. John, *The Boss,* chap. 9.

24. The quotation appears in St. John, *The Boss,* p. 131; see also Mirskii, *Armiya i Politika,* p. 39.

25. St. John, *The Boss,* p. 159.

26. G. I. Mirsky, eminent Soviet specialist on Egypt, has provided the following very apt characterization of the rally and its role on this occasion:

The Liberation Rally is an organization, in general rather amorphous and not playing any role, but on that occasion it said its word. Perhaps for the first and the last time in all its existence the Liberation Rally revealed itself as a political force. (Mirskii, *Armiya i Politika,* p. 45).

The general secretaryship of the rally was Nasser's first official position.

27. Lacouture, *The Demi-Gods,* p. 102.

28. Quoted in Eliezer Ben-Moshe, "Middle East Scene," *New Outlook* 5 (1962): 52-55.

29. See the discussion of this basic continuity in Hurewitz, *Middle East Politics,* pp. 125-126.

30. Nutting, *Nasser,* p. 72; Mitchell, *Society,* p. 150.

31. Mitchell, *Society,* pp. 55-58; Lacouture, *Nasser,* pp. 262-263.

32. Walid Khalidi, trans. "Nasser's Memoirs of the First Palestine War," *Journal of Palestine Studies,* 2 (1973):19.

33. Ibid., pp. 19, 25-26.

34. Nutting, *Nasser,* pp. 91-97; Stephens, *Nasser,* pp. 151-157; Love, *Suez, The Twice-Fought War,* pp. 1-20; Lacouture, *Nasser,* pp. 268, 271.

35. See Safran, *From War to War,* pp. 44-46.

36. Nutting, *Nasser,* pp. 93-96; Stephens, *Nasser,* pp. 155-156; Lacouture, *Nasser,* p. 275.

37. Safran, *From War to War,* pp. 45-46; Love, *Suez,* p. 1.

38. Safran, *From War to War,* p. 80.

39. Mansfield, *Nasser's Egypt,* p. 51.

40. The Nasser quotation appears in Be'eri, *Army Officers,* p. 93; see also Laqueur, *The Soviet Union and the Middle East,* p. 214.

41. Wynn, *Nasser of Egypt,* p. 119.

42. Ibid.; Safran, *From War to War,* esp. pp. 59-83.

43. Abul-Fath, *L'Affaire Nasser,* p. 51.

44. Safran, *From War to War,* p. 51.

45. Lacouture, *Nasser*, pp. 169-170; Sadat, *In Search of Identity*, p. 143.

46. UAR Information Department, *Nasser's Speeches, 1962*, p. 107.

47. Ministry of Information, State Information Service, *The October Working Paper Presented by Mohamed Anwar el Sadat*, April 1974 (Cairo, n.d.).

48. Raymond William Baker, "Nasser's Egypt" (Ph.D. diss., Harvard University, 1972), pp. 59-60.

2. BUILDING A POLITICAL-ECONOMIC ORDER

1. *Al-Ahram*, Jan. 14, 1966.

2. Nasser, *The Philosophy of the Revolution*, pp. 106-107.

3. *Al-Ahram*, Jan. 14, 1966.

4. *Al-Ahram*, Nov. 20, 1964; Mansfield, *Nasser's Egypt*, p. 184. Financial statistics will be given throughout in U.S. dollar equivalences converted at the prevailing official rates. Those rates for the period 1952 through 1978 are the following: 1952 to 1955, one Egyptian pound equal to $2.862; 1956 to 1961, $2.838; 1962 to 1972, $2.30; 1973 to 1978 (January), $2.5556 (International Monetary Fund, *International Financial Statistics*). For aggregate data that involve figures from time periods with different exchange rates, weighted average rates have been calculated on the basis of the number of years at each individual rate.

It should be noted also that in September 1973 the Egyptian government established a parallel market (in which the exchange rate differed from the official rate). Its use was gradually broadened until by 1977 it was widely applied. The exchange situation has been further complicated by a free-market exchange, both white and black. However, given the nature of the Egyptian pound figures converted, I have chosen to use the official rate throughout.

5. UAR Information Department, *Address by President Gamal Abdel Nasser at the opening meeting of the second session of the National Assembly, Cairo, November 12, 1964* (Cairo, n.d.), pp. 7-9, 23-24; Stephens, *Nasser*, pp. 182, 253, 310, 435. Nasser explained his protection of Egypt's interests in this way:

We also cooperate with the world in order to be of benefit and to draw benefit. What we mean by being of benefit is that, for example, when we get a loan of L.E. 400 million and we are asked for loans amounting to L.E. 10 million, we can give them because we are not selfish. We took loans from America, from the Soviet Union, from Japan, from Germany, from Czechoslovakia, from Yugoslavia, from Rumania, as was published in the papers. Then we gave out loans. We gave loans to Mali; we are building a hotel and roads in Mali. We gave a loan of 6 or 7 million pounds to Guinea. (UAR Information Department, *Address, Nasser, Nov. 12, 1964*, p. 9.)

6. *Al-Ahram*, Oct. 9, 1974.

7. The Egyptian journalist Ahmed Bahaeddin has laid bare the deception characteristic of the Nasser years:

Modern states are not established by purchasing modern equipment or modern factories, but by organizing our work and changing our habits and traditions. This reminds me of the story of a very rich bedouin who had a very expensive tent in which he had all kinds of modern equipment such as transistor radios, refrigerators, air conditioners, and so on. But most unfortunately, the bedouin had not changed his habits, traditions, or ideas. (*al-Musawwar,* July 28, 1967, p. 9.)

The quotations (emphasis added) are from Ministry of Information, State Information Service, *The October Working Paper Presented by President Mohamed Anwar el Sadat* (Cairo, n.d.), pp. 95-96.

8. UAR Information Department, *President Gamal Abdel Nasser's Speeches and Press Interviews, January-December, 1962* (Cairo, n.d.), pp. 154-162.

9. Be'eri, *Army Officers in Arab Politics and Society,* p. 426.

10. Cited in O'Brien, *The Revolution in Egypt's Economic System,* p. 68; see also p. 71.

11. See Marx's discussion of the class character of a peasantry in "The Eighteenth Brumaire of Louis Napoleon" in Feuer, *Basic Writings on Politics and Philosophy,* pp. 338-339; for a recent confirmation of this view, see Harik, *The Political Mobilization of Peasants,* esp. pp. 186-205.

12. Mirskii, *Armiya i Politika v Stranakh Azii i Afriki* [*The Army and Politics in the Countries of Asia and Africa*], p. 61.

13. *Al-Ahram,* March 15, 1968 (emphasis added).

14. Quoted in Be'eri, *Army Officers,* pp. 94-95.

15. Naguib, *Egypt's Destiny,* p. 87; St. John, *The Boss,* p. 107.

16. Abul-Fath, *L'Affaire Nasser,* pp. 123-124.

17. St. John, *The Boss,* p. 48; Be'eri, *Army Officers,* p. 85; Nasser, *The Philosophy,* p. 38.

18. Abul-Fath, *L'Affaire Nasser,* pp. 123, 228, 229.

19. G. Mirsky, "Arab East: Moment of Truth," *New Times* 46-47 (1967):27; Abul-Fath, *L'Affaire Nasser,* p. 229.

20. Abul-Fath, *L'Affaire Nasser,* p. 133; Wheelock, *Nasser's New Egypt,* p.31.

21. Jean Lacouture, "Nasserism in Uniform," *New Outlook* 4 (5) (March-April 1961), p. 8.

22. Be'eri, *Army Officers,* pp. 111-112; the quotation is from Wynn, *Nasser of Egypt,* p. 61.

23. Bernard Vernier, "La République arabe unie," in Léo Hamon, *Le Role extramilitaire de l'armée dans le tiers monde,* p. 127; Be'eri, *Army Officers,* p. 429; Hurewitz, *Middle East Politics,* p. 134.

24. UAR Information Department, *Nasser's Speeches, 1962,* p. 72; see Safran, *From War to War,* p. 148 and, for the official Egyptian view, *al-Ahram,* Jan. 7, 1966.

25. Hansen, *Economic Development in Egypt,* p. 1.

26. Lafif Lakhdar, "Une Révolution conduite par la petite bourgeoisie," *Démocratie nouvelle,* Feb. 1968, p. 68; UAR Information Department, *Nasser's Speeches, 1962,* pp. 76, 156.

27. UAR Information Department, *Address, Nasser, Nov. 12, 1964,* p. 16; UAR Information Department, *Address by President Gamal Abdel Nasser at*

Port Said on the occasion of the return of our troops from Yemen (Cairo, n.d.), p. 7.

28. Malcolm Kerr, "The United Arab Republic: The Domestic, Political, and Economic Background of Foreign Policy," in Hammond and Alexander, *Political Dynamics in the Middle East,* pp. 205-206.

29. Nasser's hopes for the campaign in Yemen were expressed in these words: "The Yemeni Revolution was able to tip the balance, bring back the initiative to the Arab revolutionary power and force reactionism to be in the defensive position" (UAR Information Department, *Address by President Gamal Abdel Nasser at the meeting of the National Assembly's ordinary session, Cairo, March 26, 1964* [Cairo, n.d.], p. 32). See also Kerr, "The United Arab Republic," p. 205; UAR Information Department, *Nasser's Speeches, 1961,* p. 315.

30. *Al-Ahram,* Aug. 27, 1962, p. 7.

31. *Al-'Ammal,* Sept. 1967, pp. 4-6. The case of Magdi Hasanayn provides the most glaring example of such leniency. A member of the Free Officers association and reputedly an intimate of Nasser, Hasanayn was made head of the widely trumpeted Liberation Province, the most impressive of the regime's early desert reclamation and rural development projects. Fantastic wastefulness in expenditures for the project coupled with conspicuous personal display of the director resulted in public censure and eventual dismissal of Hasanayn in the autumn of 1957. Too much should not be made of such a case of the abuse of office, but Hasanayn's fate does tell a great deal about the regime's attitude toward such deviations on the part of the military. Having resigned his commission in the army, in the summer of 1958 Hasanayn reportedly held the position of manager of the National Cement Company. And *al-Akhbar* of July 15, 1966, reported his appointment to the ambassadorship of Czechoslovakia (see Be'eri, *Army Officers,* pp. 324-325). The quotation is from *al-Ahram,* Oct. 31, 1968.

32. See Meyer-Ranke, *Der Rote Pharao,* pp. 64-65, and Bernard Vernier, "R.A.U.," in Hamon, *Le Role extramilitaire,* p. 126.

33. "Vues due Caire: Les leçons de la défaits," *Démocratie nouvelle,* Feb. 1968, p. 42; Igore Belyaev and Evgennii Primakov, "Kogda Voina Stoit u Doroga" ["When War Stands in the Street"], *Za Rubezhom* 27 (1967):7-8. Of the military training programs, Anouar Abdel-Malek reports that "those who expressed the desire, and they were numerous, were detached to take courses at the universities especially in the faculties of law, economics, political science, and business administration." Particularly important was the setting up in 1961 of a military-technical faculty "whose seven year curriculum was designed to train managerial staffs both of officers and of civilian engineers" (Abdel-Malek, *Egypt,* pp. 176-177).

34. Mirskii, *Armiya i Politika,* p. 89; Belyaev and Primakov, "Kogda Voina Stoit," pp. 7-8.

35. UAR Information Department, *Address, Nasser, Nov. 12, 1964,* p. 39.

36. UAR Information Department, *Address, Nasser, March 26, 1964,* pp. 28, 38; O'Brien, *The Revolution,* pp. 131-132.

37. O'Brien, *The Revolution,* p. 87; the Sabry quotation is from *al-Ishtiraki,* Dec. 24, 1966, pp. 9-12.

38. The National Planning Committee was established to "prepare a long

term plan for social and economic development which would mobilize public and private effort.'' It was composed of some two hundred officials assisted by various foreign experts. Unlike previous planning bodies, which had included representatives of the private sphere, this one was purely public in composition. The Mixed Committee on Economic and Financial Problems was one of six established to plan Egypt's economy. The difference of opinion on growth rates cited was probably related to the inclusion of representatives from the private sector on the mixed committees but not on the National Planning Committee. See O'Brien, *The Revolution,* pp. 85-88 and 104-105.

39. UAR Information Department, *Address, Nasser, Nov. 12, 1964,* p. 24.

40. Hansen, *Economic Development,* p. 72.

41. Arnold Hottinger, ''How the Arab Bourgeoisie Lost Power,'' *Journal of Contemporary History,* 3 (1968):118-119; O'Brien, *The Revolution,* pp. 214-215.

42. Hottinger, ''How the Arab Bourgeoisie Lost Power,'' p. 119.

43. UAR Information Department, *Address by President Nasser on the seventh anniversary of the Unity at the popular rally held by the Arab Socialist Union, February 21, 1965* (Cairo, n.d.), p. 11.

44. The first Nasser quotation is from Wheelock, *Nasser's New Egypt,* p. 53; the second, from *al-Ahram,* Dec. 6, 1957, is quoted in Be'eri, *Army Officers,* p. 392.

45. G. I. Mirskii, ''Gamale Abdel Nasser,'' *Mezhdunarodnye Ekonomiya i Mezhdunarodnye Otnosheniya* 7 (1961):114; the quotations are from UAR Information Department, *Nasser's Speeches, 1961,* pp. 311-312.

46. Malcolm Kerr, *The Arab Cold War, 1958-1964,* p. 30.

47. Ibid., p. 21.

48. UAR Information Department, *Nasser's Speeches, 1961,* pp. 78-79.

49. Kerr, *The Arab Cold War,* p. 32; UAR Information Department, *Nasser's Speeches, 1961,* p. 315.

50. *Al-Ahram,* Dec. 29, 1962; Safran, *From War to War,* pp. 74-78.

51. G. Mirsky, ''The U.A.R. Reforms,'' *New Times,* 4 (1962):12-14.

52. Ibid.; O'Brien, *The Revolution,* p. 213.

53. *Al-Ahram,* July 29, 1960; the quotations are from Mirsky, ''The U.A.R. Reforms,'' p. 14.

54. Hottinger, ''How the Arab Bourgeoisie Lost Power,'' p. 120; Hansen, *Economic Development,* p. 73.

3. BUREAUCRATIC FEUDALISM

1. Salem has written over a dozen plays, several of which are very revealing social commentary. Students of modern Egypt are grateful to John Waterbury for his excellent translations of several of Salem's plays in the *American Universities Field Staff Reports. The Well of Wheat* is translated in vol. 19, no. 2, May 1974. The quotations from the play given here are from the Waterbury translation, pp. 12-13, 15-16, 16-17.

2. *Al-Ahram,* Dec. 18, 1964.

3. Hansen, *Economic Development in Egypt,* p. 55. Premier Aly Sabry confided to a foreign diplomat in 1966, after the second five-year plan, that the

plan had been carried out 150 percent in the services sector—that is, the bureaucracy—but only 50 percent in the production sector (Lacouture, *Nasser,* p. 254).

4. Malcolm Kerr, "The United Arab Republic: The Domestic, Political, and Economic Background of Foreign Policy," in Hammond and Alexander, *Political Dynamics in the Middle East,* p. 37; Patrick O'Brien, "Nasser's Economic Legacy," *The New Middle East,* Sept. 1971, p. 22.

5. For the best-argued statement of this position, see Leonard Binder, "Egypt: The Integrative Revolution," in *Political Culture and Political Development,* Lucien Pye and Sidney Verba, editors (Princeton, 1965), p. 401.

6. The position developed here may be contrasted with the influential views of James Heaphey, who has argued:

> The setting of rapid economic development as a national goal impels the elite in an underdeveloped country to envision the country in terms of an organizational model . . . In such a situation an administrative logic is more realistic than a political logic, so administrative concepts are more prevalent in the elite's vision of the nation-state than are political concepts. ("The Organizations of Egypt: Inadequacies of a Nonpolitical Model for Nation-Building," *World Politics* 28 [1966]:177.)

It is true that official pronouncements on public policy suggest that the character of the new regime was determined by experience in dealing with practical problems understood in an administrative or organizational framework. Ideological pronouncements, then, are typically cast in terms of administrative logic. Analysts who rely on such evidence make an unwarranted transference from official pronouncements to official behavior. Official pronouncements comprise largely self-serving, post-facto rationalizations. Furthermore, the formal ideology that frequently structures such pronouncements has consistently occupied a relatively unimportant place in Egyptian politics and has little value in the understanding of domestic policies.

7. For all its importance the role of the bureaucracy under Nasser should not be exaggerated. It is misleading to state, as some analysts have done, that Nasser's political system can be understood as one where "only one tightly controlled structure exists, the bureaucracy, engaged in all the functions of nation-building." Reference to the bureaucracy as "one tightly controlled structure" suggests a cohesiveness that is largely illusory. Such a formula also seems to assign the bureaucracy a key role by intent rather than by default (Amos Perlmutter, "Egypt and the Myth of the New Middle Class: A Comparative Analysis," *Comparative Studies in Society and History,* 10 (1967):61-62).

8. *Al-Ahram,* Nov. 6, 1961, March 6, and Dec. 18, 1964; Charles Issawi, *Egypt in Revolution,* p. 74.

9. Binder, "Egypt: The Integrative Revolution," p. 423; *al-Ahram,* March 13, 1964.

10. *Al-Ahram,* Oct. 25, 1968.

11. Hurewitz, *Middle East Politics,* p. 134. One glimpse of the ugly side of bureaucratic politics in Egypt came in June 1967 when Salah Nasr, an important chief of intelligence in the early sixties, was sentenced to ten years at hard labor for having ordered the arrest and torture of a prominent journalist (*New York Times,* June 28, 1976).

12. *Al-Ahram,* March 6 and 13, and Dec. 18, 1964.

13. Be'eri, *Army Officers in Arab Politics and Society,* p. 427; *al-Ahram,* Dec. 25, 1964.

14. In an article in *al-Ahram* of March 13, 1964, Haikal wrote:
The new administrative bodies created originally to bypass the old apparatus and to rejoin the hopes of the masses behind its back had become the greatest and most powerful instruments for national action.
See also Be'eri, *Army Officers,* p. 431.

15. *Al-Ahram,* April 2, 1973; the quotations are from John Waterbury, "Manpower and Population Planning in the Arab Republic of Egypt, Part IV," *American Universities Field Staff Reports,* vol. 17, no. 5, p. 1.

16. *Al-Ahram,* April 2, 1973.

17. Ibid.

18. Waterbury, "Manpower and Population Planning," pp. 1, 7.

19. *New York Times,* April 26, 1977.

20. Khaled Mohieddine, "Le parti qu'il nous faut construire," *Démocratie nouvelle,* Feb. 1966, p. 117; *al-Ahram,* Dec. 1, 1967.

21. *Al-'Ammal,* Sept. 1967; Avraham Ben-Tzur, "The Economic Crisis in Egypt," *New Outlook* 7 (1967):63-64.

22. *Al-Ahram,* March 13 and Dec. 25, 1964.

23. See the two-part study by Dr. Kamal Dasuqi in *al-Ahram* of Aug. 25 and 27, 1962; also Mohieddine, "Le parti qu'il nous faut construire," p. 121.

24. Adib Dimitri, *al-Katib* 79 (1967):44-54.

25. Dr. Muhammad Anis, *al-Jumhuriyyah,* Sept. 14, 1967.

26. Dimitri, *al-Katib* 79 (1967):44-54; *al-Ahram,* Oct. 23, 1961.

27. Anis, *al-Jumhuriyyah,* Sept. 14, 1967, p. 5.

28. *Al-Katib* 61 (1966):2-30.

29. *Al-Ahram,* Oct. 31, 1968, p. 4.

30. Mohieddine, "Le parti qu'il nous faut construire," p. 120; "Vues du Caire: Les leçons de la défaite," *Démocratie nouvelle,* Feb. 1968, p. 45; *al-Mussawwar,* June 23, 1967.

31. Abd al-Rah'man al'Charqawi, "Notre résponsabilité intellectuels révolutionnaires, *Démocratie nouvelle,* Feb. 1968, p. 62.
This mounting tension in the last years of Nasser's rule between the military/police and the leftists is a theme that has received significant treatment in Soviet commentaries on Egyptian developments. Unfortunately, on this issue the Soviet specialists do not identify their sources of information. By virtue of the generally high quality of his studies of Egyptian politics, it is perhaps of interest to record a highly provocative opinion of G. Mirsky. In an article in a scholarly Soviet periodical Mirsky discusses the admittedly peculiar arrangement whereby members of the "political apparatus" within the Arab Socialist Union were to remain anonymous. He charges that such anonymity was designed "to protect them from a repression on the part of anti-socialist elements." Mirsky concludes that such a prospect was the outgrowth of the "dual power," by which he meant the independent position enjoyed by the military under Marshal Amer ("Novaya

Revolyutsiya v OAR'' [''The New Revolution in the UAR''], *Mezhdunarodnye Ekonomiya i Mezhdunarodnye Otnesheniya* 1 (1969):46).

32. *Al-Ahram,* Dec. 1, 1967.

4. NASSER'S SEARCH FOR A NEW WAY

1. UAR Information Administration, *Arab Political Encyclopedia, July-December 1965* (Cairo, n.d.), pp. 64, 67.

2. Ibid., p. 71; M. H. Haikal, *al-Ahram,* Jan. 15, 1965.

3. Mansfield, *Nasser's Egypt,* pp. 224-240. For Sadat's harsh judgments on these efforts, see *In Search of Identity,* pp. 130-131.

4. Mustafa Teiba, *al-Tali'ah,* Dec. 1965, pp. 40-44; *al-Ahram,* Feb. 11, 1966. See also Sadat, *In Search of Identity,* pp. 157-160.

5. UAR Information Department, *Address by President Gamal Abdel Nasser at the meeting of the National Assembly's ordinary session, Cairo, March 26, 1964* (Cairo, n.d.), p. 39; UAR Information Department, *Address by President Gamal Abdel Nasser at the opening meeting of the second session of the National Assembly, Cairo, November 12, 1964,* (Cairo, n.d.), pp. 52-53.

6. See St. John, *The Boss,* p. 52 for an account of this incident.

7. See the argument by M. H. Haikal in an important *al-Ahram* editorial of April 5, 1968; also Be'eri, *Army Officers in Arab Politics and Society,* p. 322. The journalists are Igore Belyaev and Evgennii Primakov, ''Kogda Voina Stoit u Doroga'' [''When War Stands in the Street''], *Za Rubezhom* 27 (1967):7.

8. See the account of the trials by E. Primakov, ''March 30 Program,'' *New Times* 17 (1968):5; also *al-Ahram,* April 5, 1968; Sadat, *In Search of Identity,* pp. 168-169.

9. Cited by Mustafa Teiba, *al-Tali'ah,* Dec. 1965, pp. 40-44.

10. M. H. Haikal, *al-Ahram,* April 10, 1964; UAR Information Department, *Address by President Gamal Abdel Nasser at the historical meeting of the National Assembly, Cairo, January 20, 1965* (Cairo, n.d.), p. 4.

11. *Al-Ishtiraki,* Dec. 24, 1966.

12. UAR Information Department, *President Gamal Abdel Nasser's Speeches and Press Interviews, July-September, 1960* (no publication information), p. 53. British commentator Peter Mansfield reports: ''Foreign observers had the utmost difficulty in gaining any clear picture of it [the structure of the union] even from senior Egyptian officials'' (*Nasser's Egypt,* p. 230). Soviet specialist Mirsky believes that the union had really no purpose at all (*Armiya i Politika v Stranakh Azii i Afriki* [*The Army and Politics in the Countries of Asia and Africa*], p. 61.

13. UAR Information Department, *Address, Nasser, Jan. 20, 1965,* p. 4.

14. The Haikal quotation appeared in *al-Ahram,* April 5, 1968; the Sadat quote is from his *In Search of Identity,* p. 168.

15. *Al-Tali'ah,* March 1965; *al-Ahram,* Feb. 4, 1966.

16. *Al-Ahram,* March 13, 1964.

17. Haikal's Friday editorials for 1964-1965 reflect a rather explicit consid-

eration of the Leninist experience; a random example is *al-Ahram,* March 6, 1964. See also V. I. Lenin, *What Is To Be Done* (New York, 1929), p. 112.

18. *Al-Tali'ah,* Dec. 1965, pp. 56-67.

19. Ibid., pp. 45-55.

20. *Al-Ahram,* Dec. 18, 1964.

21. For a detailed treatment of the fate of the Egyptian left under Nasser, see Abdel-Malek, *Egypt,* pp. 69-70, 133-134. The telegram is cited in Lacouture, *Nasser,* p. 159.

22. Lacouture, *Nasser,* pp. 228-229.

23. See Leonard Binder, "Political Recruitment and Participation in Egypt," in Joseph LaPalombara and Myron Weiner, editors, *Political Parties and Political Development* (Princeton, 1965), p. 229.

24. *Al-Tali'ah,* Dec. 1965, pp. 5-12.

25. *Mahadir Jalsat Mubahathat al-Wahda* [*Proceedings of the Unity Talks*] (Cairo, 1963), p. 163.

26. Representative samples are *al-Jumhuriyyah,* May 3 and 4, 1967.

27. *Rose al-Yusuf,* May 3, 1965, pp. 8-10. For the complete Sabry statement, see a three-part interview in *Rose al-Yusuf,* Sept. 5, 12, and 19, 1966.

28. Lenin, *What Is To Be Done,* p. 33.

29. *Al-Ahram,* Dec. 18, 1964.

30. Gamal Abdel Nasser, *Battles and Achievements of the Political and Social Revolution* (no publication information), p. 36; UAR, State Information Service, *The Charter,* p. 5.

31. *Al-Ahram,* March 6, 1964; UAR Information Department, *President Gamal Abdel Nasser's Speeches and Press Interviews, January-December, 1962* (Cairo, n.d.), pp. 181, 192.

32. UAR Information Department, *Nasser's Speeches, 1962,* pp. 211-212; UAR Information Department, *Address, Nasser, Nov. 12, 1964,* p. 15; *al-Ahram,* Nov. 15, 1968. Much later, Sadat was to claim that the charter had been intended by Nasser merely to divert popular attention from the collapse of the union with Syria (*In Search of Identity,* pp. 162, 195).

33. "U.A.R.: Home Front," *New Times* 50 (1968):10.

34. UAR Information Department, *Address, Nasser, Nov. 12, 1964,* pp. 48-49; *Akher Saa,* Sept. 6, 1967, p. 11.

35. *Al-Jumhuriyyah,* June 5, 1969. For a similar argument, but with a technocratic slant, see Ahmad Bahaeddine, *al-Musawwar,* June 23, 1967.

36. Quoted in Eliezer Ben-Moshe, "Difficulties of Socialism in Egypt," *New Outlook* 5 (1962):52-53.

37. Mirsky, "U.A.R.: Home Front," p. 10.

38. UAR Information Department, *Address, Nasser, Nov. 12, 1964,* pp. 40-41.

39. UAR Information Department, *Address, Nasser, Jan. 20, 1965,* pp. 10-11; *al-Ahram,* Nov. 15, 1968.

40. Mahfouz, *Socialisme et pouvoir en Égypte,* pp. 172-173.

41. *Al-Tali'ah,* March 1965, pp. 9-26.

42. Ibid.; Sadat, *In Search of Identity,* p. 159.

43. UAR Information Department, *Address, Nasser, Jan. 20, 1965,* p. 4.

44. Mahfouz, *Socialisme,* p. 193.

45. *Al-Jumhuriyyah,* June 19, 1969.

46. *Al-Tali'ah,* March 1965, pp. 2-26.

47. *Rose al-Yusuf,* Sept. 5, 1966.

48. Quoted by M. H. Haikal, *al-Ahram,* Oct. 25, 1968.

49. *Al-Ahram,* April 10, 1964. (emphasis added).

50. *Al-Ahram,* Aug. 11, 1967. (emphasis added).

51. *Al-Ahram,* Feb. 11, 1966.

52. UAR Information Administration, *Arab Political Encyclopedia,* p. 68; *al-Ahram,* Aug. 11, 1967, and Sept. 13, 1968.

53. *Al-Ahram,* Oct. 25, 1968.

54. UAR Information Department, *Address, Nasser, Nov. 12, 1964,* p. 36.

5. FROM DESPAIR TO EXULTATION

1. Lacouture, *Nasser,* p. xiii.

2. Mabro, *The Egyptian Economy, 1952-1972,* p. 168.

3. John Waterbury, "A Note on Egypt: 1973," *American Universities Field Staff Reports,* Northeast Africa Series, vol. 18, no. 4, p. 4; Eric Rouleau, *Le Monde,* Oct. 1, 1971.

4. Safran, *From War to War,* p. 30.

5. See *al-Ahram,* July 27, 1966; Love, *Suez,* p. 63.

6. *Al-Ahram,* Sept. 25, 1964.

7. "The Arab-Israeli War: How It Began," *Foreign Affairs* 46 (1968), pp. 304-305.

8. Mansfield, *The Middle East,* p. 239.

9. Nasser's speech at Cairo University, April 25, 1968 (cited in Stephens, *Nasser,* p. 510).

10. Both the description and interpretation are taken from Brecher, *The Foreign Policy System of Israel,* p. 536; see also Kimche, *There Could Have Been Peace,* esp. pt. 3.

11. See Safran, "The War and the Future of the Arab-Israeli Conflict," *Foreign Affairs* 52 (1974):219-220, where this point is given historical depth.

12. John Waterbury, "The Crossing," *American Universities Field Staff Reports,* Northeast Africa Series, vol. 18, no. 6, p. 7.

13. The citation is from Heikal, *The Road to Ramadan,* p. 87.

14. See Waterbury, "The Crossing," p. 7.

15. The best general account of the working of the assembly is that by R. H. Dekmejian, "The U.A.R. National Assembly—A Pioneering Experiment," *Middle East Studies* 4 (1968). See also *Rose al-Yusuf,* June 6, 1966, p. 4.

16. UAR Ministry of Information, State Information Service, *Speeches by President Anwar el-Sadat, September 1970-March 1971* (Cairo, n.d.), p. 13.

17. Quoted in the *Arab World Weekly,* Sept. 18, 1971, p. 9.

18. Ministère de la culture et de l'information, Service de l'état pour l'information, *Discours et interviews du President Anouar el-Sadate, Avril-Décembre 1971* (Cairo, 1972), p. 74.

19. See Waterbury, "A Note on Egypt," p. 2.

20. Ministère de la culture, *Discours, 1971,* pp. 75, 225; Heikal, *Road to Ramadan,* pp. 133-134.

21. Israeli scholar Yair Evron has explained: "The official Israeli position has always been based on the assumption that the Arabs are ultimately committed to the destruction of Israel. Any apparent change in Arab attitudes (like Sadat's readiness to sign a peace agreement) should be regarded therefore as a tactical move designed to secure an Israeli withdrawal and also to bring about a change in the American position vis-à-vis Israel" (*The Middle East,* p. 210). For a discussion of these domestic problems, see Kimche, *There Could Have Been Peace,* p. 243; for a description of the dangerous results of this new Israeli unity, see Nadav Safran, "Israel's Internal Politics and Foreign Policy," in Hammond and Alexander *Political Dynamics in the Middle East,* p. 178. A good historical analysis of the U.S.-Israeli relationship is provided by Safran in *Israel,* pp. 331-599. The particulars of the post-1967 relationship are analyzed by Chomsky in *Peace in the Middle East,* p. 154.

22. *Akhbar al-Yaum,* Aug. 3, 1974; Heikal, *Road to Ramadan,* p. 173; *New York Times,* Jan. 23, 1975.

23. See the reports of Henry Tanner of the *New York Times*—for example, Feb. 6, 1975; also Sadat, *In Search of Identity,* p. 238.

24. Heikal, *Road to Ramadan,* p. 172; Sadat, *In Search of Identity,* p. 225.

25. Heikal, *Road to Ramadan,* p. 174; Drew Middleton, *New York Times,* Feb. 9, 1975; Waterbury, "The Crossing," p. 10.

26. *Rose al-Yusuf,* Jan. 31 and Feb. 14, 1972.

27. *Rose al-Yusuf,* Dec. 25, 1972; cited by Heikal, *Road to Ramadan,* pp. 95, 205.

28. *Al-Ahram,* Dec. 7, 1973, as cited by Waterbury in "The Crossing," p. 2.

6. SADAT'S EGYPT TAKES FORM

1. UAR Ministry of Information, State Information Service, *Speeches by President Anwar el-Sadat, September 1970-March 1971* (Cairo, n.d.), p. 19.

2. The *New York Times* of Jan. 3, 1974, estimated Israeli losses in the October War at twenty-five hundred. For a detailed treatment of the actual fighting, see the Insight Team of the Sunday Times, *Insight on the Middle East War.* For the diplomatic side, see Golan, *The Secret Conversations of Henry Kissinger,* pp. 3-92; Sheehan, *The Arabs, Israelis, and Kissinger,* pp. 11-217; Kalb and Kalb, *Kissinger,* pp. 450-499; Safran, *Israel,* pp. 476-505.

3. Heikal, *Road to Ramadan,* pp. 205-206.

4. See *al-Ahram,* Jan. 14 and April 5, 1974; also Sadat's address to university students in Alexandria on April 3, 1974, as cited in the *New York Times* of the following day.

After 1973 Sadat did not hesitate to use the added diplomatic clout of Egypt's demonstrated capacity for a military strike to pressure both superpowers to lend support to his diplomatic initiatives. On the 1976 anniversary of the October War, Sadat openly warned that if peaceful efforts to resolve the conflict with

Israel failed, "we shall go back once more to military conflict." High-level American diplomats, remembering how Sadat's so-called saber rattling in 1973 culminated in the October surprise attack, in 1976 were willing to grant that Sadat might find it necessary "to set a fire under the great powers." Even after the Sadat speech to the Israeli Knesset in the fall of 1977, Egypt's foreign minister was guarded about the president's repeated declaration in Jerusalem that there would be "no more war" between Egypt and Israel. Dr. Ghali explained that "no nation can possibly give up its military option" and observed that Sadat's visit had been intended to "show the Israelis that we are ready to go to the maximum to obtain peace." By the launching of a war in October 1973 and by his unprecedented gesture of peace in November 1977, Sadat proved that he could and would take hard and independent decisions perceived to be in Egypt's interest (*New York Times,* Oct. 10, 1976, and Nov. 25, 1977).

5. See Golan, *Secret Conversations,* pp. 47-50; Kalb and Kalb, *Kissinger,* 465-478; Safran, *Israel,* p. 483.

6. Mahgoub, *Democracy on Trial,* pp. 310-311.

7. UAR Ministry of Information, State Information Service, *The October Working Paper Presented by Mohamed Anwar el-Sadat, April, 1974* (Cairo, n.d.), p. 27.

8. Ibid., pp. 9-10, 43, 54.

9. Ibid., p. 61.

10. See John Waterbury, "The Opening, Part I," *American Universities Field Staff Reports,* Northeast Africa Series, vol. 20, no. 2; *al-Ahram,* Oct. 25, 1975.

11. Waterbury, "The Opening, Part I," p. 3; *al-Ahram,* Oct. 25, 1975.

12. Waterbury, "The Opening, Part I," p. 3.

13. *New York Times,* Jan. 23, 1975.

14. *Al-Ahram,* Dec. 17, 1973, in John Waterbury, "The Crossing," *American Universities Field Staff Reports,* Northeast Africa Series, vol. 18, no. 6, p. 3.

15. For details on the issues involved see Bernard Gwertzman, *New York Times,* April 7, 1975; Holden, " 'Hero of the Crossing,' " *New York Times Magazine,* June 1, 1975.

16. For the complete text of the agreement, see the *Department of State News Release,* Sept. 1, 1975, Bureau of Public Affairs, Office of Media Services.

17. See Drew Middleton, *New York Times,* May 5, Oct. 22, and Dec. 10, 1975; Henry Tanner, *New York Times,* April 19, 1974, and Feb. 6, 1975; *Le Monde,* Jan. 22, 1975; *New York Times,* Jan. 24, 1977.

18. *New York Times,* Feb. 20, 1977.

19. *New York Times,* Oct. 24, 1977; *Washington Post,* June 28, 1977.

20. See *Newsweek,* Dec. 29, 1975; *New York Times,* Nov. 26, 1975.

21. *New York Times,* Oct. 30, 1975.

22. *New Outlook* 19 (1976):63; *Middle East Economic Digest,* Feb. 6, 1976, p. 12.

23. *Middle East Economic Digest,* April 23, 1976, p. 4; Waterbury, "The Opening, Part I," pp. 1-3.

24. *Business Week,* Feb. 16, 1974, p. 71.

25. Cited in *Euromoney,* May 1975, p. 39.

26. John Waterbury, "The Opening, Part II," *American Universities Field Staff Reports,* Northeast Africa Series, vol. 20, no. 3, pp. 11-14.

27. *Middle East Economic Digest,* Oct. 3, 1975, p. 6.

28. *Middle East Economic Digest,* July 2, 1976, p. 3.

29. *The Banker* 125 (1975):301-303; *Middle East Economic Digest,* Oct. 3, 1975, p. 4.

30. *Middle East Economic Digest,* July 30, 1976, p. 3; and see John K. Cooley, *Christian Science Monitor,* Dec. 27, 1976.

31. Citations from *Business Week* Feb. 16, 1974, p. 72; and Robert L. Ferrar, "Foreign Investments in the Egyptian Economy," *Middle East Review* (winter 1975/76):63.

32. The discussion that follows is based on Ferrar, "Foreign Investments," p. 65. See also Nabil Megali, "Western Bankers Irked by Difficulties in Egypt," *Burroughs Clearing House* 59 (1975):43-44.

33. *New York Times,* Oct. 26, 1975; on the "middlemen," see the discussion by Fuad Mursi in *al-Tali'ah,* Feb. 1974, pp. 16-23.

34. *Middle East Economic Digest,* Oct. 1, 1976, p. 8; *The Banker,* 125 (1975):299; *Euromoney,* May 1975, p. 40. The quotation appears in James Dorsey, "Egypt—Where Does the Open Door Lead?" *New Outlook* 19 (1976):61-63.

35. Ferrar, "Foreign Investments," p. 65.

36. Heikal, *The Cairo Documents,* p. 344; Sadat, *In Search of Identity,* pp. 12, 73.

37. John Waterbury, "Egypt: The Politics of Dependency," in Udovitch, *The Middle East,* p. 307; Clement Henry Moore, "La Nouvelle Technocratie égyptienne," *Maghreb-Machrek* 73 (1976):41-53.

38. *Arab Record and Report,* Sept. 1-15, 1973, p. 388, and March 1-15, 1974, p. 79; *al-Nahar,* April 19 and 22, 1974; Waterbury, "Egypt," p. 327.

39. *New York Times,* Oct. 24, 1975; Waterbury, "Egypt," pp. 308-309.

40. UAR Ministry of Information, *The October Working Paper,* p. 36.

41. Heikal, *Road to Ramadan,* p. 136; Amnesty International, *Report on Torture,* pp. 226-227; Lacouture, *Nasser,* p. 360. See also Raymond William Baker, "Egypt in Shadows: Films and the Political Order," *American Behavioral Scientist* 17 (1974); John Waterbury, "The Phantoms of New Egypt," *American Universities Field Staff Reports,* Northeast Africa Series, vol. 18, no. 1.

42. *New York Times,* Feb. 23, 1974.

43. Quoted in Henry Tanner, *New York Times,* Feb. 28, 1974; see also *New York Times,* Oct. 8, 1974.

44. *Al-Musawwar,* March 15, 1974.

45. *Rose al-Yusuf,* Dec. 25, 1972.

46. *Rose al-Yusuf,* Jan. 31, 1972.

47. Quoted in *New York Times,* Jan. 6, 1975.

48. *New York Times,* Jan. 24, 1977.

49. *New York Times,* Feb. 6, 10, and 15, 1977.

50. *Al-Ahram,* Aug. 21, 1974.

51. See the interview with Musa Sabry in *Akhbar al-Yaum,* Aug. 3, 1974.

52. *New York Times,* May 9, 1974; see especially the lengthy summary of the hearings in *al-Ahram* of April 19, 1972; also *Arab Record and Report,* Feb. 1-14, 1974, p. 44.

53. *Al-Hawadith,* May 3, 1974; *New York Times,* May 9, 1974.

54. *Al-Ahram,* Oct. 25, 1974; *al-Iqtisad wa al-Muhasib,* April 1974.

55. Ministère de la culture et de l'information, Service de l'état pour l'information, *Discours et interviews du President Anouar el-Sadate, Avril-Decémbre 1971* (Cairo, 1972), pp. 142-143; *al-Ahram,* June 11, 1972; *New York Times,* Feb. 28, 1974.

56. *New York Times,* Feb. 28, 1974.

57. Waterbury, "Egypt," pp. 337-339.

58. *Wall Street Journal,* Nov. 22, 1977.

59. *Akhbar al-Yaum,* Aug. 3, 1974; *New York Times,* Dec. 24, 1976.

60. *Al-Akhbar,* May 10, 1973, and June 18, 1974; *al-Iqtisad,* July 1974.

61. *Al-Ahram,* Dec. 11, 1972; *al-Akhbar,* Feb. 20, 1972; *al-Musawwar,* April 14, 1972.

62. John Waterbury, "The Opening, Part III," *American Universities Field Staff Reports,* Northeast Africa Series, vol. 20, no. 4, p. 16.

63. See *al-Musawwar* of Jan. 21, 1972, and Sadat's speech to students in Alexandria on April 3, 1974, reported in the *New York Times* of April 4, 1974. A persuasive analysis of the reasons for Haikal's ouster is given in *al-Nahar* of Feb. 1, 1974, by the well-informed Fuad Matar.

64. *Al-Ahram,* Sept. 6, 1974.

65. *New York Times,* Nov. 12, 1976.

66. *New York Times,* Jan. 31 and Feb. 6, 1977.

67. *Al-Ahram,* Jan. 26, 1977; *New York Times,* Jan. 30, 1977.

68. *New York Times,* Feb. 26, 1977.

69. *Akhbar al-Yaum,* Jan. 22, 1977; *New York Times,* Feb. 26, 1977.

70. Holden, " 'Hero of the Crossing,' " p. 79; *New York Times,* Sept. 21 and Nov. 26, 1977.

71. *New York Times,* Feb. 26 and May 3, 1977.

7. MANAGERS AND THE NEW INDUSTRIAL ORDER

1. Patrick K. O'Brien, "Nasser's Economic Legacy," *The New Middle East,* September 1971, p. 21; UAR Information Administration, *Arab Political Encyclopedia, July-December, 1975* (Cairo, n.d.), p. 68.

2. O'Brien, *The Revolution in Egypt's Economic System,* p. ix.

In the charter the respective spheres of the two sectors are outlined as follows:

1. Social overhead capital, including railways, highways, airports, energy, dams, means of sea, land, and air transportation and other public utilities should be within the framework of public ownership.

2. Most heavy, medium, and mining industries should be part of public ownership. Such private ownership as is allowed in these spheres should be controlled by the government.

Light industry is consigned to the private sector, so long as monopoly is precluded and the public sector has a role in guiding light industry.

3. Foreign import trade must be fully controlled by the state. Private ownership is allotted up to a share of 25 per cent in export trade. Although the private sector enjoys a dominant position in domestic trade, at least one fourth of that trade is reserved to the public sector to prevent monopoly and exploitation.

4. All banks and insurance companies must be under the public sector.

5. All agricultural land ownership is restricted to one hundred feddans for an individual family. Buildings are left under private ownership, but exploitation is to be eliminated through rental regulations and progressive taxation. (UAR Information Administration, *The Charter* [Cairo, n.d.], pp. 54-55.)

3. For a history of planning in Egypt, see Abdel-Malek, *Egypt,* pp. 109-111; for a discussion of the two comprehensive plans, see Albert L. Gray, Jr., "Egypt's Ten Year Economic Plan, 1973-1982," *Middle East Journal* (winter 1976):36-48.

4. For a fuller discussion of the provisions of the laws, see Gray, "Egypt's Ten Year Economic Plan," p. 42.

5. UAR Ministry of Information, State Information Service, *The October Working Paper Presented by Mohamed Anwar el Sadat, April, 1974* (Cairo, n.d.), p. 64.

6. For a discussion of the Sidki appointment, see *al-Ahram,* Dec. 25, 1964. Details on the meetings of the committee presided over by Amer (including lists of those in attendance and agendas) appeared frequently in the press; see, for example, *al-Tali'ah,* May 1967, pp. 48-54, and *al-Ahram,* Dec. 28 and 30, 1966. See also *al-Ahram,* April 18 and 21, May 25, 1962, and March 13, 1964; Abdel-Malek, *Egypt,* p. 176; *al-Ta'bi'ah al-'Ammah wa al'Ihsa',* July 1968, pp. 1-19; Farid, *Top Management in Egypt,* p. 11.

7. Be'eri, *Army Officers in Arab Politics and Society,* p. 431; Farid, *Top Management in Egypt,* p. 32; *al-Ahram,* Sept. 26, 1963; A. Ghoneim, "Encore sur la nouvelle classe en Égypte," *Démocratie nouvelle,* April-May 1968, p. 91.

8. *Al-Ahram,* Dec. 25, 1964.

9. *Al-Tali'ah,* May 1967, pp. 48-54; *al-Jaridah al-Rasmiyyah,* Aug. 28, 1966, pp. 931-942. The quotation is from *al-Jumhuriyyah,* Dec. 10, 1964.

10. M. S. Ahmed, "Sur la révolution sociale dans un pays sousdeveloppé," *Démocratie nouvelle,* Feb. 1968, p. 144.

11. "Les nouveaux nantis," *Démocratie nouvelle,* Feb. 1968, p. 90.

12. *Al-Ahram,* March 13 and Dec. 25, 1964.

13. See Amos Perlmutter, "Egypt and the Myth of the New Middle Class: A Comparative Analysis," *Comparative Studies in Society and History* 10 (1967):61-62; Hansen, *Economic Development in Egypt,* p. 79.

14. *Al-Ahram,* Dec. 25, 1964.

15. *Al-Jumhuriyyah,* Dec. 10, 1964; *al-Ahram,* March 13, 1964.

16. Hansen, *Economic Development,* p. 79; debate on these effects in the press has been extensive. See, for example, the April 1967 issue of *al-Tali'ah,* which is devoted entirely to statements by management, union, and technical personnel on these questions as well as on broader theoretical discussions.

17. *Al-Ahram,* March 20, 1964.

18. *Al-Jumhuriyyah,* March 20, 1967.

19. Ibid.

20. *Al-Jumhuriyyah,* Dec. 10, 1964; *al-Ahram,* March 20, 1964.

21. Sabry's articles appeared daily from January to June 1967. See especially the issues of Jan. 8 and 30, Feb. 28, and April 3, 16, and 25.

22. *Al-Jumhuriyyah,* Feb. 28, and March 19 and 20, 1967.

23. *Al-Jumhuriyyah,* March 20, 1967.

24. Sabry developed his argument with a lengthy description of the new forms of exploitation that had appeared on the Egyptian scene—the emergence of groups of "expediters," suppliers, and subcontractors who at exorbitant rates offered their services to overcome bottlenecks in the functioning of the public sector. Comments on the construction industry may serve to illustrate the thrust of Sabry's views. These are taken from *al-Jumhuriyyah,* Feb. 28, March 1 and 2, and April 16, 1967:

Deviations in the construction industry, according to Sabry, typically manifest themselves in the following forms:

(a) There is widespread recourse by public-sector companies to private-sector subcontractors (who specialize in electrical installation, plumbing, and the like), despite the fact that public-sector enterprises are available that could do the work.

(b) While such a practice may appear innocent enough, it frequently constitutes a deviation, since the subcontracting firms often "belong to bigwigs directing the public sector firms." Such bigwigs assign the subcontracting firms to their own private companies and charge fabulous prices for services rendered. Sabry related that the whole operation is frequently smoke-screened with such devices as registering the ownership of the subcontracting firms under a fictional name or with minor children, in order to conceal the conflict of interest.

25. *Al-Jumhuriyyah,* March 20, 1967; *al-Katib,* April 1966, pp. 2-30.

26. For a discussion of these various control agencies and their effect on the managers, see Farid, *Top Management in Egypt,* pp. 48-51, and Hilmi Salam in *al-Jumhuriyyah,* Dec. 10, 1964, and March 20, 1967.

27. Farid, *Top Management,* p. 35. Writing in *al-Ahram* of March 20, 1964, M. H. Haikal described the effects of such behavior by the managers:

Thus their management of the enterprises which employ them is transformed into a series of questions deferred to the corporations or the cabinet of the Minister to whom they are responsible. According to them, this is the good method and the most sure. In reality, it is a hindrance to creative effort within the production units, which, in counting too heavily on the authorities separating themselves from the practical reality of the problems which arise.

28. See statute 32, *al-Jaridah al-Rasmiyyah,* Aug. 15, 1966, pp. 885-895; also *al-Ta'awun,* Sept. 15, 1968.

29. *Al-Jumhuriyyah,* March 20, 1967.

30. Statute 32, pp. 885-895; presidential decree 3309, *al-Jaridah al-Rasmiyyah,* Aug. 28, 1966.

31. *Al-Jumhuriyyah,* March 20, 1967.

32. *Al-Tali'ah,* May 1967; *al-Ahram,* April 19, 1968.

33. To be sure, it remains difficult to prove unequivocally what Nasser's motives were in fostering the four popular formations within the factory. However, there is considerable evidence that, motives aside, the four formations did rival one another and did serve effectively to counterbalance the manager's authority. Furthermore, Nasser was manifestly aware of this result and did nothing to "correct" the situation—a strong hint that he was not displeased with the arrangement. For example, during the course of high-level discussions concerning the ASU (the transcript of which was published in *al-Tali'ah* of March 1965), the question of rivalries between the Socialist Union committees and the labor unions was raised. While the seriousness of the situation was acknowledged, Nasser himself suggested that resolution of the difficulties was best postponed to a later date.

34. Hassan et al., *La Voie égyptienne vers le socialisme*, p. 396; Ibrahim Ghubashy, *al-Tali'ah*, May 1967, pp. 68-78.

35. *Al-Jaridah al-Rasmiyyah*, Aug. 15, 1966, pp. 885-895.

36. *Al-Jumhuriyyah*, March 19, 1967.

37. *Al-Jumhuriyyah*, March 20, 1967.

38. For a more complete discussion of the procedures for electing members, see *al-Jumhuriyyah*, April 7, 1967.

39. Gray, "Egypt's Ten Year Economic Plan," p. 42.

40. The quotations are from *al-Ahram al-Iqtisadi*, Feb. 1, 1967; *al-Ahram*, March 20, 1964; *al-Tali'ah*, May 1967, pp. 68-78.

41. Amin Ezz ed-Din, "La révolution de juillet et les ouvriers," in Hassan et al., *La voie égyptienne*, p. 398.

42. *Al-Tali'ah*, May 1967, pp. 68-78.

43. *Al-Ahram*, July 28, 1967.

44. Cited in John Waterbury, "The Opening, Part I," *American Universities Field Staff Reports*, Northeast Africa Series, vol. 20, no. 2, p. 11; also UAR Ministry of Information, *The October Working Paper*, p. 59.

45. UAR Ministry of Information, *The October Working Paper*, p. 58.

46. Ibid., p. 59.

47. *Al-Ahram*, Nov. 1, 1974; *al-Tali'ah*, March 1974; Waterbury, "The Opening, Part I," p. 13.

48. UAR Ministry of Information, *The October Working Paper*, pp. 57-58.

49. For details on the problems created by the arrival of the big banks in Egypt, see Waterbury, "The Opening, Part II," *American Universities Field Staff Reports*, Northeast Africa Series, vol. 20, no. 3, pp. 9-10.

50. *Al-Ahram*, April 6, 1972, and April 1 and 2, 1973.

8. AGRICULTURAL COOPERATIVES

1. Hansen, *Economic Development in Egypt*, pp. 84-85; Mabro, *The Egyptian Economy, 1952-1972*, pp. 229-230; al-Barawy, *Economic Development in the United Arab Republic (Egypt)*, p. 86; Nassar Saad, "Structural Changes and Socialist Transformation in Agriculture of the U.A.R. (Egypt)," *L'Égypte contemporaine* 60 (1969):263.

2. *Al-Ahram*, July 14, 1964. (In the seventies, however, there were extensive reports that this agricultural land area was eroding as a result of the use of

agricultural land for housing, industrial works, and so forth. There have also been charges that the land reclamation figures were exaggerated. *Akhbar al-Yuam,* June 18 and 29, 1974.) See also Hansen, *Economic Development,* pp. 18-23.

3. Malcolm Kerr, "The United Arab Republic: The Domestic, Political, and Economic Background of Foreign Policy," in Hammond and Alexander, *Political Dynamics in the Middle East,* p. 215; UAR State Information Service, *The Charter* (Cairo, n.d.), p. 58. The Nasser citation is from an interview with correspondent Eric Rouleau, *Le Monde,* Sept. 18, 1963.

4. Safran, *Egypt in Search of Political Community,* p. 196; Issawi, *Egypt in Revolution,* pp. 280-281.

5. Patrick O'Brien, "Nasser's Economic Legacy," *The New Middle East,* Sept. 1971, p. 22; Hansen, *Economic Development,* p. 69.

6. U.A.R. Information Service, *The Charter,* p. 72; Mansfield, *Nasser's Egypt,* p. 205.

7. See O'Brien, *The Revolution in Egypt's Economic System,* pp. 76-77, 98; al-Barawy, *Economic Development,* p. 116.

8. Al-Barawy, *Economic Development,* pp. 117-118.

9. Warriner, *Agrarian Reform and Community Development in the U.A.R.,* p. 45.

10. *Al-Ahram,* July 29, 1963.

11. O'Brien, *The Revolution,* p. 51.

12. The discussion of the land reforms is based on Gabriel Baer, "New Data on Egypt's Land Reform," *New Outlook* 10 (1967):29; Anouar Abdel-Malek, "La Réforme agraire en Égypte (R.A.U.): problèmes et perspectives," *Développement et civilisations,* 22 (1965):23. The Nasser quotation is from *Arab Political Documents* (Beirut, 1964), p. 470.

13. *Al-Tali'ah,* May 1965, pp. 76-79; Harik, *The Political Mobilization of Peasants,* pp. 56-57.

14. Typical of the reports on corruption is a study in the weekly *Rose al-Yusuf* of June 10 and 24, 1963, which argues that the cooperatives are generally dominated by rich peasants who succeed in turning them into instruments of their own service to the detriment of the mass of the small farmers.

The Kamchiche affair is treated in "Interview à Kamchiche: Mme Salah Hussein," in *Démocratie nouvelle,* Feb. 1968, pp. 113-114; Michel Kamel, "Féodaux, paysans riches, et fallahs," *Démocratie nouvelle,* Feb. 1968, p. 99; Mirskii, *Armiya i Politika v Stranakh Azii i Afriki* [*The Army and Politics in the Countries of Asia and Africa*], p. 82; and *Unita,* Feb. 14, 1967. In the seventies the right-wing press revived interest in the incident, alleging that it was trumped up to advance a leftist drive in the countryside. In *In Search of Identity* Sadat argues that the village of Kamchiche had fallen into the hands of communists and Marxists, and that the charges made were false. No supporting evidence for this interpretation is offered (pp. 170-171).

15. See also O'Brien, *The Revolution,* p. 145.

16. *Al-Ahram al-Iqtisadi,* May 15, 1968.

17. *Al-Jumhuriyyah,* Jan. 25, 1967; see also A. Ghoneim, "Encore sur la nouvelle classe en Égypte," *Démocratie nouvelle,* April-May 1968, p. 88.

18. Kamel, "Féodaux, paysans riches, et fellahs," p. 102; *al-Jumhuriyyah,* Jan. 25, 1967.

19. *Al-Ahram al-Iqtisadi,* May 15, 1968.

20. *Al-Ahram al-Iqtisadi,* Feb. 15, 1967.

21. *Al-Ahram al-Iqtisadi,* May 15, 1968; Don Peretz, "Reform and Revolution in Egypt," *New Outlook* 3 (1959):15.

22. *Al-Jumhuriyyah,* Jan. 25, 1967, and June 20, 1968.

23. *Al-Ahram al-Iqtisadi,* May 15, 1968.

24. *Al-Jumhuriyyah,* Jan. 26, 1967.

25. Kamel, "Féodaux, paysans riches, et fellahs," p. 102; Gataullin, *Ekonomika OAR Na Novom Puti* [*The Economy of the UAR on a New Path*], p. 185; *Rose al-Yusuf,* June 10 and 24, 1963.

26. For the text of the new law, see *al-Jaridah al-Rasmiyyah,* Aug. 16, 1969, pp. 613-624. Citations that follow are from this text.

27. *Al-Tali'ah,* Nov. 1974.

28. *al-Musawwar,* July 13, 1973.

29. See Mabro's informed, technical discussion of an early study by the Institute of National Planning in *The Egyptian Economy,* pp. 77-80; for an overall positive assessment of their cooperative by the peasants in one village, see Harik, *The Political Mobilization of Peasants,* pp. 189-192.

30. *Al-Ahram,* March 6, 1964.

31. UAR Ministry of Information, State Information Service, *The October Working Paper Presented by Mohamed Anwar el Sadat, April, 1974* (Cairo, n.d.), pp. 61, 64-65. For a discussion of the reasoning of Sadat and his key advisers on these fundamental issues, see John Waterbury, " 'Aish: Egypt's Growing Food Crisis," *American Universities Field Staff Reports,* Northeast Africa Series, vol. 19, no. 3, esp. Dec. 1974, pp. 10-12.

9.   RURAL HEALTH CARE

1. UAR Ministry of Information, State Information Service, *The October Working Paper Presented by Mohamed Anwar el Sadat, April, 1974* (Cairo, n.d.), p. 27.

2. Akademiya Nauk S S S R, Institut Narodov Azii, *Obedinennaya Arabskaya Respublika (Spravochnik)* [*United Arab Republic (Handbook)*], p. 292.

3. J. M. Weir et al., "An Evaluation of Health and Sanitation in Egyptian Villages," *Journal of the Egyptian Public Health Association* 27 (1952):55-122.

4. Gataullin, *Ekonimika OAR Na Novom Puti* [*The Economy of the UAR on a New Path*], p. 181; Akademiya Nauk, *OAR (Spravochnik),* p. 293.

5. Akademiya Nauk, *OAR (Spravochnik),* pp. 293-294. The 382 figure is derived from data in Gataullin, *Ekonomika OAR,* p. 181, and *al-Ta'bi'ah al-Ammah wa al-Ihsa'* 3 (1965):30-42; see also *al-Akhbar,* Oct. 2, 1966, p. 4.

6. Gataullin, *Ekonomika OAR,* p. 181.

7. *Al-Ahram,* April 16, 1965; Gataullin, *Ekonomika OAR,* p. 181.

8. Wheelock, *Nasser's New Egypt,* p. 118; Gataullin, *Ekonomika OAR,* p. 181.

9. Gataullin, *Ekonomika OAR,* p. 181.

10. Statistical evidence on distribution and staffing and supply problems is in *al-Ta'bi'ah al'Ammah wa al-Ihsa'* 3 (1965):30-42.

11. *Al-Ahram,* April 16, 1965, p. 5.

12. O'Brien, *The Revolution in Egypt's Economic System,* p. 299.

13. Mansfield, *Nasser's Egypt,* p. 111; Smith et al., *Area Handbook for the United Arab Republic (Egypt)* (Washington, D.C., 1970), p. 126.

14. *Al-Ahram,* April 16, 1965, p. 5.

15. *Al-Jumhuriyyah,* Feb. 15, 16, 18, 19, 21, and 22, 1967.

16. See, as one example, O'Brien, *The Revolution,* p. 299.

17. The published record in Egyptian sources on the operation of the health care units is handily supplemented by the observations of an American researcher, James Bruce Mayfield, who toured the rural areas of the UAR in 1966-1967. Impressed with the rural doctors as an information source on administrative developments in rural Egypt, Mayfield enjoyed extensive contact with them and has recorded their perspective on the problems of the rural health programs. His thoughtful and sensitive study, *Rural Politics in Nasser's Egypt,* is invaluable for an understanding of the changes in rural life under Nasser.

18. Mayfield, *Rural Politics,* pp. 219-220.

19. *Al-Jumhuriyyah,* June 20, 1968, p. 4.

20. Tewfik el-Hakim, *The Maze of Justice* (London, 1947), p. 18.

21. Mayfield, *Rural Politics,* p. 220.

22. *Al-Tali'ah,* Sept. 1966, p. 41; *al-Jumhuriyyah,* June 20, 1968, p. 4.

23. Mayfield, *Rural Politics,* pp. 222-223.

24. Ibid., p. 225.

25. *Al-Ishtiraki,* Oct. 29, 1966, pp. 12-17.

26. Ibid.

27. Ibid.

28. Mayfield, *Rural Politics,* pp. 121-122.

29. *Al-Jumhuriyyah,* Dec. 11, 1961.

30. *Al-Tali'ah,* Sept. 1966; see also *al-Jumhuriyyah,* June 20, 1968, p. 4.

31. *Al-Jumhuriyyah,* Dec. 11, 1961.

32. *Al-Ishtiraki,* Oct. 29, 1966, pp. 12-17.

33. Akademiya Nauk, *OAR (Spravochnik),* p. 296. Impressionistic evidence from Egyptian sources does indeed suggest that the already low 18 percent figure is inflated. For example, Ahmed Tawfik comments in *al-Tali'ah* of September 1966 that "the combined unit, the supposed center for government services, rarely has any peasants in it; they never go there unless it is absolutely necessary." Similarly, the 1968 *al-Jumhuriyyah* study found that the units "lack facilities" and that "work is carried out in an inefficient routine," resulting in the loss of peasant confidence in the health units.

34. See Mabro, *The Egyptian Economy, 1952-1972,* p. 159; UAR State Information Service, *The Charter,* pp. 83-84; UAR Ministry of Information, *The October Working Paper,* p. 98.

35. *Al-Akhbar,* Jan. 20 and Oct. 19, 1971.

36. *Al-Ahram,* April 1, 1973.

37. *Al-Akhbar,* June 18, 1973.

10.   THE REGIME AND THE REVOLUTION

1. Quoted in John Waterbury, "The Opening, Part III," *American Universities Field Staff Reports,* Northeast Africa Series, vol. 20, no. 4, p. 3.

2. UAR Information Administration, *Arab Political Encyclopedia, July-December, 1965* (Cairo, n.d.), p. 68; UAR Information Department, *Address by President Gamal Abdel Nasser at the opening meeting of the second session of the National Assembly, Cairo, November 12, 1964* (Cairo, n.d.), p. 36; Patrick K. O'Brien, "Nasser's Economic Legacy," *The New Middle East,* Sept. 1971, p. 22.

3. UAR Information Department, *Gamal Abdel Nasser's Speeches and Press Interviews;* citation from Mustafa Teiba, *al-Tali'ah,* Dec. 1965, pp. 40-45.

4. UAR Information Department, *Gamal Abdel Nasser's Speeches and Press Interviews, Address by President Gamal Abdel Nasser at the opening meeting of the third ordinary session of the UAR National Assembly, Cairo, November 15, 1965.*

5. The quotations are from Eliezer Ben-Moshe, "Difficulties of Socialism in Egypt," *New Outlook* 5 (1962):52-53; A. M. Goichon, "Le plan de rénovation sociale de la campagne égyptienne," *Orient* 20 (1961):11; Sadat, *In Search of Identity,* p. 210.

6. Quoted in Waterbury, "The Opening, Part III," p. 1.

7. *Middle East Economic Digest,* April 23, 1976, p. 3.

8. *Al-Ahram,* Oct. 25, 1974.

9. *New York Times,* Nov. 21 and 27, 1977.

10. Mayfield, *Rural Politics in Nasser's Egypt,* p. 96.

11. Sharkawy, *Egyptian Earth,* p. 191. The quotation is from Mansfield, *Nasser's Egypt,* p. 246.

12. Quoted in P. J. Vatikiotis, "Egypt Adrift: A Study in Disillusion," *New Middle East,* March 1973, pp. 8, 10.

Selected Bibliography

I. EGYPTIAN NEWSPAPERS AND PERIODICALS

Egypt has the largest press in the Arab world, with approximately four hundred newspapers and periodicals published. The following have been especially useful in the preparation of this book: daily newspapers—*al-Ahram, al-Akhbar, al-Jumhuriyyah, Egyptian Gazette, Progrès égyptien;* periodicals—*Akher Saa, al-Ahram al-Iqtisadi, al-Ishtiraki, al-Katib, al-Musawwar, al-Tali'ah, Rose al-Yusuf.* Specific articles drawn from these sources are fully identified in notes.

II. OFFICIAL PUBLICATIONS OF THE EGYPTIAN GOVERNMENT

The Egyptian government regularly puts out about one hundred twenty official publications, most of which are in Arabic. The following have been particularly important as sources: *al-Amn al-'Ammah wa al-Ihsa', al-Jaridah al-Rasmiyyah,* and *al-Ta'bi'ah al-'Ammah wa al-Ihsa'.* In addition, the Ministry of Information regularly publishes English-language versions of the important speeches and press interviews of Egypt's president; these have been used whenever available.

III. SELECTED BOOKS

A complete bibliography of the books and articles used for this study is impossible here. The text is annotated to provide some guidance to the wealth of relevant material in specialized journals (in Arabic, Russian, and various Western languages.) The following is a list of books in Western languages that might prove of interest to the general reader.

Abdel-Malek, Anouar. *Egypt: Military Society, The Army Regime, the Left, and Social Change under Nasser.* Translated by Charles Lam Markmann. New York: Vintage Books, 1968.
———. *Ideologie et renaissance nationale de l'Égypte moderne.* Paris: Éditions Anthropos, 1969.
———. *La Pensée politique arabe contemporaine.* Paris: Éditions du Seuil, 1970.
Abul-Fath, Ahmed. *L'Affaire Nasser.* Paris: Plon, 1962.

Ahmad, Jamal Mohammed. *The Intellectual Origins of Egyptian Nationalism.* London: Royal Institute of International Affairs, 1960.

Akademiya Nauk SSSR. Institut Narodov Azii. *Obedinennaya Arabskaya Respublika (Spravochnik)* [*United Arab Republic (Handbook)*]. Moscow: Nauka, 1968.

Allen, Richard. *Imperialism and Nationalism in the Fertile Crescent: Sources and Prospects of the Arab-Israeli Conflict.* New York: Oxford University Press, 1974.

Amin, G. A. *Food Supply and Economic Development with Special Reference to Egypt.* London: Cass, 1966.

Ammar, Hamed. *Growing up in an Egyptian Village: Silwa, Province of Aswan.* New York: Octagon Books, 1966.

Amnesty International. *Report on Torture.* New York: Farrar, Straus and Giroux, 1975.

Ayrout, Henry Habib. *The Egyptian Peasant.* Boston: Beacon Press, 1963.

Badeau, John S. *The American Approach to the Arab World.* New York: Harper & Row, 1968.

Baer, Gabriel. *A History of Landownership in Egypt, 1800-1950.* New York: Oxford University Press, 1962.

———. *Egyptian Guilds in Modern Times.* Jerusalem: Israel Oriental Society, no. 8, 1964.

———. *Studies in the Social History of Modern Egypt.* Chicago: University of Chicago Press, 1969.

Barawy, Rashed al-. *The Military Coup in Egypt: An Analytical Study.* Cairo: Renaissance Bookstore, 1952.

———. *Economic Development in the United Arab Republic (Egypt).* Cairo: Anglo-Egyptian Bookshop, 1970.

Be'eri, Eliezer. *Army Officers in Arab Politics and Society.* New York: Praeger-Pall Mall, 1970.

Berger, Morroe. *Bureaucracy and Society in Modern Egypt.* Princeton, New Jersey: Princeton University Press, 1957.

———. *Military Elites and Social Change: Egypt since Napoleon.* Princeton, New Jersey: Center for International Studies, Princeton University, 1960.

———. *The Arab World Today.* Garden City, New York: Doubleday, 1964.

———. *Islam in Egypt Today: Social and Political Aspects of Popular Religion.* New York: Cambridge University Press, 1970.

Berque, Jacques. *Egypt: Imperialism and Revolution.* London: Faber and Faber, 1972.

Binder, Leonard. *The Ideological Revolution in the Middle East.* New York: Wiley, 1964.

Blackman, Winifred, S. *The Fellahin of Upper Egypt.* London: Cass, 1968.

Brecher, Michael. *The Foreign Policy System of Israel: Setting, Images, Process.* New Haven, Connecticut: Yale University Press, 1972.

Chomsky, Noam. *Peace in the Middle East? Reflections on Justice and Nationhood.* New York: Vintage Books, 1974.

Colombe, Marcel. *L'Évolution de l'Égypte, 1924-1950.* Paris: Maison-neuve, 1951.

Copeland, Miles. *The Game of Nations: The Amorality of Power Politics.* New York: Simon and Schuster, 1969.

Cremeans, Charles D. *The Arabs and the World: Nasser's Arab Nationalist Policy.* New York: Praeger, 1963.

Cromer, Lord. *Modern Egypt.* Vols. 1 and 2. London: MacMillan, 1908.

Crouchley, A. E. *The Economic Development of Modern Egypt.* London: Longmans, Green, 1938.

Dekmejian, Hrair R. *Egypt under Nasir: A Study in Political Dynamics.* Albany: State University of New York Press, 1971.

Dilthey, Wilhelm. *Pattern and Meaning in History: Thoughts on History and Society.* H. P. Rickman, editor. New York: Harper, 1962.

Estier, Claude. *L'Égypte en révolution.* Paris: René Juillard, 1965.

Evron, Yair. *The Middle East: Nations, Superpowers, and Wars.* New York: Praeger, 1973.

Fakhouri, Hani. *Kafr el-Elow: An Egyptian Village in Transition.* New York: Holt, Rinehart and Winston, 1972.

Farid, Saleh. *Top Management in Egypt: Its Structure, Quality and Problems, P-4291.* Santa Monica, California: Rand Corporation, 1970.

Feuer, Lewis S., editor. *Basic Writing on Politics and Philosophy: Karl Marx and Friedrich Engels.* Garden City, New York: Doubleday, 1959.

Fisher, Sydney N., editor. *Social Forces in the Middle East.* Ithaca, New York: Cornell University Press, 1955.

————, editor. *The Military in Middle Eastern Society and Politics.* Columbus: Ohio State University Press, 1963.

Gadalla, Saad M. *Land Reform in Relation to Social Development, Egypt.* Columbia: University of Missouri Press, 1962.

Gataullin, M. F. *Ekonomika OAR Na Novom Puti* [*The Economy of the UAR on a New Path*]. Moscow: Mysle, 1966.

Ghanem, Fathy. *The Man Who Lost His Shadow.* Translated by Desmond Stewart. London: Chapman, 1966.

Gibb, H. A. R. *Modern Trends in Islam.* Chicago: University of Chicago Press, 1947.

————. *Mohammedanism.* 2nd ed. London: Oxford University Press, 1954.

Golan, Matti. *The Secret Conversations of Henry Kissinger: Step-by-Step Diplomacy in the Middle East.* New York: Quadrangle, 1976.

Halpern, Manfred. *The Politics of Social Change in the Middle East and North Africa.* Princeton, New Jersey: Princeton University Press, 1963.

Hammond, Paul, and Alexander, Sidney, editors. *Political Dynamics in the Middle East.* New York: American Elsevier, 1972.

Hamon, Léo, editor. *Le Role extramilitaire de l'armée dans le tiers monde.* Paris: Presses Universitaires de France, 1966.

Hanna, Sami A., and Gardner, George H. *Arab Socialism.* Salt Lake City: University of Utah Press, 1969.

Hansen, Bent. *Economic Development in Egypt*. RM-5961 FF. n.p. Rand Corporation, 1969.

——— and Marzouk, Girgis A. *Development and Economic Policy in the U.A.R. (Egypt)*. Amsterdam: North-Holland Publishing Company, 1965.

Harbison, Frederick, and Abdelkader, Ibrahim. *Human Resources for Egyptian Enterprise*. New York: McGraw-Hill, 1958.

Harik, Ilya. *The Political Mobilization of Peasants: A Study of an Egyptian Community*. Bloomington: Indiana University Press, 1974.

Harris, Christina Phelps. *Nationalism and Revolution in Egypt*. Stanford, California: Hoover Institute on War, Revolution, and Peace, 1964.

Harris, George L., editor. *Egypt*. Country Survey series. New Haven, Connecticut: Human Relations Area Files Press, 1957.

Hassan, Abdel Razek, et al. *La Voie égyptienne vers le socialisme*. Cairo: Dar al-Naaef, n.d.

Heikal, Mohamed. *The Cairo Documents: The Inside Story of Nasser and His Relationship with World Leaders, Rebels, Statesmen*. New York: Doubleday, 1973.

———. *The Road to Ramadan*. New York: Quadrangle, 1975.

Holt, P. M. *Egypt and the Fertile Crescent, 1516-1922*. Ithaca, New York: Cornell University Press, 1966.

———, editor. *Political and Social Change in Modern Egypt*. London: School of Oriental and African Studies, 1967.

Hourani, Albert H. *Middle East Affairs: Number Four*. St. Anthony's Papers no. 17. London: Oxford University Press, 1965.

———. *Arabic Thought in the Liberal Age, 1789-1939*. London: School of Oriental and African Studies, 1967.

Hurewitz, J. C. *Middle East Politics: The Military Dimension*. New York: Praeger, 1969.

Hussein, Mahmoud. *Class Conflict in Egypt, 1945-1970*. New York: Monthly Review Press, 1973.

Insight Team of the Sunday Times. *Insight on the Middle East War*. London: André Deutsch, 1974.

Issawi, Charles. *Egypt at Mid-Century: An Economic Survey*. London: Oxford University Press, 1954.

———. *Egypt in Revolution: An Economic Analysis*. London: Oxford University Press, 1963.

Joesten, Joachim. *Nasser: The Rise to Power*. London: Odhams Press, 1960.

Johnson, John J., editor. *The Role of the Military in Underdeveloped Countries*. Princeton, New Jersey: Princeton University Press, 1962.

Kalb, Marvin, and Kalb, Bernard. *Kissinger*. Boston: Little, Brown, 1974.

Kammash, Magdi M. el-. *Economic Development and Planning in Egypt*. New York: Praeger, 1968.

Kardouche, G. K. *The U.A.R. in Development: A Study in Expansionary Finance*. New York: Praeger, 1967.

Kerr, Malcolm. *Egypt under Nasser*. Headline series. New York: Foreign Policy Association, 1963.

————. *The Arab Cold War, 1958-1964: A Study of Ideology in Politics*. London: Oxford University Press, 1965.

————. *Islamic Reform*. Berkeley and Los Angeles: University of California Press, 1966.

————. *The United Arab Republic: The Domestic Political and Economic Background of Foreign Policy*. RM-5967-FF. n.p. Rand Corporation, 1969.

————. *Regional Arab Politics and the Conflict with Israel*. RM-5966-FF. n.p. Rand Corporation, 1969.

Khouri, Fred J. *The Arab-Israeli Dilemma*. Syracuse, New York: Syracuse University Press, 1968.

Kimche, Jon. *There Could Have Been Peace*. U.S.A.: Dial Press, 1973.

Lacouture, Jean. *The Demi-Gods: Charismatic Leadership in the Third World*. New York: Alfred A. Knopf, 1970.

————. *Nasser*. New York: Alfred A. Knopf, 1973.

Lacouture, Jean, and Lacouture, Simone. *Egypt in Transition*. London: Methuen, 1958.

Landes, David S. *Bankers and Pashas: International Finance and Economic Imperialism in Egypt*. New York: Harper & Row, 1969.

Laqueur, Walter Z. *The Soviet Union and the Middle East*. London: Routledge & Kegan Paul, 1959.

————, editor. *The Middle East in Transition: Studies in Contemporary History*. New York: Praeger, 1958.

Lewis, Bernard. *The Arabs in History*. New York: Harper and Brothers, 1960.

————. *The Middle East and the West*. New York: Harper Torchbooks, 1964.

Little, Tom. *Egypt*. London: Ernest Benn, 1958.

Love, Kennett. *Suez, the Twice-Fought War*. New York: McGraw-Hill, 1969.

Mabro, Robert. *The Egyptian Economy, 1952-1972*. London: Clarendon Press, 1974.

Mahfouz, el Kosheri. *Socialisme et pouvoir en Égypte*. Paris: R. Pichon et R. Durand-Auzias, 1972.

Mahfouz, Naguib. *God's World: An Anthology of Short Stories*. Minneapolis: Bibliotheca Islamica, 1973.

Mahgoub, Mohamed. *Democracy on Trial: Reflections on Arab and African Politics*. London: Deutsch, 1974.

Mansfield, Peter. *Nasser's Egypt*. England: Penguin Books, 1969.

————. *Nasser*. London: Methuen, 1969.

————. *The British in Egypt*. London: Weidenfeld and Nicolson, 1971.

————. *The Middle East: A Political and Economic Survey*. London: Oxford University Press, 1973.

Marcuse, Herbert. *Negations: Essays in Critical Theory*. Boston: Beacon Press, 1968.

Matykhin, I. S. *Obedinennaya Arabskaya Respublika: Ekonomiya i Vneshnyaya Torgovlya [United Arab Republic: The Economy and Foreign Trade]*. Moscow: Mezhdunarodyne Otnosheniya, 1966.

Mayfield, James B. *Rural Politics in Nasser's Egypt: A Quest for Legitimacy*. Austin: University of Texas Press, 1971.

Mead, Donald C. *Growth and Structural Change in the Egyptian Economy.* Homewood, Illinois: Richard D. Irwin, 1967.

Memmi, Albert. *Portrait du colonisé: précédé du portrait du colonisateur.* Correa: Buchet/Chastel, 1957.

———. *L'Homme dominé.* Paris: Gallimard, 1968.

Meyer-Ranke, Peter. *Der Rote Pharao.* Hamburg: Christian Wegner Verlag, 1964.

Mills, C. Wright. *The Sociological Imagination.* London: Oxford University Press, 1959.

Mirskii, G. I. *Armiya i Politika v Stranakh Azii i Afriki* [*The Army and Politics in the Countries of Asia and Africa*]. Moscow: Nauka, 1970.

Mitchell, Richard P. *Society of the Muslim Brothers.* London: Oxford University Press, 1969.

Moore, Barrington. *Social Origins of Dictatorship and Democracy: Lord and Peasant in the Making of the Modern World.* Boston: Beacon Press, 1967.

Nagi, M. H. *Labor Force and Employment in Egypt.* New York: Praeger, 1971.

Naguib, Mohammed. *Egypt's Destiny: A Personal Statement.* Garden City, New York: Doubleday, 1955.

Nasser, Gamal Abdel. *The Philosophy of the Revolution.* n.p. 1954.

Nieuwenhiujze, C. A. O. van. *Social Stratification in the Middle East: An Interpretation.* Leiden: Brill, 1965.

———. *Sociology of the Middle East.* Leiden: Brill, 1971.

Nutting, Anthony. *Nasser.* London: Constable, 1972.

O'Brien, Patrick. *The Revolution in Egypt's Economic System: From Private Enterprise to Socialism, 1952-1965.* London: Oxford University Press, 1967.

Owen, Edward R. J. *Cotton and the Egyptian Economy.* Oxford: Clarendon Press, 1969.

Parsons, Talcott, and Shils, Edward A., editors. *Toward a General Theory of Action.* Cambridge, Massachusetts: Harvard University Press, 1951.

Perlmutter, Amos. *Military and Politics in Israel: Nation-Building and Role Expansion.* New York: Praeger, 1969.

———. *Egypt: Praetorian State.* New Brunswick, New Jersey: Transaction Books, 1974.

Popper, Karl. *The Logic of Scientific Discovery.* New York: Harper & Row, 1959.

———. *The Open Society and Its Enemies.* Princeton, New Jersey: Princeton University Press, 1962.

———. *Conjectures and Refutations: The Growth of Scientific Knowledge.* New York: Harper & Row, 1963.

———. *The Poverty of Historicism.* New York: Harper Torchbooks, 1964.

———. *Objective Knowledge: An Evolutionary Approach.* Oxford: Clarendon Press, 1972.

Quraishi, Zaheer Masood. *Liberal Nationalism in Egypt: Rise and Fall of the Wafd Party.* Allahabad, India: Kitab Mahal, 1967.

Ra'anan, Uri. *The USSR Arms the Third World: Case Studies in Soviet Foreign Policy.* Cambridge, Massachusetts: MIT Press, 1969.

Rejwan, Nissim. *Nasserist Ideology: Its Exponents and Critics.* New York: John Wiley & Sons, 1974.

Riad, Hassan. *L'Égypte nasserienne*. Paris: Éditions de Minuit, 1964.

Rivlin, Helen Anne B. *The Agricultural Policy of Muhammad Ali in Egypt*. Cambridge, Massachusetts: Harvard University Press, 1961.

Rodinson, Maxime. *Israel and the Arabs*. New York: Pantheon Books, 1968.

Rubinstein, Alvin Z. *Red Star on the Nile*. Princeton, New Jersey: Princeton University Press, 1977.

Saab, Gabriel S. *The Egyptian Agrarian Reform, 1952-1962*. London: Oxford University Press, 1967.

Saber, Ali. *Nasser en procès: Face à la nation arabe*. Paris: Nouvelles Éditions Latine, 1968.

Sadat, Anwar al-. *Revolt on the Nile*. New York: John Day, 1957.

———. *In Search of Identity*. New York: Harper & Row, 1977 and 1978.

Safran, Nadav. *Egypt in Search of Political Community: An Analysis of the Intellectual and Political Evolution of Egypt, 1804-1952*. Cambridge, Massachusetts: Harvard University Press, 1961.

———. *The United States and Israel*. Cambridge, Massachusetts: Harvard University Press, 1963.

———. *From War to War: The Arab-Israeli Confrontation, 1948-1967*. New York: Pegasus, 1969.

———. *Israel: The Embattled Ally*. Cambridge, Massachusetts: Harvard University Press, 1978.

St. John, Robert. *The Boss: The Story of Gamal Abdel Nasser*. New York: Mc-Graw-Hill, 1960.

Sharkawi, A. R. *Egyptian Earth*. London: William Heinemann, 1962.

Sheehan, Edward R. F. *The Arabs, Israelis, and Kissinger: A Secret History of American Diplomacy in the Middle East*. New York: Reader's Digest Press, 1976.

Smith, Harvey H., et al. *Area Handbook for the United Arab Republic (Egypt)*. Da Pam 550-43. Washington, D.C.: U.S. Government Printing Office, 1970.

Smith, Wilfred Cantwell. *Islam in Modern History*. New York: New American Library, 1957.

Stephens, Robert. *Nasser: A Political Biography*. London: Penguin Press, 1971.

Stevens, Georgianna G., editor. *The United States and the Middle East*. Englewood, New Jersey: Prentice Hall, 1963.

Stewart, Desmond. *Young Egypt*. London: Allan Wingate, 1958.

Thompson, Jack H., and Reischauer, Robert D., editors. *Modernization of the Arab World*. Princeton, New Jersey: D. Van Nostrand Company, 1966.

Tignor, Robert L. *Modernization and British Colonial Rule in Egypt, 1882-1914*. Princeton, New Jersey: Princeton University Press, 1966.

Udovitch, A. L., editor. *The Middle East: Oil, Conflict & Hope*. Lexington, Massachusetts: D. C. Heath, 1976.

Ulam, Adam. *The Unfinished Revolution*. New York: Vintage Books, 1964.

Vatikiotis, Panagiotis J. *The Egyptian Army in Politics: Pattern for New Nations?* Bloomington: Indiana University Press, 1961.

———, editor. *Egypt since the Revolution*. New York: Praeger, 1968.

———. *The Modern History of Egypt*. London: Weidenfeld and Nicolson, 1969.

Vaucher, Georges. *Gamal Abdel Nasser et son équipe.* Vols. 1 and 2. Paris: René Juillard, 1959 and 1960.

Vernier, Bernard. *Armée et politique au Moyen-Orient.* Paris: Payot, 1966.

Wallerstein, Immanuel. *Africa: The Politics of Independence. An Interpretation of Modern African History.* New York: Vintage Books, 1961.

———. *Social Change: The Colonial Situation.* New York: John Wiley & Sons, 1966.

Warriner, Doreen. *Agrarian Reform and Community Development in the U.A.R.* n.p. Dar al-Taawon Publishing and Printing House, 1961.

Wheelock, Keith. *Nasser's New Egypt.* New York: Praeger, 1960.

Wilber, Donald N. *United Arab Republic: Egypt: Its People, Its Society, Its Culture.* New Haven, Connecticut: HRAF Press, 1969.

Wynn, Wilton. *Nasser of Egypt: The Search for Dignity.* Cambridge: Arlington Books, 1959.

Index